REVISION WORKBOOK

Obligations:
THE LAW OF TORT

Third Edition

DR VICKNESWAREN KRISHNAN
LLB (Hons), LLM, MA, Barrister, ACI Arb, AIPFM, AFSALS, ACII, PhD

OLD BAILEY PRESS

OLD BAILEY PRESS
at Holborn College, Woolwich Road,
Charlton, London, SE7 8LN

First published 1997
Third edition 2004

ISBN 1 85836 558 9

British Library Cataloguing-in-Publication.

A CIP Catalogue record for this book is available from the British Library.

Printed and bound in Great Britain.

Contents

Acknowledgement

Some questions used are taken or adapted from past University of London LLB (External) Degree examination papers and our thanks are extended to the University of London for their kind permission to use and publish the questions.

Caveat

The answers given are not approved or sanctioned by the University of London and are entirely our responsibility.

They are not intended as 'Model Answers', but rather as Suggested Solutions.

The answers have two fundamental purposes, namely:

a) to provide a detailed example of a suggested solution to an examination question; and

b) to assist students with their research into the subject and to further their understanding and appreciation of the subject.

Introduction

This Revision WorkBook has been designed specifically for those studying the law of tort to undergraduate level. Its coverage is not confined to any one syllabus, but embraces all the major law of tort topics to be found in university examinations.

Each chapter contains a brief introduction explaining the scope and overall content of the topic covered in that chapter. There follows, in each case, a list of key points which will assist the student in studying and memorising essential material with which the student should be familiar in order to fully understand the topic.

Additionally in each chapter there is a key cases and statutes section which lists the most relevant cases and statutory provisions applicable to the topic in question. These are intended as an aid to revision, providing the student with a concise list of materials from which to begin revision.

Each chapter usually ends with several typical examination questions, together with general comments, skeleton solutions and suggested solutions. Wherever possible, the questions are drawn from the University of London external law of tort papers, with recent questions being included where possible. However, it is inevitable that, in compiling a list of questions by topic order rather than chronologically, not only do the same questions crop up over and over again in different guises, but there are gaps where questions have never been set at all.

Undoubtedly, the main feature of this Revision WorkBook is the inclusion of as many past examination questions as possible. While the use of past questions as a revision aid is certainly not new, it is hoped that the combination of actual past questions from the University of London LLB external course and specially written questions, where there are gaps in examination coverage, will be of assistance to students in achieving a thorough and systematic revision of the subject.

Careful use of the Revision WorkBook should enhance the student's understanding of the law of tort and, hopefully, enable you to deal with as wide a range of subject matter as anyone might find in a law of tort examination, while at the same time allowing you to practise examination techniques while working through the book.

Introduction

Studying the Law of Tort

The law of tort, covering as it does the legal duties that one person owes to another, is an inherently fascinating area. In particular, the cases that a student comes across can be readily understood and appreciated from a factual point of view as they concern (relatively speaking) day-to-day situations. However, a problem immediately arises of the sheer volume of information and data that is contained in a textbook of tort law. A factor which contributes to this volume is that tort is basically a case law subject, ie it is a subject in which the general principles and detailed rules have been laid down by judgments of the courts over a period of years, often in a rather haphazard manner due to accidents of litigation. It is, therefore, vital that the student extracts (with the help of his lectures and textbooks!) the general principles from this mass of cases. This is by no means an easy task, and many rules in tort have exceptions, but without a framework of clear principles in which to place cases which illustrate the workings of the principles and their limitations, understanding and progress will be difficult.

In addition to the judge-made law, tort has a number of statutes which have extended, refined and often changed the common law, such as the Animals Act 1971, the Occupiers' Liability Acts of 1957 and 1984 and the Consumer Protection Act 1987. These and other relevant statutes must clearly form part of the data bank from which the student erects his framework of principles of the law of tort.

Yet another problem awaits the student of the law of tort, namely that certain areas of the law are still being developed by the courts, and whilst in law generally it is advisable to keep up to date, in certain areas of tort it is absolutely essential. Thus in recent years the courts have restated and/or refined the law as regards duty of care in situations involving third parties and rescuers, for instance. Hence it is imperative that students ensure that they are kept abreast of recent developments.

To summarise, the student of the law of tort needs to have a good grasp of the principles of tort law as laid down by the cases and statutes. In addition, a good knowledge of case law is required to explain and illustrate the working of these principles in practical situations. Fortunately, both these requirements can be satisfied by a study of one set of materials, but the student should be particularly careful not to fall into the trap of memorising lists of cases with no clear understanding of the ratio decidendi therein.

Finally the student should, wherever possible, study the original sources, ie the original cases and statutes. However learned or illustrious a textbook author is, the textbook is essentially a secondhand version of the facts. Given the amount of material in the tort syllabus, this is a counsel of perfection, but it is well worth following whenever time permits. In particular, when a student encounters difficulties, a reading of the original authorities will often make not only the point being checked clear, but several others.

Studying the Law of Tort

Revision and Examination Technique

Revision Technique

Planning a revision timetable

In planning your revision timetable make sure you do not finish the syllabus too early. You should avoid leaving revision so late that you have to 'cram' – but constant revision of the same topic leads to stagnation.

Plan ahead, however, and try to make your plans increasingly detailed as you approach the examination date.

Allocate enough time for each topic to be studied. But note that it is better to devise a realistic timetable, to which you have a reasonable chance of keeping, rather than a wildly optimistic schedule which you will probably abandon at the first opportunity!

The syllabus and its topics

One of your first tasks when you began your course was to ensure that you thoroughly understood your syllabus. Check now to see if you can write down the topics it comprises from memory. You will see that the chapters of this WorkBook are each devoted to a syllabus topic. This will help you decide which are the key chapters relative to your revision programme, though you should allow some time for glancing through the other chapters.

The topic and its key points

Again working from memory, analyse what you consider to be the key points of any topic that you have selected for particular revision. Seeing what you can recall, unaided, will help you to understand and firmly memorise the concepts involved.

Using the WorkBook

Relevant questions are provided for each topic in this book. Naturally, as typical examples of examination questions, they do not normally relate to one topic only. But the questions in each chapter will relate to the subject matter of the chapter to a degree. You can choose your method of consulting the questions and solutions, but here are some suggestions (strategies 1–3). Each of them pre-supposes that you have read through the author's notes on key points and key cases and statutes, and any other preliminary matter, at the beginning of the chapter. Once again, you now need to practise working from memory, for that is the challenge you are preparing yourself for. As a rule of procedure constantly test yourself once revision starts, both orally and in writing.

Strategy 1

Strategy 1 is planned for the purpose of quick revision. First read your chosen question carefully and then jot down in abbreviated notes what you consider to be the main points at issue. Similarly, note the cases and statutes that occur to you as being relevant for citation purposes. Allow yourself sufficient time to cover what you feel to be relevant. Then study the author's skeleton solution and skim-read the suggested solution to see how they compare with your notes. When comparing consider carefully what the author has included (and concluded) and see whether that agrees with what you have written. Consider the points of variation also. Have you recognised the key issues? How relevant have you been? It is possible, of course, that you have referred to a recent case that is relevant, but which had not been reported when the WorkBook was prepared.

Strategy 2

Strategy 2 requires a nucleus of three hours in which to practise writing a set of examination answers in a limited time-span.

Select a number of questions (as many as are normally set in your subject in the examination you are studying for), each from a different chapter in the WorkBook, without consulting the solutions. Find a place to write where you will not be disturbed and try to arrange not to be interrupted for three hours. Write your solutions in the time allowed, noting any time needed to make up if you are interrupted.

After a rest, compare your answers with the suggested solutions in the WorkBook. There will be considerable variation in style, of course, but the bare facts should not be too dissimilar. Evaluate your answer critically. Be 'searching', but develop a positive approach to deciding how you would tackle each question on another occasion.

Strategy 3

You are unlikely to be able to do more than one three hour examination, but occasionally set yourself a single question. Vary the 'time allowed' by imagining it to be one of the questions that you must answer in three hours and allow yourself a limited preparation and writing time. Try one question that you feel to be difficult and an easier question on another occasion, for example.

Misuse of suggested solutions

Don't try to learn by rote. In particular, don't try to reproduce the suggested solutions by heart. Learn to express the basic concepts in your own words.

Keeping up-to-date

Keep up-to-date. While examiners do not require familiarity with changes in the law during the three months prior to the examination, it obviously creates a good impression if you can show you are acquainted with any recent changes. Make a habit of looking through one of the leading journals – *Modern Law Review*, *Law Quarterly Review* or the *New Law Journal*, for example – and cumulative indices to law reports, such as the *All England Law Reports* or *Weekly Law Reports*, or indeed the daily law reports in *The Times*. The *Law Society's Gazette* and the *Legal Executive Journal* are helpful sources, plus any specialist journal(s) for the subject you are studying.

Examination Skills

Examiners are human too!

The process of answering an examination question involves a communication between you and the person who set it. If you were speaking face to face with the person, you would choose your verbal points and arguments carefully in your reply. When writing, it is all too easy to forget the human being who is awaiting the reply and simply write out what one knows in the area of the subject! Bear in mind it is a person whose question you are responding to, throughout your essay. This will help you to avoid being irrelevant or long-winded.

The essay question

Candidates are sometimes tempted to choose to answer essay questions because they 'seem' easier. But the examiner is looking for thoughtful work and will not give good marks for superficial answers.

The essay-type of question may be either purely factual, in asking you to explain the meaning of a certain doctrine or principle, or it may ask you to discuss a certain proposition, usually derived from a quotation. In either case, the approach to the answer is the same. A clear programme must be devised to give the examiner the meaning or significance of the doctrine, principle or proposition and its origin in common law, equity or statute, and cases which illustrate its application to the branch of law concerned. Essay questions offer a good way to obtain marks if you have thought carefully about a topic, since it is up to you to impose the structure (unlike the problem questions where the problem imposes its own structure). You are then free to speculate and show imagination.

The problem question

The problem-type question requires a different approach. You may well be asked to advise a client or merely discuss the problems raised in the question. In either case, the most important factor is to take great care in reading the question. By its nature, the question will be longer than the essay-type question and you will have a number of facts to digest. Time spent in analysing the question may well save time later, when you are endeavouring to impress on the examiner the considerable extent of your basic legal knowledge. The quantity of knowledge is itself a trap and you must always keep within the boundaries of the question in hand. It is very tempting to show the examiner the extent of your knowledge of your subject, but if this is outside the question, it is time lost and no marks earned. It is inevitable that some areas which you have studied and revised will not be the subject of questions, but under no circumstances attempt to adapt a question to a stronger area of knowledge at the expense of relevance.

When you are satisfied that you have grasped the full significance of the problem-type question, set out the fundamental principles involved.

You will then go on to identify the fundamental problem (or problems) posed by the question. This should be followed by a consideration of the law which is relevant to the problem. The source of the law, together with the cases which will be of assistance in solving the problem, must then be considered in detail.

Very good problem questions are quite likely to have alternative answers, and in advising a party you should be aware that alternative arguments may be available. Each stage of your answer, in this case, will be based on the argument or arguments considered in the previous stage, forming a conditional sequence.

If, however, you only identify one fundamental problem, do not waste time worrying that you cannot think of an alternative – there may very well be only that one answer.

The examiner will then wish to see how you use your legal knowledge to formulate a case and how you apply that formula to the problem which is the subject of the question. It is this positive approach which can make answering a problem question a high mark earner for the student who has fully understood the question and clearly argued their case on the established law.

Examination checklist

a) Read the instructions at the head of the examination carefully. While last-minute changes are unlikely – such as the introduction of a compulsory question or an increase in the number of questions asked – it has been known to happen.

b) Read the questions carefully. Analyse problem questions – work out what the examiner wants.

c) Plan your answer before you start to write.

d) Check that you understand the rubric before you start to write. Do not 'discuss', for example, if you are specifically asked to 'compare and contrast'.

e) Answer the correct number of questions. If you fail to answer one out of four questions set you lose 25 per cent of your marks!

Style and structure

Try to be clear and concise. Fundamentally this amounts to using paragraphs to denote the sections of your essay, and writing simple, straightforward sentences as much as possible. The sentence you have just read has 22 words – when a sentence reaches 50 words it becomes difficult for a reader to follow.

Do not be inhibited by the word 'structure' (traditionally defined as giving an essay a beginning, a middle and an end). A good structure will be the natural consequence of setting out your arguments and the supporting evidence in a logical order. Set the scene briefly in your opening paragraph. Provide a clear conclusion in your final paragraph.

Table of Cases

Table of Statutes and Other Materials

Chapter 1

Introduction and Liability

1.1 Introduction

A tort is a civil wrong which is not solely a breach of contract or a breach of trust, and which gives rise to civil proceedings to enforce a right.

The law of tort is concerned with the legal duties that individuals owe to each other and with the legal rights that the law will protect.

1.2 Key points

Liability

A tort is some act by the defendant which, without just cause or excuse, causes some form of 'harm' to the claimant. 'Harm' is used here in a legal sense and two concepts must be examined.

Damnum sine injuria – damage without wrong

There are many kinds of harm of which the law takes no account, and so any damage suffered is damage without wrong, eg invasion of privacy, competition between traders. *Bradford Corporation* v *Pickles* [1895] AC 587 is the leading case where although damage was caused to the claimant it was caused only by the defendant exercising his legal rights and was therefore not actionable.

Injuria sine damne – wrong without damage

Here behaviour is actionable even though no damage has been caused. There are two kinds of tort; those which are actionable only on proof that actual damage resulted, eg negligence, and those which are actionable per se, eg trespass to land, libel which are actionable even though no actual damage follows.

Malice

Malice in the sense of an improper motive is relevant to certain torts only, eg malicious falsehood, nuisance in certain situations and some defences to defamation. But as a general rule motive is irrelevant in that a good motive is no justification for an illegal act and a bad motive does not make a legal act wrongful. See *Bradford Corporation* v *Pickles* (above) where the motive for the defendant's lawful actions was to coerce the claimant into buying the defendant's land at the defendant's price.

1.3 Key cases and statutes

- *Bradford* v *Pickles Corporation* [1895] AC 587
  Where there is a lawful excuse, there wil be no cause for action

- *Donoghue* v *Stevenson* [1932] AC 562
  The concept of duty of care or 'neighbour' principle was established

- *Smith* v *Littlewoods Organisation Ltd* [1987] AC 241
  The court will draw the extent of the duty owed by one person to another in any given circumstance

- Civil Liability (Contribution) Act 1978 – more than one person may be made liable to the same claimant

- Congenital Disabilities (Civil Liability) Act 1976 – Parliament vested a right of action in any child born alive for injuries suffered in the womb

1.4 Questions and suggested solutions

QUESTION ONE

'English law does not acknowledge a single tort of intention in the same sense that it acknowledges the existence of the tort of negligence.' (Markesinis and Deakin.)

Explain and discuss.

University of London LLB Examination
(for External Students) Law of Tort June 2000 Q2

General Comment

This is quite a wide question that requires the candidate to compare and contrast tortious liability with other forms of tortious liability that are based on intention. There must be a comparative element in the answer, and the discussion should not deal with only negligence.

Skeleton Solution

Introduction – the basis of tortious liability – remedy in tort – the nature of other liability based on intention – remedies in such cases – a comparative analysis.

Suggested Solution

As far as the law of tort is concerned, Salmond and Heuston (*Law of Tort* (5th edn, 1999) contend that 'the law in general asks merely what the defendant has done, not why he did it'. Therefore, it follows that the defendant's motive or intention is irrelevant (usually) to his liability in tort. For example, in the tort of defamation, it is said that the defamatory words must be 'maliciously' published, but this is regarded as mere verbiage. It has been established that even an innocent publication will suffice to give rise to a tortious action for defamation.

Jones (*Tort* (7th edn, 2000)) states that malice can have two meanings in tort: first, intentional wrongdoing, and second, improper motive. Intention refers to the defendant's knowledge that the consequences of his conduct are bound to occur, where the consequences are desired or, if not desired, are foreseen as a result. Recklessness for instance is always categorised with intention, where it is used to signify the defendant's advertence to a risk that the consequences will result from his act, although the House of Lords in cases such as *R* v *Lawrence* [1982] AC 510 and *R* v *Reid* [1992] 1 WLR 793 has stated that recklessness can include some forms of inadvertence.

As Jones rightly observes, as far as tort is concerned the concept of intention has not created the problems that have bedevilled the criminal law. The much wider range of liability for careless conduct or negligence has, to a large extent, removed the need for fine distinctions. In the tort of negligence, if a defendant is responsible when he ought to have foreseen that harm would result from his actions, it becomes irrelevant whether in fact he did foresee the possibility of harm, or even whether he desired it, unlike criminal law, where the culpability or intention must be proved by the prosecution to secure a conviction.

The tort of negligence has, ever since the case of *Donoghue* v *Stevenson* [1932] AC 562, itself developed into a general principle of liability which is distinct and exclusive from other torts which have some connotation or link or relationship with the concept of intention. In negligence, a duty of care must be owed. That duty must have been breached and must result in consequential damage, either in the form of a physical injury or property damage. If this is the case, then the defendant will be liable to the claimant. The usual remedy is that of damages. Negligence can relate to misfeasance or non-feasance, and has nothing or little to do with intention.

But, be that as it may, there are, however, other torts which involve the intentional infliction of harm. These torts will now be analysed briefly. Some of these torts do inevitably overlap with criminal law, for example the torts of trespass to the person and to land.

Battery, for example, is a tort which clearly cannot be committed in the absence of intent. Battery is the direct act of the defendant which causes contact with the claimant's body without the claimant's consent. The court in *Letang* v *Cooper* [1965] 1 QB 232 said that intent to harm is an essential element for this tort, and, in *Miller* v *Jackson* [1977] QB 966, the court held that this particular tort cannot be committed negligently. The House of Lords in *Stubbings* v *Webb* [1993] 2 WLR 120 subsequently emphasised the distinct and separate nature of the tort of trespass.

Trespass to land is defined as a direct interference with the possession of another's land, without lawful justification. One of the essential elements of this tort is intention. The defendant must have intended to enter the land, but need not have intended to trespass. Hence, it is no defence to show that the defendant was unaware that the land belonged to somebody else: *Conway* v *George Wimpey & Co Ltd* [1951] 2 KB 266. It is, however, a defence to show that he had no intention of entering the land, as in *Smith* v *Stone* (1647) Style 65.

It was held in *Wilkinson* v *Downton* [1897] 2 QB 57 that where the defendant intentionally inflicts, or wilfully does, an act calculated to cause physical damage to the claimant, and has in fact caused such harm, a cause of action arises in tort.

There are other torts which cover the infliction of economic harm, such as deceit and malicious falsehood, which are also intention based. In the tort of deceit, for instance, the court in *Pasley* v *Freeman* (1789) 3 TR 51 stated that where a person makes a wilful and reckless statement to another with the intention that the other shall act in reliance upon that statement, and the other does in fact rely on the statement to his or her detriment, liability arises in tort. It must be mentioned that the tort of deceit has similarities with the tort of negligent misstatement and the contractual concept of fraudulent misrepresentation. Deceit, of course, is more appropriate where the parties are in a non-contractual relationship. Malicious falsehood involves the making of a false statement, with malice, to a person other than the claimant, which causes damage to the claimant; the court in *Ratcliffe* v *Evans* [1892] 2 QB 524 emphasised the requirement of malice or intention. An honest belief would therefore negate the presumption of an intention: *Balden* v *Shorter* [1933] Ch 247.

The economic tort of conspiracy is yet another tort which requires an intention on the part of the conspirators to pursue a common aim or objective. This was illustrated in *Lonrho plc* v *Fayed* [1991] 3 WLR 188.

Inducing a breach of contract is also an economic tort which requires knowledge and intention on the part of the defendant. The court in *Merkur Island Shipping Corp* v *Laughton* [1983] 2 AC 570 stated that this tort cannot be committed negligently. Intimidation is another tort which has intention as one of its core elements: *Rookes* v *Barnard* [1964] AC 1129. Another good example would be the tortious act of interference with trade by unlawful means. In *Associated British Ports* v *Transport and General Workers Union* [1989] 1 WLR 939, the court held that it was the presence of an intent to injure which turned a non-actionable inducement of breach into unlawful means.

Whilst the remedy is purely damages in the tort of negligence, for all the other torts requiring intention, the remedy could also include injunctions as well as mere damages. Hence, it is submitted that whilst negligence may be viewed as singular, there is not, on a comparative basis, a simple tort of intention in the same sense.

QUESTION TWO

'The general rule is that, if conduct is presumptively unlawful, a good motive will not exonerate the defendant, and that, if conduct is lawful apart from motive, a bad motive will not make him liable.' (Winfield and Jolowicz.)

Discuss this statement. Should the law of tort attach more importance to the defendant's motives?

University of London LLB Examination
(for External Students) Law of Tort June 1990 Q2

General Comment

A question that raises the relevance of motive or intention in the commission of a tort. A distinction must be drawn between motive in criminal law (which must essentially be proven) and motive in the civil law of tort which need not be proven in order to find liability on the part of the tortfeasor.

Skeleton Solution

The nature of the law of tort – different types of tort – relevance of motive – nuisance – economic torts – breach of contract – conversion – conclusion as to irrelevance of motive.

Suggested Solution

Perhaps the best known case on lawful conduct not being made unlawful by a bad motive is *Bradford Corporation* v *Pickles* [1895] AC 587, where the defendant was held not liable for intentionally intercepting water flowing through his land via undefined channels. The defendant's motive in doing this was to coerce the claimant into buying the defendant's land at the defendant's price, and it was held that as his act was lawful his motive could not make it unlawful. This was re-emphasised by the House of Lords a few years later in *Allen* v *Flood* [1898] AC 1. *Chapman* v *Honig* [1963] 2 QB 502, where a landlord maliciously served a notice to quit on a tenant, and *Wyld* v *Silver* [1963] 1 QB 169, where persons exercised a long-defunct right to hold a fair solely to prevent the erection of buildings for which planning permission had been granted, are more modern examples.

Clearly, however, there are some areas of the law of tort where motive is relevant. Thus malice will have to be shown in malicious prosecution or malicious falsehood, and in defamation the presence of malice will destroy the defence of fair comment or qualified privilege.

Another area in which motive is relevant is nuisance. While malice is by no means an essential ingredient of this tort, the presence of malice may mean that an interference is deemed unreasonable, as in *Hollywood Silver Fox Farm* v *Emmett* [1936] 2 KB 468 where the defendant was held to have committed a nuisance when he acted maliciously, and it seems clear that in the absence of malice no nuisance would have been found. *Christie* v *Davey* [1893] 1 Ch 316 is a similar example of malice being taken into account.

Finally, it is in the area of economic torts that motive may be relevant. Thus in *Mogul Steamship* v *McGregor, Gow & Co* [1892] AC 25, it was held that the motive of the defendant was irrelevant and a cause of action would only arise where the defendant's action was unlawful. A few years later in *Allen* v *Flood* [1898] AC 1 the House of Lords reached a similar conclusion. However, in *Quinn* v *Leatham* [1901] AC 495 the House of Lords held that a tort had been committed where the defendants acted lawfully but with a malicious motive. The anomalous finding in *Quinn* has been confined to cases of conspiracy to injure. Motive is relevant to this tort which can be carried out (inter alia) by the doing of a lawful act by unlawful means by two or more persons: *Mulcahy* v *R* (1868) LR 3 HL 306, 317. This leads to the strange conclusion that if an individual carried out the acts they would be lawful, ie the motive would be irrelevant, but if carried out by more than one person the acts would become actionable because of the motive, as in *Huntley* v *Thornton* [1957] 1 WLR 321 where the reason for denying the claimant employment was to uphold the dignity of certain union officials. By contrast in *Crofter Hand Woven Harris Tweed* v *Veitch* [1942] AC 435, where the defendants' motive was to protect their members' interests, it was held no action would lie.

In the tort of inducing a breach of contract, the relevant defences were summarised in *Edwin Hill & Partners* v *First National Finance Corporation* [1989] 1 WLR 225. It was stated that absence of malice was irrelevant (*South Wales Miners' Federation* v *Glamorgan Coal* [1905] AC 239), but that a moral duty to induce a breach of contract, as in *Brimelow* v *Casson* [1924] 1 Ch 302, was a defence, so again motive may be relevant.

Lastly, in the tort of interference with trade by unlawful means, it was held in *Lonrho plc* v *Fayed* [1991] 3 All ER 303 that an essential ingredient of this tort was an intent to harm the claimant where lawful means are used or to direct the unlawful act against the claimant, so again motive is relevant here.

Thus it can be seen that while traditionally the law has disregarded motive, there are some important exceptions to this rule in both nuisance and defamation and in the relatively new and still developing area of economic torts the courts seem more ready to pay attention to the defendant's motives.

The difficulty of attaching more importance to the defendant's motives is that often the criterion used in fixing liability is objective, rather than subjective, as well as the difficulty of ascertaining the defendant's motive, especially as unreasonable behaviour does not necessarily prove the existence of malice. As public law (eg planning law) controls a person's freedom to act in detriment to the interests of the community, and the law of tort regulates behaviour between individuals, it might seem an unwarranted infringement on personal liberty to delve into a person's motives and make lawful acts unlawful. Even greater problems could arise if unlawful acts were to be made lawful because of a good motive; eg an employer removes a guard from dangerous machinery to enable the employee to work faster and obtain higher wages – the employee is injured and would not have been if the guard had been kept in place. Should the employer's good motive exonerate him? On the other hand why should a malicious defendant be able to rely on a defence of justification in defamation? The reliance on motive would also tend to create uncertainty as regards the liability of a particular defendant.

Overall, therefore, it is submitted that a case has not been made out for attaching more importance in tort to the defendant's motives.

QUESTION THREE

Discuss the proposition that the law of tort attaches too little significance to motive or purpose as a basis of liability.

> University of London LLB Examination
> (for External Students) Law of Tort June 1993 Q5

General Comment

A general question raising the relevance of motive in the commission of civil wrongs or torts. Examples of the different types of tort need to be discussed with emphasis on the irrelevance of motive.

Skeleton Solution

Definition of terms – the general rule as to motive – exceptions: nuisance; defamation – discussion.

Suggested Solution

The law of torts may be seen as a number of specific rules prohibiting certain kinds of harmful behaviour, such as negligence, trespass or defamation. Depending upon one's viewpoint, there may be a fundamental general principle underlying these rules that it is wrongful to cause harm to others. In *Mogul Steamship Co Ltd* v *McGregor, Gow & Co* [1892] AC 25, Bowen LJ said that whenever someone intentionally caused harm without lawful justification or excuse, liability should follow. That was not the case at the time and nor is it that straightforward today. In truth, the mental element will often play a small part in establishing liability in tort.

One has to consider carefully the terms. By motive or purpose, one means the ulterior reason behind the act, which frequently will be malice. This is not the same as intention, which is the mental element immediately behind the particular act. To take an example: A sees B, a child, shoplifting so he slaps B across the face. This is a trespass to B's person. A's intention was to strike him. However, his motive or purpose may have been to punish him. Without the intention, this would not have amounted to a battery; the motive is no defence. Of course, there will be a grey area where the terms merge. The word 'purpose' perhaps connotes a longer-term intention and is sometimes used synonymously with intention. However, what we are concerned with in this question is how important is the underlying reason in tort.

One can say immediately that the presence of a malicious motive will not generally make an otherwise lawful act actionable (*Allen* v *Flood* [1898] AC 1), nor will it exonerate the defendant who has acted unlawfully. One can further state that, with some exceptions, the defendant's motive will generally be irrelevant. In negligence, for example, my ulterior reason for driving negligently so as to cause an accident will count for nothing.

One exception is private nuisance. A spiteful motive – in other words, malice – can make interference with a person's use and enjoyment of land unreasonable and therefore an actionable nuisance. In *Christie* v *Davey* [1893] 1 Ch 316, the defendant was held liable for deliberately and maliciously banging on a party wall to annoy the claimant, a teacher of music. Again, in *Hollywood Silver Fox Farm Ltd* v *Emmett* [1936] 2 KB 468, a defendant who deliberately caused guns to be fired near the claimant's boundary in order to scare his foxes during breeding time was held liable. Both of these activities might not have amounted to a nuisance in the absence of malice.

Another exception is defamation, where the defence of qualified privilege can be defeated by proving malice, as can the defence of fair comment. Malice in the former may mean not only an improper purpose but a lack of belief in the truth of the statement subject to the qualified privilege. In the latter, malice refers to an evil motive, as in *Thomas* v *Bradbury, Agnew & Co Ltd* [1906] 2 KB 627, where a book reviewer's demeanour in the witness box showed personal hostility to the claimant.

There are certain torts which depend upon proof of intention – such as conspiracy, inducing breach of contract, intimidation – but it remains the case that motive as an element is the exception. In which case, should it have greater significance? To take negligence again: the imposition of a duty is largely based upon objective criteria and the foresight of the reasonable man. Whether or not one can say there is a general duty of care following cases such as *Murphy* v *Brentwood District Council* [1991] 1 AC 398 is questionable, nevertheless there is a large body of case law which establishes the parameters of negligence and any extension of that duty is by analogy. Motive is incompatible with recognition of that duty. As a defence, it would allow the claimant to say that, although he was negligent, his motives were such as to override this liability. However, one can argue that a person is no less negligent and the damage is not reduced merely by the fact that the defendant had a positive motive or purpose.

One is considering motive as a positive factor here. As a negative factor, there is more scope for saying that it should have greater significance. While it is unlikely that existing torts will change to include it, motive may have an important role in developing torts. The tort of harassment was recognised by the Court of Appeal in *Khorasandjian* v *Bush* [1993] 3 WLR 476 and this is an area where motive or purpose may prove to be an important element. Similarly, if a tort of privacy is established, the motive of the tortfeasor may well be significant.

It is difficult to say whether there is too little significance attached to motive, although undoubtedly it has little relevance in many areas. If tort is made up of various rules prohibiting certain types of behaviour, then the motive of the tortfeasor in behaving in that way is inevitably of relatively little importance.

One reason that perhaps justifies this approach is that motive is largely an area which is governed by criminal laws and to encroach into it by establishing tortious principles based on motive or intention would be to upset the established principles of criminal liability.

Chapter 2

Parties and Types of Liability

2.1   Introduction

2.2   Key points

2.3   Key cases and statutes

2.4   Questions

2.1 Introduction

This chapter briefly discusses who can sue and be sued, and the situation where there is more than one defendant.

2.2 Key points

Parties

a) Minors can sue in tort, as can an unborn child both at statute law, Congenital Disabilities (Civil Liability) Act 1976, and at common law: *B* v *Islington Health Authority* [1992] NLJ 565, and spouses may sue each other. A minor cannot be sued in tort if the effect would be to enforce a legally unenforceable contract against him: *Jennings* v *Rundall* (1799) 8 Term Rep 335.

b) Note the position of the Crown and members of the armed forces. In law a company is a person, so a company may sue and be sued, and is often the defendant in a tort action as companies are vicariously liable for the torts committed by their employees in the course of their employment: see *Matthews* v *Ministry of Defence* [2003] 1 All ER 689 and *Multiple Claimants* v *Ministry of Defence* [2003] EWHC 1134 which provide useful illustrations.

c) Unincorporated associations, such as clubs, have no legal personality and so cannot sue or be sued: *Robertson* v *Ridley* [1989] 1 WLR 872.

d) Trade unions have some of the attributes of legal entities and can be sued, but they cannot sue in defamation: *EETPU* v *Times Newspapers* [1980] QB 585.

e) A witness in a case cannot subsequently file a negligence action against the police. The case of *Darker* v *Chief Constable of the West Midlands Police* [2000] 4 All ER 193 (HL) provides a useful illustration.

Types of liability

Independent liability

If the claimant is damaged by two separate torts he may sue each defendant separately in respect of the damage suffered: *Baker* v *Willoughby* [1970] AC 467.

Several liability

If the tortfeasors act independently and cause the same damage to the claimant, each tortfeasor is separately liable for the damage (although the claimant can only recover damages once): *The Koursk* [1924] P 140.

Joint liability

a) Here two tortfeasors damage the claimant following a shared intent. Joint liability can also arise in vicarious liability eg where an employer is held vicariously liable for the tort of his employee. Here both employer and employee are jointly liable. Each tortfeasor is liable for the damage, but the claimant can only recover once.

b) Under the Civil Liability (Contribution) Act 1978, judgment against one tortfeasor does not bar a subsequent action against another joint tortfeasor, nor is there any rule against recovery of contribution between joint tortfeasors. See *K* v *P* [1993] 1 All ER 521 for a wide interpretation of the scope of the 1978 Act.

c) Limitation periods. The Limitation Act 1980 governs the time period in which tortious actions can be brought. Sections 2, 11, 14 and 33 are of particular relevance and importance.

2.3 Key cases and statutes

- *B* v *Islington Health Authority* [1992] NLJ 565
  Minors have a right to sue in law

- *Baker* v *Willoughby* [1970] AC 467
  The claimant may sue more than one defendant if blame can be apportioned as appropriate

- *Darker* v *Chief Constable of the West Midlands Police* [2000] 4 All ER 193
  A witness cannot subsequently sue the police in negligence

- *EETPU* v *Times Newspapers* [1980] QB 585
  Trade unions, though not strictly legal entities, may sue in some instances – for instance, in defamation

- *Matthews* v *Ministry of Defence* [2003] 1 All ER 689 (HL)
  On the extent of Crown immunity

- *Multiple Claimants* v *Ministry of Defence* [2003] EWHC 1134
  On the extent of Crown immunity

- Civil Liability (Contribution) Act 1978 – distributes liabilities amongst blameworthy tortfeasors

- Congenital Disabilities (Civil Liability) Act 1976 – newborn children have the 'locus' to sue

- Limitation Act 1980 – defines the time periods within which actions must be initiated in court

2.4 Questions

Questions are rarely set on the above specific points, although a knowledge of them is frequently implicit in examination questions.

Chapter 3
General Defences

3.1   Introduction

3.2   Key points

3.3   Key cases and statutes

3.4   Questions and suggested solutions

3.1 Introduction

Although each tort will have a number of defences that are specific to that tort (eg in negligence that no duty of care was owed) there are a number of defences that are common throughout the law of tort.

3.2 Key points

Necessity

This defence exists: *Cope* v *Sharpe* [1912] 1 KB 496; *Rigby* v *Chief Constable of Northamptonshire* [1985] 1 WLR 1242; [1985] 2 All ER 985, although it is not much favoured by the courts: *Southwark London Borough Council* v *Williams* [1971] Ch 734. The case of *Monsanto plc* v *Tilly* [2000] Env LR 313 also provides a useful example.

Statutory authority

Where a statute authorises an act, no action will lie either for doing that act or for any necessary consequence of the act: *Vaughan* v *Taff Vale Railway* (1860) 5 H & N 679. See *Allen* v *Gulf Oil Refining* [1981] AC 1001 on the liberal interpretation of such statutes, but note *Hampson* v *Department of Education and Science* [1990] 2 All ER 513.

Consent or volenti non fit injuria

This defence, usually known as the volenti defence, is based on the maxim 'volenti non fit injuria' – no wrong is done to one who consents. This is a complete defence.

Clearly few problems will occur where harm is intentionally inflicted on a consenting person. However, problems can arise where harm is accidentally inflicted: acceptance of the risk of injury must be voluntary with no constraints (*Bowater* v *Rowley Regis Corporation* [1944] KB 476; *Smith* v *Baker* [1891] AC 325) and there must be express or implied agreement between the claimant and defendant that the claimant will accept the risk of injury: *Nettleship* v *Weston* [1971] 2 QB 691; *Pitts* v *Hunt* [1990] 3 WLR 542; *Morris* v *Murray* [1990] 3 All ER 801.

Note the possible application of the Unfair Contract Terms Act 1977 to any agreement; that mere knowledge of the danger is insufficient to establish the defence (see *Smith* v *Baker* (above)); that the defence does not apply to rescue cases (*Haynes* v *Harwood* [1935] 1 KB 146); the effect of s149(3) Road Traffic Act 1988 (*Pitts* v *Hunt* [1990] 3 WLR 542), and the fact that if the 1988 Act is inapplicable, eg as between an aircraft pilot and his passenger, that the volenti defence can be successful: *Morris* v *Murray* [1990] 3 All ER 801.

Illegality (*ex turpi causa non oritur actio*)

If a claimant suffers damage because of the defendant's tort while participating in a crime, no action will lie on the grounds of public policy – ex turpi causa non oritur actio – no right of action arises from a bad cause (*Ashton* v *Turner* [1981] QB 137; *Pitts* v *Hunt* [1990] 3 WLR 542), but note *Tinsley* v *Milligan* [1993] 3 WLR 126 in which the House of Lords rejected the 'affront to public conscience' test as a general guide to barring recovery. The Court of Appeal's decision in *Clunis* v *Camden and Islington Health Authority* [1998] QB 978 also lends support to this contention.

Mistake

Although it is not a general defence in a tort action, it can operate as a defence – for instance, an honest but mistaken belief in the truth of a statement will negative liability in deceit.

Limitation

Statute has intervened to impost time limits within which an action in tort must be brought against the defendant. Section 2 of the Limitation Act 1980 bars all actions brought after six years from the date on which the claimant's cause of action accrued. Other relevant sections are ss11, 14 and 33. Noteworthy cases include: *Byrne* v *Hall Pain & Foster* [1999] 2 All ER 400 and *James* v *East Dorset Health Authority* (2001) 59 BMLR 196.

Contributory negligence

The Law Reform (Contributory Negligence) Act 1945 creates a partial defence where the defendant can prove that the claimant contributed to his injury through his own fault. The court can reduce damages to the extent that it thinks just and reasonable to reflect the claimant's fault: see *Jayes* v *IMI (Kynoch) Ltd* [1985] ICR 55 for an illustration.

The Court of Appeal has applied s1 of this Act in the case of *Sahid Foods Ltd (In Liquidation)* v *Paskin Kynakides Sands (A Firm)* (2004) The Times 23 January.

3.3 Key cases and statutes

- *Byrne* v *Hall Pain & Foster* [1999] 2 All ER 400 (CA)
  Time begins to run from the date of damage, in tort

- *James* v *East Dorset Health Authority* (2001) 59 BMLR 196
  Date of damage is deemed to be the date of the actual knowledge of the damage

- *Monsanto plc* v *Tilly* [2000] Env LR 313
  The defence of 'necessity' is very restrictively interpreted in tort

- *Pride Valley Foods Ltd* v *Hall and Partners* (2001) 76 Com LR 1
  The court apportioned 50 per cent fault on the claimants in applying the Law Reform (Contributory Negligence) Act 1945

- *Sahid Foods Ltd (In Liquidation)* v *Paskin Kynakides Sands (A Firm)* (2004) The Times 23 January
  Illustrates how the court applies the Law Reform (Contributory Negligence) Act 1945

- Law Reform (Contributory Negligence) Act 1945 – establishes a partial defence

- Limitation Act 1980 – sets out the time period within which actions in tort should be commenced

3.4 Questions and suggested solutions

QUESTION ONE

a) Discuss the concept of necessity as a defence to an action in trespasss.

b) Hilda enters hospital for major abdominal surgery. Ingrid, the surgical registrar, describes the nature of the operation to her and she signs a form consenting to the surgery. During the operation Ingrid notices that Hilda's appendix is diseased and is likely to cause her serious problems in a year or two. She therefore removes it. Hilda is annoyed when she discovers that this has happened.

Advise her.

University of London LLB Examination
(for External Students) Law of Tort June 1998 Q8

General Comment

Candidates would have needed a very detailed knowledge of the defences to actions in trespass, particularly in respect of trespasses to the person, in order to do justice to this question. It is therefore unsurprising that few candidates chose to answer this question in the exam.

Skeleton Solution

a) Discuss the limited nature of the defence of necessity to actions in both trespass to property and to the person, using past cases by way of illustration.

b) Discuss whether the removal of Hilda's appendix might have been covered by the terms of her original written consent – if Hilda's consent was not expressly provided, might the courts imply such consent? – finally, discuss whether the defence of necessity might justify additional procedures being carried out where other medical conditions are discovered during an operation.

Suggested Solution

a) Necessity is, by definition, an extremely limited defence in trespass as it allows a defendant to lawfully protect his, or another's, person or property, even though the result is that an innocent person suffers a loss in the process. It is likely that the defence will only be available in emergency situations where it is necessary for private citizens to avert immediate and serious dangers to life or property, and where the citizen acts reasonably in all the circumstances. Thus, defendants who take personal action, when a call to the emergency services would have been a reasonable alternative course of action, are unlikely to avail themselves of the defence.

On this basis, campaigners against field trials of genetically modified plants had no defence to an action in trespass after entering land to destroy some of the crops, even though they claimed such action was necessary to raise public awareness and to protect the public: *Monsanto plc v Tilly* [2000] Env LR 313. In *Southwark London Borough Council v Williams* [1971] Ch 734 necessity was also held to be no defence to actions in trespass brought against homeless persons squatting in empty local authority housing, Lord Denning stating that otherwise, necessity '... would be an excuse for all sorts of wrongdoing. So the courts must, for the sake of law and order, take a firm stand.'

However, necessity has been successfully used as a defence to trespass to property in a variety of circumstances such as the following.

i) The prevention, by diversion, of flood water from entering a defendant's land, with the result that a neighbour's land was flooded: *Home Brewery plc v William Davis & Co (Loughborough) Ltd* [1987] QB 339.

ii) The prevention of a plague of locusts from entering the defendant's land (achieved by entering the land of a third party) with the result that the insects re-entered the claimant's land, destroying crops: *Greyvensteyn v Hattingh* [1911] AC 355.

iii) The firing, by a police officer, of a CS gas cylinder into a building in order to flush out a dangerous psychopath: *Rigby v Chief Constable of Northamptonshire* [1985] 2 All ER 985. However, whilst the defence was held to apply in the circumstances, damages were awarded against the defendant as the officer responsible was found to have been negligent in firing the cylinder without having fire fighting equipment to hand.

iv) The throwing of goods overboard in a storm in order to save the passengers on a ship: *Mouse's Case* (1609) 12 Co Rep 63.

Necessity is also a limited defence to trespasses against the person. Most cases have arisen where medical treatment has been administered without a patient's consent, but even here the courts have taken an extremely restrictive approach to the availability of the defence, the sanctity of the human body being a fundamental basic principle.

Necessity would be applicable in those circumstances where a doctor is forced to give medical treatment to an unconscious patient in order to preserve life or prevent permanent damage to health. It might also extend to the administration of treatment to a conscious adult who is temporarily or permanently incompetent to give consent by reason of mental illness or because of the undue influence of others. For example, in *F* v *West Berkshire Area Health Authority* [1989] 2 All ER 545 the House of Lords allowed the defence of necessity to justify the sterilisation of a 36-year-old woman who was a voluntary patient in a mental hospital. It was held that the defence would be available in similar circumstances where a reasonable body of medical opinion was in favour of allowing the treatment in the best interests of the patient. Not only would treatment be justified in order to save life or to prevent permanent injury, but also in cases of routine medical treatment.

However, the defence will not operate where a mentally competent patient refuses life-saving treatment provided there is a full understanding of the consequences of that decision. This principle extends to the refusal of a caesarean section, even if that would mean the death of the mother's unborn child: *Re M B (Caesarean Section)* [1997] 147 NLJ 600. Nor could the defence be used to justify the force-feeding of prisoners on hunger strike: *Secretary of State for the Home Department* v *Robb* [1995] Fam 127.

b) The issues to be decided here are whether Hilda has in fact given her consent (express or implied) to the removal of her appendix and if not, whether its removal by the hospital was justified on the grounds of necessity. The basic position was stated by Lord Brandon in *F* v *West Berkshire Area Health Authority*:

> 'At common law, a doctor cannot lawfully operate on adult patients of sound mind … without their consent. If a doctor were to operate on such patients, or give them other treatment, without their consent, he would commit the actionable tort of trespass to the person.'

In other words, the hospital may have committed a battery on Hilda in going beyond the scope of the original abdominal surgery. Whether such a battery has taken place here will depend upon the scope of the defences available to the hospital.

Did Hilda provide her express consent to the removal of her appendix?

We are told that Hilda signed a consent form covering, at the very least, major abdominal surgery. Such written consents normally contain a declaration, on the part of the patient, that the nature and effect of the treatment has been explained to them, and provided that the patient has in fact been advised of the broad nature of the operation by a doctor, consent will have been lawfully given. Whether Hilda has expressly consented to the removal of her appendix appears, therefore, to depend upon how closely this further procedure matched the precise nature of the operation previously explained to her. It is possible that the diseased appendix related to the condition originally requiring surgery, in which case Hilda's actual consent is more likely to authorise the removal of the organ. Another possibility is that the original written consent may have authorised such further treatment as the doctor considered necessary or desirable in the circumstances. Such a wording, if present, would appear to cover the removal of the appendix.

Did Hilda impliedly consent to the removal of her appendix in the circumstances?

Consent to a course of medical treatment can sometimes be implied from the claimant's conduct, eg where a patient holds out her arm in order to receive an injection. It is clearly much more difficult to imply such consent if a patient is unconscious when the need for a consent first arises. It might be thought that the courts would approach the issue on the basis of whether a reasonable person would have wanted their appendix removed during an operation for some other matter, given that it's removal would have been inevitable at some stage in the future. This would obviously depend upon whether any additional risks were involved. However, the courts prefer to approach these questions according to the defence of necessity rather than upon issues of implied consent (*F* v *West Berkshire Area Health Authority*), and it is submitted that this is the likely basis on which the hospital would have to justify their actions.

Can the removal of the appendix be justified by the defence of necessity?

It has already been noted that that a doctor would be justified in administering urgent, necessary medical treatment where a patient is unconscious and not known to object to it. However, this exception appears to be confined to cases where immediate action is necessary to preserve life or prevent permanent damage to health. It is clear that Hilda's diseased appendix does not pose any immediate threat to her health, and on this basis, it is submitted that she ought to have been given the opportunity to provide her consent to the procedure, even if that meant a further operation.

There does not appear to be any explicit UK authority on whether consent to one medical procedure justifies another. Whilst the issue was considered by the Canadian courts in *Marshall* v *Curry* [1933] 3 DLR 260 and *Murray* v *McMurchy* [1949] 2 DLR 442 (and resolved as suggested above), the question was expressly left open in *F* v *West Berkshire Area Health Authority* by Lord Goff. It is submitted that necessity will be no defence in the circumstances described.

QUESTION TWO

Fergus is employed as a driver by the Egmont Engineering Co. It is a company rule that only their employees may be carried in their vehicles. A notice is displayed on the dashboard of Fergus's van, reading:

> 'Egmont employees only in this van. The company can accept no liability towards any other persons riding in this vehicle.'

One day Fergus has to drive to the premises of a supplier to collect some materials. George, an employee of a firm of electrical contractors repairing machinery at the Egmont plant, asks if he can have a lift to collect some supplies urgently needed for their repairs. Fergus agrees, but on the way he is gripped by severe chest pains, George asks him, 'Are you feeling well enough?' Fergus replies, 'Yes, just a touch of indigestion.' George allows him to continue to drive. A few minutes later Fergus loses control of the van and crashes into a lamp-post. George is thrown out of the van and is severely injured. He had not been wearing a seat belt because he felt trapped if he did so. If he had been wearing a belt, his injuries would have been slight.

It is later discovered that Fergus had had a heart attack and he can now remember nothing of the accident.

Advise George.

Written by the Author

General Comment

A general problem on negligence, and particularly the tort of vicarious liability. It also raises the defences of contributory negligence and volenti non fit injuria as appropriate.

Skeleton Solution

Elements of the tort of negligence – reasonable person test – element of vicarious liability – defence of contributory negligence – defence of volenti non fit injuria – relevance of UCTA 1977 as regards exclusion of liability.

Suggested Solution

George will base his action on Fergus' negligence, and may be in a position to sue Fergus' employers should they be vicariously liable.

He must first prove that Fergus owed him a duty of care to take reasonable steps for his safety while he is a passenger, and a duty of care has been found to exist between passenger and driver in cases such as *Froom* v *Butcher* [1975] 3 WLR 379. Since Fergus should have George in his reasonable contemplation as he may be harmed by his carelessness, it is submitted that he is under a duty of care. A breach of that duty will be proved if a reasonable man would not have acted in the same way: *Blyth* v *Birmingham Waterworks* (1856) 11 Ex 781. On the facts, it is not per se a breach that Fergus lost control of the vehicle, but a reasonable and prudent driver may, on feeling unwell, pull into the side of the road and stop his vehicle, especially if he had a passenger, and so Fergus is in breach by continuing to drive when he feels unwell. Res ipsa loquitur has no application here since the reason for Fergus' loss of control is ascertainable: *Barkway* v *South Wales Transport* [1950] AC 185. Fergus' breach has caused George's injuries, so that negligence has prima facie been made out.

The second issue is whether Egmont Engineering Co is vicariously liable for Fergus' negligence. Fergus must be their employee, which is apparent from the facts, but it must also be determined whether he is 'in the course of employment'. This phrase has in recent times been construed by the courts very liberally. The question to be asked is whether Fergus was performing an act which he was authorised to do or which was reasonably incidental to his employment, even though he may have been doing it in an unauthorised manner; if he was his employers will be liable.

The fact that Fergus undoubtedly knew of his employers' prohibition on the carrying of non-employees is, it is submitted, by no means decisive. In *Limpus* v *London General Omnibus Co* (1862) 1 H & C 526, contrary to his employers' express instructions, a bus driver obstructed buses from a rival company and caused an accident; it was held that the employers were still vicariously liable because the driver's act was merely a wrongful act of carrying out an authorised act, ie the driving of buses, and was not an act which he was not employed to do at all. The prohibition related to the mode of performing his job and not to the scope of his employment: see *Beard* v *London General Omnibus Co* [1900] 2 QB 530.

A contrary view was taken as to a prohibition in *Twine* v *Bean's Express* [1946] 1 All ER 202, a case with facts similar to those in George's case, except that in *Twine* a hitchhiker was given a lift. It was held that an employee giving a lift to an unauthorised person is acting outside the course of his employment. Since the claimant was a trespasser, the employers owed him no duty of care. The latter reason now seems erroneous in the light of *British Railways Board* v *Herrington* [1972] 2 WLR 537 and the Occupiers' Liability Act 1984, where a modified duty of care was held to apply to trespassers, but the main distinction is that the court in *Twine* based vicarious liability on a duty of care owed by the employer to the claimant, a view which today has lost favour, so that modern courts examine instead the employer/employee relationship.

The decision in *Twine* was disapproved of by a majority of the Court of Appeal in *Rose* v *Plenty* [1976] 1 WLR 141 where the trespassory status of the claimant in the milk-float was regarded as irrelevant, and in any event the presence of the boy was in effect furthering the employer's interests in helping to deliver milk.

It is submitted that *Rose* is the preferable decision to apply in this case so that the prohibition relates only to the way in which Fergus is to carry out his job as a driver and it is immaterial that George is a trespasser. It may further be argued that George's presence is indirectly furthering Egmont's interests, since he is an employee of contractors repairing machinery at the Egmont plant. As long as Fergus has not deviated from his route, he is not on a frolic of his own.

Egmont's notice should also be read in the light of s2 of the Unfair Contract Terms Act 1977, so that the employers could not rely on the notice to the extent that it purports to exclude liability for death or personal injury caused by negligence.

Fergus and Egmont would be able to claim contributory negligence against George on two possible grounds. The clearest is his failure to wear a seatbelt and he must face a reduction in his damages of 20 per cent – 15 per cent since his injuries would have been slight had he worn one (*Froom v Butcher* (above)). His aversion to seatbelts is unlikely to affect this, per Denning MR in Froom, unless his aversion amounted to a 'phobia': *Condon v Condon* [1978] RTR 473. He may also have acted without regard for his own safety by allowing Fergus to continue driving when he felt unwell; this case is different from decisions such as *Owens v Brimmell* [1977] QB 859 where the claimant knew of the defendant's disability (drunkenness) before he accepted a lift, so that this ground is less certain to succeed.

Volenti may also be raised against George for accepting a lift in view of the notice displayed in the van. For this defence to succeed, George must have voluntarily submitted to the risk of injury, and must have had knowledge of the danger. It is therefore unlikely to succeed on these facts, since George, by ignoring the notice, has not consented to the risk of injury by Fergus' negligence: s2(3) Unfair Contract Terms Act 1977.

Chapter 4

Vicarious Liability

4.1   Introduction

4.2   Key points

4.3   Key cases and statutes

4.4   Questions and suggested solutions

4.1 Introduction

The term vicarious liability means that one person takes the place of another as regards liability. Although the matter also arises in relation to principal and agent and partnership, the most important and commonest example of vicarious liability is that an employer is liable for the torts committed by an employee who is acting in the course of his employment.

From this statement it follows that we must be able to identify an employer and an employee and decide just what is meant by 'acting in the course of employment'. The decision by the House of Lords in *Lister* v *Hesley Hall Ltd* [2001] 2 All ER 769 provides a useful discussion as to whether the employers were found liable for the torts of their employee. In this case the employers (a school) were found to be vicariously liable for the sexual abuse committed by their employee. Another recent case involving schools is *Ramsay Elshafey* v *Kings School of Macclesfield* (2003) 147 SJ 1338.

4.2 Key points

Employer

In simple terms the person who has the right to hire and fire. In practice this gives rise to few difficulties, except where an employee is loaned out by his original employer to a third party. Here the onus lies on the original employer to rebut the presumption that he, and not the third party, remains the employer.

This can be done by showing that the third party had, at the relevant moment, the right to control the way in which the work was done: *Mersey Docks & Harbour Board* v *Coggins & Griffith* [1947] AC 1. It is a difficult presumption to rebut; the original employer may run foul of the Unfair Contract Terms Act 1977: compare *Phillips Products* v *Hyland* [1987] 2 All ER 620 with *Thompson* v *T Lohan (Plant Hire) Ltd* [1987] 2 All ER 631.

Employee

Original test: a person was an employee if his employer has the right to control not only what work he does but the way in which that work is done: *Yewens v Noakes* (1880) 6 QBD 530.

a) The test is right of control not whether any actual control is exercised: used by the House of Lords in *Smith v Stages* [1989] 2 WLR 529; [1989] 1 All ER 833. In *Lane v Shire Roofing* (1995) The Times 25 February the Court of Appeal stated that in the case of skilled employees the question should be broadened to: whose business was it? Was it the workers' or the employers'?

b) Other tests which have been suggested include:

   i) whether the person is employed as part of the business and his work is done as an integral part of it: *Stevenson, Jordan & Harrison v MacDonald & Evans* [1952] 1 TLR 101.

   ii) whether the person is in business on her own account: *Market Investigations v Minister of Social Security* [1969] 2 QB 173; [1969] 2 WLR 1; *Andrews v King* (1991) The Times 5 July.

c) The present approach of the courts is not to seek any single test which will apply in all cases, but to look at all the facts of the particular case. The reason for seeking to define an employee is not to recognise an employee as such, but rather to be able to distinguish between an employee and an independent contractor (see later).

Course of employment

a) The employer is liable for any torts of the employee that he authorises or ratifies.

b) In addition he is liable for any wrongful or unauthorised modes of doing an authorised act.

c) In other words, the employer is not only responsible for what he authorised the employee to do but for how the employee does it.

d) The employer will only escape liability in this respect if the employee goes outside the course of his employment, ie if the employee's act is not so connected with the authorised act as to be a mode of doing it but is an independent act of the employee: compare *Century Insurance v Northern Ireland Road Transport Board* [1942] AC 509 with *Beard v London General Omnibus Co* [1900] 2 QB 530. However, this is not a strict rule and may be subject to exceptions; see *Mattis v Pollock (t/a Flamingo's Nightclub)* [2003] 1 WLR 2158 concerning the actions of a nightclub bouncer.

e) Two particular problems – frolics and detours and the effect of an express prohibition by the employer.

   i) Frolics and detours, eg a driver who departs from an unauthorised route – has this action taken the employee outside the course of his employment? *Joel v*

Morrison (1834) 6 C & P 501 and *Williams* v *A & W Hemphill Ltd* 1966 SLT 259 are examples of this test and its application and should be compared with *Whatman* v *Pearson* (1868) LR 3 CP 422.

ii) The related problem of whether employees travelling to and from work are in the course of their employment: see *Smith* v *Stages* (above) (note criteria applied do not apply to salaried employees).

iii) Express prohibitions – clear from the definition of course of employment it follows that any prohibition that the employer has placed on the conduct of the employee will not restrict the course of employment.

iv) However, the law does allow the employer to limit acts which lie within the course of employment, but not to restrict the mode of performing acts within the course of employment: compare *Limpus* v *London General Omnibus Co* (1862) 1 H & C 526 and *Beard* v *London General Omnibus Co* (above).

v) The problem – how one defines the 'act' the employee is employed to do. In *Conway* v *George Wimpey & Co Ltd* [1951] 2 KB 266 and *Twine* v *Bean's Express* [1946] 1 All ER 202 the 'act' was defined very narrowly, but in *Rose* v *Plenty* [1976] 1 WLR 141; [1976] 1 All ER 97 a more liberal interpretation was used.

vi) The current attitude of the courts seems to be to adopt this wide interpretation where the employee acts carelessly, but to adopt a narrow interpretation of the act the employee was employed to do when considering a deliberate wrongful act by the employee.

f) In considering intentional wrongful acts by the employee, the courts take a restrictive approach to the course of employment: see *Heasmans* v *Clarity Cleaning* [1987] IRLR 286; *Irving* v *The Post Office* [1987] IRLR 289; *General Engineering Services* v *Kingston & St Andrews Corp* [1989] 1 WLR 69; [1988] 3 All ER 867.

g) Note that where the employer is held vicariously liable he can recover an indemnity from the employee under statute (s1(1) Civil Liability (Contribution) Act 1978) and at common law: *Lister* v *Romford Ice & Cold Storage Co* [1957] AC 555.

Principal and agent

The principal is liable for the agent's acts which are carried out in the course of the agency: difficulty – determining whether or not an 'ad hoc' agency has arisen creating the relationship of principal and agent. Compare *Ormrod* v *Crossville Motor Services* [1953] 1 WLR 1120 and *Morgans* v *Launchbury* [1973] AC 127.

Independent contractors

An employer is not liable for the torts of an independent contractor because he does not control the independent contractor: see *Morgan* v *Incorporated Central Council of the Girls'*

Friendly Society [1936] 1 All ER 404 and *D & F Estates* v *Church Commissioners* [1989] AC 177; [1988] 3 WLR 368.

Partnership

Sections 10 and 12 of the Partnership Act 1890. See also the relevance of Limited Liability Partnerships Act 2000 within context.

4.3 Key cases and statutes

- *Century Insurance* v *Northern Ireland Road Transport Board* [1942] AC 509
  Distinguishes between 'authorised' and 'unauthorised' acts of an employee

- *Lister* v *Hesley Hall Ltd* [2001] 2 All ER 769 (HL)
  Illustrates the extent to which an employer may be found liable

- *Lister* v *Romford Ice & Cold Storage Co* [1957] AC 555
  Employer may recover an indemnity from the 'negligent' employee

- *Mattis* v *Pollock (t/a Flamingo's Nightclub)* [2003] 1 WLR 2158
  Club was vicariously liable for bouncer's actions

- *Mersey Docks & Harbour Board* v *Coggins & Griffith (Liverpool) Ltd* [1947] AC 1
  Illustrates who the employer is in cases of employee secondment

- *Morgans* v *Launchbury* [1973] AC 127
  A principal may be found liable for the wrongful or negligent actions of the agent

- *Ramsay Elshafey* v *Kings School of Macclesfield* (2003) 147 SJ 1338
  Court found school vicariously liable for its pupil's action

- *Trotman* v *North Yorkshire County Council* [1999] LGR 584
  Exemplifies what may or may not be defined as falling within the definition of 'the course of employment'

- *Yewens* v *Noakes* (1880) 6 QBD 530
  Sets out the test in defining an 'employee'

- Civil Liability (Contribution) Act 1978 – employer may seek an indemnity from the employee

- Limited Liability Partnerships Act 2000 – allows partners to limit the extent of their financial liability to the other partners and to the partnership

- Partnership Act 1890 – sets out liability as between partners

4.4 Questions and suggested solutions

QUESTION ONE

Jim is a lorry driver employed by Slapdash Carriers Ltd. His assistant was ill one day and he asked Kyle and Leo, two office boys, to load up his lorry as he had a lot of other things to attend to. All three of them know that office workers are forbidden by their employer to do so. Nevertheless they loaded some barrels on to the lorry and locked the tailgate. Jim had to deliver the load to the premises of International Thumbscrews plc. When he lowered the tailgate, a barrel rolled out and struck Melvyn, an employee of International Thumbscrews, who was waiting to unload the consignment.

Melvyn was permanently paralysed and will not be able to return to work. He has also had to give up his hobbies of snooker and cricket. He had been a valued employee and Thumbscrews provided him with a car and paid for adaptations to his flat. He became extremely irritable and aggressive as the result of his injuries and his girlfriend left him. His mother Noreen has, however, given up her job to care for him permanently.

Advise Melvyn (i) if he has a cause of action in tort and (ii), if so, how the damages will be assessed.

University of London LLB Examination
(for External Students) Law of Tort June 2001 Q6

General Comment

This is a two-part question. The first requires an analysis of the law on vicarious liability and the relevance of the concept of 'res ipsa loquitor' in relation to Melvyn. The second part of the question requires an assessment of damages under the various heads.

Skeleton Solution

The principles establishing liability under vicarious liability: the employer/employee relationship; the course of employment; the role of Kyle and Leo; the role of Jim; res ipsa loquitor – assessment of damages: special damages; general damages.

Suggested Solution

The most important and commonest example of vicarious liability can be found in the employer/employee relationship: an employer is liable for the torts committed by an employee who is acting in the course of his employment. An employer/employee relationship is thus essential and must therefore be primarily established,

On the facts of this question, it is clear that Jim is an employee of Slapdash Carriers and was employed as a lorry driver. Second, it must be established that the tort committed by Jim was done within the course of employment. This is also easily provable, as the question states that Melvyn suffered the injury when Jim went to unload the delivery from his lorry.

Therefore Melvyn, a third party, suffered an injury caused by Jim's negligence. This would implicate Jim's employer, Slapdash Carriers, on the basis of vicarious liability. However, what might arise as a potential problem is the fact that Slapdash Carriers may deny liability on the basis that, as Kyle and Leo were office boys and thus had no authority (express or implied) to load the barrels onto the lorry, that took them outside of the course of employment. In *Century Insurance Co* v *Northern Ireland Road Transport Board* [1942] AC 509 it was stated that the employer will only escape liability if the employee goes outside the course of his employment, ie if the employee's act is not connected with the authorised act, as to be an independent act of the employee. Therefore, Slapdash Carriers may claim that Kyle and Leo were doing something other than that for which they had been employed. They were doing an unauthorised act. Whilst that argument may be acceptable in relation to Kyle and Leo, what about the role of Jim? It might be argued that Jim had improperly carried out his work by delegating the task of loading to Kyle and Leo. Jim was in fact doing something that he was authorised to do, but in a wrongful way: *Limpus* v *London General Omnibus Co* (1862) 1 H & C 526. On this basis, Slapdash Carriers would most certainly be vicariously liable. There is no problem establishing negligence on the part of Kyle, Leo and Jim. The barrrels had been negligently loaded so as to roll out as soon as the tailgate was lowered. This raises the doctrine of 'res ipsa loquitor', otherwise known as 'the thing that speaks for itself'. If something is so obvious, there is no need to prove it: *Scott* v *London and St Katherine Docks Co* (1865) 3 H & C 596.

Therefore, Melvyn would have no problem establishing a case under vicarious liability. If, on the other hand, Melvyn can establish that his employers have failed to provide him with a safe system of work, as in *Walker* v *Northumberland County Council* [1994] 1 All ER 737, then Melvyn may have a case against his employers, International Thumbscrews, under employer's liability. But there is little on the facts of this case to suggest this possibility. The next issue to be considered is the various heads of damage that would be available to Melvyn in his personal injury claim. Melvyn has, as a result of the accident, become permanently paralysed.

Briefly, damages in personal injury claims are divided in two distinct groups. First 'special damages'. This includes pecuniary loss up to the date of trial; it can also include costs of medical care, equipment, loss of earnings and other such expenses that the court might consider to be reasonable under the circumstances.

Second, 'general damages' or 'future damages'. This includes pecuniary loss such as future earnings, medical costs, costs of care, special facilities and costs of adapting the home. It also includes non-pecuniary loss, such as pain and suffering and loss of amenities. Non-pecuniary losses are difficult to quantify and awards are based entirely on arbitrary calculations. However, guidance is normally sought from authoritative works in the area, such as Kemp and Kemp, for instance. Loss of earnings are calculated by multiplying the multiplicand (the claimant's annual net loss) by a multiplier (a notional figure representing the number of years the court feels the award should cover).

Therefore, Melvyn would be able to recover all of the following:

a) the loss of earnings – both actual and future or prospective loss;

b) all medical and other expenses that have been reasonably incurred, such as travelling expenses, the cost of special equipment or of employing someone to carry out domestic duties which the claimant is no longer able to perform;

c) the loss of pension rights;

d) pain and suffering in respect of his injuries (permanent paralysis); and

e) loss of faculty and amenity, such as loss of job satisfaction, loss of leisure activities and hobbies and loss of family life (all are relevant in Melvyn's case).

Melvyn may also recover insofar as the car and the adaptations to his flat are concerned, but as this has been paid for by his 'compassionate' employers, the court will not allow double recovery (unless it is being claimed to reimburse his employers). Melvyn will not be able to claim for Nora's loss of earnings, but he would be able to claim for the cost of permanent care.

QUESTION TWO

Gina is a qualified word processor who is registered with Paperjam, a word processing agency. She is at present working at Macro & Merge Ltd, who have recruited her through Paperjam to cover for a member of staff on sick leave. On returning from lunch one day, she saw a man, whom she did not know, alone in the office loading computers onto a trolley. She struck him in the stomach, winding him and ran out locking the office door. The man was Hugo, who was employed by the maintenance department of Macro & Merge, and he was removing the computers in the course of his work. Hugo was known to his employers to suffer from asthma and to be prone to blackouts during which he sometimes needed assistance. Hugo had a very severe asthmatic attack and passed out. He has suffered permanent damage to his health.

Advise Hugo as to any claims in tort.

University of London LLB Examination
(for External Students) Law of Tort June 1999 Q7

General Comment

This ought to have been a relatively straightforward question for those candidates who were familiar with the torts of trespass to the person. In addition, it is always necessary to consider the possibility of employer's liability in negligence where injuries are sustained by an employee in the course of employment.

Skeleton Solution

Discuss Gina's liability for claims in battery and false imprisonment – are Hugo's injuries too remote given his unusual physical susceptibility? – examine the defences of lawful arrest to a claim of false imprisonment and self-defence to a claim in battery – if Gina has committed a tort against Hugo, are either Macro & Merge Ltd or Paperjam vicariously liable? – who was Gina employed by? – was her attack in the course of her employment? – are Macro & Merge Ltd liable in negligence on the basis of a breach of the duty to provide a safe system of work? – were Hugo's injuries too remote to recover for, given his unusual physical susceptibility?

Suggested Solution

Claims against Gina

Gina's liability in tort is relatively easy to establish in these circumstances. Hugo may have claims in battery and false imprisonment.

Battery

Battery is the intentional and direct application of unlawful force to another. The elements of battery are easily satisfied in this case. The contact with Hugo's stomach was a direct act on the part of Gina, ie a direct cause of her act of striking him. The act itself was intentional rather than merely accidental or negligent: *Letang v Cooper* [1965] 1 QB 232. The force used by Gina is certainly likely to be regarded as unlawful in that it was either hostile in the circumstances: *Wilson v Pringle* [1987] QB 237 or without lawful excuse, lacking Hugo's consent: *Re F (Mental Patient: Sterilisation)* [1990] 2 AC 1. Battery, along with other trespass related torts, is actionable per se, without the need to prove any injury to the claimant.

False imprisonment

This is the infliction of bodily restraint which is not expressly or impliedly authorised by law. Once again, the elements of false imprisonment appear to be present in the circumstances described. The confinement of the claimant must be such that his liberty is totally restrained: *Bird v Jones* (1845) 7 QB 742 with no reasonable means of escape. An issue here is whether Hugo was aware of his apparent confinement to the office after Gina's attack. Early authority appeared to suggest that false imprisonment is not committed where the claimant is unaware of any restriction placed upon his freedom: *Herring v Boyle* (1834) 1 Cr M & R 377. The modern approach, however, seems to be that a person can be falsely imprisoned whilst unconscious, although any award of damages will be purely nominal unless the claimant suffers some other form of harm as a result: *Murray v Ministry of Defence* [1988] 2 All ER 521. It is submitted that Gina's intentional locking of the office door almost certainly gives rise to a claim for false imprisonment, and that Hugo is likely to be entitled to compensatory damages for any period of awareness of his confinement before he passed out, and possibly after he came to, and the fact that the harm he suffered following Gina's attack was aggravated by his on-going confinement without medical treatment.

Remoteness

Battery and false imprisonment are trespasses against the person, and as such are actionable per se without the need to prove any injury to the claimant. This means that Hugo can recover for all the injuries resulting from Gina's unlawful acts, whether or not they were foreseeable, including any direct harm caused by the impact to his stomach, the suffering caused by the winding and the subsequent asthma attack, and the injuries resulting in permanent damage to Hugo's health.

Defences

The main defence to a claim of false imprisonment is lawful arrest. Section 24(4) Police and Criminal Evidence Act 1984 allows anyone, including a private citizen, to make an arrest where they have reasonable grounds for suspecting that an arrestable offence is being committed (even if, in fact, there is no offence). It will be for Gina to justify any arrest on the balance of probabilities, unless she is to be found liable for false imprisonment. She will have to establish that she actually believed Hugo was in the course of committing a theft (an arrestable offence), and further, that she had reasonable grounds to suspect that he was doing so. It is this latter aspect which may cause problems for Gina. It could be argued that an objective observer would take the view that Gina's initial suspicion did not turn into a reasonable one, because she failed to challenge Hugo as to his presence in the office and to ask to see some identification. Macro & Merge Ltd appear to be a large employer, and Gina as a temporary member of staff clearly cannot expect to recognise everyone in the office. However, the question of reasonable suspicion is one which will have to be determined in all the circumstances of the case.

There is a further question as to the lawfulness of any arrest carried out by Gina, in that the provision of some information to the suspect upon arrest is normally necessary, unless the fact and grounds for arrest are obvious: *Christie* v *Leachinsky* [1947] AC 573. In other cases, probably such as this, Gina would be required to give sufficient information to inform Hugo as to the factual and legal basis of the accusation against him. In the absence of such an explanation, there will be no valid lawful arrest.

It is unlikely that Gina will be able to raise self-defence to a claim of battery against Hugo. Gina would effectively have to establish the existence of a defence in tort of 'mistaken self-defence of the property of another', requiring considerable expansion of the existing authorities in this area.

Claims against Macro & Merge Ltd and Paperjam

Vicarious liability

Whilst Gina's liability in tort appears to be easily established, Hugo will want to claim against an organisation which is better placed to compensate him than a temporary employee. Gina's employer will almost certainly carry an insurance policy to meet such a claim. The two main issues that arise here relate to the identity of Gina's employer at the time of the incident and whether Gina was acting in the course of her employment when she attacked Hugo.

Who is the employer?

It is unclear whether Gina is employed on a temporary basis by Macro & Merge Ltd, or on an ongoing basis by the agency that supplied her. The modern approach is for the courts to consider a range of factors and to examine all the circumstances of Gina's working relationship as against each potential employer. Such factors, none of which are conclusive on their own, will include the following.

a) Who paid Gina's wages and National Insurance contributions in return for her work and skill?

b) Who had the authority to exercise a sufficient degree of control over the manner in which Gina did her work?

c) Who could dismiss Gina?

d) How long was she hired out for?

Was Gina in the course of her employment when she attacked Hugo?

Assuming, for a moment, that Gina is an employee of Macro & Merge Ltd, she will be impliedly authorised (although not legally bound) to protect her employer's property, provided that her actions are not so outrageous that a reasonable employer would not have contemplated them as being within the scope of employment. For example, an employee was held to be acting in the course of his employment when he struck a boy whom he reasonably believed to be in the course of steeling goods belonging to his employer: *Polland v Parr & Sons* [1927] 1 KB 236. If the employee acts so excessively beyond what is necessary to deal with the emergency (eg were Gina to have shot Hugo) then the employee steps beyond the scope of his employment. This fact was considered in *Mattis v Pollock (t/a Flamingo's Nightclub)* [2003] 1 WLR 2158, where a bouncer's actions bound his employers on the basis of vicarious liability.

It is submitted, on this basis, that Gina is acting in the course of her employment with Macro & Merge Ltd. However, it may be one stage too far removed to suggest that she is acting in the course of any employment with Paperjam, the agency which supplied her, when acting to protect Macro & Merge Ltd's property against what she assumed was a theft.

Employers' liability

Macro & Merge Ltd may be liable in negligence for a breach of their non-delegable duty to devise and operate a safe system of work. Such a duty may arise in view of their knowledge of Hugo's asthmatic condition, his susceptibility to blackouts and his subsequent need for occasional assistance. The particular characteristics of a claimant are relevant in deciding how a reasonable employer ought to have discharged its duty. In *Paris v Stepney Borough Council* [1951] AC 367 for example, an employer's failure to provide an employee, who was already blind in one eye, with safety goggles amounted to a breach of this duty due to the serious possible (and actual) consequences of the employee sustaining further eye injury. Thus it could be argued that Macro & Merge Ltd's failure to ensure that Hugo was accompanied at all times by another member of staff amounts to a breach of the duty to provide a safe system of work. Clearly, injury to Hugo was foreseeable as a result of the failure to provide adequate supervision, and so it does not matter that the extent of Hugo's injuries, and the precise way in which they occurred, could not have been foreseen: *Hughes* v *Lord Advocate* [1963] AC 837.

QUESTION THREE

Describe, and explain the purpose of, the concept of vicarious liability. Consider what, if any, development of the concept is appropriate now that the pattern of employment is changing and many people do not work for a single permanent employer.

University of London LLB Examination
(for External Students) Law of Tort June 1997 Q2

General Comment

In such a question, the narrative and descriptive of parts of the question should be dealt with fairly shortly. The essential points, such as necessary relationships and course of employment, judicial controls, etc, should be covered, but the candidate should take a vigorous approach to the real problems and possible solutions that follow from rapidly changing patterns of occupation. Consideration of alternative safeguards, such as statutory schemes, insurance, etc, might be discussed.

Skeleton Solution

The origins and nature of vicarious liability – the significance of employment situations as distinct from independent contractor situations – the social and economic arguments involved – changes in working patterns and the implications for vicarious liability – suggested changes and developments to the doctrine – legislative intervention and insurance arrangements.

Suggested Solution

The modern doctrine of vicarious liability has its historical roots in the idea that the master should be liable for the torts of his servant, if committed 'within the course of employment'. This pattern of liability to third parties within a close and well-known relationship has remained to modern times, and vicarious liability will still arise only in such relationships as employer/employee or principal/agent. There remains also the requirement that the tort should be committed within the course of employment or, with agents, within some express or implied or ostensible authority: *Storey* v *Ashton* (1869) LR 4 QB 476 (employees); *Lloyd* v *Grace, Smith & Co* [1912] AC 716 (agency). The question of just what distinguishes an employee from some other form of contractor has occupied the courts to a very considerable extent and, after several attempts at a satisfactory rationale, such as the 'control test' (*Yewens* v *Noakes* (1880) 6 QBD 530) and the 'in business on own account' test from *Market Investigations Ltd* v *Minister of Social Security* [1969] 2 QB 173 (still used for taxation purposes), the modern view seems to prefer the three-stage approach favoured by MacKenna J in *Ready Mixed Concrete (South East) Ltd* v *Minister of Pensions* [1968] 2 QB 497 as being more appropriate to the question of vicarious liability for torts.

The question of 'course of employment' can be seen from the cases as being one that the courts consider a matter for decision by them rather than one which is dictated by the employer and the terms of employment. This is highlighted by cases on the effect of express prohibitions, such as the contrasting cases of *Twine* v *Bean's Express Ltd* [1946] 1 All ER 202 and *Rose* v *Plenty* [1976] 1 WLR 141. It is clear that the court will be the final arbiter of what is an 'unauthorised act' so as to take the matter outside the course of employment, preferring, on occasion, to find that the matter is an 'unauthorised mode of doing an authorised act' as in *Limpus* v *London General Omnibus Co Ltd* (1862) 1 H & C 526.

A finding that an employment relationship subsists is usually much more advantageous to the third party victim of a tort because the alternative, that the tortfeasor is an independent contractor, means that the general vicarious liability of the employer for torts within the course of employment is replaced by an altogether narrower range of liabilities under which one independent contractor is, by way of exception to the general rule, liable for torts committed by an independent contractor employed by him. If the tort falls outside this narrower band of exceptional situations, the victim will only have a remedy against the direct tortfeasor who may sometimes be unable to satisfy a judgment.

The legal rationale for vicarious liability seems, at bottom, to come down to a matter of 'social convenience and rough justice': per Lord Pearce in *Imperial Chemical Industries Ltd* v *Shatwell* [1965] AC 656. It seems logical that liability should fall jointly upon the primary tortfeasor and the person best able to profit from the other's labours and who, as employer, is in an infinitely better position to obtain insurance cover at sensible rates; the employer will be the one best able to assess the range of risk, scale of damage and the quality of employee required for the employment.

The doctrine of vicarious liability arose over a period in which the distinction between employee and self-employed was obvious and clear. Over the last few decades, patterns of business and occupation have changed to an unprecedented degree, with a large part of the adult working population becoming increasingly involved in part-time and short-period engagements. In combination with the business attractiveness of reducing employed labour forces this has led to many situations where the true working relationship is often extremely unclear. Examples of this can be seen in the *Ready Mixed Concrete* and *Market Investigations* cases. In many cases, the very reason for these changes is to restrict the liabilities to others, including third parties. Clearly, as matters stand, this will reduce the possibilities for vicarious liability, especially where the use of individual independent contractors replaces an employee workforce. This has gone hand-in-hand with a perceived increase in the use of the so-called 'masters indemnity' against the tortfeasor employee as seen in *Lister v Romford Ice and Cold Storage Co Ltd* [1957] 1 All ER 125, probably at the instance of the insurers.

Is there, then, anything that can be done to help the third party in such circumstances? A possibility might be to extend the liability for the torts of independent contractors to the situation where, if the damage to a third party were reasonably foreseeable had it been caused by an employee, the fact that an independent contractor is used will not prevent a joint liability arising. This might be combined with a statutorily implied term into any such contract that, in the event that the parties had not agreed upon which party provides third-party cover, the liability will be deemed to be joint. In any event, the matter would require legislation; short of this, matters will have to progress naturally and only time will show how useful vicarious liability will be in the future.

QUESTION FOUR

Luke is unemployed but has enrolled on a government training scheme. He is sent three days each week for work experience to the offices of Newfield Industries plc. The office manager Matilda was sent to a conference one day in a town forty miles away and was told to take the company car. She asked Luke to go with her as part of his work experience. She also thought that she might be drinking and that Luke could then drive the car, but did not tell Luke this. Both Luke and Matilda knew that he was not allowed to drive the company car. On the way back Matilda stopped for a drink at a pub and asked Luke to take over the driving. Luke drove out of the pub car park without looking and caused Neil, a passing motor cyclist, to swerve. Neil struck a tree and was seriously injured.

Advise Neil as to any rights of action in tort.

University of London LLB Examination
(for External Students) Law of Tort June 1994 Q8

General Comment

This is a question that involves a consideration of the relationship between employer and employee, and the way in which tortious acts fit into that relationship.

Skeleton Solution

Negligence – vicarious liability – employer/employee – course of employment.

Suggested Solution

It is possible from a consideration of the parties mentioned in the question to discern a number of people who, on face value, could be considered responsible for Neil's accident. These range from Luke, the obvious cause of the accident, through to Newfield Industries, the party most likely to be able to bear any costs, and even to an external body, like the Motor Insurance Bureau.

It seems appropriate to begin with Luke, as the driver of the car that caused the accident. The central difficulty with Neil initiating proceedings against any individual defendant is that they will either be impecunious or certainly not in a financial position to meet any claim. So, the issue of culpability becomes submerged in the reality of the economic situation and highlights that this problem involves discussion of practicalities as well as academic points. In the light of Luke's unemployed status, it seems unlikely that he will be able to compensate Neil. It seems probable that the same will apply to Matilda who, although she is in employment, is not likely to be in a position to pay the sorts of sums that can be involved in serious personal injury actions.

It then falls to consider Newfield Industries plc, who would be in a much better position to meet the claim, if not through any insurance they may have, then certainly through their position to pass on any losses. This, in essence, is the heart of the problem, namely whether Newfield Industries can be held vicariously liable for the actions of Luke and of Matilda. In order for the courts to find in favour of Neil, there are certain hurdles that such a claim must surmount. First, Newfield Industries will only be held responsible if a wrongful act has been committed by another person. There must have been a tortious act. It is difficult to see that there is any other interpretation to place on the incident in the light of the facts given in the question. Support for this proposition can also be found in *Mattis* v *Pollock (t/a Flamingo's Nightclub)* [2003] 1 WLR 2158.

Second, Newfield Industries will only be responsible if it is possible to show a special relationship existing between them and the wrongdoer. This relationship has to be one recognised by law, and in reality this limb of liability only relates to the relationship between employer and employee. Matilda would obviously fall into the category of employee on the factual situation under discussion. There are, however, problems in relation to Luke and whether he is an employee of Newfield Industries. It seems probable that they would try to argue that any responsibility for Luke does not lie with them because he is on work experience as part of his government training scheme. In general terms, where an employer (A) 'lends' an employee to another employer (B), if that employee then commits a tortious act, it is difficult for A to shift any responsibility onto the temporary employer (B). It remains, however, a question of fact and it appears that the circumstances in this case would not allow Newfield Industries to deny that they controlled Luke. This being the case it seems undeniable that Luke would be seen as operating within the necessary special relationship.

The final hurdle will, in this case, prove the most difficult for Neil to establish, namely that Newfield Industries should be held vicariously liable for the actions of Luke. Neil needs to establish that Luke was acting in the course of his employment and so found a connection between Luke's act and his special relationship with Newfield Industries. This involves considering a mixed question of law and of fact and considering whether, at the time of the accident, Luke and Matilda were undertaking unauthorised deviations from their work. It was in *Joel* v *Morrisson* (1834) 6 C & P 501 that the courts considered that a 'master' will not be liable for a 'servant's' actions, if the servant is on a frolic of his own. It is therefore for the courts to establish what is meant by a 'frolic of his own'. There is a suggestion in *Williams* v *A & W Hemphill Ltd* 1966 SLT 259, a Scottish case, that the actions must be solely for the selfish purposes of the employee. It therefore seems that stopping for a drink at the pub could not be seen as incidental to the journey and doing so takes the detour outside the course of their employment. It would also appear that the intentionally wrongful act by both Luke and Matilda, in allowing Luke to drive while knowing he was not permitted to do so, would take their actions outside the course of employment. Therefore, Neil appears not to have any recourse against Newfield Industries plc. However, mention should be made of *Ilkiw* v *Samuels* [1963] 1 WLR 991, where a lorry driver allowed a third party to move his lorry without ensuring that he was able and insured to do it. The employers were vicariously liable because the lorry driver was employed not only to drive the lorry but to be in charge of it. Likewise, it might be possible to argue that Matilda was in a similar position. The potential scope of an action against Newfield Industries would be limited but in advising Neil on a purely practical basis, it may be worth, at the very least, initiating proceedings.

Finally, for the sake of completeness and bearing in mind the difficulties that Neil would face in tackling Newfield Industries plc, mention must be made of the Motor Insurers' Bureau (MIB). Neil may find that in the event of his failing to succeed in levelling the blame for his accident at Newfield Industries, the MIB may meet the unsatisfied judgment, if Luke was not insured to drive the car that caused the accident.

QUESTION FIVE

The Moonshine Home is a private convalescent hospital. It has a permanent nursing staff, but recruits temporary nursing assistance from Mrs Nightingale's Agency when it is needed to cover for staff holidays and sickness. The agency pays the salary to its nurses and charges a fee to the hospitals which use its services. Florence was sent from the agency for two weeks as a night nurse at the Moonshine Home. On her first night George, a patient, asked Florence to give him an extra dose of his medicine as he found that it helped him to sleep. Florence told him that she was not allowed to do so without authority from a doctor. George told her untruthfully that the doctor had said that he could have an extra dose whenever he needed it and that the regular nurse had several times administered one. Florence therefore gave him an extra dose. The medicine had a stimulating effect on the heart and the extra dose caused George to suffer a non-fatal heart attack.

Advise George.

University of London LLB Examination
(for External Students) Law of Tort June 1986 Q6

General Comment

Another example of a question on vicarious liability that overlaps with negligence. Whilst the discussion of negligence is essential, it must, however, be remembered that emphasis should be placed on establishing the legal principles relating to vicarious liability.

Skeleton Solution

Negligence – Florence negligently gives George an extra dose of medicine causing a heart attack – Florence sent to work in hospital by a nursing agency which is vicariously liable for her conduct – facts indicate that Florence an employee of nursing agency – this raises further issue as to whether burden of liability can be shifted to hospital under the principle of lending a servant, this is unlikely on the facts – further issue arises as to whether Florence was acting within scope of her employment at relevant time – this appears to be so.

Suggested Solution

It is hardly in dispute that Florence was negligent in giving George an extra dose of his medicine merely because he requested it. As a qualified nurse she would be expected to measure up to the standard of proficiency which could be expected of an ordinary competent nurse and to conform to practices accepted as proper by a responsible section of her profession: see *Bolam* v *Friern Hospital Management Committee* [1957] 1 WLR 582. I doubt if she was conforming with proper practices in giving a patient a dose of medicine without first checking to see if it was prescribed for him in his medical records, or asking the doctor whose authority was necessary in the first place or by merely giving it to him because he asked for it.

There would appear to be little that Florence could do in defending a claim by George in negligence except, perhaps, alleging that he was contributorily negligent. Such a claim would be based on the ground that he had been less careful for his own safety than he otherwise ought to have been. Any damages he might obtain would be reduced to the extent that the court considered that he was to blame for his own misfortune: see *Nance* v *British Columbia Electric Railway* [1951] AC 601 and the Law Reform (Contributory Negligence) Act 1945. It is doubtful if contributory negligence would have any success here because if George was ill he may have been in no fit state to consider his safety. In any event, the real cause of his injury is the administration of the extra dose rather than his asking for it. Florence could have easily refused to give it.

Having decided that there is a case in negligence against Florence the next issue is who George should sue. Obviously, he could sue Florence but it is likely that she could not pay any damages awarded against her because she probably has limited financial means. The question therefore arises whether George should sue the Moonshine Home or the Nightingale Agency on the basis that one of them is vicariously liable for

Florence's negligence. An employer is vicariously liable for the tort of his employee or 'servant' where the tort is committed in the course of employment. It would appear that Florence was an employee of the Nightingale Agency since they paid her a salary and, it appears, directed her what to do. There are a number of tests to determine an employer/employee relationship; these include the 'control' test and the 'business integration' test. The former test is based on whether the alleged employee can be told not only what to do but how to do it: see *Yewens* v *Noakes* (1880) 6 QBD 530. This test is satisfactory for menial positions but is rather unsatisfactory where the alleged employee has a special skill which the employer does not have as, for example, in the case of a hospital employing doctors and nurses. See *Moren* v *Swinton and Pendlebury BC* [1965] 1 WLR 576. The courts appear to have ignored the difficulties of the control test and in cases concerning hospital doctors have held that the hospital authorities are vicariously liable for their negligence. See *Cassidy* v *Ministry of Health* [1951] 2 KB 343. On this basis the Moonshine Home would be vicariously liable for Florence if she was their employee and, if this is so, it is difficult to see why the Nightingale Agency should be in a different position if other terms of Florence's contract with them are consistent with an employer/employee relationship. The 'business integration' test was formulated by Denning LJ in *Stevenson, Jordan & Harrison Ltd* v *MacDonald & Evans* [1952] 1 TLR 101 and is used to distinguish a contract of service from a contract of services. If a person is employed as part of the business and his work is an integral part of it he is an employee under a contract of service. Considering this test in the present case it would appear that Florence is an employee of the Nightingale Agency. However, it would be appropriate to see if Florence's contract with the Nightingale Agency is consistent with this conclusion, whether she is paid gross or net of tax, if Nightingale pay employers' national insurance contributions for her, pay towards pensions schemes etc. It also seems unlikely that Florence is in business on her own account: see *Market Investigations* v *Minister of Social Security* [1969] 2 QB 173; *Andrews* v *King* (1991) The Times 5 July.

If, as appears to be the case, Florence is an employee of the Nightingale Agency this does not necessarily mean that they are liable for her negligence. It may be that in the circumstances of this case the principles concerning lending a servant apply so that the Moonshine Home is instead vicariously liable for Florence. The principles of this rule were considered by the House of Lords in *Mersey Docks and Harbour Board* v *Coggins and Griffith (Liverpool) Ltd* [1947] AC 1 and under it, it appears that a permanent employer may be able to shift the burden of responsibility to a temporary employer. Factors which will be considered relevant to the application of the rule include whether machinery was lent with the employee, the duration of service with the temporary employer, who pays the employee, contributes towards his national insurance and pension schemes and who has the power of dismissal. In my view Nightingale Agency would not be able to invoke this rule because the period of service was too short, being two weeks only, and it seems Nightingale continued to pay Florence etc and merely collected a fee from the Moonshine Home for her services.

Thus, the proper party to sue here is the Nightingale Agency. This does not solve all difficulties because an employer is only vicariously liable for the acts of an employee if they are done in the course of the employment. Florence gave George medicine which should only have been given on the authority of a doctor so it is arguable that she acted outside the scope of her employment. I doubt if such an argument would be successful since Florence is not prohibited from giving George medicine but merely prohibited from giving it to him except on the authority of a doctor. The case is one where a prohibition exists which regulates the manner in which Florence performs her duties rather than one which defines or limits the sphere of her employment. In *Rose v Plenty* [1976] 1 WLR 141 a prohibition on a milkman allowing small boys to ride on his milkfloat was treated as regulating the course of employment rather than its scope. However, the decision of the House of Lords in *Lister* v *Hesley Hall* [2001] 2 All ER 769 provides a useful example of what factors the court takes on board in determining the liability of an employer. It is difficult to see how as a matter of law, the present case could be viewed differently. The case *Mattis* v *Pollock (t/a Flamingo's Nightclub)* [2003] 1 WLR 2158 lends further support to this contention.

Chapter 5

Negligence: Duty of Care

5.1   Introduction

5.2   Key points

5.3   Key cases and statutes

5.4   Questions and suggested solutions

5.1 Introduction

In tort the word negligence has two meanings: it can be a mode of committing certain acts, and negligence in this sense means carelessness; or it can be an independent tort, and it is this we shall now consider.

The tort of negligence has been defined as 'the breach of a legal duty to take care which results in damage, undesired by the defendant, to the claimant' (Winfield & Jolowicz). The tort has three elements.

a) The defendant must owe the claimant a duty of care.

b) The defendant must be in breach of this duty.

c) Damage must have been caused to the claimant by the defendant's breach and such damage must not be too remote.

The first element of the tort will be considered in this chapter and the second and third elements in subsequent chapters.

5.2 Key points

The general principle is the neighbour principle as formulated in *Donoghue* v *Stevenson* [1932] AC 562: 'You must take reasonable care to avoid acts or omissions which you can reasonably foresee would be likely to injure your neighbour. Who, then, in law is my neighbour? The answer seems to be – persons who are so closely and directly affected by my act that I ought reasonably to have them in contemplation as being so affected when I am directing my mind to the acts or omissions which are called in question.'

Development

The neighbour principle was taken further by Lord Wilberforce in *Anns* v *Merton London Borough Council* [1978] AC 728 when he proposed a two-tier test.

First: as between the alleged wrongdoer and the person who has suffered damage is there a sufficient relationship of proximity or neighbourhood such that, in the reasonable contemplation of the former, carelessness on his part may be likely to cause damage to the latter, in which case a prima facie duty of care arises.

Second: if the first question is answered affirmatively are there any considerations which ought to negative or reduce or limit the scope of the duty or the class of persons to whom it is owed or the damages to which a breach of it may give rise?

The effect of this two-tier test was to expand considerably the scope of the tort of negligence, but the test has been the subject of much judicial criticism. The *Anns* two-tier test was subsequently overruled in *Murphy* v *Brentwood District Council* [1990] 3 WLR 414 and replaced by the three-part test or incremental approach in *Caparo Industries plc* v *Dickman* [1990] 2 AC 605.

Current formulation

In *Peabody Donation Fund Governors* v *Sir Lindsay Parkinson & Co Ltd* [1985] AC 210 Lord Keith introduced the requirement that it should be just and reasonable that a duty of care should exist. Subsequent cases have emphasised this just and reasonable criterion, see especially *Davis* v *Radcliffe* [1990] 2 All ER 536.

Note the formulation of the test for duty of care by the House of Lords in *Caparo Industries plc* v *Dickman* [1990] 2 AC 605, namely that there are three criteria for the imposition of a duty of care:

a) foreseeability of damage – *Bourhill* v *Young* [1943] AC 92; *Topp* v *London Country Bus (South West) Ltd* [1993] 3 All ER 448;

b) proximity of relationship – *Hill* v *Chief Constable of West Yorkshire* [1998] 2 All ER 238;

c) reasonableness or otherwise of imposing a duty – *Peabody Donation Fund Governors* v *Sir Lindsay Parkinson & Co Ltd* [1985] AC 210; *Hemmens* v *Wilson Browne* [1993] 4 All ER 826. The House of Lords reiterated support for this contention in *Rees* v *Darlington Memorial Hospital NHS Trust* [2004] 1 AC 309. See also *JD* v *East Kent Community NHS Trust* [2003] 3 All ER 1167 on the same principle.

In particular, in determining whether there was a relationship of proximity between the parties, the court, guided by situations in which the existence, scope and limits of a duty of care had previously been held to exist rather than a single general principle, would determine whether the particular damage suffered was the kind of damage which the defendant was under a duty to prevent and whether there were circumstances from which the court could pragmatically conclude that a duty of care existed, adopting the dictum of Brennan J in *Sutherland Shire Council* v *Heyman* (1985) 60 ALR 1.

The problem the courts have found with Lord Wilberforce's test is that it is so easy to satisfy the first requirement that too much is left to the second requirement, ie to a policy decision.

Note that *Anns* has been overruled on its facts by the House of Lords in *Murphy* v *Brentwood District Council* [1990] 2 All ER 908; in *Murphy* the House noted that reservations had been expressed regarding the two tier test and stated a preference for the incremental approach of *Sutherland Shire Council*, although in *Ravenscroft* v *Rederiaktiebolaget Transatlantic* [1991] 3 All ER 73 Ward J held at first instance that the two-tier test had been overruled by *Murphy*.

The courts have also held that where the claimant has an alternative remedy, eg in contract or where there are statutory regulations covering the situation, that a duty of care should not be imposed which would have the effect of taking the law beyond contractual agreement or Parliamentary intention, eg *Greater Nottingham Co-operative Society* v *Cementation Piling & Foundations* [1989] QB 71; [1988] 2 All ER 971 (contractual agreement); *Reid* v *Rush & Tomkins Group plc* [1990] 1 WLR 212; [1989] 3 All ER 228 (contractual agreement); *Curran* v *Northern Ireland Co-ownership Housing Association* [1987] AC 718 (regulations); *Mills* v *Winchester Diocesan Board of Finance* [1989] 2 All ER 317 (regulations); *Marc Rich* v *Bishop Rock Marine* [1995] 3 WLR 227 (Hague-Visby Rules).

In *Yuen Kun Yeu* v *Attorney-General of Hong Kong* [1988] AC 175 and *Hill* v *Chief Constable of West Yorkshire* [1989] AC 53; [1988] 2 WLR 1049 it was emphasised that mere foreseeability of harm was insufficient to impose a duty of care. Those cases decided between 1978 and 1985 in which a duty was imposed on the grounds of pure foreseeability can no longer be supported – see, for example, the criticism of *JEB Fasteners* v *Marks, Bloom & Co* [1983] 1 All ER 583 by Lord Bridge in *Caparo* (above). The incremental approach was considered by the Court of Appeal in *Law Society* v *KPMG Peat Marwick* [2000] 4 All ER 540.

Negligent misrepresentation or misstatement

The courts have been reluctant to impose a duty of care as regards the careless making of statements as opposed to liability for careless acts. But in *Hedley Byrne & Partners Ltd* v *Heller & Co Ltd* [1964] AC 465 the House of Lords held that a duty to take care in making statements could arise. Normal *Donoghue* principles were not applied as a strict application of these principles would have led to too great a liability. Instead it was held that a duty of care would arise where there was a special relationship between the parties. For such a relationship to arise the following requirements are needed.

a) The representor must have a special skill. Although the Privy Council in *Mutual Life* v *Evatt* [1971] AC 793 took a narrow view of this criterion, the Court of Appeal has followed the more liberal minority view: *Esso Petroleum Co Ltd* v *Mardon* [1976] 1 QB 801; *Howard Marine and Dredging* v *Ogden* [1978] QB 574.

b) The representee must reasonably rely on the representation. Note that the Privy Council has taken a narrow view of this criterion also: *Royal Bank Trust Co (Trinidad) Ltd* v *Pampellonne* [1987] 1 Lloyd's Rep 218. If such reliance is absent the claimant may, in exceptional cases, rely on ordinary *Donoghue* principles: *Ross* v *Caunters*

[1980] Ch 287. In this context *Chappell* v *Somers & Blake* [2003] 3 All ER 1076 provides a useful illustration.

c) The defendant must have some knowledge of the type of transaction in question: eg *Smith* v *Eric Bush (A Firm)* [1989] 2 WLR 790; [1989] 2 All ER 514.

In *Caparo Industries plc* v *Dickman* (above) the House of Lords considered the situation where a person puts a statement into general circulation, as opposed to the situation where the defendant is aware of the transaction the claimant contemplated, knew the advice would be communicated to the claimant and knew it was likely that the claimant would rely on that advice (as, for example, in *Smith*, above). In the former case it was held that no duty would arise as the essential requirement of proximity was missing.

Note Lord Oliver's analysis of *Hedley Byrne* in *Caparo* and the application of *Caparo* in *Al-Nakib Investments* v *Longcroft* [1990] 3 All ER 321, *Morgan Crucible* v *Hill Samuel* [1991] 1 All ER 148 and *James McNaughton Paper Group* v *Hicks Anderson & Co* [1991] 1 All ER 134; note especially the factors elucidated by Neill LJ in *James McNaughton* from his analysis of the cases as being relevant to the imposition or otherwise of a duty of care.

Principles of negligent misstatement were received by the courts in the following cases: *Williams* v *Natural Life Health Foods* [1998] 2 All ER 577; *Welton* v *North Cornwall District Council* [1997] 1 WLR 570; *Gorham* v *British Telecommunications plc* [2000] 4 All ER 867; and *Standard Chartered Bank* v *Pakistan National Shipping Corp* [2000] 3 WLR 1692 (CA).

Pure economic loss

Because of the 'floodgates' argument the courts have held that no liability in negligence can arise for pure economic loss: *Cattle* v *Stockton Waterworks* (1875) LR 10 QB 453, ie economic loss which is not consequent on damage to the person or property of the claimant. However, in 1983 in *Junior Books Ltd* v *The Veitchi Co Ltd* [1983] AC 520 recovery was allowed for pure economic loss as between the owner of a building and a nominated sub-contractor. Note that this case was decided before the retreat from *Anns* (above) when foreseeability of damage played a greater part in the imposition of a duty of care: see Chapter 4.

The courts have consistently refused to apply *Junior Books* since 1986: see for example *Muirhead* v *Industrial Tank Specialities Ltd* [1986] QB 507; *Aswan Engineering Establishment Co* v *Lupdine Ltd* [1987] 1 All ER 135; *Simaan General Contracting* v *Pilkington Glass* [1988] QB 758; [1988] 2 WLR 761; *Greater Nottingham Co-operative Society* v *Cementation Piling & Foundations* [1989] QB 71.

In the House of Lords in *D & F Estates* v *Church Commissioners* [1989] AC 177; [1988] 3 WLR 368 it was said of *Junior Books* that 'the decision cannot be regarded as laying down any principle of general application in the law of tort' per Lord Bridge, and that it was 'really of no use as an authority on the general duty of care' per Lord Oliver, and perhaps the strongest criticism of all in *Simaan Contracting* where it was said that the case had been 'the subject of so much analysis and discussion with differing explanations of the basis of the case that the case cannot now be regarded as a useful pointer to any development of law … Indeed I find it difficult to see that future citation from *Junior Books* can ever serve any useful purpose': per Dillon LJ.

It thus seems unlikely that *Junior Books* will be applied in the future, and in *Nitrigin Eirann Teoranta* v *Inca Alloys* [1992] 1 All ER 854 the High Court again refused to apply *Junior Books* holding that that case was 'unique'. See also *Lancashire & Cheshire Association of Baptist Churches* v *Howard & Seddon Partnership* [1993] 3 All ER 467.

Note that in the above discussion we are considering pure economic loss resulting from a negligent act; pure economic loss resulting from a negligent misstatement is, of course, recoverable under *Hedley Byrne* (see above). However, in three further cases in the House of Lords it was held that *Hedley Byrne* covered negligent acts and omissions as well as negligent statements where there has been a voluntary assumption of responsibility towards the defendant: *Henderson* v *Merrett Syndicates* [1994] 3 WLR 761; *Spring* v *Guardian Assurance* [1994] 3 WLR 354 and *White* v *Jones* [1995] 2 WLR 187 – see especially the speeches of Lord Goff. The issue of 'protected interests' was once again brought before the Court of Appeal in *Walker* v *Geo H Medlicott & Son* [1999] 1 WLR 727 wherein the court took account of its own judgment in *Horsfall* v *Haywards* [1999] 1 FLR 1182, and *Gorham* v *British Telecommunications plc* [2000] 4 All ER 867. Other illustrations can be found in *Hooper* v *Fynmores (A Firm)* (2001) The Times 19 July, *Dean* v *Allin & Watts* (2001) The Times 28 June and *Commissioner of Police of the Metropolis* v *Lennon* [2004] 2 All ER 266.

Nervous shock

By nervous shock or psychiatric damage, the law means mental injury or psychiatric illness, not merely grief or sorrow: *Brice* v *Brown* [1984] 1 All ER 997; *Nicholls* v *Rushton* (1992) The Times 19 June.

Originally it was held that no duty of care arose because of the fear of fraudulent claims: *Victorian Railway Commissioners* v *Coultas* (1888) 13 App Cas 222. Gradually, however, the courts retreated from this stand and allowed recovery where the claimant was in fear of her own safety: *Dulieu* v *White* [1901] 2 KB 669, or in fear for the safety of her children: *Hambrook* v *Stokes Bros* [1925] 1 KB 141. However, this area of negligence was still burdened by requirements including the fact that the claimant had to witness the accident through his own senses and had to be in the vicinity of the accident. In *McLoughlin* v *O'Brian* [1983] AC 410 the House of Lords held that the appropriate test to apply was that of reasonable foreseeability. Lord Wilberforce stated that the law must limit those situations in which the claimant could recover for nervous shock and postulated three elements which should be present for a claim to succeed. In this respect, *Wainwright* v *Home Office* [2003] 3 WLR 1137 is worthy of note.

In *Attia* v *British Gas* [1988] QB 304 the Court of Appeal allowed recovery for nervous shock following damage to property continuing the incremental approach of allowing recovery to a range of claimants, and in *Hevican* v *Ruane* [1991] 3 All ER 65 and

Ravenscroft v *Rederiaktiebolaget Transatlantic* [1991] 3 All ER 73 the claimants succeeded despite not being present at the accident or its aftermath. However, in the leading case of *Alcock* v *Chief Constable of South Yorkshire Police* [1991] 4 All ER 907 the House of Lords held a claimant could only recover from nervous shock if he satisfied both the test of reasonable foreseeability that he would be so affected because of the close relationship of love and affection with the primary victim, and the test of proximity to the tortfeasor in terms of physical and temporal connection between the claimant and the accident.

Hence a claimant may could only be able to recover if:

a) his relationship to the primary victim was sufficiently close that it was reasonably foreseeable that he might suffer nervous shock;

b) his proximity to the accident or its immediate aftermath was sufficiently close both in time and space; and

c) he suffered nervous shock through seeing or hearing the accident or its immediate aftermath.

Thus a claimant who suffered psychiatric illness not caused by sudden nervous shock through seeing or hearing the accident or its immediate aftermath, or who suffered nervous shock caused by being informed of the accident by a third party, did not satisfy the tests of reasonable foreseeability and proximity. Also, given the television broadcasting guidelines, persons who witnessed the Hillsborough disaster live on television had not suffered nervous shock induced by the sight or hearing of the event as they were not in the proximity to the event and would not have suffered shock in the sense of a sudden assault on the nervous system.

The House of Lords doubted that *Hevican* or *Ravenscroft* had been correctly decided, and *Ravenscroft* has been overruled by the Court of Appeal: [1992] 2 All ER 470.

The House of Lords also held that the class of persons who may claim for nervous shock was not limited to particular relationships such as husband and wife or parent and child.

The House also suggested that a bystander who witnesses a particularly horrific catastrophe may recover, and that in certain circumstances a claimant may recover on witnessing an event on simultaneous television. However, in *McFarlane* v *Caledonia Ltd* [1994] 2 All ER 1 the Court of Appeal held that a bystander could not recover unless he was proximate in time and place and there was a close relationship of love and affection between the claimant and the victim. Note also *Page* v *Smith* [1995] 2 WLR 644 where it was held that where the defendant was under a duty to avoid causing personal injury to the claimant, it did not matter whether the injury caused was physical or psychiatric or both; and that the control mechanisms for nervous shock only applied to secondary victims and not primary victims.

In *Frost* v *Chief Constable of South Yorkshire Police* [1997] 3 WLR 1194 it was held that an employer who causes physical injury to an employee is liable to a fellow employee who sustains nervous shock either through fear for himself or witnessing what happened to his fellow employee. This duty exists because of the employer/employee relationship, and the distinction between primary and secondary victims and the control criteria on the latter are unnecessary.

Cases on principles used to determine liability for nervous shock include: *White v Chief Constable of South Yorkshire* [1999] 2 AC 455; *W v Essex County Council* [2000] 2 WLR 601; *Hunter v British Coal Corp* [1998] 2 All ER 97; *Greatorex v Greatorex* [2000] 4 All ER 769; *Leach v Chief Constable of Gloucestershire* [1999] 1 All ER 215; and *Frost v Chief Constable of South Yorkshire* [1999] 2 AC 455.

Third parties

As regards a person's duty to prevent third parties from inflicting damage on the claimant see the House of Lords' decision in *Smith v Littlewoods Organisation* [1987] AC 241 and especially the speech of Lord Goff.

Police

Do not have any general immunity from the law: *Rigby v Chief Constable of Northamptonshire* [1985] 1 WLR 1242; *Kirkham v Chief Constable of Greater Manchester Police* [1990] 3 All ER 246 but in many negligence situations there will be insufficient proximity to impose a duty: *Hill v Chief Constable of West Yorkshire* (above); *Clough v Bussan* [1990] 1 All ER 431; *Ancell v McDermott* [1994] 4 All ER 355; *Alexandrou v Oxford* [1994] 4 All ER 328; *Osman v Ferguson* [1993] 4 All ER 344. See also *Hughes v National Union of Mineworkers* [1991] 4 All ER 278.

Many cases concerning the liability of the police have come before the courts. Some of the important ones are: *Swinney v Chief Constable of the Northumbria Police* [1997] QB 464; *Leach v Chief Constable of Gloucestershire* [1999] 1 WLR 1421; *Costello v Chief Constable of Northumbria* [1999] 1 All ER 550 (CA); *Reeves v Commissioner of Police of the Metropolis* [1999] 3 All ER 897 (HL); *Waters v Commissioner of Police of the Metropolis* [2000] 4 All ER 934 (HL); *Vellino v Chief Constable of Greater Manchester* [2001] EWCA Civ 1249; and *Orange v Chief Constable of West Yorkshire* [2001] EWCA Civ 611. The Privy Council has, however, found that the police owed a duty of care to the public with respect to police guns in *Attorney-General of the British Virgin Islands v Hartwell* [2004] 1 WLR 1273.

Judges and legal representatives

Cannot be sued for their conduct of a case: *Rondel v Worsley* [1969] 1 AC 191; *Somasundaram v Julius Melchior* [1989] 1 All ER 129; *Gran Gelato v Richcliff* [1992] 1 All ER 865; but note *Walpole v Partridge & Wilson* [1993] 3 WLR 1093. But if a legal adviser steps outside his role liability may have been imposed: *Al-Kandari v Brown* [1988] QB 665; [1988] 1 All ER 833.

The House of Lords, however, have now reversed this position. Barristers and all other legal representatives are now as liable as the next person: *Arthur J S Hall v Simons* [2000] 3 All ER 673. See also *Atwell v Michael Perry & Co* [1998] 4 All ER 65, *Kelly v Corston* [1997] 4 All ER 466 and *Griffin v Kingsmill* [1998] PNLR 157. Some cases where solicitors have been found negligent include *Williams v Fanshaw Porter & Hazelhurst* [2004] 2 All ER 616; *Humblestone v Martin Tolhurst Partnership (A Firm)* [2004] EWHC 151; *Pickersgill v Riley* [2004] 14 EGCS 140 and *Daniels v Thompson* [2004] EWCA Civ 307.

Exercise of a statutory power

A distinction is drawn between policy and operational decisions, the latter being capable of being exercised negligently: *Sheppard v Glossop Corporation* [1921] 3 KB 132; *Home Office v Dorset Yacht* [1970] AC 1004. In this light, the Court of Appeal provided a rather interesting decision in *JD v East Kent Community Health NHS Trust* [2003] 3 All ER 1167. See also the Privy Council decision in *B v Attorney-General of New Zealand* [2003] 4 All ER 833 in the same context.

In *Jones v Department of Employment* [1989] QB 1; [1988] 1 All ER 725 it was held that a civil servant owed no duty of care and remedy was via judicial review: see also *Mills v Winchester Diocesan Board of Finance* (above).

Case law

General: duty of care

- *Doherty and Others v Rugby Joinery (UK) Ltd* (2004) The Times 3 March
- *JD v East Kent Community Health NHS Trust* [2003] 3 All ER 1167
- *Law Society v KPMG Peat Marwick* [2000] 4 All ER 540
- *Rees v Darlington Memorial Hospital NHS Trust* [2004] 1 AC 309

Negligent misstatement

- *Chappell v Somers & Blake* [2003] 3 All ER 1076
- *Gorham v British Telecommunications plc* [2000] 4 All ER 867
- *Standard Chartered Bank v Pakistan National Shipping Corp* [2000] 3 WLR 1692
- *Welton v North Cornwall District Council* [1997] 1 WLR 570
- *Williams v Natural Life Health Foods* [1998] 2 All ER 577

Pure economic loss

- *Commissioner of Police of the Metropolis v Lennon* [2004] 2 All ER 266
- *Dean v Allin & Watts* (2001) The Times 28 June

- *Gorham* v *British Telecommunications plc* [2000] 4 All ER 867
- *Hooper* v *Fynmores (A Firm)* (2001) The Times 19 July
- *Horsfall* v *Haywards* [1999] 1 FLR 1182
- *Walker* v *Geo H Medlicott & Son* [1999] 1 WLR 727

Nervous shock

- *Frost* v *Chief Constable of South Yorkshire* [1999] 2 AC 455
- *Greatorex* v *Greatorex* [2000] 4 All ER 769
- *Hunter* v *British Coal Corp* [1998] 2 All ER 97
- *Leach* v *Chief Constable of Gloucestershire* [1999] 1 All ER 215
- *W* v *Essex County Council* [2000] 2 WLR 601
- *Wainwright* v *Home Office* [2003] 3 WLR 1137
- *White* v *Chief Constable of South Yorkshire* [1999] 2 AC 455

Police

- *Costello* v *Chief Constable of Northumbria* [1999] 1 All ER 550 (CA)
- *Daniels* v *Thompson* [2004] EWCA Civ 307
- *Leach* v *Chief Constable of Gloucestershire* [1999] 1 All ER 215
- *Orange* v *Chief Constable of West Yorkshire* [2001] EWCA Civ 611
- *Reeves* v *Commissioner of Police of the Metropolis* [1999] 3 All ER 897 (HL)
- *Swinney* v *Chief Constable of the Northumbria Police* [1997] QB 464
- *Vellino* v *Chief Constable of Greater Manchester* [2001] EWCA Civ 1249
- *Waters* v *Commissioner of Police of the Metropolis* [2000] 4 All ER 934 (HL)

Judges and legal representatives

- *Arthur J S Hall* v *Simons* [2000] 3 All ER 673
- *Atwell* v *Michael Perry & Co* [1998] 4 All ER 65
- *Griffin* v *Kingsmill* [1998] PNLR 157
- *Kelly* v *Corston* [1997] 4 All ER 466

Exercise of statutory duty

Refer to Chapter 9 for cases.

5.3 Key cases and statutes

- *Arthur J S Hall* v *Simons* [2000] 3 All ER 673
  Barristers have now lost their immunity and may now be sued for negligence generally

- *Attorney-General of the British Virgin Islands* v *Hartwell* [2004] 1 WLR 1273
  Privy Council held that police owe the public a duty of care

- *Caparo Industries plc* v *Dickman* [1990] 2 AC 605
  Establishes duty of care through a three-part test

- *Chappell* v *Somers & Blake* [2003] 3 All ER 1076
  A mere voluntary assumption of responsibility may give rise to a legal duty

- *D & F Estates Ltd* v *Church Commissioners* [1989] AC 177
  Recovery for pure economic loss not allowed in tort

- *Donoghue* v *Stevenson* [1932] AC 562
  The establishment of the concept of duty of care

- *Gorham* v *British Telecommunications plc* [2000] 4 All ER 867
  Reaffirmed the principles established in *Hedley Byrne* (below)

- *Hedley Byrne & Co Ltd* v *Heller & Partners Ltd* [1964] AC 465
  Sets out liability in negligent misstatement cases

- *Law Society* v *KPMG Peat Marwick* [2000] 4 All ER 540
  Reaffirmed the incremental approach of *Caparo* (above)

- *McLoughlin* v *O'Brian* [1983] AC 410
  The test in deciding recoverability in cases of nervous shock was laid down

- *Rees* v *Darlington Memorial Hospital NHS Trust* [2004] 1 AC 309
  Their Lordships reviewed the extent to which a hospital owes a duty of care

- *Rigby* v *Chief Constable of Northamptonshire* [1985] 1 WLR 1242
  Police do not have any general immunity from the law

- *Vellino* v *Chief Constable of Greater Manchester* [2001] EWCA Civ 1249
  Gives an illustration of where there might be exceptions to the general rule

- *W* v *Essex County Council* [2000] 2 WLR 601
  The court reaffirmed the principles used in deciding recovery for nervous shock or psychiatric injury

- *Wainwright* v *Home Office* [2003] 3 WLR 1137
  House of Lords placed limitations on what can constitute a claim in nervous shock

- Employers' Liability (Defective Equipment) Act 1969 – employer is liable for all defective equipment

- Factories Act 1961 – imposes strict liability on employers in certain situations

- Fires Prevention (Metropolis) Act 1774 – no liability for 'accidental' fires

- Latent Damage Act 1986 – extends the original limitation period by another three years from date of knowledge

- Limitation Act 1980 – defines limitation periods for tortious actions

5.4 Questions and suggested solutions

General – duty of care/mixed issues

QUESTION ONE

Lewis and his twin sister Megan went for a week's holiday to the seaside resort of Fishmouth where they hoped to participate in water-skiing. The weather was unsuitable, and none of the water-ski operators was prepared to venture out in the conditions. On the last day of their holiday the weather improved and Megan was determined to water-ski. Owen, one of the operators, agreed to take her out. Lewis refused to go and went for a drink in a pub near the harbour. While he was drinking, he heard a commotion from the harbour and someone rushed in to the pub, saying that there had been an accident and that the young woman who had gone water-skiing had been swept out to sea. Megan's body was not found until it was washed ashore three days later. Lewis has had a serious mental breakdown as a result of the tragedy and has not been able to complete his university course. Some water-ski operators say that they would not have gone out in the conditions, but others disagree.

Advise Lewis on his behalf and Megan's.

University of London LLB Examination
(for External Students) Law of Tort June 2001 Q2

General Comment

At a glance this question appears to focus on general negligence, but on a closer examination it also gives rise to a discussion of psychiatric injury and issues of causation and breach.

Skeleton Solution

Did Owen owe a duty of care to Megan? – was Lewis owed any duty or was he a secondary victim? – issue of breach by Owen – any defences? – Lewis's claim for psychiatric injury – the *McLoughlin* v *O'Brian* criteria – chances of recovery.

Suggested Solution

The first point is to determine whether Owen owed a duty of care to Megan. Subsequent to the *Donoghue v Stevenson* [1932] AC 562 neighbour principle, the case of *Caparo Industries plc v Dickman* [1990] 2 AC 605 established a three-stage test to determine whether a duty of care is owed. The first stage is to establish reasonable foreseeability. The second stage is to determine the proximity of relationship between the parties. The final stage is to consider the reasonableness or otherwise of imposing a duty of care under the circumstances. Applying this criteria, there is no doubt that Owen, the water-ski operator, owed his client Megan a duty of care in tort.

The more crucial issue in relation to liability is whether Owen was in breach of his duty to Megan. In considering the issue of breach several factors must be addressed. First, the test of establishing a breach of duty. In *Blyth v Birmingham Waterworks Co* (1856) 11 Ex 781 the standard of care was stated to be that of the reasonable person, and a breach of duty was defined as the omission to do something that a reasonable man would do, or doing something that a prudent or reasonable man would not do. This requires an objective assessment of the situation. The question is not whether the defendant acted reasonably, but whether a reasonable person placed in the position of the defendant would have acted as the defendant did: *Glasgow Corporation v Muir* [1943] AC 448. In considering how a reasonable person would acted, the following guidelines are material:

a) the magnitude of the risk: *Paris v Stepney Borough Council* [1951] AC 367;

b) the likelihood of the risk or injury materialising: *Bolton v Stone* [1951] AC 850;

c) the relationship of the risk to the object to be attained: *Watt v Hertfordshire County Council* [1954] 1 WLR 835;

d) the practicality of precautions taken, if any: *Knight v Home Office* [1990] 3 All ER 237;

e) the knowledge and skill of the defendant (is he/she a professional?): *Bolam v Friern Hospital Management Committee* [1957] 1 WLR 582;

f) the common practice surrounding the defendant's activity, ie was the defendant conforming to or departing from established practices: *Johnson v Bingley* (1995) The Times 28 February.

Considering the above, the facts disclose first that the weather was unsuitable for water-skiing. Second, none of the water-ski operators were prepared to venture out under those conditions. These factors obviously support the contention that Owen was in fact in breach of his duty of care. Other considerations, such as could he have negligently controlled the boat or was he incompetent in some way so as to cause the accident, are also relevant. Even if there is no negligence in Owen's management of the boat, could he have been negligent in simply venturing out in those conditions? Alternatively, was the boat sufficiently or adequately equipped to negotiate adverse weather conditions, even though the question merely states that the weather was unsuitable? What about Megan's role in the whole scenario? She had been there for a week: the bad weather had persisted and deterred water-skiing throughout her stay. But she was determined to go water-skiing even though she knew the weather was unsuitable. Could Megan's determination to go water-skiing in any way be said to attract any liability on her part? It is likely that Owen could invoke contributory negligence under the Law Reform (Contributory Negligence) Act 1945, but no more than that. In any case, above all, there is nothing on the facts to indicate that the accident was caused by the bad weather or the unseaworthiness of the boat. It could have been any extraneous factor that could have caused the accident. If this is the case, then Megan's death would be deemed as a misadventure. If, on the other hand, it isn't, then the causation argument is what will pin liability on Owen, ie 'but for' Owen taking the boat out, would Megan have suffered a fatal injury? The answer would be an obvious 'no' and that is enough, it is submitted, to establish liability on Owen's part: *Cork* v *Kirby MacLean Ltd* [1952] 2 All ER 402. Owen's standard must be compared with other water-ski operators, and on balance it is arguable that most of them would not have ventured out under those conditions, even though we are told that some would have gone nonetheless.

As such, Megan's estate or dependants may sue Owen if he is the owner, or his employers under the principles of vicarious liability if he is working for another. Section 1(1) Law Reform (Miscellaneous Provisions) Act 1934 provides for the estate of the deceased to sue the defendant. Alternatively, the dependants of the deceased may sue under the Fatal Accidents Act 1976.

Lewis has suffered a serious mental breakdown or psychiatric injury. Can he hold Owen liable for this condition? In *McLoughlin* v *O'Brian* [1983] AC 410, the court established the principles of recovery in psychiatric injury cases. Three conditions must be fulfilled. First, the claimant's relationship to the primary victim must be sufficiently close that it was reasonably foreseeable that he might suffer psychiatric injury. Second, the claimant's proximity to the accident or its immediate aftermath must be sufficiently close both in time and space. Third, the claimant must have suffered the nervous shock through seeing or hearing the accident or its immediate aftermath. In *Alcock* v *Chief Constable of South Yorkshire Police* [1992] 1 AC 310 the House of Lords held that a claimant would only recover if he satisfied both the test of reasonable foreseeabilty (that he would be so affected because of the close relationship of love and affection with the primary victim), and the test of proximity to the tortfeasor in terms of the physical and temporal connection between the claimant and the accident. Being twins, Lewis would stand a better chance of establishing a special closeness with Megan. As far as proximity is concerned, Lewis was there, and although he did not see or hear the accident directly, he came within its immediate aftermath. No one else had gone water-skiing that day. It was only Owen, who had taken his sister Megan, who had done so. On the basis of *McLoughlin* v *O'Brian* [1983] AC 410 it is submitted that Lewis would be able to recover for psychiatric injury as against Owen.

Priest in the charge of a church

the person who goes to church reg[...]

QUESTION TWO

Simon is a vicar. He visited Tanya, one of his parishioners, one evening in August 1998 in order to discuss church business. Tanya is a solicitor and, before he left, Simon said to her: 'Can I ask your advice on a point of law? I really just want to know if there is any point in taking it further. My daughter, Una, had a holiday job at a garden centre. She was driving stakes into the ground when one of them split and went right into her wrist. She lost quite a lot of blood, but the worst thing is that she was hoping to be a professional violinist – it looks as though she will have to give that up now. The stakes were brand new and from a good company and there didn't appear to be anything wrong with them at all'. Tanya said: 'The trouble is that she has to prove negligence and anyway she would have had to tell her boss that she was a musician and then they wouldn't have given her work like that to do. So there isn't really any point in suing, I'm afraid'.

Simon did not take the matter any further. It is now too late to bring an action against the garden centre or the manufacturer of the stake, as it is barred by lapse of time.

Advise Una.

University of London LLB Examination
(for External Students) Law of Tort June 2001 Q7

General Comment

At first glance it appears that this question is raising a discussion of the law relating to negligent misstatement, but on a deeper analysis, it raises issues of breach of duty and negligence, ie did Tanya fall below the standard of a professional lawyer, and was she negligent in the giving of advice?

Skeleton Solution

Was there a duty of care owed to Simon by Tanya? – the nature of their relationship – the setting in which the advice was given – Tanya's qualified response – was there a breach of duty on Tanya's part? – was the advice given negligently? – the lapse of time and Una's ability to sue.

Suggested Solution

The courts have been reluctant to impose a duty of care as regards the careless making of statements as opposed to liability for careless acts. But in *Hedley Byrne & Co Ltd v Heller & Partners Ltd* [1964] AC 465 the House of Lords held that a duty to take care in making a statement could arise. The normal *Donoghue v Stevenson* [1932] AC 562 principles are not applied, as a strict application of these principles would have led to too great a liability. As the court observed in *Murphy v Brentwood District Council* [1990] 3 WLR 414, it would have 'exposed the defendant to indeterminate liability to an indeterminate class for an indeterminate amount'. Instead, it was held that a duty of

mumble = अस्पष्ट बोल रहा हूँ।

care would arise where there was a special relationship between the parties. For such a relationship to arise, several factors deserve analysis.

The representor must have a special skill

Case law reveals that the courts will only deem that such a duty exists if the defendant possesses skill in the area of advice given, as in the case of *Mutual Life and Citizens Assurance Co* v *Evatt* [1971] AC 793. Hence, there will be no liability usually for advice of an uninformed and inexpert character. This, of course, means that in a purely social context setting, such a duty would not arise, but in *Chaudry* v *Prabhaker* [1989] 1 WLR 29 the court held that this point may be rebutted if the circumstances reveal that carefully considered advice was being sought.

The representee must reasonably rely on the representation

The person making the statement should be aware that, at the time the statement was made, there would be reasonable reliance on the part of the recipient. Therefore, if a negligent statement did not influence the claimant's judgment then there is obviously no liability: *JEB Fasteners Ltd* v *Marks, Bloom and Co* [1983] 1 All ER 583, and more recently, *Lambert* v *West Devon Borough Council* [1997] 1 All ER 424. The issue is whether such a reliance is reasonably foreseeable, as was the case in *Smith* v *Eric S Bush* [1989] 2 WLR 790. Further, in *Ross* v *Caunters* [1980] Ch 297 the court held that if such a reliance is absent, the claimant may, in exceptional cases, rely on the *Donoghue* [1932] AC 562 principles.

The representor must have some knowledge of the type of transaction in question

In *Caparo Industries plc* v *Dickman* [1990] 2 AC 605 the House of Lords considered the situation where a person puts a statement into general circulation, as opposed to the situation where the defendant is aware of the transaction the claimant contemplated, knew the advice would be communicated to the claimant and knew that it was likely that the claimant would rely on that advice. In *Caparo*, however, it was held that there was no duty owed as the essential requirement of proximity was missing.

On an application of these principles, the following observations can be made. First, on the existence of a special relationship: Tanya is a professional lawyer, but Simon was not there for the purpose of seeking legal advice. The advice was given in a semi-social setting and, although both Simon and Tanya were meeting for professional purposes, these concern church business and not Simon's personal concerns. This rebuts the existence of a special relationship. But it should be noted that Simon was merely asking for advice on a preliminary question as to whether there may be any point in taking his case further. Did Tanya have a special skill, which she knew if communicated would be relied on? Tanya was a lawyer but was she a personal injury expert? The manner in which she responded to Simon, ie without any qualification or reservation, would in fact give rise to such an assumption. Tanya clearly stated there was no hope or point as there was no chance of a successful claim. Surely, at that point, she must have known that Simon would rely on her representation. Hence, a duty exists.

The next point to consider is whether Tanya was in breach of her duty of care to Simon. The advice given by Tanya would certainly seem to be wrong. Had Tanya properly considered the issues, she would have realised that there would have been strict liability on the part of the garden centre if a claim was to be pursued under the Consumer Protection Act 1987, or alternatively pursuing a claim under the Employers' Liability (Defective Equipment) Act 1969. In neither of these cases would Una have had to prove negligence. Further, the fact that Tanya said that Una should have told her employer that she was a musician would yield no fruitful result, as any other employee in similar circumstances would equally have been affected. Therefore, employers' liability is evident. On the basis of *Paris* v *Stepney London Borough Council* [1951] AC 367, it is clear that employers are expected to take extra precautions for an employee who might be vulnerable to any injury which would not affect most other employees. Hence, even if the initial argument is not acceptable, knowledge of the fact that Una was a musician might nonetheless implicate the garden centre, but that really would not make any difference, because an employer owes a duty to ensure that the employee is placed in a safe and secure working environment with proper plant and equipment. Was the advice given by Tanya therefore negligent? The standard of care is that of another equally qualified lawyer or solicitor in similar circumstances. Would a reasonable solicitor have reacted in the same way to Simon's enquiry: see *Bolam* v *Friern Hospital Management Committee* [1957] 1 WLR 582.

On the basis of *Blyth* v *Birmingham Waterworks Co* (1856) 11 Ex 781, it is submitted that Tanya was negligent. The advice was for the benefit of Una, and Tanya knew this. The situation is therefore comparable to that in *Hedley Byrne* itself. Clearly Simon would not be able to sue as he has in no way suffered any loss, but Una may be able to sue on the basis that there was foreseeability, proximity on the basis of *Ross* v *Caunters* [1980] Ch 297 and *White* v *Jones* [1995] 2 WLR 187, and finally that it is just, fair and reasonable under the circumstances to impose a duty of care on Tanya: *Peabody Donation Fund (Governors of)* v *Sir Lindsay Parkinson & Co Ltd* [1985] AC 210. Una has clearly suffered loss and damage. She, therefore, has a right of action in tort against Tanya. As far as the limitation period is concerned, an action should have been brought against the party causing the injury within a three-year period: s11(4) Limitation Act 1980 but the court has a discretionary power to disapply the limitation period under s33 Limitation Act 1980, but this may be defeated, as Una's physical injury was patent and there was nothing preventing her from seeking proper legal advice from any other solicitor.

QUESTION THREE

Joseph collected his car from the Knock-u-Down garage after its annual service. He drove out of the garage and into a busy road. Before he had got up any speed, a pedestrian, Leila, crossed a pedestrian crossing ahead of him. Joseph applied the brakes but the car did not stop. He was able to swerve and bring the car to a halt without any damage, but Leila was struck a glancing blow and fell over. Leila was taken to the casualty department of the local hospital, where the nurse at reception accorded her a low priority and she had to wait several hours for attention. When she was eventually called, she found that she could not stand up. It was found that she had sustained a more serious back injury than at first thought, and she is likely to suffer permanent paralysis. If she had been given a suitable support and seen promptly, these consequences would probably have been avoided. Joseph, who was of a very nervous disposition, was shocked by the accident and has suffered a permanent breakdown in his mental health. It has been established that the garage had failed to reconnect the brakes before the car was returned to Joseph.

Advise Joseph and Leila.

University of London LLB Examination
(for External Students) Law of Tort June 2000 Q8

General Comment

The question raises general issues in relation to an action in negligence. Candidates should be vigilant and rope in the garage as a party to the action, and not merely focus on Joseph. The other pertinent issue is whether Joseph can recover for psychiatric injury against the garage.

Skeleton Solution

Negligence: duty of care, breach, loss or damage; foreseeability; causation; remoteness – garage's liability to Leila: hospital's liability, if any; if so, the effect of that on garage's liability – psychiatric injury: principles establishing recovery in *McLoughlin* v *O'Brian*; is Joseph a primary or secondary victim? – garage's liability to Joseph.

Suggested Solution

Winfield and Jolowicz (Winfield and Jolowicz, *Law of Tort* (16th edn, 2002) (Chapter 1)) define the tort of negligence as: 'the breach of a legal duty to take care which results in damage, undesired by the defendant, to the claimant'. In order to succeed in an action for negligence, the claimant has to satisfy three primary elements:

a) that the defendant owed the claimant a duty of care;

b) that the defendant breached that duty; and

c) that as a result of the defendant's breach, the claimant suffered loss or damage which is not too remote.

The crucial issue here for Leila is whether she can bring an action against Joseph. Looking at the facts of the case, there is no suggestion that Joseph was negligent or fell below the standard of care expected of a reasonably competent driver. On yet closer examination, the facts seem to rule out negligence on the part of Joseph and point inescapably to liability on the part of the garage. The question clearly states that Knock-u-Down garage was negligent in leaving the car with the brakes unconnected. Was Leila their neighbour, based on the 'neighbour' principle enunciated in *Donoghue v Stevenson* [1932] AC 562 so that the garage owed her a duty of care? Yes, surely the garage must know or foresee that if the car was not roadworthy, then there would be other victims apart from the owner alone. Therefore, Leila was a foreseeable victim and on that basis was owed a duty of care. Applying *Caparo Industries plc v Dickman* [1990] 2 AC 605, there is no problem establishing proximity and foreseeability. Knock-u-Down garage failed to discharge their duty properly in leaving the brakes unconnected. Therefore, they are in breach of their duty, and it is that breach that causes loss and damage to Leila consequently. It is therefore just, fair and reasonable to impose a duty on Knock-u-Down garage: *Peabody Donation Fund Governors v Sir Lindsay Parkinson & Co Ltd* [1985] AC 210. Leila would be able to bring an action directly against Knock-u-Down garage for negligence.

However, the garage may only be liable for the initial injury sustained by Leila, and not the ultimate injury. This is dependent on whether there could be any liability attributed to the hospital in failing to prioritise Leila's case as urgent. The facts disclose that the nurse at casualty diagnosed Leila's case as one of low priority, which meant that Leila had to wait for several hours to be seen. For there to be any liability on the hospital's part, it must be proven that they fell short of their duty of care to Leila. Was the hospital in breach of their duty to Leila? It is submitted not, on the basis that there were not any physical injuries suffered by Leila apart from the glancing blow. Presumably Leila was still standing and was not showing any other signs or symptoms apart from mere discomfort. This may have led the nurse to conclude that there was no urgent treatment required. The issue is one of breach and causation. Would any other nurse have acted in the same way on the basis of *Bolam v Friern Hospital Management Committee* [1957] 1 WLR 582? The standard of care owed by this nurse must be judged according to the standard of care expected of nurses of equal standing. The *Bolam* [1957] 1 WLR 582 test was given approval in *Shakoor v Situ* [2000] 4 All ER 181. In deciding breach, the House of Lords in *Paris v Stepney Borough Council* [1951] AC 367 remarked that the seriousness of the injury must be taken into account. On that basis, since the nurse could not see any patent serious injury, she did the right thing by according Leila a low priority. This would probably be the same course of action taken by another nurse under the same circumstances. This, however, does not break the chain of causation and Knock-u-Down garage will still be liable to Leila.

If, on the other hand, it can be established that the hospital was indeed in breach of its duty of care to Leila in failing to sufficiently diagnose the extent of her injury, by successfully using the 'but for' test as established in *Barnett v Chelsea and Kensington Hospital Management Committee* [1969] 1 QB 428, then Knock-u-Down garage's liability could be limited to the initial injuries only and the hospital would be liable for the subsequent and ultimate injury suffered by Leila on the basis of *Baker v Willoughby* [1970] AC 467. The court is empowered under the Civil Liability (Contribution) Act 1978 to apportion liability as between as many defendants as may be relevant and appropriate or blameworthy.

As far as Joseph's claim for psychiatric injury against Knock-u-Down garage is concerned, Joseph would have to satisfy the principles of recovery for **psychiatric** injury as laid down in the celebrated case of *McLoughlin* v *O'Brian* [1983] AC 410. Joseph will only be able to recover if:

a) his relationship to the primary victim was sufficiently close that it was reasonably foreseeable that he might suffer nervous shock; and

b) his proximity to the accident or its immediate aftermath was sufficiently close both in time and space; and

c) he suffered nervous shock through seeing or hearing the accident or its immediate aftermath.

On a strict application of these principles, it is evident that Joseph would not be able to satisfy the first condition and would not be able to recover for nervous shock. However, the decision of *Page* v *Smith* [1995] 2 WLR 644 would prove otherwise. In this case, it was held that where the defendant was under a duty to avoid causing personal injury to the claimant, it did not matter whether the injury caused was physical, psychiatric or both; and that the control mechanisms for nervous shock only applied to secondary victims and not primary victims. This therefore implicates Knock-u-Down garage. Another possibility is to proceed on the basis of the decision in *Frost* v *Chief Constable of South Yorkshire Police* [1999] 2 AC 455, in which it was held that where the defendant causes the claimant to suffer psychiatric injury either through fear for himself (which is not the case as far as Joseph is concerned), or through witnessing what happened directly (which is the case here), there there could be liability. Joseph is filled with fear that he was the sole cause of all that has happened to Leila, when in fact it is Knock-u-Down garage's negligence that has produced these consequences. Hence, his fear has been induced by the garage's negligence, and this gives rise to liability. Therefore Joseph would be able to successfully bring an action against Knock-u-Down garage for negligence.

QUESTION FOUR

Juliet is a doctor who works for the Laburnam Street Surgery, a National Health Service practice in an inner city area. Because there have been several attacks on doctors on night call, the practice has an arrangement with Owlish Security Services to provide a guard to drive the doctor's car. Juliet is called out one night to a patient living in a large block of flats. She went into the flats leaving Dale, a guard from the security firm, sitting in the driver's seat. Two men attacked the car. One of them distracted Dale's attention by trying to open the back door. While Dale dealt with him, the other opened the passenger door, removed a pad of prescription forms which Juliet had left in the glove compartment and ran off. Juliet did not discover the loss until the next day. Meanwhile the thieves had given some prescription forms to their friends, one of whom, Liam, used a form to obtain a supply of drugs from a pharmacy. Liam suffered permanent brain damage as a result of taking the drugs.

Advise Liam's father.

University of London LLB Examination
(for External Students) Law of Tort June 1998 Q2

General Comment

This would have proved a popular question for candidates involving, as it did, consideration of the elements of the tort of negligence. Candidates should have appreciated that this was not a question concerning the duty of care owed by doctors to their patients. An analysis of the current authorities involving possible duties to prevent harm arising from the deliberate wrongful acts of third parties was required. Much of the discussion should have centred around the existence or otherwise of a duty of care, and related issues of causation and remoteness.

Skeleton Solution

Primary liability of Juliet – did she owe a duty to safeguard the prescription forms to prevent them from falling into the wrong hands? – was there a breach of duty? – did the intervening criminal conduct of the thieves and/or Liam's own decision to use the prescription to obtain the drugs amount to a novus actus interveniens? – was Liam contributory negligent? – was Dale also liable in negligence (on similar grounds)? – vicarious liability – were the partners of the surgery liable for Juliet's wrongdoing? – if Dale was negligent, who was his employer?

Suggested Solution

Primary liability of Juliet

The issue here is whether Juliet could be said to owe a duty to safeguard property in her control so that it could not be used to injure others. The establishment of such a duty of care, together with the further issue of whether, in law, Juliet could be said to have caused Liam's injuries, are fraught with difficulty.

Duty of care

Following the case of *Caparo Industries plc v Dickman* [1990] 2 AC 605 there is now a three-stage test in order to determine whether a duty of care arises in a novel situation.

a) The harm suffered by Liam must have been reasonably foreseeable. It is submitted that there is no great problem with this test. A reasonable person would surely have foreseen that the blank prescriptions might be the subject of a theft in an inner city area in which the incidence of crime necessitated the hiring of a security guard. It must also have been reasonably foreseeable that stolen prescriptions would inevitably fall into the wrong hands and be used to obtain supplies of drugs, the dangerous consequences of which are obvious.

b) There must have been a relationship of proximity between Juliet and Liam. The application of this test is far more problematic. There is no pre-existing relationship between Juliet and Liam. In addition, this is a case of non-feasance on the part of Juliet, ie a failure to safeguard property in her control so as to prevent it from falling into the wrong hands. It is unlikely that any positive duty to look after the prescription forms arises unless, possibly, she has been issued with guidelines as to their security. In the case of non-feasance, duties to prevent harm arising from the deliberate wrongful acts of third parties are only created in exceptional circumstances. There is no general common law duty to this effect.

Lord Goff, in *Smith* v *Littlewoods Organisation Ltd* [1987] AC 241, identified four situations in which such an exceptional duty might arise (although he conceded that there might be others) the most analogous of which are as follows.

i) Where there is a special relationship between the defendant and the third parties who inflict damage by criminal activity. Such a duty was held to exist in *Home Office* v *Dorset Yacht Co Ltd* [1970] AC 1004 in which damage done by escaped inmates of a Borstal institution was held to be recoverable, the escape arising from the negligent supervision of the inmates by three Borstal officers. However, a special relationship only arose in that case as a result of the statutory duties placed on Borstal authorities to control their trainees. In this case Juliet clearly has no responsibility in respect of the two men who attacked the car, and therefore it is submitted that no liability arises for their wrongful act under this exception.

ii) Where the defendant knows, or has the means to know, that a third party is creating a danger on his property and he fails to take reasonable steps to abate the danger. Thus in *Smith*, the defendants were not held liable in respect of their failure to prevent vandals from entering their unoccupied premises and starting a fire which spread to the claimant's property. Although their Lordships conceded that there is a general duty on occupiers to ensure that their premises are not a source of danger to neighbouring properties, this did not extend to preventing vandals from doing damage where a reasonable person would not have foreseen that steps were necessary to make the premises lockfast. In *Smith*, a reasonable person in the defendant's position would not have foreseen the need to secure the premises, as the defendant had no notice that vagrants were regularly in the building or that fires had previously been started there.

Lord Goff's approach was subsequently followed by the Court of Appeal in *Topp* v *London Country Bus (South West) Ltd* [1993] 3 All ER 448 in which the defendant was held not to be liable for a hit and run incident caused by joyriders who stole the defendant's minibus, even though the vehicle had been left unlocked with the key in the ignition awaiting a relief driver. It could be argued that, since Juliet knew of the high incidence of attacks on doctors in the area, she failed to take reasonable steps to abate the danger, especially if the previous attacks were with a view to obtaining blank prescriptions. She might, for example, have taken a smaller number of prescription forms with her rather than a whole pad, and taken some extra steps to secure them, such as locking them away in the glove compartment or in the boot of the car.

c) It must be fair, just and reasonable for the court to impose a duty of care in all the circumstances of the case. This is, of course, difficult to assess. The court might be persuaded to extend the duty recognised in *Smith* to Juliet's circumstances as the facts are clearly analogous. These three factors were considered by the House of Lords in *Rees* v *Darlington Memorial Hospital NHS Trust* [2004] 1 AC 309. Such an incremental development would not appear to fall foul of policy considerations, such as the need to prevent a flood of possible similar claims.

Breach

The factors relevant to whether Juliet's conduct fell below that to be expected of the reasonable person have been discussed above, when considering whether she failed to take reasonable steps to abate the danger.

Causation and remoteness

There is no doubt that Juliet's failure to safeguard the prescription forms was a factual cause of Liam's injuries. There is, however, a major issue as to whether, as a matter of law, she should be held liable for the damage which she has in fact caused. There are two possible intervening events (novus actus interveniens) which may serve to break the link between Juliet's possible negligence and Liam's injuries.

a) The intervening criminal conduct of the two men who stole the prescription forms. In *Home Office* v *Dorset Yacht Co Ltd* Lord Reid stated:

> 'Where human action forms one of the links between the original wrongdoing and the loss suffered by the plaintiff, the action must at least have been something very likely to occur if not to be regarded as a novus actus interveniens.'

This proposition is clearly closely related to the question of whether Juliet owed a duty to take reasonable steps to prevent the possibility of a theft, given her knowledge of the likelihood of attacks in the area. It is submitted that if Juliet owes a duty to Liam similar to that which was identified in *Smith*, then the damage caused by the third parties will not be regarded as too remote a consequence of a breach of that duty. The issues of duty, causation and remoteness are closely linked in situations such as these.

b) The intervening decision of Liam to use the stolen prescription form in order to obtain a supply of drugs. The unreasonable intervening conduct (going beyond a matter of pure contributory negligence) of the claimant will amount to a novus actus interveniens: *McKew* v *Holland & Hannen & Cubitts (Scotland) Ltd* [1969] 3 All ER 1621. It is submitted that Liam's actions fall well within the scope of this rule, and his loss will therefore be treated as too remote from any negligence on the part of Juliet to warrant recovery.

Defences

In the unlikely event that Juliet were to be held liable for Liam's injuries, Liam's damages would undoubtedly be substantially reduced having regard to his share in the responsibility for the loss: s1(1) Law Reform (Contributory Negligence) Act 1945. Clearly Liam was very much at fault in using the stolen prescription to obtain the drugs and in subsequently consuming them.

Primary liability of Dale

The basis for the possible liability of Dale will be very similar to that of Juliet, although some differences apply. It is submitted that a duty to safeguard property left in his control will only arise if Dale was aware of the presence of the prescription forms in the glove compartment. The fact that Dale remained in the car might indicate that Juliet had left him there for the purpose of guarding the forms rather than to provide personal protection for her upon entering the block of flats. On the other hand, the lapse in time before discovering that the forms had gone missing might indicate that Dale's attention hadn't been drawn to the presence of the forms in the first place.

If one of Dale's functions was to safeguard the prescription forms, then his failure to lock the passenger door whilst waiting in this particular neighbourhood would be an additional factor suggesting a breach of duty.

Vicarious liability

If Juliet has been negligent in failing to safeguard the forms, then the other partners in the Laburnam Street Surgery will liable to the same extent under the Partnership Act 1890.

Dale's employer will also be vicariously liable for any negligence on his part. The fact that he may have been discharging his duties in a negligent or careless manner will not take him outside the course of his employment: *Century Insurance Co v Northern Ireland Road Transport Board* [1942] AC 509. The only question remaining is whether Dale is an employee of Owlish Security Services, the agency which supplied him, or of the Laburnum Street Surgery. The modern approach is for the courts to consider a range of factors in relation to each potential employer such as:

a) who provided Dale's wage or other remuneration;

b) who paid his national insurance contributions;

c) who directed Dale as to the mode of performance of his work to such a degree as to make the other his employer;

d) who had the power to dismiss Dale; and

e) how long has Dale worked for the Laburnum Street Surgery?

There is little evidence in the question as to Dale's true position, although the fact that he drives the doctor's car, rather than one supplied by Owlish Security, is some indication that he may be an employee of the surgery.

QUESTION FIVE

Hettie was a patient at the Manpool Hospital. Ian, the junior doctor in her ward, decided that to combat an infection she should receive a daily course of injections. In entering the details in the computer he put the decimal point in the wrong place. When Jane, the newly qualified nurse in the ward, gave Hettie her injections, she was surprised by the dosage but was too shy to question it. She therefore gave Hettie the dose shown, which was ten times that which was appropriate. Within a few hours Hettie's face, arms and legs had become extremely painful, swollen and grotesquely disfigured. Hettie's brother, Kevin, came to visit her next day. He had not been told of her appearance and was extremely shocked. Both Jane and Kevin have suffered severe psychiatric damage.

Advise Hettie, Jane and Kevin.

University of London LLB Examination
(for External Students) Law of Tort June 1997 Q1

General Comment

This question requires a consideration of breach of duty and, in particular, the 'reasonable man' standard applicable to medical professionals. The effect of lack of experience, and the distinction between prognosis and treatment, should be discussed, as should the vicarious liability of the hospital authority. The question of nervous shock/psychiatric injury should be given reasonable prominence; in particular the sibling relationship and the time-scale/causative aspects.

Skeleton Solution

Duty; breach of duty; the 'reasonable man' standard – the *Bolam* test; prognosis and treatment; the duties owed by Ian and Jane – inexperience and the need to acquire expertise – nervous shock; primary and secondary victims – siblings as secondary victims/'mere bystanders' – the time gap and causation – vicarious liability of the hospital.

Suggested Solution

There is overwhelming authority for the proposition that a medical professional or a health authority will owe a duty of care to patients undergoing treatment; the necessary foreseeability, proximity and 'just, fair and reasonable' aspects of a duty are patently present. The real question is of the standard of care required to discharge the duty or, conversely, below which a breach of duty occurs. The case law has put a gloss upon a 'reasonable man' objective standard so that the test to apply to medical professionals is that of McNair J in *Bolam* v *Friern Hospital Management Committee* [1957] 1 WLR 582, that of 'the ordinary skilled man exercising and professing to have that special skill'. This test has found great favour with the English courts and has been held to apply not simply to medical professionals but to other types of professional and, indeed, to any situation where one is exercising skill and expertise: see *Bolitho* v *City and Hackney Health Authority* (1997) The Times 27 November.

We are not told whether Ian has discussed the proposed injections with Hettie or not. This raises the point whether any failure to consult Hettie or to advise her about possible effects would, in itself, constitute negligence. *Sidaway* v *Board of Governors of the Bethlem Royal Hospital* [1985] AC 871 shows that the same test should apply to giving advice about proposed treatment as to the standard required in giving treatment, ie the *Bolam* test. Ian will be measured against this. On balance, in failing to spot a very significant error in time, he would be likely to be found to have fallen below the standards of any body of reasonably competent medical professionals and, as a consequence, to have breached his duty towards Hettie. The question of any duty owed to Kevin is dealt with below.

The same *Bolam* reasoning will apply to Jane as a nurse. The question might be raised as to whether the standard should be lowered to allow for her relative inexperience (or, indeed, that of Ian). This will not be a factor; this much is clear from *Wilsher* v *Essex Area Health Authority* [1988] AC 1074. There is no room for a sliding scale varying with experience.

The damage to both Jane and Kevin is psychological in nature and this can create problems because of restrictive judicial attitudes towards recovery for this type of damage. The first question is whether the sufferer is categorised as a primary victim, ie one who suffers psychiatric damage as a result of a sudden shock to the system caused by the negligence of the tortfeasor. Here, there is little problem for Hettie's recovery because there are no special restrictive mechanisms at work, and recovery is based upon simple *Donoghue* v *Stevenson* [1932] AC 562 principles as in *Dulieu* v *White* [1901] 2 KB 669 and *Page* v *Smith* [1995] 2 All ER 736. The test is one of reasonable foreseeability of any type of physical (including mental) damage to such victims. By contrast, where a sufferer is a secondary victim, ie one who suffers shock because of danger or harm caused to another by the negligence of the tortfeasor, the special restrictions imposed by *McLoughlin* v *O'Brian* [1983] AC 410, as explained and extended by *Alcock* v *Chief Constable of South Yorkshire* [1991] 3 WLR 1057, come into play.

There are two problems raised by these cases in the situation in question. The first one is the categorisation of the victims. Hettie is arguably a primary victim, although we are not told of the precise means or process by which her condition arose. There would be no difficulties for her in the light of *Page* v *Smith* in that, provided some harm to her person was foreseeable, the precise type need not be foreseeable. Kevin can only, on the given facts, be a secondary victim. According to the House of Lords, such a victim must stand in such a relationship to the person harmed or in danger as would exhibit the sort of ties of love and affection to be found between spouses or between parents and children. This is a question of fact in the particular circumstance, according to *Alcock*. If the relationship is not this close, Kevin is likely to be equated with a 'mere bystander' and unable to recover: *McFarlane* v *E E Caledonia* [1994] 2 All ER 1.

Jane is in a rather anomalous position. She is possibly to be considered as a 'mere bystander' but it is more likely that her damage results from her knowledge of involvement in Hettie's injury. She would find assistance from her employee status as equating to a 'professional rescuer' within *Frost* v *Chief Constable of South Yorkshire* [1997] 3 WLR 1194 and from *Dooley* v *Cammell Laird & Co* [1951] 1 Lloyd's Rep 271.

The second problem raised by the House of Lords' cases is that of the closeness in time and space between the negligence giving rise to shock-causing event and the time at which the secondary victim observes the result and is shocked. Where there is no subsequent negligence by the original tortfeasor, the passage of time beyond the 'immediate aftermath' tends to bar recovery as in *Alcock*; there are too many possibilities for novus actus interveniens. Here, there seems to be no such problem because the fact of permitting visitors (or any unprepared person) to see such a shocking sight is, arguably, a quite separate act of negligence in itself. There might be defence arguments of novus actus interveniens, if, for example, Kevin had sought Hettie out without notifying anyone of his presence.

The hospital, as employers of Ian and Jane, will almost certainly be vicariously liable for such torts as they have committed within the course of their employment. There is nothing here to suggest that they were acting otherwise than in the course of employment. If the hospital system was at fault in allowing Kevin to visit Hettie unprepared, its liability will be primary.

Negligent misstatement/pure economic loss

QUESTION SIX

'Can a mere failure to speak ever give rise to liability in negligence under the *Hedley Byrne* principles? In our view it can, but subject to the all important proviso that there has been on the facts a voluntary assumption of responsibility in the relevant sense, and a reliance on that assumption' (*Banque Financière de la Cité CA* v *Westgate Insurance Co Ltd* [1990] 1 QB 665).

Discuss.

Written by the Author

General Comment

A general essay question on the principles of negligent misstatement after Hedley Byrne. Students must display a good knowledge of recent cases.

Skeleton Solution

Duty of care situation in instances of negligent misstatement – the principle enunciated in *Hedley Byrne* – an examination of cases post *Hedley Byrne* – present status quo – particular focus involving situations where the giver of the advice is silent or does not speak.

Suggested Answer

It has long been established that as regards careless acts the law will impose liability on the *Donoghue* v *Stevenson* [1932] AC 562 principle, but it will not impose liability in respect of omissions. Liability in negligence is confined to misfeasance and not non-feasance: see, for example, the speech of Lord Goff in *Smith* v *Littlewoods Organisation* [1987] AC 241, where his Lordship stated this general rule and identified four exceptions. By analogy, in negligent misstatement, one might assume that while liability may arise in respect of a negligent misstatement, no liability will arise from a failure to speak. Essentially, the statement from *Banque Financière* says that no liability will attach to a failure to speak subject to just one exception, namely where there has been a voluntary assumption of responsibility in the relevant sense and reliance on that assumption.

In *Candler* v *Crane Christmas* [1951] 2 KB 164 the courts were not prepared to extend duty of care to instances involving negligent misstatements. However, subsequently the position changed in *Hedley Byrne & Co Ltd* v *Heller & Partners Ltd* [1964] AC 465 where it was held that in order to succeed the claimant must show that the defendant had particular knowledge or skill or expertise. Second, it must be proven that the defendant knew or ought to have known that the claimant would rely on the statement/s and that it was reasonable to do so. Finally, it must be demonstrated that there was a 'special relationship' (one which is akin to contract), without any disclaimer of liability.

A further point worh pursuing is what the Court of Appeal meant by the phrase 'voluntary assumption of responsibility' as in *Smith* v *Eric S Bush (A Firm)* [1990] 1 AC 831. In *Smith* it was stated that the phrase can only have any meaning if it is understood as referring to the circumstances in which the law will deem the maker of the statement to have assumed responsibility to the person who acts on the advice, which essentially has turned the test from a subjective to an objective one.

It is this interpretation which is of relevance in so far as the quotation in the instant question is concerned. Therefore, it is arguable that what was said in *Banque Financière de la Cité CA* v *Westgate Insurance* [1990] 1 QB 665 is susceptible to rephrasing; by saying that a failure to speak can give rise to liability only where the law will deem the non-speaking party to have assumed responsibility (voluntarily) to the other, ie a failure to speak will give rise to liability only where a duty to speak arises.

However, the Court of Appeal has decided in several recent cases that a duty can be owed in the absence of a voluntary assumption of responsibility. In *Banque Financière* itself the court held that in an appropriate case the court could hold that having regard to the special circumstances and the relationship between the parties, a defendant could be treated in law (even though not in fact) as having assumed a responsibility towards the claimant. This principle can be seen in cases such as *White v Jones* [1995] 2 AC 207 and *Welton v North Cornwall District Council* [1997] 1 WLR 570. More recently the House of Lords in *Gorham v British Telecommunications plc* [2000] 4 All ER 867 and *Grimm v Newman and Another* [2003] 1 All ER 67 reiterated the principle enunciated in *Hedley Byrne* and emphasised that the criteria for the imposition of a duty of care in situations where there is evidence of negligent misstatement are: a voluntary assumption, reasonable reliance and some element of a fiduciary based relationship.

It would seem, therefore, that the quotation in the question is incomplete to a certain degree, in that it makes no reference to those situations where the defendant is deemed to have assumed a duty or responsibility, unless one reads 'voluntary assumption of responsibility' to include these situations.

QUESTION SEVEN

In 1997 Gigantic Industries plc contracted with Superdig Ltd to reconstruct their factory premises. The plans included the building of a light railway to carry finished goods from the factory to the distribution warehouse on another part of the site from which they were despatched throughout the country. Under sub-contracts Superdig engaged Hugetrains Ltd to build the light railway and also engaged Maxigardens Ltd to landscape the site. Maxigardens planted a large selection of trees and shrubs. The weather has been much warmer since 1997 than was forecast then, and during exceptionally hot weather in 1999 the railway line buckled, damaging a train travelling on it. The line was out of action for some weeks. The trees and shrubs have grown so as to overhang the railway line, and the Health and Safety Executive reported in 1999 that they obscured the line of vision of drivers to such an extent that they threatened the safety of those operating the railway. Accordingly Gigantic Industries had to have many trees felled, shrubs removed and a large area replanted at considerable expense.

Superdig Ltd have gone out of business. Advise Gigantic Industries as to the possibility of an action against Hugetrains and Maxigardens.

University of London LLB Examination
(for External Students) Law of Tort June 2000 Q6

General Comment

This is a question on pure economic loss and the principles governing the recovery of such loss. Matters are made difficult by the fact that the main contractors, Superdig, have gone out of business, leaving Gigantic Industries to question whether they can proceed against the sub-contractors in tort.

Skeleton Solution

The general principles of the tort of economic loss – recovering economic loss in tort – the relevance of *Junior Books Ltd* v *The Veitchi Co Ltd* – negligence in relation to railway line – physical damage to train and economic loss – liability of Maxigardens for economic loss caused by tree plantings.

Suggested Solution

In the late 1970s and early 1980s, a number of successful attempts were made to circumvent limitations in the law of contract by framing the cause of action in the tort of negligence. Two such cases were *Ross* v *Caunters* [1980] Ch 297 and *Junior Books Ltd* v *The Veitchi Co Ltd* [1983] AC 520. Academics seem divided over the justification of such circumvention. *Jaffey* [1985] 5 Leg Studies 77 states that it goes against the established rules of privity of contract, whilst *Markesinis* [1987] LQR 354 on the other hand argues for a possible expansion of tort law.

However, in the late 1980s, and certainly in the 1990s, a string of cases emerged to bring this expansion of the tort of negligence to a grinding halt. In its place has been inserted a new restrictive approach. Such a restrictive approach can clearly be seen in cases such as *Yuen Kun Yeu* v *Attorney-General of Hong Kong* [1988] AC 175 and *Curran* v *Northern Ireland Co-ownership Housing Association Ltd* [1987] AC 718. The culmination of this restrictive approach can be seen in the decision of the House of Lords in *D & F Estates Ltd* v *Church Commissioners* [1989] AC 177, where it was held that damages in tort did not generally extend to the cost of repairing the defect in the product itself; such a claim lay, if at all, in contract. Cases such as *Junior Books* and *Anns* v *Merton London Borough Council* [1978] AC 728, which had allowed the recovery of damages in tort in respect of repairing the defect in the product itself, were held to be anomalous cases, which their Lordships felt were not to be extended. Hence, there is no recovery for pure economic loss.

In the instant case, if Superdig had not gone out of business and were still solvent traders, Gigantic Industries would have no problem at all in framing an action for breach of contract, but Superdig are insolvent and have gone out of business. The question, therefore, is whether Gigantic Industries can file a claim against Hugetrains for the buckled railway line and the damaged train. There is also the issue of the line being out of action for some weeks, generating a loss of revenue. It this recoverable as well?

The second question relevant to Gigantic Industries is whether there is any liability on the part of Maxigardens, who have planted trees and shrubs along the railway line which have overgrown to the extent that they are posing a threat, resulting in additional expense as a result of felling, removing and replanting. Each issue will now be dealt with in turn.

Liability of Hugetrains

Hugetrains were contracted by Superdig to build a railway line for Gigantic Industries. Hugetrains did build a railway line, but it buckled under exceptionally hot weather. Did Hugetrains owe Gigantic Industries any duty of care in constructing the railway line free from any defect or free from negligence? Hugetrains were in the business of building trains. They should have foreseen and guarded against extreme weather conditions. It is no defence, nor it would not be logical or sensible, to say that the railway line could only be used in mild weather conditions. The weather in the United Kingdom is unpredictable, and the added benefit of hindsight would compound the issue of foreseeability. On this basis, it could be said that Hugetrains owed Gigantic Industries a duty of care, that they breached that duty, and as a result Gigantic Industries suffered loss and damage. Any physical injury or damage is recoverable, but not pure economic loss flowing from the negligence. Whilst Gigantic Industries would be able to recover for the damage to the train and all other consequential losses flowing from it on the basis of *Spartan Steel and Alloys Ltd* v *Martin & Co (Contractors) Ltd* [1973] 1 QB 27, the defective railway line and loss of revenue resulting from the railway line being out of action for some weeks would amount to economic loss. Unless Gigantic Industries is able to show reliance on their part and an assumption of responsibility and the existence of a fiduciary relationship on the part of Hugetrains, it is highly suspect that Gigantic Industries would be able to recover for pure economic loss.

Liability of Maxigardens

The trees and shrubs planted by Maxigardens along the railway line have overgrown and have begun to overhang the railway line. The trees and shrubs, although described by the Health and Safety Executive as posing a threat to drivers of trains and other potential users as well as to those operating the railway line, have not caused any physical injury to any person or property damage. There seems to be no possibility of any negligent act on the part of Maxigardens in planting these trees and shrubs. They seem to have discharged their contractual obligations properly. The duty to maintain the trees and shrubs falls to Gigantic Industries themselves as owners, and there is nothing on the facts to suggest otherwise. Hence the cost of felling the trees, removing the shrubs and replanting a large area amounts to pure economic loss and is thus irrecoverable on the basis of *Lancashire & Cheshire Association of Baptist Churches* v *Howard & Seddon Partnership* [1993] 3 All ER 467.

QUESTION EIGHT

'… in *Henderson* v *Merrett Syndicates Ltd*, it was settled that the assumption of responsibility principle enunciated in the *Hedley Byrne* case is not confined to statements but may apply to any assumption of responsibility for the provision of services.' (*Williams* v *Natural Life Health Foods Ltd* per Lord Steyn.)

Discuss this statement and comment on the use of the concept of 'assumption of responsibility' as the basis of liability.

University of London LLB Examination
(for External Students) Law of Tort June 1999 Q3

General Comment

This question would have suited those candidates who were keeping themselves fully up to date with current developments in tortious liability in the House of Lords. Such contemporary developments are always possible areas for examination, although a more in-depth analysis and comment upon the law will usually be required to compensate for predictability. Candidates should have concentrated their efforts on describing recent case law concerning liability for the provision of services, rather than the historical development of the *Hedley Byrne* principles relating to negligent misstatements. The two cases mentioned in the question were obvious starting points.

Skeleton Solution

Describe the notion of 'assumption of responsibility' as a criterion for liability in respect of negligent statements under *Hedley Byrne* – explain how the concept has been used to extend liability to the provision of services – discuss specific examples, in particular *Henderson; White* v *Jones; Williams* – criticise the concept of 'assumption of responsibility' as a basis for liability, describing the different attitudes of the judges to it.

Suggested Solution

In *Hedley Byrne & Co Ltd* v *Heller & Partners Ltd* [1964] AC 465 the House of Lords established that pure economic loss, suffered as a consequence of reasonable reliance by the claimant upon the defendant's negligent statement, is recoverable.

All of their Lordships justified their decisions upon the basis of one party having assumed a responsibility towards the other. Lord Devlin in particular held that the 'special relationship' necessary for a duty of care to arise occurred in relationships which 'are equivalent to contract'; that is, there is an assumption of responsibility in circumstances in which, but for the absence of consideration, there would be a contract. Lord Devlin also stated: 'Cases may arise in the future in which a new and wider proposition, quite independent of any notion of contract, will be needed'.

This essay will concentrate on how notions of 'assumption of responsibility' have been used by the courts since *Hedley Byrne* to extend the principles established in that case to the negligent performance of services in addition to negligent statements and advice. Such extensions were made in order to do individual justice in cases where the claimants concerned had suffered pure economic loss, and would therefore have been unable to recover under normal negligence principles.

The extension of the Hedley Byrne *principle to the provision of services*

A suggestion that *Hedley Byrne* was not simply to be confined to 'statement' cases came in the judgments of Lord Oliver in *D & F Estates Ltd* v *Church Commissioners* [1989] AC 177 and Lord Keith in *Murphy* v *Brentwood District Council* [1990] 3 WLR 414. Their Lordships classified the decision of the House of Lords in *Junior Books Ltd* v *The Veitchi Co Ltd* [1983] 1 AC 520 as an example of *Hedley Byrne*-type liability. However, *Junior Books* was a case concerning the recovery for economic loss arising from a defective product rather than a negligent statement.

The extension of *Hedley Byrne* principles to cover negligently provided services is, perhaps, unsurprising. Many professional services are based wholly or partly upon the giving of advice. A significant extension of liability eventually occurred in *Henderson* v *Merrett Syndicates Ltd* [1994] 3 WLR 761, a case arising out of the losses suffered by Lloyd's 'names' following advice given by their underwriting agents as to the risks involved. The House of Lords decided that a duty of care would exist where a person assumed responsibility to perform professional or quasi-professional services for another who relied on those services. Lord Goff stated:

> '... though *Hedley Byrne* was concerned with the provision of information and advice, the example given by Lord Devlin ... and his and Lord Morris's statement of principle show that the principle extends beyond the provision of information and advice to include the performance of other services.'

The scope of this extended duty will necessarily be limited, because service providers are only likely to assume responsibility to specific individuals, or to a limited class of specific recipients, in respect of their services. Thus, liability can be maintained within acceptable bounds.

Similarly, in *White* v *Jones* [1995] 2 WLR 187 Lords Goff and Browne-Wilkinson applied *Hedley Byrne* in order to impose liability upon a solicitor who had negligently failed to carry out instructions in preparing a new will, resulting in financial loss to the intended beneficiaries. The lack of privity of contract between the solicitors and beneficiaries did not prevent a claim in negligence, because a 'special relationship' arose between the parties, the defendant having assumed a responsibility for the economic welfare of the beneficiaries. A point of particular difficulty in this case was that the beneficiaries could not necessarily be said to have relied upon the defendant's expertise as a matter of fact, given that beneficiaries are usually unaware of the provisions which have been made for them in a will. However, in order to allow the beneficiaries a claim, their Lordships held that reliance is not a necessary condition for the creation of a 'special relationship' in every case under the extended *Hedley Byrne* principle.

White v *Jones*, therefore, clearly indicates that *Hedley Byrne* principles may be extended to the provision of services, even if those services were provided at the request of a third party.

The case of *Williams* v *Natural Life Health Foods Ltd* [1998] 2 All ER 577 involved a claim for substantial economic losses following the failure of a franchisee's natural health business. It was claimed that the loss arose from negligent advice provided by the franchisor, a company run by the defendant (who was the principal shareholder and managing director). However, the franchisor had been wound-up and dissolved, and so the claimants sued the defendant, attempting to prove that he had personally assumed responsibility for the negligent advice. On the facts, the House of Lords held that the defendant had not assumed personal responsibility for the advice and the claim failed.

Lord Steyn confirmed that 'assumption of responsibility' is the basis for liability under the extended *Hedley Byrne* doctrine. The test is an objective one, not depending upon the state of mind of the defendant but upon evidence of statements or conduct which conveyed to the claimants that the defendant was willing to assume personal responsibility for them. Lord Steyn held that reliance by the claimants on the assumption of responsibility is necessary to establish causation. However, the test is not whether, in fact, the claimant relied upon the assumption of responsibility, but whether it was reasonable to rely on the defendant to take personal responsibility in all the circumstances.

Thus it can be seen that recovery for pure economic loss arising from the negligent provision of services is now possible under English law. The *Hedley Byrne* test as applied to negligent misstatements has, by necessity, been adapted to apply more easily to the provision of services. For example, reliance by the claimant, as a question of fact, could not be established in many situations involving the provision of services.

The concept of 'assumption of responsibility' as the basis of liability

It was once thought that the 'assumption of responsibility' test was nothing more than a convenient phrase to describe the situation in which a duty of care would be recognised or imposed by the law. In *Caparo Industries plc v Dickman* [1990] 2 AC 605 Lord Oliver stated that 'it was not intended to be a test for the existence of the duty ... It tells us nothing about the circumstances from which such attribution arises'. However, as we have seen, there have been attempts to adapt the test as a criterion for liability in other cases concerning pure economic loss arising from the provision of services.

One criticism of the current concept of 'assumption of responsibility' as a test for liability is that it is too uncertain and imprecise to provide useful guidance to trial judges in future cases. As such, it could simply be used as a tool to justify a finding of liability when the court feels that the justice of the situation requires such a conclusion. This makes it hard for lawyers advising the parties to predict the outcome of a dispute, thus possibly necessitating expensive litigation. However, the Court of Appeal has, in *Commissioner of Police of the Metropolis v Lennon* [2004] 2 All ER 266, held that a voluntary assumption of responsibility does in fact attract legal liability.

There is evidence supporting the view that the concept might simply be used as a tool to justify liability in the authorities already discussed. In *White v Jones* Lord Goff openly admitted that he was motivated to achieve practical justice, because a lack of privity of contract would have denied the beneficiaries a claim. The testator's estate had suffered no loss and so a claim for breach of contract would not have been sustainable on the facts. The defendants would escape liability for their admitted negligence unless the court was prepared to impose a concurrent duty in tort.

The formulation of 'assumption of responsibility' by Lord Steyn in *Williams* is also unsatisfactory in that it cannot explain all the cases. For example, in *Smith* v *Eric S Bush (A Firm)* [1990] 1 AC 831 the defendant surveyors, instructed by a building society, had sought to avoid liability to the claimant house purchaser by the use of a disclaimer. Nonetheless, the claimant was held to be entitled to rely upon the valuer's report, even though the disclaimer said that the survey was prepared for the benefit of the building society and not the claimant. Surely, it could not be said that the surveyor had shown a willingness to assume a personal responsibility to the house purchaser by statements or conduct, given the clear wording of the disclaimer? Lord Steyn regarded *Smith* v *Bush* as an awkward case decided on special facts, which was very much based on the need to 'yield to practical justice'.

Perhaps a more coherent version of the 'assumption of responsibility' is that formulated by Lord Browne-Wilkinson in *White* v *Jones*. This would involve liability based upon 'a conscious assumption of responsibility for the task' which benefits the claimant, rather than 'a conscious assumption of legal responsibility to the claimant for its careful performance'. Such a formulation would avoid the difficulties associated with Lord Steyn's approach when it comes to explaining cases such as *Smith* v *Bush*. Alternatively, it has been suggested that the *Donoghue* v *Stevenson* [1932] AC 562 conception of proximity, which asks whether the claimant was a person 'so closely and directly affected by my act that I ought reasonably to have them in contemplation', would provide a suitable alternative criterion in cases like these: Cooke, John, *Law of Tort* (4th edn, 1999).

QUESTION NINE

Every month a national newspaper The Clarion publishes the serial numbers of premium bonds which have won large prizes in that month's draw. Louisa read the list one month, checked her numbers and saw that one of her bonds had won a prize of £100,000. A week earlier in her public library she had been reading a copy of The Dabbler, a weekly periodical which gives investment advice. She remembered readers being advised to consider purchasing shares as soon as possible in Dentache plc, whose research scientists were said to be on the brink of a revolutionary new technique for arresting tooth decay. This information was seriously misleading and The Dabbler published a correction in the next issue, but Louisa had not read this. Louisa immediately decided to invest a large part of her prize money in Dentache plc and purchased shares to the value of £80,000.

In the list of prizewinners in The Clarion two digits had been transposed incorrectly and Louisa had not won a prize. The shares in Dentache plc have not risen in value.

They fell slightly after she purchased them, but have now risen to the price at which she purchased them.

Advise Louisa.

University of London LLB Examination
(for External Students) Law of Tort June 1998 Q3

General Comment

This question requires more thought, and possibly a more detailed analysis of the facts. Candidates needed to know the rules necessary to impose liability for economic loss caused by negligent advice and information, and be able to apply them to a set of rather awkward facts. Different approaches to structure are also possible here. Candidates should make some observations about the different economic losses that arise in this case, and whether they were all recoverable, bearing in mind the general aim of damages in tort. Such discussion would normally be reserved until the end of a question. However, candidates could set the scene by making it clear from the outset which losses Louisa might have been able to recover (if at all).

Skeleton Solution

Identify, in relation to the aims of damages in tort, which losses Louisa might be able to recover following her reliance on negligent information and advice – discuss whether Louisa was owed a duty of care by The Dabbler in respect of economic losses caused by reliance on negligent investment advice (investigate whether a 'special relationship' existed between them and whether Louisa reasonably relied on their advice) – discuss whether Louisa was owed a duty of care by The Clarion in respect of economic losses caused by reliance on negligently provided information.

Suggested Solution

This question concerns potential liability for economic loss caused by negligent advice and information. It is more difficult to impose liability for negligent statements than for negligent actions: careless words can spread rapidly resulting in a proliferation of claims and potentially unlimited financial losses. Therefore, policy considerations have led to the introduction of rules which limit the class of potential claimants in such cases. The mere foresight of harm arising from negligent advice is insufficient to establish a duty of care.

Which losses might Louisa be able to recover in negligent misstatement?

It should be noted from the outset that, even if duties of care can be established in this case, Louisa is unlikely to be able to claim for all the potential losses she has suffered. This is because the aim of damages in tort is to restore the claimant to the position she would have been in had the tort never been committed (the 'reliance' interest). There have been very few tort cases in which the claim resulted in an award of damages to protect the 'expectation' interest, ie by putting the claimant into the position she would have been in had the defendant properly carried out their obligation. One exceptional category of cases have arisen in relation to the negligent execution of a testator's instructions by a solicitor in the preparation of a will: see *Ross* v *Caunters* [1980] Ch 297 and *White* v *Jones* [1995] 2 WLR 187. However, these cases appear to represent a very limited exception to the general rule.

The losses accruing to Louisa in this case seem to be as follows.

a) The loss of interest/investment income on the £80,000 which Louisa would have earned had she not withdrawn the funds to invest in Dentache plc shares.

b) The administration costs of buying (and possibly selling) the shares.

c) Any loss resulting from a fall in the value of Dentache plc shares. It should be noted that Louisa has not actually made a loss, since the price of these shares has recovered, and it is submitted that she may now be under a duty to mitigate her loss by selling the shares in order to prevent future loss from accruing (assuming she is to claim in negligent misstatement).

d) The failure to make an economic gain, ie a profit from the Dentache plc shares, which would have been made had the information quoted in The Dabbler been correct.

The loss in (d) above clearly relates to the expectation interest, and is not recoverable in negligent misstatement. The restoration of Louisa to the position she was in before any tort took place would require the courts to ensure that Louisa had suffered neither financial loss nor financial gain. It is submitted that it would not be fair, just and reasonable to expect the maker of a statement to be held responsible for a lack of financial gain arising from negligent advice. As a matter of policy, it might be thought that those who 'gamble' in the hope of making a profit should be expected to accept the risk of making a loss.

Is Louisa owed a duty of care by The Dabbler in respect of the (pure) economic losses arising from the negligent investment advice?

The development of this area of law has been heavily influenced by trends in judicial policy and therefore the decisions have not always been consistent. However, some common requirements can be deduced from the body of case law, starting with the House of Lords' decision in *Hedley Byrne & Co Ltd* v *Heller & Partners Ltd* [1964] AC 465.

A duty of care arising from a negligent misstatement can only be established if the following two criteria apply.

a) There must have been a special relationship (of close proximity) between the claimant and the defendant.

   The existence of such a relationship is dependent upon a variety of factors. It has been suggested that a relationship 'equivalent to contract' must exist between the claimant and defendant before the defendant will be held to have voluntarily assumed responsibility to the claimant. See the judgments of Lord Devlin in *Hedley Byrne* and Lord Templeman in *Smith* v *Eric S Bush (A Firm)* [1990] 1 AC 831. In the instant case, it could be argued that such a relationship might exist between The Dabbler and those who purchase copies of it from a retailer. Whether such a relationship could be said to exist in respect of those who simply read the magazine in a public library is more difficult to say. In *Caparo Industries plc* v *Dickman* [1990] 2 AC 605 Lord Oliver defined the range of persons to whom a duty is owed in terms of the purpose for which the statement was made. He identified four necessary elements for the existence of a duty of care, as explained below.

i)   The advice must be required for a purpose which is either specified in detail or described in general terms, and this purpose must be expressly or inferentially made known to the advisor when the advice is given.

The whole purpose of The Dabbler is to give investment advice to its readership, and this would of course have been known to the editorial staff. However, whether the purpose is simply to give general investment advice (to point readers in the right direction) or to give specific information about companies is unclear. It could be argued that the information concerning Dentache plc was very specific, and the fact that the magazine advised its readers to consider purchasing shares 'as soon as possible' might indicate that The Dabbler had voluntarily assumed responsibility to their readership in respect of the accuracy of this information.

On the other hand, it could be argued that the advice being given was simply to 'consider' purchasing shares in Dentache plc, and therefore the purpose was to suggest that readers might make an investment after undertaking further research and possibly obtaining a second opinion. It must be remembered that the rules, as a matter of policy, are intended to reduce the potential class of claimants. The losses accruing to The Dabbler and other similar periodicals would potentially be unlimited if every reader were permitted to recover for financial losses following reliance on poor investment advice. In *James McNaughten Paper Group plc* v *Hicks Anderson & Co* [1991] 1 All ER 134 Neill LJ identified, as an additional relevant factor, the size of any class of persons to which the advisee belongs. It is submitted that it is unlikely that the courts would impose a duty of care on The Dabbler in respect of the advice honestly given, as the potential class of claimants would be very large.

ii) The advisor must know (expressly or inferentially) that the advice will be communicated to the claimant, either specifically or to a member of an ascertained class, in order that it should be used by the advisee for that purpose. It is submitted that The Dabbler must be aware that its potential readers are likely to include those who visit public libraries.

iii) It must be expressly or inferentially known that the advice communicated is likely to be acted upon by the advisee for that purpose without independent enquiry (see below on 'reasonable' reliance).

iv) The advice must be acted upon by the advisee to his detriment.

The advice given must be formal considered advice. 'Off the cuff' advice or 'passing comment' will not usually give rise to a special relationship. However, it is submitted that written advice contained in a magazine whose purpose it is to inform its readership of investment decisions must be regarded as formal considered advice. The person giving the advice must usually possess some special skill/knowledge: *Esso Petroleum Co Ltd* v *Mardon* [1976] 1 QB 801. It can be assumed that those who write for The Dabbler have some expertise in the field of investment decisions, or at least hold themselves out as doing so.

b) It must have been reasonable for the claimant to rely on the defendant's statement.

Louisa clearly relied on the advice she had read, as she was influenced to invest on the strength of it. It is unlikely, however, that her reliance was reasonable. It has already been pointed out that the purpose of such a magazine might only have been to inform general investment decision-making by pointing readers in the right direction. It would seem unreasonable for Louisa to make such a large investment without undertaking further research or even seeking independent financial advice. This is particularly the case given that Louisa's decision was based upon her recollection of an article in a magazine which was published a week earlier. The price of shares in Dentache plc might already have increased following the earlier publicity and the investment might no longer be regarded as a good one.

It is submitted, therefore, that Louisa is not owed a duty of care by The Dabbler in respect of the advice given, in that no special relationship arose between them (the advice arguably not having been provided for the purpose of making specific investment decisions) and in any event, it would have been unreasonable for Louisa to rely on the advice in the circumstances.

Even if a duty was owed by The Dabbler to its readers, it could be argued that the duty was discharged by the printing of a correction in the first available issue, at least in respect of losses sustained after publication.

Is Louisa owed a duty of care by The Clarion in respect of the misprint?

The failure to correctly transpose the serial numbers of the winning premium bonds also gives rise to difficulty. In applying the criteria identified by Lord Oliver in *Caparo* it seems likely that a special relationship did arise between The Clarion and Louisa. The newspaper knew that the information they gave would be used by readers for the purpose of checking their serial numbers. It is also clear that Louisa relied on this information to her detriment.

However, the main issue is whether it can be said that Louisa reasonably relied on the printed information. Surely the newspaper could reasonably expect Louisa to receive official confirmation of her win, or at least to confirm the numbers from another source, before relying on the information. There is also some authority to suggest that the courts may draw a distinction between the mere passing on of information and the giving of advice based upon that information: see the Privy Council case of *Royal Bank Trust Co (Trinidad) Ltd* v *Pampellonne* [1987] 1 Lloyd's Rep 218. The mere printing of winning serial numbers might simply be regarded as the passing on of information, and therefore, would not give rise to any duty of care.

Psychiatric injury (nervous shock)

QUESTION TEN

A party of schoolchildren from London went on a week's adventure holiday in Devon. One afternoon they went on a river expedition organised by Titanic Cruises. Twelve of the children were on a boat piloted by Amos, an employee of Titanic Cruises. As the boat approached a dangerous section of river, the steering mechanism failed and Amos was unable to stop the boat being carried towards a weir. The boat crashed over and everyone was thrown overboard and carried down by a raging current. Bianca was standing on the bank. She tried to climb down the bank but saw at once that she would herself be carried away. She watched helplessly as the children were carried past. Most children were drowned, but two together with Amos were rescued. News of the tragedy was given on the evening news bulletin together with an emergency contact number in Exeter. Cleo telephoned the number from London to ask about her daughter Daphne, who had been on the expedition, and was told that Daphne had drowned. This was a mistake; Daphne had not been on the trip that afternoon.

Amos, Bianca and Cleo have all suffered psychiatric injury.

Advise them.

University of London LLB Examination
(for External Students) Law of Tort June 1999 Q4

General Comment

This should have been a relatively straightforward question for those candidates who revised the law concerning the recovery of compensation for psychiatric injury, provided they were up to date with the most recent case developments. It must of course be remembered that 'nervous shock' is a type of damage rather than a tort, and therefore candidates would first have needed to identify the basis upon which the defendant might be held liable to those involved in the accident.

Skeleton Solution

Identify and discuss the basis for liability – elements of negligence: duty; breach (res ipsa loquitur); causation; remoteness of damages – discuss each potential claim for recovery in respect of psychiatric illness: Amos as a primary victim; Bianca and Cleo as secondary victims – does Cleo have an alternative claim for a negligent statement made by the Exeter authorities?

Suggested Solution

Basis for liability

It appears that Titanic Cruises may well be liable in negligence to the primary victims of the accident, ie Amos and the children, on the basis of their apparent failure to properly maintain the boat, if indeed this was the case. The elements of the tort of negligence are briefly as follows.

a) The defendant must have owed the claimant a duty of care.

The modern approach for determining whether a duty of care should be imposed in a novel case was recommended by the House of Lords in *Caparo Industries plc* v *Dickman* [1990] 2 AC 605. The question is approached in the three stages shown below.

i) Assuming Titanic had failed to properly maintain the boat, were the consequences of that failure reasonably foreseeable? It would have to be proved that the failure of the steering mechanism was a reasonably foreseeable consequence of a failure to properly maintain the boat. If this were the case, it is submitted that the resulting inability to properly navigate the boat in fast moving rapids would almost inevitably result in a crash, causing injury to the occupants of the boat.

ii) Was the relationship between the defendant and the claimant(s) sufficiently proximate? This requirement is easily satisfied on the facts, because it is the negligent infliction of physical injury which itself appears to create the required degree of proximity.

iii) Would it be 'fair, just and reasonable' in all the circumstances for the courts to impose a duty of care? This requirement is heavily influenced by policy considerations, and it is submitted that it would certainly be fair, just and reasonable to impose a duty of care upon Titanic in these circumstances. Titanic are likely to be insured against claims arising from its business activities, and to allow this type of claim would certainly not result in an opening of the 'floodgates of litigation'. It might be argued that imposing a duty in these circumstances will encourage other similar operators to take care.

b) The defendant must be in breach of that duty.

This involves deciding whether Titanic's conduct fell short of the standard of care which would have been adopted by reasonable persons in the circumstances. The amount of care required in each particular case will depend upon different factors, such as the likelihood of people suffering injury from the hazard, balanced against the practicality of taking precautions in terms of cost and otherwise: *Bolton* v *Stone* [1951] AC 850. The extent of the potential damage may also be relevant.

In this case, the maxim 'res ipsa locquitur' (the thing speaks for itself) may apply, as the facts appear to be sufficient to give rise to an inference of negligence on Titanic's part. If such were the case, the court would not require the claimant to give detailed evidence regarding Titanic's failure to maintain the boat. Instead, it would fall to Titanic to rebut the inference of negligence.

For the maxim to apply, the claimant must show that Titanic was in control of the thing (ie the boat) which caused the loss or damage, and that the accident was of such a nature that it would not have occurred in the ordinary course of events with proper care. It might be suggested that a steering defect would have been unlikely to occur had the boat been properly maintained. Finally, the cause of the accident must be unknown in that it cannot be easily explained. This criterion may apply assuming that no cause can readily be advanced for the failure of the steering mechanism.

c) The breach of duty must have caused the claimant to suffer reasonably foreseeable damage/loss.

Assuming that the failure of the steering mechanism resulted from a breach of a duty owed by Titanic, there can be no doubt that the deaths of the children and the psychiatric injuries suffered by the various claimants were direct factual causes. The question as to whether the psychiatric injuries were reasonably foreseeable is dealt with below. The following analysis assumes that Titanic were negligent in respect of physical harm suffered by Amos and the other primary victims of the accident.

Can Amos recover as a primary victim of the accident?

The law relating to the recovery of compensation for psychiatric illness in tort makes a distinction between primary and secondary victims. Primary victims are those who are physically threatened by the negligence, and either suffer personal injury or are put in fear of suffering injury. A secondary victim is someone who is a witness to the consequences of a negligent act or omission in respect of a primary victim.

Amos is a primary victim as he was directly involved in the accident and must have feared for his own life and/or was an active participant in an accident caused by Titanic's negligence: *Dooley* v *Cammell Laird & Co Ltd* [1951] 1 Lloyd's Rep 271. This level of direct involvement in the accident automatically establishes a relationship of proximity between Amos and Titanic. The fact that Amos is Titanic's employee does not automatically give him the status of a primary victim. In *White* v *Chief Constable of South Yorkshire* [1999] 1 All ER 1 the House of Lords decided that an employer is not under a duty to protect employees from psychiatric injury unless the employer is in breach of a duty to protect employees from physical harm. Assuming that Titanic were negligent in respect of the latter, there is no requirement that Amos' psychiatric injury should have been reasonably foreseeable and Amos will be able to recover compensation accordingly. It does not matter whether or not Amos actually suffered physical injury: it is sufficient that physical harm was reasonably foreseeable in the circumstances, even if psychiatric harm was not: *Page* v *Smith* [1995] 2 WLR 644.

Can Bianca recover as a primary victim of the accident?

Bianca is a secondary victim of Titanic's negligence in that she was a mere bystander or witness to the accident rather than an active participant: *Robertson* v *Forth Bridge Joint Board* (1995) The Times 13 April. She was not put in fear for her own safety, as it is for this reason that she desisted in her initial attempts to climb down the bank of the river. Bianca is therefore in the position of having to show, in addition, that her psychiatric injury was a reasonably foreseeable consequence of Titanic's negligence. This will require Bianca to satisfy a number of extra criteria which were first established in the case of *McLoughlin* v *O'Brian* [1983] 1 AC 410 and subsequently refined in *Alcock* v *Chief Constable of South Yorkshire* [1992] 1 AC 310. These criteria have been imposed in order to limit the class of potential claimants in such cases. The criteria are as follows.

a) It must have been reasonably foreseeable that Bianca would suffer psychiatric illness as her relationship with at least one of the primary victims was sufficiently close.

   This would normally require a relationship based upon close ties of love and affection between the claimant and the primary victim, comparable to those of a normal parent, spouse or child. Whilst three of the Lords in *Alcock* suggested obiter that claims by unrelated bystanders might not be excluded where a particularly horrific catastrophe occurs within very close range, this suggestion was not subsequently followed by the Court of Appeal in *McFarlane* v *Caledonia Ltd* [1994] 2 All ER 1. The Court reasoned that to exclude the requirement of close ties of love and affection between the claimant and primary victim would be to base the test for recovery upon foreseeability alone.

   It is the requirement for a relationship of proximity which almost certainly excludes Bianca's claim in the instant case, given that she appears to be unrelated to any of the primary victims. The other criteria for recovery in *Alcock* would, however, have been satisfied in Bianca's case.

b) The claimant must have been proximate in both time and space to the accident or its immediate aftermath.

c) The psychiatric injury must have been sustained through direct perception of the accident (or its immediate aftermath) with the claimant's own unaided senses.

Can Cleo recover as a secondary victim of the accident?

Any claim by Cleo for psychiatric injury as a secondary victim of Titanic's negligence would certainly be excluded under the aforementioned criteria in *Alcock*. Whilst the relationship between parent and child is one of sufficient proximity (see *McLoughlin*), Cleo was neither close in time and space to the accident or its immediate aftermath, nor did she perceive the events with her own unaided senses. A news report cannot equate with the direct sight or hearing of an event, and being told about an accident does not, by itself, suffice.However, whilst Cleo might not have a claim against Titanic under the present state of the law, she might have a claim against the Exeter authorities on the basis of their incorrect statement, provided it could be established that they owed a duty of care to callers on the emergency number to take reasonable care to give accurate information. The court was vigilant in *Wainwright v Home Office* [2003] 3 WLR 1137 not to extend the types of case which could qualify as nervous shock cases.

QUESTION ELEVEN

Aileen and Betty have entered their cars in a rally of vintage and veteran cars from London to Dover. As Aileen reaches the foot of a hill, a car ahead of her stalls. She knows that, if she stops or slows down, she will have great difficulty in restarting on the hill and so she pulls out sharply in order to get past. Betty, who is driving immediately behind with Carla as her passenger, is unable despite careful driving to avoid colliding with Aileen's car. The cars are only slightly damaged, but Carla is thrown forward and hits the dashboard. Carla complains that she is in severe pain, but Betty tells her not to make a fuss and that they must push on in order to reach the finishing line. When they reach the terminus of the rally, Carla is taken to hospital where it is discovered that she has suffered serious internal injuries. She requires major surgery and a long period of convalescence. It is probable that, if she had sought medical assistance when the accident happened, she would have made a quick recovery.

Advise Carla.

University of London LLB Examination
(for External Students) Law of Tort June 2001 Q8

General Comment

A question of this nature would evidently be a hit with candidates as it requires a discussion of general issues of negligence, such as a duty of care, breach and consequential loss. Care has to be taken, however, in analysing each party's role and contribution in determining liability. As there are several parties involved, a structured appraisal is necessary.

Skeleton Solution

Aileen: is she negligent?; standard of care of competitors in a rally such as this – Betty: did she fail in her duty?; could she have obtained medical assistance sooner for Carla? – the effect of Betty's act or omission on the scope of Aileen's liability – is Carla contributorily negligent?

Suggested Solution

Each party's liability will now be assessed in turn.

Aileen

There is no problem in establishing that Aileen owed a duty of care to all other competitors in the rally of vintage and veteran cars which were travelling from London to Dover. Applying the principle in *Donoghue v Stevenson* [1932] AC 562, it is evident that all the other competitors would be defined as a proper 'neighbour' to Aileen. Further, the *Caparo Industries plc v Dickman* [1990] 2 AC 605 elements seem to have been discharged as well. There is foreseeability, proximity and it is just, fair and reasonable under the circumstances of the case for there to be the imposition of a duty of care.

The enquiry should be, however, one of a breach of duty. Did Aileen fall below the standard of care expected of her? And, if so, what is the standard of care expected of a competitor in such a rally? Answering these questions will determine if Aileen was negligent. The standard of care is that of a reasonable person. In *Blyth v Birmingham Waterworks Co* (1856) 11 Ex 781, a breach of duty was defined as an omission to do something that a reasonable and prudent man would do, or doing something that a reasonable and prudent man would not do. This is an objective test. Thus, as regards drivers of motor vehicles, it was held in *Nettleship v Weston* [1971] 2 QB 691 that a learner driver or impaired driver is judged by the standard of the reasonably competent driver. Aileen's manner of driving and her reasons for such driving (that she would have difficulty in restarting on the hill) clearly indicate negligence on her part. Aileen, therefore, is a potential defendant for Carla.

Betty

Betty is driving immediately behind Aileen. Betty has Carla as a passenger. When Aileen pulled out sharply, Betty, despite careful driving, collided into Aileen's car. Although the cars were only slightly damaged, Carla was thrown forward onto the dashboard and was complaining of severe pain. Despite Carla's complaint, Betty carried on driving, telling Carla not to make a fuss. Clearly her main aim was to finish the rally and reach the end. This blatantly careless attitude is clearly negligent. Betty owed her passenger, Carla, a duty of care and she breached that duty of care by not stopping the car to see if Carla was okay, or, alternatively, to seek medical assistance. Clearly, another reasonable person in Betty's shoes would have done just that. Applying *Glasgow Corporation v Muir* [1943] 2 AC 448, the breach is evident on Betty's part. Under the principle of passenger liability, Betty owed Carla a non-delegable duty to ensure her safety at all times during conveyance. Betty has evidently failed to discharge this duty. Carla would be able to recover against her successfully, in the first instance, for all her injuries. On the issue of causation, it must be remembered that despite the defendant owing the claimant a duty of care and being in breach of that duty, the defendant will not be liable unless his/her conduct has caused the claimant's damage, and that damage is not too remote in law. The test that is generally used in determining causation is the 'but for' test, as illustrated in *Cork v Kirby MacLean Ltd*

[1952] 2 All ER 402. Therefore, but for Betty's failure in seeking immediate medical assistance for Carla, would Carla still have suffered the injuries she sustained? The question states that had medical assistance been sought at the time of the accident, Carla would have probably made a quick recovery. Clearly Betty's omission in not seeking immediate medical help causes a problem in applying the but for test: *McWilliams* v *Sir William Arrol & Co Ltd* [1962] 1 WLR 295, but on the balance of probabilities, negligence can be made out against Betty: *Fairchild* v *Glenhaven Funeral Services* [2001] EWCA Civ 1881. The fact that Betty's breach did in fact materially contribute to Carla's injury would be significantly relevant following *McGhee* v *National Coal Board* [1973] 1 WLR 1.

Potentially, therefore, as far as Carla is concerned, there are two defendants, Aileen and Betty, who have successively and in their own independent way caused Carla's injury. The court may apportion liability on the basis of the Civil Liability (Contribution) Act 1978. Additionally, the court may adopt the approach taken in *Baker* v *Willoughby* [1970] AC 467 in finding each of the defendants liable to the extent of their involvement. Therefore, Aileen may only be liable to Betty for the damage to Betty's car, and Betty may be wholly responsible to Carla for Carla's injuries.

All that remains is to see whether Betty would have any defence available. If Carla was not wearing her seat belt, then Betty could invoke contributory negligence on the basis of *Froom* v *Butcher* [1976] QB 286, and under the Law Reform (Contributory Negligence) Act 1945. Apart from this defence, there is no indication on the facts of any other defence being available.

Chapter 6
Negligence: Breach of Duty

6.1   **Introduction**

6.2   **Key points**

6.3   **Key cases and statute**

6.4   **Questions and suggested solutions**

6.1 Introduction

The standard of care is that of the reasonable person: *Blyth* v *Birmingham Waterworks Co* (1856) 11 Ex 781 where breach of duty was defined as the omission to do something that a reasonable man would do, or doing something that a prudent or reasonable man would not do.

This is an objective test; the question is not did the defendant act reasonably, but would a reasonable person, placed in the position of the defendant, act as the defendant did: *Glasgow Corpn* v *Muir* [1943] AC 448. Thus, as regards drivers of motor vehicles, a learner or impaired driver is judged by the standard of the reasonably competent driver: *Nettleship* v *Weston* [1971] 2 QB 691; *Roberts* v *Ramsbottom* [1980] 1 All ER 7.

6.2 Key points

Guidelines

In considering how a reasonable person would act some guidelines are used.

a) The seriousness of the injury risked: eg *Paris* v *Stepney Borough Council* [1951] AC 367.

b) The likelihood of the injury occuring, as the defendant is only required to guard against reasonable possibilities, not highly unlikely possibilities: see *Blyth* v *Birmingham Waterworks Co* (above); *Bolton* v *Stone* [1951] AC 850.

c) The relationship of the risk to the object to be attained: eg *Daborn* v *Bath Tramways* [1946] 2 All ER 333; *Watt* v *Hertfordshire County Council* [1954] 1 WLR 835.

d) The practicability or cost of precautions: eg *Latimer* v *AEC Ltd* [1953] AC 643; *Knight* v *Home Office* [1990] 3 All ER 237. In this context also see *Bottomley* v *Secretary and Members of Todmorden Cricket Club* (2003) The Times 13 November concerning the liability of a cricket club.

e) Conforming to common practice, which is evidence though not conclusive proof of lack of carelessness: eg *Knight* v *Home Office* (above); *Johnson* v *Bingley* (1995) The Times 28 February; and *Vowles* v *Evans* (2003) The Times 13 March where a referee's failure to apply the rules of the game attracted liability.

f) Any special relationship between the claimant and defendant, such as spectator and participant in a sport: *Wooldridge* v *Sumner* [1963] 2 QB 43.

g) Defendant is a child. There is no English authority as to whether the standard of a reasonable person or a lesser standard is to be used. In Australia the standard of a reasonable child was used: *McHale* v *Watson* [1966] ALR 513. Note that for contributory negligence the courts do apply a different standard for children (see Chapter 8) which supports the Australian approach.

h) Emergencies. Where the defendant acts in an emergency, the standard of care takes into account all the circumstances of the situation: *Jones* v *Boyce* (1816) 1 Stark 493.

i) Professionals. A person who claims to possess a special skill is judged by the standard of a reasonable person having that skill: *Bolam* v *Friern Hospital Management Committee* [1957] 1 WLR 582; *Hughes* v *Waltham Forest Health Authority* (1990) The Times 9 November. There has been a surge of cases involving breach of duty on the part of health authorities: *Greenfield* v *Irwin* (2001) The Times 6 February; *McFarlane* v *Tayside Health Board* [1999] 4 All ER 961; *Nunnerly* v *Warrington Health Authority* (1999) The Times 26 November; *Parkinson* v *St James & Seacroft University Hospital NHS Trust* [2001] 2 All ER 97; *Penney* v *East Kent Health Authority* (1999) The Times 25 November; and *Shakoor* v *Situ* [2000] 4 All ER 181.

j) Foreseeability. In all cases the harm to the claimant must have been foreseeable by a reasonable person: *Roe* v *Minister of Health* [1954] 2 QB 66.

Proof of the breach

The claimant must prove, on the balance of probabilities, that the defendant was in breach of his duty. Note the effect of s11(1) Civil Evidence Act 1968 and *Wauchope* v *Mordecai* [1970] 1 WLR 317.

A problem may arise where the cause of the accident is known only to the defendant. In such situations the claimant may seek to rely on the maxim res ipsa loquitur – the thing speaks for itself. In *Scott* v *London and St Katherine Docks* (1865) 3 H & C 596 it was said it applies where the thing is shown to be under the management of the defendant and the accident is such as in the normal course of things does not happen if those who have the management use proper care. The maxim does not apply where all the facts are known, as it depends on the absence of explanation: *Barkway* v *South Wales Transport Co* [1950] 1 All ER 392.

It has been suggested that as the maxim raises the inference that the defendant was in breach of his duty, the defendant must rebut this inference, ie that the maxim reverses the burden of proof. Despite *Henderson* v *Henry E Jenkins & Sons* [1970] AC 282 and

Ward v *Tesco Stores Ltd* [1976] 1 WLR 810, the Privy Council has held that the burden of proof does not shift to the defendant but rests on the claimant throughout the case: *Ng Chun Pui* v *Lee Chuen Tat* [1988] RTR 298.

6.3 Key cases and statute

- *Blyth* v *Birmingham Waterworks Co* (1856) 11 Ex 781
  Court gave a definition of what amounts to a breach of duty

- *Bolam* v *Friern Hospital Management Committee* [1957] 1 WLR 582
  The standard of care of professionals is to be judged according to professionals of equal standing

- *Bolton* v *Stone* [1951] AC 850
  The practicality of precautions taken is also a factor to be considered on deciding breach

- *Bottomley* v *Secretary and Members of Todmorden Cricket Club* (2003) The Times 13 November
  Practicality of precautions is an important factor in establishing the existence of a duty of care

- *Glasgow Corporation* v *Muir* [1943] AC 448
  The issue of breach is to be decided on an objective basis

- *Jones* v *Boyce* (1816) 1 Stark 493
  The standard of care is adjusted in emergencies

- *McHale* v *Watson* [1966] ALR 513 (Australian case)
  Standard of care relating to children is a question of fact to be decided objectively by the court

- *Nettleship* v *Weston* [1971] 2 QB 691
  The standard of care of a learner or impaired driver is judged by the standard of a reasonably competent driver

- *Nunnerley* v *Warrington Health Authority* (1999) The Times 26 November
  The standard of care of professionals is to be judged according to professionals of equal standing

- *Paris* v *Stepney Borough Council* [1951] AC 367
  In deciding breach, the seriousness of the injury risked is to be taken into account

- *Parkinson* v *St James & Seacroft University Hospital NHS Trust* [2001] 2 All ER 97 (CA)
  The standard of care of professionals is to be judged according to professionals of equal standing

- *Scott* v *London & St Katherine Docks Co* (1865) 3 H & C 596
  If something is so obvious, it will speak for itself – res ipsa loquitur

- *Shakoor* v *Situ* [2000] 4 All ER 181
  The standard of care of professionals is to be judged according to professionals of equal standing

- *Vowles* v *Evans* (2003) The Times 13 March
  Non-conformity to common rules attracted liability

- *Wauchope* v *Mordecai* [1970] 1 WLR 317
  Claimant must prove the defendant's breach of duty on the balance of probabilities

- *Wooldridge* v *Sumner* [1963] 2 QB 43
  The relationship between the claimant and the defendant is also material in considering breach

- Civil Evidence Act 1968 – claimant may use the defendant's 'criminal' convictions as proof in his civil action to prove negligence

6.4 Questions and suggested solutions

QUESTION ONE

In January Agnes was aged 85 and living in her own home which she owned. Her daughter Brenda thought that she was becoming too frail and forgetful to continue living on her own and wanted her to get a place in sheltered accommodation run by the local council. The council said that Agnes's condition would have to be independently assessed by the two doctors, one appointed by Brenda and one chosen by the council. The two doctors, Cyril (Brenda's nominee) and Daniel, visited Agnes. She was lively during the visit and the doctors reported that she was a fit and robust lady, in good condition for her age and well able to live on her own. She was refused a place in the sheltered housing.

Brenda immediately had expensive work done to adapt her own home so that her mother could come and live with her. However in April before she was able to move Agnes wandered out one night, could not find her way home and fell over in the darkness breaking both hips. She has been in hospital ever since and is unlikely to be well enough to go to live with Brenda.

Advise Agnes and Brenda.

University of London LLB Examination
(for External Students) Law of Tort June 1994 Q3

General Comment

At first glance, this question may appear to be a professional negligence question. However, in reality it requires the student to address all the elements of the tort of negligence, namely duty, breach, causation and loss. It is framed in such a way as to raise doubts under each of these heads.

Skeleton Solution

Did the council owe a duty of care? – if so, what is the extent of that duty and to what extent did the council fulfil its duty? – did the doctors owe a similar duty of care? – breach: did the council breach its duty? – did the doctors breach theirs? – was this series of events caused by any breach of duty by the council and/or the doctors? – loss – Agnes suffered physical injury – Brenda carried out expensive work on her home in preparation for her mother's arrival – that expense appears to have been wasted – was the injury to Agnes and/or the financial loss to Brenda foreseeable?

Suggested Solution

Agnes and her daughter Brenda first approached the council with a view to moving Agnes into council-run sheltered accommodation in January. Before the council would provide a place, they required an independent medical assessment of Agnes by two doctors, one appointed by Brenda, and one appointed by the council.

Following the assessment by the two doctors, opining that Agnes was fit and capable of living alone, the council refused to provide sheltered housing. Brenda immediately had expensive work done to adapt her home so that her mother could move in. Before Agnes could move in, however, she wandered out one night in April, could not find her way home, and fell over in the darkness, breaking her hips. It is now unlikely that Agnes will move into Brenda's house.

The facts outlined in the question suggest a possible claim in negligence against the council and/or the doctors. The tort of negligence has been defined by Winfield and Jolowicz (*The Law of Torts* (13th edition) p72) in the following terms:

'Negligence as a tort is the breach of a legal duty to take care which results in damage, undesired by the defendant, to the plaintiff.'

At this stage of my advice to Agnes and Brenda, it is necessary to consider whether the council, and/or the doctors owed any duty of care to either Agnes, and/or Brenda.

A duty of care is imposed on a party in the following terms, set out by Lord Atkin in the seminal case of *Donoghue* v *Stevenson* [1932] AC 562:

'You must take reasonable care to avoid acts or omissions which you can reasonably foresee would be likely to injure your neighbour. Who, then, in law is my neighbour? The answer seems to be – persons who are closely and directly affected by my act that I ought reasonably to have them in contemplation as being so affected when I am directing my mind to the acts or omissions which are called in question.'

If a duty exists, it is necessary to define the extent of that duty. According to Lord Keith in the decision of the House of Lords in *Peabody Donation Fund Governors* v *Sir Lindsay Parkinson & Co Ltd* [1984] 3 WLR 953:

'The true question in each case is whether the particular defendant owed to the particular plaintiff a duty of care having the scope which is contended for, and whether he was in breach of that duty with consequent loss to the plaintiff.'

Brenda was obviously concerned about Agnes, and as a result she went to the council. In those circumstances, it would appear that the council was aware of Brenda's concerns, and owed a duty of care to both Agnes and Brenda, such duty being of the nature of ensuring that Agnes was offered sheltered accommodation if she needed it.

The council, in my opinion, discharged that duty by providing a system whereby two independent doctors, including one nominated by Brenda, were appointed to assess the need, if any, of Agnes. It is difficult to argue that the council could have done any more for Agnes and/or Brenda.

Having been appointed, the two doctors also owed a duty of care to Agnes and/or Brenda, to assess Agnes for the purpose of recommending whether or not she needed sheltered accommodation. The level of that duty was laid down by McNair J in *Bolam v Friern Hospital Management Committee* [1957] 1 WLR 582 as follows:

> 'Where you get a situation which involves the use of some special skill or competence, then the test as to whether there has been negligence or not is not the test of the man on the top of the Clapham omnibus, because he has not got this special skill. The test is the standard of the ordinary skilled man exercising and professing to have that special skill … he is not guilty of negligence if he has acted in accordance with a practice accepted as proper by a responsible body of medical men skilled in that particular act.'

Thus, in order to determine whether or not Cyril and Daniel (the doctors) breached their respective duties, it would be necessary to consider precisely what they did in purporting to assess Agnes, and whether or not their assessment technique complied with 'a practice accepted as proper by a responsible body of medical men'.

Even if it could be shown that the doctors, and either or both of them, acted negligently in assessing that Agnes was able to live alone, it would still be necessary to show that their breach of duty caused the loss and injury suffered by Agnes and Brenda.

Agnes wandered out of her home and fell over. These events took place only three months after Brenda first approached the council. It is not evident from the facts given in the question how quickly Agnes would have been re-housed if the assessment had recommended her move. If she would not have been moved in that short period of time in any event, the doctors' breach, if found, would not have caused her injury.

This is the 'but for' test as stated by Lord Denning in *Cork* v *Kirby MacLean Ltd* [1952] 2 All ER 402 as follows:

> '… if the damage would not have happened but for a particular fault, then the fault is the cause of the damage; if it would have happened just the same, fault or no fault, the fault is not the cause of the damage.'

Equally, the doctors could argue that their acts or omissions caused Agnes to remain at home, but did not cause her to go out and get lost and/or injured. The level of Agnes' disability at the time of the assessment and the foreseeability of such an occurrence would determine whether or not the doctors' acts or omissions were causative of the injury.

Brenda's loss was immediate, in that she acted on the report of the doctors by adapting her home. If the doctors were negligent, they caused her loss. However, Brenda cannot be said to have relied upon the expertise of the doctors, in that her actions indicate that she did not agree with their assessment. Thus her expenditure does not fall into the *Hedley Byrne & Co Ltd v Heller & Partners Ltd* [1964] AC 465 category of cases.

Brenda may still be able to claim for the expenditure by relying on *Ross v Caunters* [1980] Ch 297 pure economic loss. That case could not be accommodated within the *Hedley Byrne* doctrine because the claimant had not relied upon the skill of the defendant. But the claimant did suffer pure economic loss (as has Brenda) and in finding for the claimant Megarry VC relied upon the judgments of Mason and Gibbs JJ in *Caltex Oil (Australia) Pty Ltd v The Dredge 'Willemstad'* (1976) 11 ALR 227. However, a different decision was reached in *Chappell v Somers & Blake* [2003] 3 All ER 1076 where an executrix's claim against a solicitor succeeded.

The test which they posited was that the defendant should be held liable for economic loss caused by his negligent conduct when he can reasonably foresee that the specific claimant, as opposed to a general class of persons, will suffer financial loss as a result of his negligence.

Whether or not Brenda's financial expenditure could have been foreseen by the doctors will depend on their degree of knowledge of her relationship with Agnes, and her plans in the event of a refusal to re-house by the council.

The doctors might argue that even if the expenditure could be foreseen, the fact that it was wasted was not caused by their negligence. So, if Agnes' injuries were not caused by the doctor's negligence, nor could the fact of the wasted costs be caused by the doctors' negligence.

This brings the whole question of foreseeability into issue. A defendant is only liable for losses which directly result from his negligence in circumstances where some loss is foreseeable.

In Agnes' case the distinction between the tests laid down in *Re Polemis and Furness, Withy & Co* [1921] 3 KB 560 (directness of loss) and *Overseas Tankship (UK) Ltd v Morts Dock & Engineering Co, The Wagon Mound (No 1)* [1961] AC 388 (reasonably foreseeable loss) is of importance.

The essential question is whether it could be foreseen that Agnes would suffer any physical damage if she was not placed in sheltered accommodation. If so, according to the *Polemis* test, if the doctors were negligent, they would be liable for her injuries if it was a direct result of their negligent assessment.

The *Wagon Mound (No 1)* test requires that the risk of loss suffered must be reasonably foreseeable to the reasonable man, and not a risk that the reasonable man would dismiss as being far-fetched.

Again, the question of foreseeability of physical injury caused by Agnes wandering out of her house is a question of fact, and would depend on the level of knowledge of the doctors regarding Agnes' tendency to wander and to get lost, and the likelihood of her falling down and becoming injured.

In conclusion, it is apparent that both Agnes and Brenda face a number of obstacles if they are to prove that the doctors in this case have been negligent. Even if negligence is established, they face similar difficulties in proving causation and foreseeability of the loss and damage they have suffered.

QUESTION TWO

Mrs White was admitted to hospital with breathing difficulties. That evening Dr Green decided to perform an emergency operation and insert a device in her windpipe. She was then transferred to intensive care under Nurse Brown. Nurse Brown was a temporary nurse hired from the Florence Agency. The agency paid her remuneration and the hospital paid a fee to the agency. Nurse Brown was instructed to summon a doctor if there was any change in Mrs White's condition. She was a very experienced nurse who had previously worked in a specialist clinic where she had tended people in Mrs White's condition. When Mrs White's windpipe became temporarily obstructed, she attempted to clear it herself but was unsuccessful. Mrs White died.

Most doctors would not have performed surgery when Dr Green did but would have waited until it was clear that she was not responding to other treatment, but some would have acted as he did. It is not clear whether Mrs White would have recovered from the emergency if Nurse Brown had summoned help or if she would have died anyway.

Advise Mrs White's executors.

University of London LLB Examination
(for External Students) Law of Tort June 1993 Q7

General Comment

This is a fairly specific question on medical negligence which also covers issues concerning vicarious liability. Quite a technical question which requires the student to have a thorough knowledge of the law relating to both areas.

Skeleton Solution

Medical negligence: the duty of care; the standard of care – negligence of nurse: breach and causation – vicarious liability.

Suggested Solution

Dr Green has performed an emergency operation on Mrs White who subsequently dies. The first point to establish is the basis on which her executors can claim. Under the Law

Reform (Miscellaneous Provisions) Act 1934 s1(1) all causes of action vested in a person on her death survive for the benefit of the estate and any damages recovered form part of the estate of the deceased.

Turning to Dr Green's actions, we are concerned with possible medical negligence. The duty of care of the medical practitioner has been considered in numerous cases. In *R v Bateman* (1925) 94 LJKB 791 it was said that 'he owes a duty to the patient to use diligence, care, knowledge, skill and caution in administering the treatment'. The standard of this care is that of the ordinary competent medical practitioner who is exercising the ordinary degree of professional skill: *Chin Keow v Government of Malaysia* [1967] 1 WLR 813. Further, in *Bolam v Friern Hospital Management Committee* [1957] 1 WLR 582, McNair J said that a practitioner was not guilty of negligence, 'if he acted in accordance with practice accepted as proper by a responsible body of medical men skilled in that particular art ... merely because there was a body of opinion who would take a contrary view'.

Applying the law to the facts, we are told that most doctors would not have performed surgery when Dr Green did, although some would have done. Presuming this minority view is also held by a body of responsible medical practitioners, the fact that Dr Green has not followed the common practice will not be sufficient to show negligence. Indeed, it was held in *Maynard v West Midlands Regional Health Authority* [1984] 1 WLR 634, in the House of Lords, that negligence ought not to be established by the judge having to choose between two bodies of respectable professional opinion. This was confirmed recently in *Bolitho v City & Hackney Health Authority* [1998] AC 232.

The operation was an emergency, therefore it is most likely that Mrs White's consent could not be obtained. Impliedly, however, she consented to allow herself to be treated in consideration for a promise that Dr Green would exercise proper care and skill. Had her express consent been obtained, there would have been further issues as to the amount of information disclosed to her (per *Sidaway v Board of Governors of the Bethlem Royal Hospital* [1985] AC 871).

It would appear, then, that Dr Green has not acted in breach of his duty of care in carrying out the operation and has not been negligent. Even if that were not the case, one would still have to consider the questions of causation and remoteness, since Mrs White dies some time after the operation. Dr Green is not liable for the negligence of nurses at the hospital when they are not employed by him and it is submitted that, even if he were in breach of his duty of care, the actions of Nurse Brown may well act as an intervening cause to make Mrs White's death too remote.

If we now consider Nurse Brown's liability, we can ask the question, why did Mrs White die? There seem to be two linked answers. First, she may have died because Nurse Brown failed to summon a doctor to deal with the obstruction; second, she may have died as a result of Nurse Brown's failure to clear the obstruction herself. The omission to summon a doctor would have to be 'the omission to do something which a reasonable man ... would do', to be in breach of the duty of care: *Blyth v Birmingham*

Waterworks Co (1856) 11 Ex 781. Certainly, there was an instruction to summon a doctor upon any change in the patient's condition and that is an important factor against Nurse Brown. But it may be that a reasonable nurse, judged by the standard of the reasonably competent nurse, would have considered this temporary obstruction too minor a change in the patient's condition to justify a doctor's attendance. Further, Nurse Brown's failure to clear the obstruction may not, in itself, be evidence of any negligence on her part. These are largely questions of fact and expert opinion.

We are also told that there is a chance that Mrs White would have died anyway. That being so, we may not be able to say that 'but for' Nurse Brown's negligence, Mrs White would not have died: *Barnett* v *Chelsea and Kensington Hospital Management Committee* [1969] 1 QB 428. It would be for the claimant executors to prove on the balance of probabilities that negligence was the cause of death. The test of causation was reviewed and reaffirmed in *Fairchild* v *Glenhaven* [2003] 1 AC 32.

Supposing that Nurse Brown is liable, she could be sued in her personal capacity. However, on the basis of suing 'the deepest pocket', the executors will want to know whether they can sue the Florence Agency and/or the hospital (ie whichever body manages the hospital). Nurse Brown is employed by the Florence Agency but works under the hospital's direction. Whether or not the agency remains vicariously liable for Nurse Brown's torts depends to an extent on the construction of the contract between the agency and the hospital. In *Mersey Docks and Harbour Board* v *Coggins & Griffith (Liverpool) Ltd* [1947] AC 1 it was held that if the servant when doing the negligent act, is merely exercising the discretion vested in him by the general employer and not obeying the specific directions given by the particular employer, he remains the servant of the general employer. It is difficult to draw the line on the facts of this case, but it is submitted that the general employer, the agency, may well remain vicariously liable.

However, while they can be sued by the executors, the hospital also owes a primary duty to its patients which it cannot delegate to employees or agencies: see *Gold* v *Essex County Council* [1942] 2 KB 293. If a nurse working in the hospital has been negligent, then the hospital is itself liable. On the issue of hospital liability, the following cases compound the approach taken by the courts in earlier decisions: *Penney* v *East Kent Health Authority* (1999) The Times 25 November; *Nunnerly* v *Warrington Health Authority* (1999) The Times 26 November; and *McFarlane* v *Tayside Health Board* [1999] 4 All ER 961 (HL).

A final point with regard to vicarious liability concerns the nature of Nurse Brown's act. If she has been merely careless or negligent then obviously the agency cannot avoid liability. However, if they can show that her actions were wilfully wrong, that may take her actions out of the course of her employment. In other words, she is employed to do X and if she does it carelessly, the agency is still liable. But if she does Y, which she has been specifically instructed not to do, that may extinguish liability. Case law has not been so straightforward, however, and, again, the dividing line is hard to draw (see, for example, *Twine* v *Bean's Express Ltd* (1946) 62 TLR 458 and *Rose* v *Plenty* [1976] 1 WLR

141). On the facts of this case, it does not appear that her failure to obey an instruction was so much a wilful wrong as a considered judgment.

In conclusion, I would advise the executors that their action in negligence lies against the agency and the hospital, but that it is not at all clear that Nurse Brown has, in fact, acted negligently.

QUESTION THREE

Shelley is a consultant psychiatrist. Keats is referred to him suffering from anxiety and depression. Shelley correctly diagnoses the nature of his illness and prescribes a course of injections of 'Poesy', a newly developed drug. Shelley knows that there is a risk of heart trouble developing in patients receiving 'Poesy' but does not tell Keats as he thinks it would worry him unnecessarily as Keats is in extremely good physical health. An article in a recent specialist medical journal concerned with the study of the blood has suggested that there is evidence of blood disorders developing in persons being treated with 'Poesy', but Shelley has not read this. Keats develops a blood complaint three months after starting treatment, but the cause cannot be ascertained.

Advise Keats.

University of London LLB Examination
(for External Students) Law of Tort June 1985 Q1

General Comment

A typical question on negligence but one which requires focus on the 'breach of duty' element, particularly the standard of care required of professionals as opposed to the 'reasonable person'.

Skeleton Solution

The factors which must be considered are what is the nature of the duty owed to Keats, what is the standard of care, has there been a breach of duty and did this breach cause Keats's loss?

Suggested Solution

Keats will be advised to bring a case in negligence against Shelley, for which he will have to prove: (a) that Shelley owed him a duty of care; (b) that he was in breach of that duty; and (c) that the breach caused Keats' damage or injury, both in fact and in law.

The main difficulties which Keats will encounter here, it is submitted, are in proving (a) that Shelley is in breach of his duty, although he certainly has an arguable case on this point, and (b) that Shelley's breach caused his damage.

As far as the duty of care is concerned, a duty was recognised between a doctor and his patient even before *Donoghue* v *Stevenson* [1932] AC 562 was decided, but the problem raised by Keats's case is whether Shelley is under a duty to warn his patient of the risks involved in the proposed course of treatment. The courts, in medical negligence cases, have to consider on the one hand the patient's right of self-determination over what happens to his body, as against the doctor's desire to act in the patient's best interests, which sometimes the patient may not be in the best position to judge. Furthermore, the courts are also aware of the adverse consequences to the medical profession of a too highly demanding duty of care which would result in over-caution, and would hinder rather than help. An analysis of the case law reveals that there is no absolute duty on a doctor to reveal any risk inherent to treatment which he may prescribe. This factor must be balanced with the issue of causation as did the House of Lords in *Bolitho* v *City & Hackney Health Authority* [1998] AC 232.

This duty was discussed by the House of Lords in *Sidaway* v *Board of Governors of the Bethlem Royal Hospital* [1985] AC 871; [1985] 1 All ER 643. The ratio of this case stated that a medical practitioner is under a duty to disclose to a patient 'any substantial risk involving grave adverse consequences inherent in the surgery or other treatment', which he proposes to carry out. Lord Scarman there took the view that the duty to warn was limited to 'material risks' (following *Canterbury* v *Spence* (1972) 464 F2d 772), concluding that a doctor would not be in breach of his duty if he formed the opinion that a warning would be detrimental to the patient's health. Applying this view to the facts of Keats' case, it may be argued that Shelley is not under a duty to warn Keats of the risk of heart trouble if he believes that such a warning would worry Keats unnecessarily. Evidence of the degree of the risk involved is essential here in order to determine with certainty whether that risk may be said to be material or substantial; on the facts of *Sidaway* the risk was assessed at 1 to 2 per cent, which was evidently insufficient to be 'substantial'. Yet in the Canadian case of *Reibl* v *Hughes* (1980) 114 DLR (3d) 1 a 10 per cent risk of a stroke following from the operation in question was a substantial risk, and Lord Bridge took the view that in such a case, the doctor would be under a duty to disclose in the absence of any cogent reason to withhold that information.

It is submitted in the light of the above discussion, that if the risk is not substantial, Shelley will be under no duty to disclose it to Keats. There may, however, be different considerations for disclosure of the risk of blood disorders of which Shelley is unaware, and at this point, discussion of the duty of care becomes very much linked with consideration of the standard of care and current knowledge. Lord Diplock in *Sidaway* formulated a doctor's duty of care as a duty 'to exercise his skill and judgment to improve the patient's health'. It is submitted that it is a rather different case where a doctor does not disclose risks to a patient because he is unaware of them.

At this point, the standard of care must be considered. The basic test is that enunciated in *Bolam* v *Friern Hospital Management Committee* [1957] 1 WLR 582 as 'standard of the ordinary skilled man exercising and professing to have that special skill'. In *Bolitho* (see above) the House of Lords held that even if there was an opinion from an expert body justifying the actions of the surgeon as reasonable, the court may still depart from this opinion if it feels that the expert opinion is corrupt, illogical or anachronistic. Current knowledge must also be taken into account (*Roe* v *Minister of Health* [1954] 2 QB 66) in order to deal with risks which are, at the time of treatment, unforeseeable. Lord Scarman in *Sidaway* spoke out rather more strongly against the *Bolam* test than his fellow Law Lords in stating that the law imposed a duty but the medical profession imposed its own standard of care, since hitherto the courts had regard to 'responsible medical opinion' on a particular practice in determining the requisite standard: see on this point *Maynard* v *West Midlands Regional Health Authority* [1984] 1 WLR 634. The House of Lords in *Sidaway* accepted that even though non-disclosure was a proper practice, judges could still hold that disclosure is necessary if 'no reasonably prudent medical man could fail to make it'. This renders the standard of care ultimately one which is imposed by law. In *McFarlane* v *Tayside Health Board* [1999] 4 All ER 961 the House of Lords found the health authority to be in breach of their duty. Similarly, in *Shakoor* v *Situ* [2000] 4 All ER 181 the House found that standard of care expected of a professional had been breached.

Turning to the facts of Keats's case, it must be noted that the blood disorder risks have been identified in a specialist medical journal concerned with the study of the blood, and the question raised here is whether a consultant psychiatrist would be expected to read such a journal and thus to know of the risks. Keats must attempt to argue that part of a reasonable medical practitioner's duty is to be informed about the risk created by new drugs, and possibly *Roe* could be distinguished here on the basis that the microscopic flaws in the ampoules in Roe were a risk of which no one knew at the time, but in Keats's case, the risk of blood disorders is a foreseeable one, though perhaps only in a specialist sphere of medical practice. This raises a further question of how widespread knowledge must be within a profession before it will constitute current knowledge. Keats must also be prepared for Shelley to raise the point which was taken both in *Bolam* and *Maynard* v *West Midlands Regional Health Authority* that a doctor is not necessarily negligent merely because a body of medical opinion takes a view which is contrary to his own, although this may be countered by an argument that Shelley simply had no knowledge of the risks, and did not merely disagree with the facts.

Keats therefore has an arguable case that there has been a breach of duty by Shelley but he must further prove that that breach has caused the blood complaint. It is possible that this condition may have developed in any event but if it was triggered off by 'poesy', Keats could rely on the maxim that Shelley must take his victim as he finds him, as illustrated in *Smith* v *Leech, Brain & Co* [1962] 2 QB 405; [1962] 2 WLR 148 on the point of remoteness. As far as factual causation is concerned, this is a case where the 'but for' test will be of little avail in the absence of medical evidence; if the condition would have happened anyway and was not triggered off by the drug, Keats's claim will fail: *Barnett* v *Chelsea and Kensington Hospital Management Committee* [1969] 1 QB 428; [1968] 1 All ER 1068. Essentially Keats must prove that the breach by Shelley caused his injury. Traditionally claimants who have had a problem with pure causation have relied on *McGhee* v *National Coal Board* [1973] 1 WLR 1 as authority for the proposition that it is enough that the claimant shows that the defendants' breach materially increased the risk of damage or materially contributed to his injury. Unfortunately for Keats the House of Lords has taken a very restrictive approach to *McGhee* in *Hotson* v *East Berkshire Area Health Authority* [1987] AC 750 and *Wilsher* v *Essex Area Health Authority* [1988] AC 1074. As in *Wilsher* where Lord Bridge stated that *McGhee* 'laid down no new principle of law whatever but on the contrary affirmed the rule that the onus of proving causation lies on the claimant', as stated in *Fairchild* v *Glenhaven Funeral Services Ltd; Waddingtons plc* v *Leeds City Council* [2003] 1 AC 32, Keats would appear to be unable to prove causation on the facts given.

In the absence of proof of causation, Keats's claim will not succeed since he has not shown to the court that Shelley's breach of duty has caused resultant loss or damage to him. A reliance on res ipsa loquitur would not avail him since that helps to prove a breach of duty rather than causation.

Chapter 7

Negligence: Causation and Remoteness

7.1   Introduction

7.2   Key points

7.3   Key cases and statutes

7.4   Questions and suggested solutions

7.1 Introduction

Despite the defendant owing the claimant a duty of care and being in breach of that duty, the defendant will not be liable unless his conduct has caused the claimant's damage and that damage is not too remote in law.

7.2 Key points

Causation

The test generally used in determining causation is the 'but for' test in *Cork* v *Kirby Maclean* [1952] 2 All ER 402; see *Barnett* v *Chelsea and Kensington Hospital Management Committee* [1969] 1 QB 428 for a good example.

However, there are three areas in which the 'but for' test gives rise to problems.

a) Pre-existing conditions. Where the damage is caused by a pre-existing condition rather than by the defendant's breach, the defendant will not be liable for all the damage which follows: *Cutler* v *Vauxhall Motors Ltd* [1971] 1 QB 418; *Performance Cars* v *Abraham* [1962] 1 QB 33 (this is an example of the rule that a tortfeasor takes his victim as he finds him).

b) Omission. The test is difficult to apply where the breach consists of an omission, eg *McWilliams* v *Sir William Arrol & Co* [1962] 1 WLR 295.

c) Multiple causes. Where, for example, two persons cause damage to the claimant, the 'but for' test would be answered in the affirmative for both defendants. In such situations the courts take a common sense view of causation.

Proof of causation

It may not always be clear that the defendant's breach was the cause of the claimant's damage. In such situations the claimant will usually rely on *McGhee* v *National Coal Board* [1973] 1 WLR 1 in which it was held to be sufficient for the claimant to show that the defendant's breach materially contributed to the injury. Note the recent restrictive developments of *McGhee* by the House of Lords in *Kay* v *Ayrshire and Arran Health Board* [1987] 2 All ER 417, *Hotson* v *East Berkshire Area Health Authority* [1987] AC 750, *Wilsher* v *Essex Area Health Authority* [1988] AC 1074; [1988] 1 All ER 871, and the dictum of Lord Bridge in *Wilsher* that *McGhee* 'laid down no new principle of law whatever. On the contrary it affirmed the principle that the onus of proving causation lies on the claimant.'

In the Court of Appeal case of *Fairchild* v *Glenhaven Funeral Services Ltd; Waddingtons plc* v *Leeds City Council* [2003] 1 AC 32, it was held that the claimants could not prove on the balance of probabilities that the defendants' negligence had caused their illness.

Loss of chance

In *Allied Maples Group Ltd* v *Simmons & Simmons* [1995] 1 WLR 1602 it was held that where the claimant's loss depended on future uncertain events, the claimant could recover if he could show there was a real or substantial chance of the event occuring. See also *Stovold* v *Barlows* [1995] NLJ 1649. The case *Blue Circle Industries plc* v *Ministry of Defence* [1999] 2 WLR 295 provides a useful illustration of this concept.

Successive causes

Note the problems that can occur here, as exemplified by *Baker* v *Willoughby* [1970] AC 467 and *Jobling* v *Associated Dairies* [1982] AC 794. In *Murrell* v *Healy* [2001] 4 All ER 345, the Court of Appeal held that any earlier recovery must be offset from the instant case, so long as they fall under the same head(s) of loss.

Remoteness of damage

Once duty, breach and causation have been established, one must ascertain whether all the damage suffered by the claimant can be recovered or whether some or all of it is too remote. The case *Sutradhar* v *Natural Environment Research Council* (2004) The Times 19 March illustrates this point clearly.

For intentional damage the defendant is liable for all the damage which follows: *Quinn* v *Leatham* [1901] AC 495; *Doyle* v *Olby (Ironmongers) Ltd* [1969] 2 QB 158; and *Lagden* v *O'Connor* (2003) The Times 5 December, where the House of Lords found that the claimant could claim for additional costs as a result of his impecuniosity.

For unintentional damage the test for remoteness is reasonable foreseeability: *The Wagon Mound (No 1)* [1961] AC 388.

Damage to the person

The defendant will be liable for all the damage if he could foresee some damage to the person, even if he could not foresee the extent. This is often known as the 'egg-shell skull' rule as laid down in *Dulieu* v *White* [1901] 2 KB 669 or by the maxim that a tortfeasor takes his victim as he finds him. This is an important rule and the following examples should be noted: *Smith* v *Leech, Brain* [1962] 2 QB 405; *Bradford* v *Robinson Rentals* [1967] 1 WLR 337; *Robinson* v *Post Office* [1974] 1 WLR 1176; *Hughes* v *Lord Advocate* [1963] AC 837.

The case *Jolley* v *Sutton London Borough Council* [2000] 3 All ER 409 illustrates how the House of Lords dealt with the issue of reasonable foreseeability.

Damage to property

Here the foreseeability requirement is greater, as it seems that foreseeability of damage, by itself, is insufficient but that the kind of damage needs to be foreseen: *The Wagon Mound (No 1)* (above). See also *Saleslease Ltd* v *Davis* [2000] 1 All ER (Comm) 883.

Damage which is too remote

a) If it arises from a novus causa interveniens, a new intervening cause such as the claimant's own impecuniosity: *The Liesbosch Dredger* v *Edison* [1933] AC 449. However, in *Perry* v *Sidney Phillips* [1982] 1 WLR 1297 it was said that this case was consistently being attenuated, and in *Mattocks* v *Mann* (1992) The Times 19 June that *Liesbosch* would only be applied in exceptional circumstances.

b) If it arises from a novus actus interveniens, an intervening act which breaks the chain of causation. An intervening act may arise in three ways.

   i) Act of claimant.

   If an act of the claimant amounts to a novus actus interveniens the defendant will not be liable. The defendant will have to show that the claimant's conduct has been so careless that his damage cannot be regarded as being caused by the defendant, eg *McKew* v *Holland & Hannen & Cubbitts* [1969] 3 All ER 1621 where the claimant acted unreasonably. Compare *Wieland* v *Cyril Lord Carpets* [1969] 3 All ER 1006 where the claimant acted reasonably and the defendants were held liable. See also *Slipper* v *BBC* [1991] 1 All ER 165 for an application of novus actus in defamation.

   ii) Act of nature.

   If an act of nature is independent of the negligence of the defendant, the defendant will not be liable: *Carslogie Steamship* v *Royal Norwegian Government* [1952] AC 292.

iii) Act of a third party.

If an act of a third party is the true cause of the claimant's damage, the defendant will not be liable (*The Oropesa* [1943] P 32; *Knightley* v *Johns* [1982] 1 WLR 349), but compare *Rouse* v *Squires* [1973] QB 889 and *Wright* v *Lodge & Shepherd* [1992] NLJ 1269.

An intervening act will not break the chain of causation where:

i)   it is an instinctive act done in the agony of an emergency created by the defendant's tort: *Jones* v *Boyce* (1816) 1 Stark 493; *The Oropesa* (above);

ii) the defendant places the claimant in a position in which it is reasonable for him to take the risk he did (ie a non-emergency situation): *Sayers* v *Harlow UDC* [1958] 1 WLR 623;

iii) the act which is alleged to have broken the chain of causation is one which the defendant should have foreseen and guarded against: *Stansbie* v *Troman* [1948] 2 KB 48; *Rouse* v *Squires* (above). This point was reiterated in *Normans Bay Ltd (formerly Illingworth Morris Ltd)* v *Condert Brothers (A Firm)* (2004) The Times 24 March.

7.3 Key cases and statutes

- *Baker* v *Willoughby* [1970] AC 467
  Recovery is possible against more than one defendant

- *Barnett* v *Chelsea and Kensington Hospital Management Committee* [1969] 1 QB 428
  Established the test for 'causation'

- *Cutler* v *Vauxhall Motors Ltd* [1971] 1 QB 418
  Pre-existing conditions might negate liability

- *Fairchild* v *Glenhaven Funeral Services Ltd; Waddingtons plc* v *Leeds City Council* [2003] 1 AC 32
  Reaffirmed the necessity of proving causation in order to successfully recover in tort

- *Jolley* v *Sutton London Borough Council* [2000] 3 All ER 409
  Provides an illustration of what could be 'reasonably foreseen'

- *Normans Bay Ltd (formerly Illingworth Morris Ltd)* v *Condert Brothers (A Firm)* (2004) The Times 24 March
  Defendant cannot rely on own further wrong as breaking the chain of causation

- *Overseas Tankship (UK) Ltd* v *Miller Steamship Co Pty Ltd, The Wagon Mound (No 2)* [1967] 1 AC 617
  Damage that occurs must have been foreseeable

- *Overseas Tankship (UK) Ltd* v *Morts Dock & Engineering Co, The Wagon Mound (No 1)* [1961] AC 388
  Damage caused must not be too remote

- *Sutradhar* v *Natural Environment Research Council* (2004) The Times 19 March
  Principles of remoteness must be satisfied for an action to be successful

- *Wilsher* v *Essex Area Health Authority* [1988] AC 1074
  Proof of causation is fundamental in establishing liability

- Civil Liability (Contribution) Act 1978 – apportions liability as between as many defendants as may be relevant and appropriate or blameworthy

- Law Reform (Contributory Negligence) Act 1945 – affords a partial defence to the defendant

7.4 Questions and suggested solutions

QUESTION ONE

'Causation in tort should be a matter of common sense and not of philosophical theory.'

Discuss.

University of London LLB Examination
(for External Students) Law of Tort June 1998 Q5

General Comment

It is unlikely that candidates will have had a detailed knowledge of any of the philosophical approaches to the issue of causation, and so what was required here was comment on the extent to which the rules could be said to reflect a commonsense approach to the imposition of liability. The focus was primarily on causation in fact. However, it would have been reasonable to include discussion on intervening cause, or even remoteness of damage.

Skeleton Solution

Introduce by explaining briefly the function of the rules of causation in tort – causation in fact – explain and illustrate 'but-for' test – explain how the rule runs into difficulty in cases involving multiple and successive causes and how the courts have modified their approach to achieve a result which accords with common sense – causation in law – rules on intervening act – based on common sense?

Suggested Solution

One way in which the law reflects notions of individual responsibility is by ensuring that a link exists between the conduct of a defendant (an act or an omission) and some harmful consequence before liability can be imposed. It is this link which justifies fixing the defendant with liability and requiring him to pay compensation. The nature of the link has been the subject of some philosophical debate and a number of possible approaches have been identified. However, the law has required the adoption of a small number of practical commonsense approaches which can be readily understood and applied to a range of real life factual scenarios. It is these approaches, and the extent to which they accord with common sense, which is discussed below.

The question of causation in tort can be approached in two stages. The first involves asking whether, as a matter of fact, the defendant's negligence was a cause of the claimant's loss. It is this so-called 'causation in fact' test which has received the most attention from philosophers. The second stage involves a consideration of whether, as a matter of law, the defendant ought to be held liable for the damage which he has in fact caused. Winfield and Jolowicz (*Tort* (16th edn, 2002) at p196) point out that this second stage involves the consideration of issues of fairness and legal policy.

Causation in fact

This stage merely establishes a factual link between the defendant's act or omission and the claimant's loss. The test normally adopted is the so-called 'but-for' test. In *Cork* v *Kirby MacLean Ltd* [1952] 2 All ER 402 Lord Denning stated:

> 'If the damage would not have happened but for a particular fault, then the fault is the cause of the damage; if it would have happened just the same, fault or no fault, the fault is not the cause of the damage.'

The case usually quoted to illustrate this point is *Barnett* v *Chelsea and Kensington Hospital Management Committee* [1969] 1 QB 428 in which the death of the claimant's husband was held not to have been caused by an employee doctor's refusal to examine and failure to diagnose arsenical poisoning. It was found that it would have been too late to have saved the deceased by the time he arrival at hospital in any event.

Whilst the 'but-for' test certainly represents a commonsense approach to establishing a factual link between claimant and defendant, it is nothing more than a preliminary test to eliminate truly irrelevant causes, and is almost always satisfied in practice. However, the test breaks down in cases where there is more than one cause of the harmful consequence, its application leading to a result which defies common sense. An example given by Professor Atiyah illustrates the point nicely (Cane, Peter (ed), Atiyah's *Accidents, Compensation and the Law* (4th edn, 1987)). Two fires started independently by A and B unite and spread to C's house which is destroyed. In applying the test 'but for A's negligence would C have suffered loss?' the answer would be yes, given that B's negligence would have caused the same loss in any event. The question would be resolved the same way in respect of B's negligence and thus neither party would be held liable for C's loss. However, the courts would almost certainly adopt a modified, commonsense approach in order to fix such defendants with liability. As Lord Wright said in *Yorkshire Dale Steamship Co Ltd* v *Minister of War Transport* [1942] AC 691 'causation is to be understood as the man in the street, and not as either the scientist or the metaphysician, would understand it'.

The approach of the courts has been to resolve cases involving multiple possible causes according to notions of the burden of proof. An initial case of difficulty was the House of Lords' decision in *McGhee v National Coal Board* [1973] 1 WLR 1 in which an employee was allowed to recover compensation against his employer in negligence after having contracted dermatitis, possibly through the lack of proper washing facilities at his place of work. Although the medical evidence was insufficient to establish that the skin disease had been caused by prolonged exposure to sweat and grime, recovery was still possible as the defendant's breach of duty was said to have materially increased the risk of the employee contracting the disease. It seems that this 'robust and pragmatic' approach was influenced more by considerations of policy than logic, Lord Wilberforce pointing out that (given the evidential difficulties for the claimant in establishing causation in such cases):

'It is the creator of the risk who, ex hypothesi, must be taken to have foreseen the possibility of damage, who should bear its consequences.'

However, the current approach of the courts in cases of multiple possible cause is to require that the claimant prove the defendant's negligence was a probable cause, ie a more likely cause than the possible alternatives. Thus in *Hotson v East Berkshire Area Health Authority* [1987] AC 750 the House of Lords disallowed a claim for serious disabilities arising after an accident in which a boy injured his hip joint. On the facts, there was a 25 per cent chance that the defendant's failure to promptly diagnose the condition resulted in permanent disability (and a 75 per cent chance that the condition would have developed anyway, even if the claimant had been properly treated) and so the claimant failed to prove his case. Similarly in *Wilsher v Essex Area Health Authority* [1988] 1 All ER 871, conflicting medical evidence was such that the trial judge had failed to identify whether retinal damage sustained by a patient during birth was caused by the negligent administration of an excess of oxygen by the doctor, or by a number of alternative possible non-negligent causes. The case was sent for retrial on the causation issue, the claimant being required to prove his case on the balance of probabilities. Thus, it could be said that one commonsense approach adopted in *McGhee*, allowing a claimant to recover damages in the face of the evidential difficulties in proving causation, has given way to another commonsense approach which insists that all cases must be proved on the balance of probabilities, thereby creating consistency and certainty in the law.

Another problem with the 'but-for' test occurs where the claimant's injuries are attributable to successive causes, only the first of which is related to the defendant's negligence. In *Baker v Willoughby* [1970] AC 467 the claimant suffered injury to his leg as a result of the defendant's negligence, resulting in ongoing pain and discomfort and a loss of earning capacity. The claimant took up a new job after the accident, but was shot in the same leg by armed robbers whilst at work, necessitating an amputation. The defendant argued that his liability should be limited to the loss suffered by the claimant before the date of the robbery. The argument was rejected by the House of Lords, because even if the robbers could be sued for damages, they would have taken their victim as they had found him and would only have had to compensate the claimant for the loss of a bad leg. This would be manifestly unjust as the claimant would have been left uncompensated following the robbery for the difference between a good and a bad leg. The House in *Baker* therefore adopted a commonsense approach in order to do justice to the claimant.

However, *Baker* was subsequently thrown into doubt by the decision of the House of Lords in *Jobling* v *Associated Dairies Ltd* [1982] AC 794. The defendant's liability to pay compensation in respect of the back injury sustained by the claimant at work (arising through a breach of statutory duty) was cut short by the independent onset, before trial, of a naturally occurring back condition. This condition was such that it would, in itself, have rendered the claimant unable to work. The Lords in *Jobling* were critical of the decision in *Baker*. It was noted that damages are generally reduced to take account of the 'vicissitudes of life', ie the possibility that the claimant's working life might be cut short by future events such as early death or unemployment. Where such an event took place before trial, the defendant should not be forced to continue to pay damages for future loss of earnings, as to do so would be to place the claimant in a better position than he would otherwise have been in had the tort not been committed.

There is clearly a conflict between the decisions of *Baker* and *Jobling*, although it has been suggested that Baker will continue to apply in cases involving two successive tortious causes. The decision in *Baker* was driven by a commonsense approach which aimed to prevent the claimant from being under-compensated. The decision in *Jobling* was driven by an equally logical desire to prevent the claimant from being overcompensated. It is therefore submitted that the courts will adopt a pragmatic, case-by-case analysis of causation rather than applying a uniform philosophical approach, in order to reach decisions which may be regarded as a matter of common sense. However, as we have seen, the commonsense approach of one judge can differ from another, and it should not be supposed that consistency will be found in the authorities. As Lord Sumner pointed out in *Weld-Blundell* v *Stephens* [1920] AC 956:

> 'The trial of an action for damages is not a scientific inquest into a mixed sequence of phenomena, or an historical investigation of the chapter of events ... It is a practical enquiry.'

One final area worthy of mention relates to the second stage of enquiry, ie whether, as a matter of law, the defendant ought to be held responsible for the damage which he has, in fact, caused. The starting point here might be to consider the rules relating to remoteness of damage. However, for the purposes of this essay it is more instructive to consider those situations in which the damage suffered by the claimant cannot be recovered, even though the 'but-for' test is established, because the courts consider that an intervening act has broken the link between the defendant's negligence and the claimant's loss. It is submitted that these novus actus interveniens scenarios are all firmly based upon common sense, and a desire to do justice on the individual facts of each case.

The first category is where, following the negligence of the defendant, some unreasonable act of the claimant (going beyond mere contributory negligence) renders the injury suffered too remote from the original act or omission. In *McKew v Holland & Hannen & Cubitts (Scotland) Ltd* [1969] 3 All ER 1621 the claimant, having suffered mild injury to his leg as a result of the negligence of the defendants, suffered further injury when his leg gave away on a steep flight of stairs. It was held that the claimant was unable to recover further compensation, as his unreasonable act of descending the steep stairs with no handrail broke the chain of causation.

An intervening act of nature which is independent of the negligence of the defendant may also serve to break the chain of causation. Such was the case in *Carslogie Steamship Co v Royal Norwegian Government* [1952] AC 292. Here the claimant's ship suffered extensive damage in a storm on a journey it would not otherwise have made, but for a delay caused by the defendant's negligence. The storm was treated as a supervening event, breaking the chain of causation and relieving the defendant of liability for the subsequent storm damage.

Finally, the unreasonable intervening act of a third party may break the chain of causation where it takes the form of a negligent or reckless independent cause. Thus, in *Knightley v Johns* [1982] 1 WLR 349, a negligent defendant who caused an accident, blocking a tunnel, was not held liable for injuries sustained by a police motorcyclist who was negligently instructed by the officer in charge to drive back into the tunnel against the flow of traffic.

The courts have much more discretion to exercise their common sense in these cases, by allocating blame between the two defendants whose negligence contributed towards the claimant's loss. Thus, in *Rouse v Squires* [1973] QB 889 a negligent driver jack-knifed his lorry across the road, causing an accident. Several minutes later, the second defendant negligently collided with the vehicles involved in the first accident, causing the claimant's death. It was held that both defendants' actions were operative causes of the accident and liability was allocated to the first defendant in the proportion of 25 per cent.

QUESTION TWO

'Causation should be a matter of common sense and not of legal rules.'

Discuss with reference to the law of tort.

University of London LLB Examination
(for External Students) Law of Tort June 1996 Q5

General Comment

The question requires a discussion of the law relating to causation, an analysis of the scope of the 'but for' test and its application. Although there is no right answer to a question of this nature, it is suggested that the examinee avoid a general discussion on remoteness of damage, although the areas overlap considerably and analogies may be drawn.

Skeleton Solution

But for test: acts and omissions – problems: multiple and successive causes; proof of causation.

Suggested Solution

A defendant will not be liable in tort unless it can be shown that his tortious conduct was the cause of the damage suffered by the claimant. The classic definition of causation was given by Lord Denning in *Cork* v *Kirby Maclean Ltd* [1952] 2 All ER 402:

> 'If the damage would not have happened but for a particular fault, then that fault was the cause of the damage; if it would have happened just the same, fault or no fault, the fault is not the cause of the damage.'

This is a clear legal principle which may often seem harsh in its application, eg in *Barnett* v *Chelsea and Kensington Hospital Management Committee* [1969] 1 QB 428, the claimant's husband was refused treatment at the casualty department of a hospital when he complained of vomiting. When the man subsequently died of poisoning it was held that the defendants were not liable, as the cause of death was poisoning, and the man would have died had the claimants not been negligent.

Problems arise when pre-existing conditions aggravate or diminish the damage caused by a tortfeasor, eg in *Performance Cars Ltd* v *Abraham* [1962] 1 QB 33 the defendant crashed into and damaged a Rolls Royce car. The claimant's car had already been involved in another crash, and the claimant had been awarded the cost of a respray to his car in an earlier judgment. Because the claimant had already been awarded the cost of repairing the car, it was held that the defendant had caused no additional loss to the claimant. The 'but for' test here mitigates against double recovery by the claimant, but it has also been pointed out that the maxim that the tortfeasor takes his victim as he finds him will work in favour of the tortfeasor in such scenarios.

Another difficult area involves loss caused by an omission to act rather than an act. In *McWilliams* v *Sir William Arrol & Co Ltd* [1962] 1 WLR 295 the claimant was killed in an industrial accident. Although the defendants, his employers, were in breach of their statutory duty to provide safety equipment, they were able to show that the defendant would have been unlikely to have used the equipment in any case and they were not liable. Further, Lord Keith argued in *Yuen Kun-Yeu* v *Attorney-General of Hong Kong* [1988] AC 175 that it was a principle of English law that no liability in negligence would attach to 'one who sees another about to walk over a cliff with his head in the air and forebears to shout a warning'. Lord Diplock added further in *Home Office* v *Dorset Yacht Company Ltd* [1970] AC 1004 that in the parable of the good Samaritan both the priest and the Levite who passed by on the other side of the road were guilty of an omission which was likely to cause damage to health, but added that no liability would attach to them under English law.

The problem here is not that the damage would not have occurred 'but for' the omission but that there were successive causes of damage, ie the damage to the Samaritan was initially caused by thieves, but exacerbated by the failure of anyone to help. The conduct of more than one defendant may pass the 'but for' test. This is an age-old philosophical question, well illustrated in Atiyah's *Accidents Compensation and the Law* (4th ed p99). The example provided is if two fires are started independently by A and B and these fires combine and destroy the property of C, who caused C's loss? A, B, both or neither? On a very strict application of the 'but for' test neither would be liable as the damage would have occurred without A's negligence, likewise without B's. It is in hard cases such as these that the law must contain an element of common sense. Although there is no relevant English authority on the point, in the Canadian case of *Cook* v *Lewis* [1952] 1 DLR 1 it was held that each defendant was 50 per cent liable in a similar scenario.

Cook v *Lewis* leads into one of the thorniest problems in the law of causation, that of the standard of proof. In *McGhee* v *National Coal Board* [1973] 1 WLR 1 an employer was held liable in negligence for an employee's contraction of dermatitis. The House of Lords held that the employer's failure to provide washing facilities had increased the risk of the employee contracting the disease. It was never established that the lack of facilities had actually caused the disease. This case was subsequently applied by the Court of Appeal both in *Wilsher* v *Essex Area Health Authority* [1987] 2 WLR 425 and in *Fitzgerald* v *Lane* [1987] QB 781. In both cases the defendants were held to be liable in negligence, and in both the claimant established only that the defendant's conduct had increased the risk of damage occurring (not that the conduct had actually caused the damage). Slade LJ referred in Fitzgerald to the fact that it would have been impossible in that case for the claimant to prove that the defendant actually caused the loss. The Court of Appeal seemed to be mitigating the harshness of the rules of causation, particularly in medical cases where it is often impossible to pinpoint the precise cause of a disease, the justification for this being 'broad justice'.

The tensions between the certainty of legal rules and the application of notions of fairness and justice in hard cases, or judicial discretion, is apparent in these decisions. The House of Lords has subsequently retreated from a liberal interpretation of *McGhee* in a line of cases including *Kay* v *Ayrshire and Arran Health Board* [1987] 2 All ER 417 and *Hotson* v *East Berkshire Area Health Authority* [1987] AC 750. The culmination of this process was the House of Lords' decision in the *Wilsher* appeal: [1988] AC 1074. This reversed the Court of Appeal decision and established firmly that in all cases the claimant bears the burden of proving on the balance of probabilities that his loss was caused by the defendant. Lord Bridge added that any attempt to use the decision in *McGhee* to modify this principle was 'fruitless'.

It would seem then that English law has adopted a rule-based approach to the issue of causation rather than a commonsense approach. This certainly has the advantage of certainty, however as technology advances it may become more and more difficult to establish liability against doctors, employers etc because proof of causation will become too difficult to obtain, and this may be a recipe for results which offend against common sense. The courts seem to have opted out of the debate, wishing to avoid a haphazard uneven development of the principles of law in this area. Perhaps this is a question which the legislature should consider.

QUESTION THREE

Sam is a trainee fireman with the Waterside Fire Brigade. While undergoing instruction in driving a fire engine, he was ordered by his instructor Tom to drive at high speed along a country road with his blue lights flashing and bell sounding. Sam could see that the driver of the car ahead, Ursula, had become agitated, but he kept going. Ursula panicked in trying to make room for the fire engine and collided with a lamp post. Ursula received serious eye injuries but was released immediately. Her passenger Violet was trapped in the car. Ursula needed urgent medical treatment and was taken to a nearby hospital. However, there had been a major railway accident a short time earlier and the hospital was unable to admit other casualties. Ursula was therefore removed to another hospital six miles away; the hospital was unable to save her sight, but this would have been possible if she had been able to receive prompt treatment. Violet was released after two hours. She was not seriously hurt but was taken by ambulance to hospital for examination. On the way the ambulance was involved in a further accident (without negligence on anyone's part) and Violet sustained two broken legs.

Advise Ursula and Violet.

University of London LLB Examination
(for External Students) Law of Tort June 1990 Q8

General Comment

This question examines the principles relevant to establishing liability for negligence generally, as well as, to a slight extent, vicarious liability. A thorough appreciation of negligence is therefore essential.

Skeleton Solution

Duty of care – damage and loss – causation – remoteness – foreseeability – principles of vicarious liability – 'course of employment' – any defences?

Suggested Solution

It is well established law that Sam as a driver owes a duty of care to all other road users and as this is a personal injuries case the nature of the duty of care is governed by *Donoghue* v *Stevenson* [1932] AC 562: see *B* v *Islington Health Authority* [1991] 1 All ER

825 per Potts J. In carrying out this duty of care Sam must act as a reasonable man: *Blyth v Birmingham Waterworks* (1856) 11 Ex 781; this is an objective test which means that the standard of care required of a trainee driver is the same standard as required of an experienced and competent driver: *Nettleship v Weston* [1971] 2 QB 691, and it is by this standard that Sam must be judged. When Sam drives at high speed along a country road he is prima facie in breach of his duty as a reasonable man would not act in this way. If Sam were en route to an emergency then his actions would be those of a reasonable man: *Watt v Hertfordshire County Council* [1954] 1 WLR 835, but this is not the situation here. Ursula's collision is caused by Sam's breach of duty so prima facie Sam is liable for any injuries caused. Sam may seek to argue that Ursula did not make room for the fire engine to pass, but acted instead in a careless manner and that she caused her own injuries, ie that her panic and collision was a novus actus interveniens. As Ursula has been placed in an emergency or difficult situation by Sam's negligence however, the court is unlikely to make this finding if Ursula acted reasonably in the agony of the moment, even if with hindsight she could have avoided the accident: *Jones v Boyce* (1816) 1 Stark 493. But it is open to the court to find contributory negligence on Ursula's part and to reduce any damages awarded by s1 Law Reform (Contributory Negligence) Act 1945 having regard to Ursula's fault in causing the accident. All that Sam will have to show is that Ursula failed to look after herself properly: *Davies v Swan Motor Co* [1949] 2 KB 291.

Hence Sam is liable for the eye injury initially suffered by Ursula (subject to any reduction in damages); the question arises, however, is Sam liable for Ursula's subsequent loss of sight or is the earlier railway accident a novus actus interveniens? The new act (ie the railway accident) is an act of a third party and we must decide whether this act is the true cause of Ursula's loss of sight. From the facts of the problem it seems that the loss of Ursula's sight was caused only by the delay, and so Sam would not be liable for this additional damage: *Knightley v Johns* [1982] 1 WLR 349. It is not a situation where the delay was a natural and probable consequence of the first accident and was foreseeable as in *Rouse v Squires* [1973] QB 889; instead there has been a break in the chain of causation. (Note that the question that must be decided here is one of causation and not foreseeability as Sam is liable for any personal injury that ensues in the accident as he need only foresee the kind of damage and not the extent: *Smith v Leech, Brain* [1962] 2 QB 405.) The case *Jolley v Sutton London Borough Council* [2000] 3 All ER 409 provides a good example of this.

Similarly, Sam will be liable for Violet's slight injuries suffered in the collision but not for her two broken legs, as the cause of the broken legs was a novus actus interveniens which was not a natural and probable consequence of the first collision (see above).

As we are told that Sam was undergoing instruction and is a trainee fireman, it is clear that Sam is an employee, the Waterside Fire Brigade (or the appropriate local authority) is his employer, and Sam was acting in the course of his employment. The fact that Sam was doing so in a negligent manner is irrelevant: *Century Insurance v Northern Ireland Road Transport Board* [1942] AC 509.

Thus the Waterside Fire Brigade (or the appropriate local authority) will be responsible for Sam's actions and Ursula and Violet are advised to sue the Fire Brigade in respect of the injuries first suffered in the collision; as regards the later more serious injuries they are without a remedy. Ursula and Violet should also be advised that if they failed to wear seat belts and the wearing of a seat belt would have reduced their injuries, a reduction will be made for contributory negligence on their part: *Froom* v *Butcher* [1976] QB 286; [1975] 3 WLR 379.

QUESTION FOUR

'The "but for" test is no more than an aid, for the choice of cause rests ultimately on commonsense evaluation. Dictates of commonsense lead sometimes to the disregard of the "but for" test.' (Dias and Markesinis.)

Discuss.

University of London LLB Examination
(for External Students) Law of Tort June 1988 Q8

General Comment

A question purely on causative principles crops up every now and then. Students must know the concept of causation, particularly the 'but for' test and its exceptions (omissions) well in order to gain good marks.

Skeleton Solution

But for test – *Barnett* – competing causes – role of common sense evaluation – policy – *Wilsher* – contrast between CA and HL – successive causes – contrast between *Baker* and *Jobling* – departures from 'but for' – multiple causes – omissions? – competing causes.

Suggested Solution

Causation is a particularly difficult issue in the law of tort. As the question implies the basis of the doctrine of causation is the 'but for' test but this test is not applied as a philosopher would apply it but, according to the judges, it is applied as a matter of common sense.

The application of the 'but for' test can be seen in the case of *Barnett* v *Chelsea and Kensington Hospital Management Committee* [1969] 1 QB 428. The claimant's husband went to a casualty department of a hospital complaining that he had been vomiting. The doctor refused to examine him and he was told to go home and consult his own doctor in the morning. The claimant's husband was, in fact, suffering from arsenical poisoning and he died some five hours later. The claimant sued the hospital alleging that they had been negligent in the treatment of her husband and that as a result of their negligence her husband had died. It was held that the defendants were not liable as their negligence had not caused the death of the claimant's husband. Even if the doctor had examined the husband and treated him the husband would still have died and so the defendant's negligence was not a cause of the husband's death.

In this case we can see an example of a pure application of the 'but for' test. So the general rule is that if the damage would not have occurred but for the fault of the defendant then the fault is a cause of the damage, but if it would have happened anyway the fault of the defendant is not the cause of the damage.

But it is true that the choice of cause 'rests ultimately on commonsense evaluation' provided that common sense is understood as including the judge's view of the policy issues at stake. A good illustration of these competing views of policy arises where one of a number of competing possible causes could have been the actual cause of the damage which the claimant has suffered. In *Wilsher* v *Essex Area Health Authority* [1988] AC 1074; [1988] 1 All ER 871 the claimant was born prematurely and suffered from, amongst other things, oxygen deficiency. The negligence of one of the defendant's doctors resulted in the claimant later being given an excess of oxygen. The claimant alleged that this excess of oxygen had caused incurable damage to his retina which had left him virtually blind. The problem for the claimant was that there were a number of other possible causes of the damage to his retina and none of these other possible causes were attributable to the fault of the defendants. The Court of Appeal held, applying the decision of the House of Lords in *McGhee* v *National Coal Board* [1973] 1 WLR 1, that the claimant was entitled to succeed because the defendants had materially increased the risk of damage to the claimant. Mustill LJ recognised that there was an element of policy in his judgment because he held that the effect of the decision mitigated the rigour of the rule that the claimant must prove that the breach of duty caused the loss. This policy consideration was also clearly expressed by Lord Wilberforce in *McGhee* when he said that it was the defendants, who admittedly had been at fault, who were the ones who had to shoulder the evidential difficulty of showing the cause of the loss to the claimant.

But this 'pro-claimant' approach was abandoned by the House of Lords in reversing the decision of the Court of Appeal in *Wilsher*. The House of Lords affirmed that in all cases the claimant must establish the requisite causal connection on a balance of probabilities. They rejected the approach of Lord Wilberforce in *McGhee* and said that the law required proof of fault causing damage as the basis of liability and that if the law was to be changed it was for Parliament to do it and not the courts acting out of some misplaced sense of 'justice'. In this type of case human knowledge simply does not know what was the cause of the loss and while scientific evidence can help to establish the cause of the damage it cannot prove what was actually the true cause. So inevitably the courts are left to apply a test based on their perception of common sense and their perception of the competing policy issues.

Evidence of commonsense evaluation can also be seen in the judgments of the House of Lords in *Baker* v *Willoughby* [1970] AC 467 and *Jobling* v *Associated Dairies* [1982] AC 794. In the former case the court was concerned to ensure that the claimant was not undercompensated by the application of the 'take your victim as you find him' rule. In the latter case the court knew that the crippling back disease would have overcome the claimant anyway and held that the defendants were therefore not liable for the loss of earnings after the onset of the back disease. It is true that the policies appear to conflict, in that the court in *Baker* was concerned to avoid claimant undercompensation whereas the concern in *Jobling* was to prevent claimant overcompensation, but the point to note is that in each case the court was seeking to come to a conclusion which it felt was a fair one on the facts of the case and which satisfied their view of common sense. The Court of Appeal decision in *Mattocks* v *Mann* (1992) The Times 19 June is another example of the courts' commonsense approach to the question of causation.

It is also true that on occasions these considerations of common sense or policy lead a court to disregard the 'but for' test. An example of a disregard of the 'but for' test is provided by Professor Atiyah. Two fires started independently by A and B unite and spread to C's house which is destroyed. The 'but for' test would appear to acquit both parties because if the question is asked, 'would the damage have occurred but for the negligence of A?', the answer would be 'yes' and the same answer would be given if the question is asked, 'would the damage have occurred but for the negligence of B?'. This absurd result would not, however, be reached by the courts. In *Cook* v *Lewis* [1952] 1 DLR 1 the claimant was injured by a gun shot and it was unclear which of the two defendants had caused the injury as both parties had fired shots simultaneously. It was held that both parties were liable because the burden of proof lay on the defendants to show that they had not been negligent and they had failed to discharge that burden. In this case, as Professor Fleming has noted, the law prefers a 50 per cent chance of doing injustice to the certainty of doing injustice.

But is is submitted that it is only in rare cases that the courts actually disregard the 'but for' test. In many cases they are trying to apply the 'but for' test but that test does not yield a conclusive answer on the facts of a particular case and so the courts have to apply it with a dose of common sense. A good example of this is provided where the negligence of the defendant takes the form of an omission. In *McWilliams* v *Sir William Arrol* [1962] 1 WLR 295 the claimant fell to his death at work because he was not wearing a safety belt. The defendants were in breach of their statutory duty in failing to supply safety belts but there was evidence that, even if they had supplied a safety belt, the claimant would not have worn it. Here the but for test yields no conclusive answer because we do not know what would have happened if the defendants had actually supplied the safety belts. So the court has to do the next best thing and attempt to ascertain from the parties' past practices whether the claimant would have worn a safety belt had one been supplied. The court concluded that he would not have worn one so that the defendants were not liable. However it would be a mistake to see these cases as a court disregarding the 'but for' test. Rather, as was the case in our consideration of competing causes, the court is seeking to apply the 'but for' test with due regard to considerations of common sense and the policy issues at stake.

QUESTION FIVE

'Where human action forms one of the links between the original wrongdoing of the defendant and the loss suffered by the plaintiff, that action must at least have been something very likely to happen if it is not to be regarded as novus actus interveniens breaking the chain of causation.' (*Home Office* v *Dorset Yacht Co Ltd* (1970), per Lord Reid.)

Discuss this proposition and explain how since 1970 the courts have dealt with the problem of intervening deliberate human conduct.

University of London LLB Examination
(for External Students) Law of Tort June 1993 Q6

General Comment

This is a specific question on remoteness. Students should be able to raise issues of causation and link it to foreseeability and remoteness. An appreciation of what may be tantamount to a novus actus interveniens is also essential.

Skeleton Solution

Explanation of the proposition – case law since 1970: *Lamb* v *Camden*; *Ward* v *Cannock Chase*; *Rouse* v *Squires*; *Knightley* v *Johns*; *Smith* v *Littlewoods* – conclusion.

Suggested Solution

'I feel bound to say with respect that what Lord Reid said in the *Dorset Yacht* case [*Home Office* v *Dorset Yacht Co Ltd* [1970] AC 1004] does nothing to simplify the task of deciding for or against remoteness, especially where the fresh damage complained of has been caused by the intervening act of a third party': Watkins LJ in *Lamb* v *Camden London Borough Council* [1981] QB 625.

Lord Reid's dictum in the *Dorset Yacht* case concerns the principle that the consequence is too remote if it follows a break in the chain of causation. This break in the chain of causation, or novus actus interveniens, could be as a result of a natural event (as in *Carslogie Steamship Co Ltd* v *Royal Norwegian Government* [1952] AC 292), the act or omission of the claimant (as in *McKew* v *Holland & Hannen & Cubbitts (Scotland) Ltd* [1969] 3 All ER 1621), or the act or omission of a third party. It is with this last that we are concerned.

In the leading case of *The Oropesa* [1943] P 32 – which pre-dates Lord Reid's dictum – it is said: 'to break the chain of causation it must be shown that there is something which I will call ultroneous, something unwarrantable, a new cause which disturbs the sequence of events, something which can be described as either unreasonable or extraneous or extrinsic' (per Lord Wright). In other words, the defendant's breach of duty has been followed by the truly independent, but not necessarily tortious, act of a third party which causes the claimant's damage.

Lord Reid has restated the principle in this way: unless the act of the third party was something very likely to happen, it will break the chain of causation. Therefore something that was merely foreseeable would be seen as a novus actus interveniens. As Lord Reid went on to say later in the same judgment, 'I do not think that a mere foreseeable possibility is or should be sufficient'.

There have been a number of cases on this point since 1970, but briefly one should place the *Dorset Yacht* case in context. It was an attempt to broaden the scope of the 'neighbour principle' of *Donoghue* v *Stevenson* [1932] AC 562 and Lord Reid suggested that the time had come to regard that principle as applicable in all cases where there was no justification or valid explanation for its exclusion. His obiter statement regarding third party interference was not reflected in the other speeches in that case.

However, if one turns to case law since 1970, one reaches the conclusion that it is very difficult to say where exactly the dividing line is drawn between those third party acts which terminate the defendant's liability and those which do not, but the test is essentially whether the intervening act is reasonably foreseeable.

In *Lamb* v *Camden London Borough Council* (above), the claimant's house was damaged through the defendant's negligence. The house became unoccupied and squatters moved in on two occasions, causing further damage. The Official Referee held that the squatting was a 'foreseeable' risk but not a likely one and, applying Lord Reid's speech in the *Dorset Yacht* case, he held that the damage they caused was too remote. However, whilst upholding this decision, the Court of Appeal was critical of Lord Reid's proposition, as has been noted above.

In contrast, in *Ward* v *Cannock Chase District Council* [1986] Ch 546, on similar facts, the defendants were held liable. The difference between the two may lie in the degree of wilful wrongdoing by the third party. A third party's negligence will be more foreseeable than its wilful conduct. But ultimately what the court is looking at is whether the reasonable man would foresee the intervening acts in question. While squatting may be foreseeable, the actual conduct of the squatters – particularly if it is wilfully wrong – is not a reasonably foreseeable consequence which can be attributed to the defendant's negligence.

In *Jolley* v *Sutton London Borough Council* [2000] 3 All ER 409 the House of Lords seemed to stretch the concept of foreseeability slightly.

To contrast two further cases which are factually similar: in *Rouse* v *Squires* [1973] QB 889, a lorry jack-knifed across a motorway owing to the first defendant's negligent driving. A second lorry, also being driven negligently, crashed some minutes later into the pile-up, killing someone who was assisting at the scene. The first defendant's negligence was held to have caused his death, Cairns LJ saying that, having negligently created the danger to other road users, the first defendant was responsible for the further accident, despite the second lorry driver's negligence. Only if this latter had deliberately or recklessly driven into the obstruction would the chain of causation be broken.

In *Knightley* v *Johns* [1982] 1 WLR 349, on the other hand, a subsequent collision was held too remote where the first defendant's negligent driving caused the blocking of a busy tunnel. A police inspector, who took charge, at first negligently failed to close the tunnel, but then sent a police motorcyclist (the claimant) the wrong way along the tunnel to close it. He collided with another motorist. This accident was too remote, because there had been so many errors between the initial negligence and the subsequent collision.

These cases suggest, therefore, that it is a question of fact where the line is precisely drawn, the need to draw a line and its general position being a question of policy, although policy based on common sense. As Oliver LJ said in *Lamb*: 'I confess that I find it inconceivable that the reasonable man, wielding his pick in the road in 1973, could be said reasonably to foresee that his puncturing of a water main would fill the claimant's house with uninvited guests in 1974'.

This passage from his judgment was endorsed by Lord Mackay in *Smith* v *Littlewoods Organisation Ltd* [1987] AC 241 in the House of Lords. Referring also to the speech of Lord Reid, his Lordship concluded that the only way it would be possible to persuade a judge that an outcome was not only possible but reasonably foreseeable was to show that it was also highly likely. In other words something more than mere foreseeability would be required. Despite the criticism of Lord Reid, this does not seem far from what Lord Reid was saying. It is perhaps the perennial difficulty in tort, and particularly in negligence, of trying to reach a definition using indefinable terms.

Perhaps the last word should go to Lord Denning, who said in *Lamb*: 'The law has to draw a line somewhere. Sometimes it is done by limiting the range of persons to whom duty is owed ... At other times it is done by saying that the consequence is too remote to be a head of damage ... But ultimately it is a question of policy for the judges to decide.'

Chapter 8

Contributory Negligence

8.1   Introduction

8.2   Key points

8.3   Key cases and statutes

8.4   Question and suggested solution

8.1 Introduction

Section 1 Law Reform (Contributory Negligence) Act 1945 provides that where the claimant is partly responsible for the damage suffered the damages recoverable shall be reduced to such an extent as the court thinks just and equitable having regard to the claimant's share in the responsibility for the damage. Recently, the court took on board consideration of this Act in determining liability in the case of *Sahid Foods Ltd (In Liquidation)* v *Paskin Kyriakides Sands (A Firm)* (2004) The Times 23 January.

8.2 Key points

Fault by the claimant

The claimant must be at fault or he can recover in full, see for example *Tremayne* v *Hill* [1987] RTR 131, but he need not owe a duty of care to the defendant: *Nance* v *British Columbia Electric Railway* [1951] AC 601.

Standard of care

The defendant must prove that the claimant failed to take reasonable precautions for his own safety: *Davies* v *Swan Motor Co* [1949] 2 KB 291; *Jones* v *Livox Quarries* [1952] 2 QB 608.

Children

In *Gough* v *Thorne* [1966] 1 WLR 1387 Lord Denning stated that a very young child could not be guilty of contributory negligence; see also *Yachuk* v *Oliver Blais* [1949] AC 386. However, in *Morales* v *Eccleston* [1991] RTR 151 an 11-year-old boy was held to be guilty of contributory negligence.

Workmen

The courts are reluctant to find an employee guilty of contributory negligence when he sues his employer for breach of statutory duty, eg *Caswell* v *Powell Duffryn Associated Collieries* [1940] AC 152, but are more willing to do so where the employee is suing in negligence only eg *Bux* v *Slough Metals* [1974] 1 All ER 262; *Jayes* v *IMI* [1985] ICR 155.

Rescuers

The courts are also reluctant to find contributory negligence on the part of a rescuer, although they will do so in appropriate cases, eg *Harrison* v *British Railways Board* [1981] 3 All ER 679.

Emergencies

Again the courts are reluctant to make a finding of contributory negligence against a claimant who makes a wrong decision in the agony of the moment: *Jones* v *Boyce* (1816) 1 Stark 493.

Causation

The claimant's carelessness need not contribute to the accident; it is enough if it contributes to the damage the claimant suffers.

Note, however, that the 1945 Act does not apply to cases where someone causes another to suffer loss by committing the tort of deceit (*Standard Charter Bank* v *Pakistan National Shipping Corporation* [2000] 3 WLR 1692), or any other tort involving dishonesty or conspiracy: *Corporacion Nacional del Cobre de Chile* v *Sogemin Metals Ltd* [1997] 1 WLR 1396.

Thus in *Froom* v *Butcher* [1976] QB 286; [1975] 3 WLR 379 the non-wearing of a seat belt was held to amount to contributory negligence, as was the failure of a motor cyclist to wear a helmet: *O'Connell* v *Jackson* [1972] 1 QB 270, or to wear a helmet but not to fasten the strap: *Capps* v *Miller* [1989] 2 All ER 333. If a person accepts a lift from a driver who he knows has consumed large quantities of alcohol, that too can amount to contributory negligence: *Owens* v *Brimmell* [1977] QB 859.

Apportionment

The damages are to be reduced to such an extent as the court thinks just and equitable. For seat belts *Froom* v *Butcher* (above) suggested that if the wearing of a seat belt would have completely prevented the injuries the reduction should be 25 per cent; if the seat belt would have reduced the severity of the injuries 15 per cent is appropriate.

In *O'Connell* a reduction of 15 per cent was made and in *Capps* a reduction of 10 per cent was made.

In *Pitts* v *Hunt* [1990] 3 WLR 542 it was held that for s1 of the 1945 Act to operate there must be fault on the part of both parties. This presupposes that the person suffering damage will recover some damages, and thus the claimant cannot be held 100 per cent responsible for the damage. However, the Court of Appeal in *Reeves v Commissioner of Police of the Metropolis* [1999] 3 All ER 897 found that a claimant could be found 100 per cent blameworthy. On appeal, the House of Lords held that both parties were to be equally blamed, ie at 50 per cent each, but their Lordships left the issue as an open one, as to whether 100 per cent contributory negligence is possible.

Where there is more than one defendant it was held by the House of Lords in *Fitzgerald v Lane* [1989] AC 328; [1988] 2 All ER 961 that first the apportionment between the claimant and the defendants should be decided, then the apportionment between the defendants inter se, and that at the first stage the claimant's conduct was to be compared with the totality of the defendant's conduct rather than to each defendant separately.

8.3 Key cases and statutes

* *Froom v Butcher* [1976] QB 286
  Causation on the part of the claimant must be proven

* *Harrison v British Railways Board* [1981] 3 All ER 679
  Rescuers are rarely found to be contributorily negligent

* *Jones v Livox Quarries* [1952] 2 QB 608
  Defendant must prove that claimant failed to take reasonable precautions

* *Morales v Eccleston* [1991] RTR 151
  The court will decide if a child can be guilty of contributory negligence

* *Reeves v Commissioner of Police of the Metropolis* [1999] 3 All ER 897
  The issue of whether there can be a finding of 100 per cent contributory negligence was left open by the Law Lords

* *Sahid Foods Ltd (in Liquidation) v Paskin Kyriakides Sands (A Firm)* (2004) The Times 23 January
  Illustrates the application of s1 Law Reform (Contributory Negligence) Act 1945

* *Tremayne v Hill* [1987] RTR 131
  Claimant must be at 'fault' for contributory negligence to apply

* Civil Liability (Contribution) Act 1978 – apportions liability as between 'blameworthy' defendants

* Law Reform (Contributory Negligence) Act 1945 – affords the partial defence of contributory negligence to a defendant

8.4 Question and suggested solution

Plodders Ltd are a firm which arranges light removals. Kieran works for them as a driver. Kieran uses his own van which he maintains himself and to which he attaches a sign reading, 'Plodders Ltd' when he is working for them. Plodders provide Kieran with overalls and with the equipment needed for loading and unloading goods. He is allowed to take someone with him to assist. On Sunday he was instructed that on the following day he was to travel to Rochester (some miles outside London) to pick up some furniture and bring it back to London. He was told not to go until the afternoon as there would be no-one at home until 2.00 pm. Kieran however decided to leave early so as to spend the morning visiting the cathedral and castle. He took his friend Patrick with him. As he drove into Rochester about 15 mph faster than permitted and rounded a curve in the road he had to brake suddenly to avoid a cyclist ahead of him. The van skidded off the road and down an embankment. Kieran and Patrick were trapped in the van. The cyclist, Camilla, a nurse, jumped over the railings at the edge of the road down to where the van had fallen. She landed on some broken glass which had been concealed by bushes. Kieran was uninjured, but Patrick suffered very serious injuries and Camilla was badly cut and off work for several weeks.

Advise Patrick and Camilla whether they have causes of action against (a) Kieran and (b) Plodders Ltd.

University of London LLB Examination
(for External Students) Law of Tort June 1995 Q8

General Comment

A question requiring a discussion on the partial defence of contributory negligence, particularly on rescuers. There is also an overlap with vicarious liability to ascertain extent. A good appreciation of both areas is essential.

Skeleton Solution

Introduction – contributory negligence – rescuers – vicarious liability – control test – multiple test – course of employment – conclusion.

Suggested Solution

Patrick has suffered personal injuries as a result of Kieran's negligent driving. Whether he recovers damages against Kieran or Plodders Ltd depends upon the application of the rules of vicarious liability. The same rules apply in Camilla's case, although as a rescuer, she is in a special category of claimant.

Dealing first with Camilla's status as a rescuer, the reason this is relevant is that the defendant(s) may argue that she was contributorily negligent in jumping over the railings and therefore placing herself in a potentially dangerous situation. If a claimant is found to be guilty of contributory negligence then his damages are reduced accordingly under the Law Reform (Contributory Negligence) Act 1945. It is possible for a rescuer to be found guilty of contributory negligence, but it happens rarely. One such case was *Harrison* v *British Railways Board* [1981] 3 All ER 679 in which a railway guard was injured whilst rescuing a passenger who had attempted to board a moving train. The court found that the guard was guilty of contributory negligence by virtue of the fact that he had failed to reduce the danger by not carrying out procedures required by the terms of his employment. However, in the vast majority of cases there will be no such finding. For instance, in *Sahid Foods Ltd* v *Paskin Kyriakides* (2004) The Times 23 January, the court found the claimant to be 50 per cent blameworthy. If a defendant creates a perilous situation, it is foreseeable that a brave passer-by will attempt a rescue. There are a number of cases which illustrate this principle. In *Brandon* v *Osborne, Garrett & Co* [1924] 1 KB 548 the claimant was injured by a falling sheet of glass when she attempted to pull her husband out of the way. It was held that she was not guilty of contributory negligence. In *Haynes* v *Harwood* [1935] 1 KB 146 the claimant, a policeman, was injured whilst trying to stop a bolting horse. The horse had been left unattended in the street and had been frightened by a child throwing a stone at it. It was held that the act of the child and the subsequent rescue attempt were both foreseeable and therefore the claimant was not guilty of contributory negligence. Applying these principles to Camilla's case it is highly likely that any award of damages she may receive will not be reduced because of contributory negligence.

Turning to the vicarious liability issue, in practice Patrick and Camilla would issue proceedings against both Kieran and Plodders Ltd in the alternative. As a matter of substantive law, however, certain tests need to be applied in order to determine which party is liable. The first point to establish is whether Kieran is an employee of Plodders Ltd in the traditional master and servant context, or an independent contractor, as the principles of liability are different.

It is often said that an employee is employed under a contract of service, whereas an independent contractor is employed under a contract for services. However, this simplistic approach does not explain the fundamental difference between the two types of contract. The courts have struggled to devise the definitive test and it seems that the different tests are all relevant but that each case will be decided upon its own facts. In *Ferguson* v *Dawson (John) and Partners (Contractors) Ltd* [1976] 1 WLR 346 it was held that if the employer controls the type of work to be done and the manner in which it is to be done then it is likely to be a contract of service. This became known as the 'control test' but it has fallen out of favour in recent years with the rise of specialised and highly skilled areas of work in which the employee is left to decide how to carry out the work.

In *Ready Mixed Concrete (South East) Ltd* v *Minister of Pensions and National Insurance* [1968] 2 QB 497 a more precise test was developed. It was held that, for a contract of service, three conditions must be satisfied. First, the employee must agree to provide his work and skill for his employer in return for wages, second, he must agree to be under the control of his employer, and third, the terms of the contract must be consistent with it being a contract of service. The most comprehensive test, the multiple test, was that used in *Market Investigations Ltd* v *Minister of Social Security* [1969] 2 QB 173. This is a two-stage test in which the first question to ask is whether the worker is providing a service as a person in business on his own account. If so, then he is not an employee. The factors to be taken into account are whether the worker provides his own equipment, whether he is responsible for hiring his own helpers, his degree of financial risk, and his degree of responsibility for investment and management.

In Kieran's case, applying the above tests seems to suggest that he is an independent contractor working under a contract for services. This is borne out by the facts that he uses his own van, and that he chooses his own helpers. Against this is the fact that Plodders Ltd provide him with overalls and equipment. However, in the overall context, Kieran is highly likely to be found to be an independent contractor. If this is the case, then he will be liable in negligence to Patrick and Camilla, rather than Plodders Ltd, as it is trite law that an employer is not liable for the negligent acts of independent contractors.

If, on the other hand, the court finds that Kieran is an employee of Plodders Ltd then, prima facie, Plodders will be liable. For the employer to be liable the tort must be committed in the course of the employee's employment. This is a question of fact in each case, but the courts tend to adopt a somewhat liberal approach as a matter of public policy. The reason for this is that the employer is better able to pay damages as he is insured against such risks, whereas employees in the vast majority of cases are not. If, however, the employee's act is wholly unconnected to his employment, then he will be liable rather than his employer. In *Joel* v *Morrison* (1834) 6 C & P 501 the court used the phrase 'was the employee on a frolic of his own?' to describe the situation where the employee acts outside the course of his employment. An example of such a case is *Beard* v *London General Omnibus Co* [1900] 2 QB 530 in which a bus conductor drove a bus in the absence of the driver and the employer was held not liable as he was clearly acting outside his employment. This can be contrasted with *Limpus* v *London General Omnibus Co* (1862) 1 H & C 526 in which a bus driver who raced his employer's bus was held to be acting within his employment as he was still driving the bus, the task for which he was employed.

Applying these principles to the present case, if the court finds that Kieran is an employee of Plodders Ltd then he was acting within the course of his employment as he was doing what he was employed to do even though he was driving too fast. Accordingly, Plodders would be liable for Kieran's negligent driving.

Chapter 9

Breach of Statutory Duty and Employers' Liability

9.1   Introduction

9.2   Key points

9.3   Key cases and statutes

9.4   Questions and suggested solutions

9.1 Introduction

A breach of statutory duty may give a cause of action in tort. The problem is, what statutes give rise to such an action? The statute may expressly exclude a civil right, eg the Guard Dogs Act 1975, or the statute may give a cause of action where none previously existed. Usually, however, the statute is silent as to whether or not it gives rise to an action in tort.

9.2 Key points

Breach of statutory duty

a) Does the breach give rise to a tort?

i) To answer this question the courts must find the intention of Parliament. See the child care cases where the courts attempted to ascertain the intent of Parliament: *X v Bedfordshire County Council* [1995] 3 WLR 152.

This area has received a lot of attention from the courts. The following decisions are important: *Barrett v Enfield London Borough Council* [1999] 3 All ER 193 (the House of Lords held that a local authority owed non-delegable child care duties where a court care order is concerned); *Phelps v Hillingdon London Borough Council* [2000] 3 WLR 776, *Jarvis v Hampshire County Council* [2000] 2 FCR 310 and *G (A Child) v Bromley London Borough Council* [2000] Ed CR 49 (these cases illustrate the extent of duty owed by local authorities); and *S v Gloucestershire County Council, L v Tower Hamlets London Borough Council* [2000] 3 All ER 345. The question of the duty of care owed by schools and their respective local authorities has been raised in respect of bullying both within and outside of school: see *Bradford-Smart v West Sussex County Council* [2002] ELR 139. A local council was found liable for the actions of its social workers in *A* v *Essex County Council* [2004] 1 FLR 749. A similar decision was reached by the Privy Council in *B* v *Attorney-General of New Zealand* [2003] 4 All ER 833.

The other related and relevant issue is whether there is any breach under the European Convention on Human Rights committed by these local authorities if they are found to be in breach of their statutory duty. In *Osman* v *United Kingdom* [1999] 1 FLR 193 the European Court had suggested strongly that to impose a 'no duty of care in tort' might be equivalent to the grant of an immunity. *Osman* was, of course, a controversial decision and attracted both judicial and extra-judicial criticism. However, in a more recent decision (*Z and Others* v *United Kingdom* (2001) The Times 31 May) the European Court has, it seems, retreated from some of the bolder statements in *Osman*.

  ii) In *Lonrho* v *Shell Petroleum Co (No 2)* [1982] AC 173 Lord Diplock stated that the initial presumption was that if the statute contained an obligation together with a means of enforcing that obligation (eg a criminal penalty) then the obligation could not be enforced in any other way. See, however, the Court of Appeal's approach in the case of *Kane* v *New Forest District Council* [2001] 3 All ER 914.

  iii) There are two exceptions to this presumption, namely where the statute was enacted for the benefit of a particular class of persons, and where the statute created a public right and the claimant had suffered damage over and above the damage suffered by the public at large.

b) Remedy within statute.

  i) If the Act imposes a duty but provides no remedy for breach, the presumption is that breach gives rise to an action in tort, eg *Thornton* v *Kirklees Metropolitan Borough Council* [1979] QB 626.

  ii) If the Act provides a remedy it is harder to show that breach gives the right to sue: *Atkinson* v *Newcastle Waterworks* (1877) 2 Ex D 441, although a civil action was allowed in *Groves* v *Lord Wimborne* [1898] 2 QB 402. In *Todd* v *Adams* [2002] 2 Lloyd's Rep 293 the Court of Appeal held that the action could not succeed as the Act in question had already provided a remedy within the Act.

c) Note also the effect of an existing common law remedy on the readiness or otherwise of the courts to hold that a civil remedy lies for a breach of statute; compare *Phillips* v *Britannia Hygienic Laundry* [1923] 2 KB 832 with *Monk* v *Warbey* [1935] 1 KB 175.

d) Statutes for the benefit of a class.

  i) The claimant has an action in tort if he is a member of that class; the problem is what constitutes a class of persons.

  ii) It is clear that employees are a class of persons as regards industrial safety legislation: *Groves* v *Lord Wimborne* (above). But see *Richardson* v *Pitt-Stanley* [1995] 2 WLR 26.

iii) This apart, however, it seems difficult to ascertain what is meant by a class: see *Phillips* v *Britannia Hygienic Laundry* (above) and *McCall* v *Abelesz* [1976] QB 585, and note *Cutler* v *Wandsworth Stadium* [1949] AC 398; *West Wiltshire District Council* v *Garland* [1995] 2 WLR 439.

e) Additional damage.

The second exception in *Lonrho* v *Shell Petroleum* (above) is where the statute creates a public right and a particular person suffers particular, direct and substantial damage other and different from that suffered by the rest of the public. Note the restricted interpretation of this exception in *Lonrho* v *Shell Petroleum* (above).

f) Scope of statute.

The claimant must prove three things:

i) the act which caused the damage is regulated by statute;

ii) he is one of the persons the Act is intended to protect;

iii) the damage suffered is of the kind the Act was intended to prevent.

See the leading case of *Gorris* v *Scott* (1874) LR 9 Exch 125.

Employers' liability

Employers owe various duties to their employees at common law and under a number of statutes. The common law duties are often described as four separate duties, although some authors prefer to say that an employer owes his employee the common duty of care in all the circumstances of the case. In any event, we shall describe the four common law duties if only as examples of the overall duty of care.

Competent staff

The employer owes a duty to his employees to select competent fellow employees: see *Hudson* v *Ridge Manufacturing Co* [1957] 2 QB 348 and compare *Smith* v *Crossley Bros* (1951) 95 SJ 655.

Proper plant and equipment

The employer must provide properly maintained plant and equipment: *Smith* v *Baker* [1891] AC 325. Note the effect of the Employers' Liability (Defective Equipment) Act 1969 and the ruling of the House of Lords in *Coltman* v *Bibby Tankers* [1988] AC 276 that the term 'equipment' in the 1969 Act is not restricted to parts of a larger entity.

Safe place of work

The employer must provide a safe place of work, but this is not an absolute duty and merely requires the employer to take reasonable steps to provide a safe place of work: *Latimer* v *AEC Ltd* [1953] AC 643; *Gitsham* v *Pearce* [1992] PIQR 57. However, this position must now be reviewed in light of the House of Lords' decision in *Fairchild* v *Glenhaven Funeral Services Ltd*; *Waddingtons plc* v *Leeds City Council* [2003] 1 AC 32 where the claimants' actions against their employers was successful.

Safe system of work

The employer is also under a duty to provide a safe system of work: *General Cleaning Contractors* v *Christmas* [1953] AC 180. In the case of *Walker* v *Northumberland County Council* [1994] 1 All ER 737 this was held to cover a duty not to cause an employee psychiatric damage by the volume and character of the employee's workload, where such psychiatric damage was foreseeable.

Note that the duty the employer owes to his employee is an individual duty to each and every individual employee, and must take into account the attributes of that particular employee: *Paris* v *Stepney Borough Council* [1951] AC 367.

Note also that this duty is a personal non-delegable duty, and the employer cannot discharge his duty merely by entrusting it to another person: *McDermid* v *Nash Dredging and Reclamation* [1987] AC 906; *Morris* v *Breaveglen* [1993] ICR 766.

The duty is only to safeguard the employee's physical safety; it does not extend to protecting the employee's economic welfare: *Reid* v *Rush & Tompkins* [1990] 1 WLR 212.

Finally, note the different attitudes of the courts to contributory negligence on the part of an employee as regards employers' breach of statutory duty and breach of common law duties (see Chapter 8) and the fact that an employer many owe a duty of care to members of an empolyee's family: *Hewett* v *Alf Brown's Transport* [1992] ICR 530.

9.3 Key cases and statutes

- *A* v *Essex County Council* [2004] 1 FLR 749
  A local council liable for the actions of its employees

- *B* v *Attorney-General of New Zealand* [2003] 4 All ER 833
  Privy Council held that social workers attracted liability that could implicate their employers

- *Barrett* v *Enfield London Borough Council* [1999] 3 All ER 193
  Local authority owes a non-delegable duty in respect of child care

- *Fairchild* v *Glenhaven Funeral Services Ltd* [2003] 1 AC 32
  Employers need to do what every other reasonable employer would do in respect of their employees, particularly by ensuring that they discharge their primary obligations

- *G (A Child)* v *Bromley London Borough Council* [2000] Ed CR 49
  Illustrates the extent of duty owed by local authorities

- *Jarvis* v *Hampshire County Council* [2000] 2 FCR 310
  Illustrates the extent of duty owed by local authorities in respect of providing education in schools

- *Kane* v *New Forest District Council* [2001] 3 All ER 914
  Parliamentary intention must be strictly interpreted

- *Latimer* v *AEC Ltd* [1953] AC 643
  Illustrates the duties owed by an employer to employees

- *McDermid* v *Nash Dredging & Reclamation Co Ltd* [1987] AC 906
  Employers owe a non delegable duty to employees

- *Osman* v *United Kingdom* [1999] 1 FLR 193
  European Court held that to impose a 'no duty of care' in tort would be granting immunity to public bodies

- *Phelps* v *Hillingdon London Borough Council* [2000] 3 WLR 776
  Illustrates the extent of duty owed by local authorities

- *S* v *Gloucestershire County Council; L* v *Tower Hamlets London Borough Council* [2000] 3 All ER 345
  Illustrates the extent of duty owed by local authorities in respect of providing education in schools

- *Todd* v *Adams* [2002] 2 Lloyd's Rep 293
  If the Act of Parliament provides a remedy, then there is no right to sue in tort

- *X* v *Bedfordshire County Council* [1995] 3 WLR 152
  Court's primary duty is to define the intentions of Parliament

- Guard Dogs Act 1975 – statute may provide a remedy where none previously existed

- Employers' Liability (Compulsory Insurance) Act 1969 – all employees must be insured by employers (a strict duty)

- Employers' Liability (Defective Equipment) Act 1969 – imposes a strict duty on employers in respect of plants and equipment

- Highways Act 1980 – imposes a strict duty on local authorities in respect of motorways/roads under their care

9.4 Questions and suggested solutions

QUESTION ONE

Peggy is aged 75 and disabled. The social services department of her local council, the

Doomtown Borough Council, provides her with several forms of assistance, including its 'Meals on Wheels' service, which delivers a midday meal to her every day. Because she has very limited savings, these services are provided free of charge. The department knows that she suffers from diabetes and that it is therefore vital that she has meals at regular times. One day a new driver on the 'Meals on Wheels' service went to the wrong address and, receiving no reply, left the meal intended for Peggy outside. At 1.00pm Peggy telephoned the social services department to say that her meal had not been delivered. She left a message on the answering machine. The receptionist did not listen to the recorded messages until 3.30pm. By that time Peggy had collapsed. A neighbour heard the noise of her fall, but, because she had fallen immediately inside the front door of her flat, could not get in. There was a long delay in reaching Peggy and she lapsed into a coma, from which she is unlikely to recover.

Advise whether Peggy has a claim in tort.

University of London LLB Examination
(for External Students) Law of Tort June 2001 Q3

General Comment

This is a question on the breach of duty by a social services department. It raises a discussion of the broader area of breach of statutory duty. Although there aren't any specific cases on this type of responsibility assumed by the council, candidates should be able to draw a conclusion from comparable cases. Ultimately, is the council liable to Peggy?

Skeleton Solution

Has the council assumed a duty of care towards Peggy? – did they know of Peggy's vulnerability? – have they discharged their duty of care? – breach of that duty – loss and damage – remedy.

Suggested Solution

Lord Browne-Wilkinson in *X v Bedfordshire County Council* [1995] 3 WLR 152 stated that a person who has suffered damage as a result of the breach of a statutory duty may have an action in tort. This has been described as 'an action for breach of statutory duty simpliciter'. As far as English law is concerned, this is a specific form of common law action which is distinct from the tort of negligence, even where the negligence action is based on a common law duty of care arising either from the imposition of a statutory duty, or from the performance of it. It must be remembered that a mere careless performance of a statutory duty, does not in itself give rise to any cause of action in the absence of either a 'right of action for breach of duty simpliciter' or a common law duty of care in negligence.

The question does not offer any information as to whether there is a specific statute involved which provides for the provision of a 'meals on wheels' service by the

Doomtown Borough Council (although such a duty may be implied from the Local Government Acts). Hence a common law negligence approach is to be preferred in determining the issues: whether the council has in fact assumed a duty of care over Peggy, and whether Doomtown Borough Council is in breach of that duty, as a result of which Peggy has suffered serious injury.

From the facts, it is evident that the council has assumed a responsibility towards Peggy, aged 75, by agreeing to provide her with a midday meal every day. The council appears to have assessed Peggy's case and decided to provide her with this service free of charge: surely the council are exercising a discretion either under the auspices of a statute, or under the common law powers of a public authority in terms of the provision of services to deserving and entitled members of the public or community concerned. On the basis of this relationship, Doomtown Borough Council have assumed responsibility towards Peggy, and as such owe her a duty of care. Clearly they are aware of Peggy's history and medical condition and as such they should have appreciated her vulnerability. The principles of liability as established under *Caparo Industries plc* v *Dickman* [1990] 1 All ER 568 appear to have been satisfied in this instance. There is reasonable foreseeability and there is a relationship of proximity. Surely then, it must be just, fair and reasonable to impose a duty of care under the circumstances. An examination of the relevant case law in this area is therefore essential before the issue can be conclusively determined.

In *X* v *Bedfordshire County Council* [1995] 3 WLR 152, the court decided that where a statute imposes general administrative functions on public bodies, and involves the exercise of broad administrative discretion following subjective decisions, it was highly unlikely that Parliament intended to create a private law right of action. This, however, does not (it must be said) preclude an action for negligence. In *Geddis* v *Proprietors of the Bann Reservoir* (1878) 3 App Cas 430, it was stated that where a public authority acts in the exercise of a statutory power, then negligence may be held to be actionable and will defeat a defence of statutory authorisation.

Another interesting case is *Kent* v *Griffiths* [2000] 2 WLR 1158, where the Court had to decide whether the ambulance service owed a duty of care to an individual when the service was summoned to render assistance to that individual. The Court of Appeal held that the ambulance service does owe a duty of care to those to whom it is summoned for assistance. This duty arises once the service 'accepts the call' for assistance. Similarly, in *Barnett* v *Chelsea and Kensington Hospital Management Committee* [1969] 1 QB 428, the court observed that a hospital accident and emergency department owes a duty of care to those who seek its assistance, and cannot simply turn away patients without accepting responsibility in the tort of negligence.

In *Costello* v *Chief Constable of the Northumbria Police* [1999] 1 All ER 550 the court held that a police inspector who witnessed an attack on a female police officer by a female prisoner owed that police officer a duty of care, as he had assumed a responsibility to her. Conversely, in *Leach* v *Chief Constable of Gloucestershire Constabulary* [1999] 1 All

ER 215 the Court of Appeal held that the police do not owe a duty of care to protect an 'appropriate adult' from mental or psychological harm.

As far as fire services are concerned, the case of *Capital and Counties plc v Hampshire County Council and Digital Equipment Co Ltd* [1997] 2 All ER 865 bears significant relevance. In this case the Court of Appeal held that, except in a case where a fire service negligently increased the damage or caused additional damage, there is no proximity of relationship between the fire brigade and the building owner in respect of negligence in the tackling of a fire.

The keyword in all the cases discussed above is negligence. So long as negligence is established, the action is sustainable. In Peggy's case, there is a clear assumption of responsibility and there is sufficient evidence on the facts to support the argument that the council was in breach of its duty.

In relation to the neighbour, there is no liability accruing, as the neighbour had in no way assumed liability towards Peggy (either before the incident or even when he/she went to offer help). Peggy therefore can sue Doomtown Borough Council for negligence.

QUESTION TWO

The Food Standards Act 1999 has established the Food Standards Agency. Under s6 it has the functions of '(a) developing policies … relating to matters connected with food safety or other interests of consumers in relation to food; and (b) providing advice, information or assistance in respect of such matters to any public authority'.

The chief executive of the Agency has asked you to prepare a report for its first meeting explaining the circumstances in which the Agency might be held liable in tort in the discharge of these functions. Write the report.

University of London LLB Examination
(for External Students) Law of Tort June 2000 Q1

General Comment

This looks like a straightforward question on negligent or faulty advice on food safety, but as there is a statute involved, namely the Food Standards Act 1999, it requires consideration of the tort of breach of statutory duty.

Skeleton Solution

Nature of a breach of statutory duty – does it impose liability in tort? – relevant principles in establishing liability – examples of cases where liability has been imposed – remedies.

Suggested Solution

It would appear from the facts of the question that the Food Standards Agency is a creature of statute and hence is to be treated as a public body for all intents and purposes. Under common law, a public body owes a duty of care in respect of all its functions and obligations that affect others. Therefore, to establish negligence at common law on the basis of *Donoghue* v *Stevenson* [1932] AC 562 would be an easy task. But one is not dealing with the ordinary principles of common law. Rather, there is a statute, namely the Food Standards Act (FSA) 1999, which is the subject matter of the question. The FSA 1999 sets out the duties, functions and obligations of the Food Standards Agency. Thus, any liability on its part (the Agency's) must be determined on the basis of its breach of statutory duty.

The Food Standards Agency, it would seem, has essentially two basic statutory functions. One is to develop policies related to matters connected with food safety and other interests of consumers in relation to food, and the other involves the provision of advice, information and assistance in respect of such matters to any public authority.

The Agency therefore not only deals with consumers who are members of the public, but it also deals with public authorities and other corporations, such as manufacturers and producers. In discharging its statutory functions, the Agency has to balance both these interests so as to avoid any possible conflict. On the one hand, if it is not sufficiently interventionist, public health might be comprised, resulting in the outbreak of serious diseases. On the other, if it is too interventionist, it may damage the commercial interest of food producers, or even add to production costs unnecessarily. For example, in *Welton* v *North Cornwall District Council* [1997] 1 WLR 570 the local authority was held liable where an environmental health officer negligently required the owner of food premises to undertake unnecessary works to secure compliance with the Food Standards Act 1990. It is also arguable that where a public body takes on the role of providing a quasi-professional service, which corresponds to a service that might well be provided by the private sector (such as the provision of information, advice and assistance, for example), the authority can be liable for negligence in the provision of that service. In *E (A Minor)* v *Dorset County Council* [1995] 3 WLR 152, the House of Lords held that a local authority could be both directly liable in negligence and vicariously liable for the negligence of an educational psychologist in assessing a child's special educational needs.

The crucial point is not the breach of the statutory duty itself, but whether the breach gives rise to a cause of action in tort. The statute may expressly exclude a civil right, for example, as in the Post Office Act 1969 and the Guard Dogs Act 1975, or the statute may provide a cause of action where none previously existed, for instance as in the Race Relations Act 1976. However, it is quite common for the statute to be silent as to whether or not it gives rise to an action in tort. Therefore, it is for the courts to determine the intentions of Parliament by construing the words or provisions of the statute in question. There are two presumptions in this context. First, if the Act in question imposes a duty but provides no remedy for the breach, then the presumption is that the breach would give rise to an action in tort, as confirmed by the court in *Thornton* v *Kirklees Metropolitan Borough Council* [1979] QB 626. The second presumption is that if the Act provides a remedy (civil or criminal), then it is harder or more onerous to show that the breach gives rise to a cause of action in tort. Recently, in *Todd* v *Adams* [2002] 2 Lloyd's Rep 293, the Court of Appeal held that an action could not succeed in tort as the Act in question had already provided a remedy itself.

However, every case has to be decided on its own facts and merits, and the court has on previous occasions held that, notwithstanding a remedy within the statute, a civil action in tort was nonetheless possible: *Groves* v *Lord Wimborne* [1898] 2 QB 402.

As such, the Food Standards Agency, in exercising its statutory functions, ought to be vigilant and diligent so as not to fall below the standards of legitimate expectation. If a breach of duty of care at common law is actionable, then the breach of a statutory duty would impose a higher duty, perhaps even strict liability. For example, if the Agency develops a policy (negligently) which results in an outbreak of a serious disease amongst some consumers, then an action in tort for compensation would undoubtedly result. The claimant(s) would have to establish three things. First, the act which caused the damage is regulated by statute; second, the claimant(s) belong to the class of people which the Act intended to protect; and, third, the damage suffered is of the kind that the Act intended to prevent. These principles were highlighted and confirmed in the case of *Gorris* v *Scott* (1874) LR 9 Exch 125. As mentioned earlier, there is not a consistent or uniform principle which has been enunciated to determine the remedy in tort for a breach of statutory duty. The courts have said 'yes' in some cases and 'no' in others. Two principles, however, lie at the heart of this area. One is parliamentary intention and the second is judicial construction, or the interpretation of that intention.

The other related and relevant issue is whether there is any breach under the European Convention on Human Rights committed by these public bodies if they are found to be in breach of their statutory duty. The Human Rights Act 1998 now provides a remedy in respect of breaches of duty by a public body. In *Osman* v *United Kingdom* [1999] 1 FLR 193, the European Court of Human Rights strongly suggested that to impose 'no duty of care in tort' might be equivalent to the grant of an immunity to public bodies and local authorities. *Osman* was, of course, a controversial decision which attracted both judicial and academic criticism. The question in the end is for the courts to decide on the basis of what is just, fair and reasonable under the circumstances.

QUESTION THREE

The (fictitious) Industrial Premises (Alcohol Restriction) Regulations 1999 provide: 'No alcoholic substance shall be taken into or consumed within any premises to which these regulations apply'. The regulations apply to the premises of Goat & Sheep Ltd. Alf, who works at Goat & Sheep, buys four bottles of wine at lunchtime, brings them back to work and places them in a bag on top of the cabinet in the recreation room.

During the lunch break, Bill and Clive, who also work at Goat & Sheep, and Des, a lorry driver who has been delivering supplies there, are sitting in the recreation room throwing a frisbee to each other. When Bill throws the frisbee, it strikes the bag containing the wine bottles. They are shattered; broken glass falls on Clive and Des, who are cut, and each of them loses an eye.

Advise Clive and Des.

University of London LLB Examination
(for External Students) Law of Tort June 1999 Q6

General Comment

This is a question that requires candidates to sift through a number of possible claims in tort arising from the facts, and to concentrate on those which show the most promise. Note that the balance of the discussion should relate to breach of statutory duty rather than common law negligence.

Skeleton Solution

Breach of statutory duty – discuss whether the regulations might allow for the bringing of private civil actions in tort, either expressly or by presumption – examine the elements of a breach of statutory duty – identity of the defendant? – was a duty owed to the claimants? – were the injuries suffered of a type contemplated by the regulations? – did any breach of duty cause the damage complained of? – were Goat & Sheep Ltd vicariously liability for breach of statutory duty (if duty imposed only upon employees)? – liability in negligence – did Bill owe Clive and Des a duty of care, and if so, was it broken? – were Clive and Des contributory negligent? – was Alf negligent in leaving the bottles on top of the cabinet? – were Goat & Sheep Ltd vicariously liable for any negligence on the part of Alf or Bill? – employer's liability of Goat & Sheep Ltd?

Suggested Solution

Breach of statutory duty

The first issue to be decided in this question is whether a possible breach of the duty contained in the Industrial Premises (Alcohol Restriction) Regulations 1999 can give rise to private civil actions for breach of statutory duty in respect of the injuries suffered by Clive and Des. Such an action might lie against Goat & Sheep Ltd or Alf, depending upon whether the duty is imposed upon employers or employees. If a duty falls upon employees, there is the further question of whether Goat & Sheep Ltd can be vicariously liable for the breach of statutory duty of one of its employees.

Does an action for breach of statutory duty lie at all?

One possibility is that the regulations may expressly state whether or not civil liability will arise from their breach. If civil claims are possible, then it will be necessary to apply the elements of the tort. If not, then no action for breach of statutory duty will be possible.

If the regulations make no mention of the possibility of civil actions, then the court will have to determine whether, on their true construction, they were intended to confer a right of action in tort upon the claimant for their breach. The general rule was laid down by the House of Lords in *Lonrho Ltd v Shell Petroleum Co Ltd (No 2)* [1982] AC 173 . Where the legislation creates an obligation and a specified means for enforcing performance of that obligation, for example by criminal penalty, there is an initial presumption that performance cannot be enforced in any other way. However, as an exception to this general rule, the courts will presume a right of action for breach of statutory duty where an obligation has been imposed for the benefit of a class of people, such as employees. Such a right may be held to exist even if the legislation does provide for criminal penalties in the event of breach: *Groves v Lord Wimborne* [1898] 2 QB 402.

The Industrial Premises (Alcohol Restriction) Regulations 1999 are clearly designed to provide safety in employment and thus intended to benefit employees as a class of people. Even if the regulations do not expressly confer a right to bring a civil claim for their breach, there will certainly be a presumption to this effect.

Elements of breach of statutory duty: identity of the defendant

It is unclear from the brief quote from the regulations as to whether the duty is imposed upon employers (to prevent employees from bringing alcohol on to industrial premises and consuming it there) or upon employees, or both. This of course is a matter of interpretation. If the duty falls wholly upon employees, then an action for breach of statutory duty lies against Alf only. If, on the other hand, the duty falls wholly or partly upon employers, then Goat & Sheep Ltd are potentially liable.

Duty must be owed to the claimant

Assuming that the duty does fall upon employers, it seems likely that the regulations may only have been passed to benefit employees. Des is not an employee of Goat & Sheep Ltd. As such, only Clive would be able to claim in respect of a breach of the regulations. A similar result was arrived at by the court in *Hartley v Mayoh & Co* [1954] 1 QB 383 in which a fireman's widow was unable to claim for breach of statutory duty against the defendant, in whose factory her husband had been killed, because the regulations concerned only conferred a duty upon 'persons employed'.

Injury must be of a kind which the legislation is intended to prevent: Gorris *v* Scott *(1874) LR 9 Exch 125*

A further problem arises in respect of the manner in which Clive and Des's injuries occurred. It seems likely that the regulations were intended to prevent injuries sustained in the workplace caused by employees under the influence of alcohol, and not by accidents caused by the smashing of unattended bottles in incidents such as the one described. Clearly, the injuries suffered by Clive and Des would have been identical whether or not the bottles left on top of the cabinet contained alcohol. It is submitted that Clive and Des's injuries may therefore be of a type which these regulations were not intended to prevent. Such was the case in *Nicholls v Austin (F) (Leyton) Ltd* [1946] AC 493 in which a workman was unable to claim for breach of statutory duty under the Factories Act 1961 for injuries sustained when a component flew out of a machine whilst in use. The requirement that the machinery should be securely fenced was intended to prevent the workers from making contact with the machine and not vice versa.

However, Winfield and Jolowicz (*Tort* (16th edn, 2002) at p261) point out that the modern approach is not to apply this requirement too strictly, and that if the damage suffered by the claimant was of the kind that the regulations were designed to prevent, then it does not matter that the precise method by which the injuries occurred was not contemplated by the legislation. Such an approach would be consistent with the decision of the House of Lords in *Hughes v Lord Advocate* [1963] AC 837.

A breach of the legislation has caused the damage complained of

The duty is framed in absolute terms: 'no alcoholic substance shall be taken into' and therefore Alf's action in leaving the bag containing the wine in the recreation room appears to give rise to a breach of duty. The breach has certainly caused Clive and Des's injuries in fact, and it has already been pointed out above that according to Hughes, the injuries are unlikely to be regarded as too remote to recover for. However, it might be argued that the conduct of the claimants, Clive and Des, in playing frisbee in the recreation room was so unreasonable as to amount to a novus actus interveniens, breaking the chain of causation: *McKew v Holland & Hannen & Cubitts (Scotland) Ltd* [1969] 3 All ER 1621. It is more likely, however, that Clive and Des will be regarded as partly at fault for their loss, and that any damages awarded will be reduced according to an apportionment of blame under the Law Reform (Contributory Negligence) Act 1945.

Vicarious liability

If the regulations are construed as imposing duties upon employees, then the question arises as to whether Goat & Sheep Ltd could be held vicariously liable for Alf's breach of statutory duty. It has never been positively decided whether vicarious liability could exist in these circumstances, and the better approach may be for the courts to decide that a duty is imposed upon both employer and employee by the regulations. A major problem in the establishment of vicarious liability in this case is whether Alf can really be said to have been acting in the course of his employment when he brought alcohol onto Goat & Sheep Ltd's premises for his own purposes.

Negligence

Liability of Bill

It must first be considered whether Bill owes a duty of care to Clive and Des. The three part test to determine whether such a duty exists was stated in *Caparo Industries Ltd plc* v *Dickman* [1990] 2 AC 605. The first requirement is that the injuries suffered by the claimant must have been reasonably foreseeable, secondly that a close relationship of proximity existed between Bill and the claimants, and finally that it should be fair, just and reasonable in all the circumstances for the courts to impose a duty. It is arguable that a reasonable person would have foreseen some form of injury resulting from the throwing of a frisbee in an enclosed space, especially with glass or loose objects in the vicinity (although the wine bottles were concealed in a bag). The courts will readily hold that a relationship of proximity is present where physical injury has been sustained by the claimant, and it is relevant that a pre-existing relationship exists between the parties here. The most difficult element to satisfy in these circumstances is likely to be the fair, just and reasonable element of the duty test, although it is submitted that there are no specific policy considerations why Clive and Des should be denied a claim.

As to whether Bill's conduct fell below the standards to be expected of the reasonable person, it is submitted that the decision to participate indoors in an outdoor activity is in itself likely to give rise to a breach of duty to take reasonable care. It cannot be said that the risk of harm being inflicted is so unlikely that that no breach has taken place: *Bolton* v *Stone* [1951] AC 850.

No issues of causation appear to arise here. However, it is almost certainly the case that Clive and Des's voluntary involvement in the game will be regarded as a partial cause of the injuries they have suffered, and that any damages awarded will be reduced 'to such extent as the court thinks just and equitable having regard to the claimant's share in the responsibility for the damage': s1(1) Law Reform (Contributory Negligence) Act 1945. It will be for Bill to prove that Clive and Des's injuries resulted from a risk which their own fault or negligence exposed them to, and that this negligence contributed towards their injuries. It is submitted that the observations above relating to the existence of Bill's own breach of duty apply equally to Clive and Des, and that a court would probably regard them as being equally responsible for the injuries they suffered.

Once again, it is highly unlikely that Bill could be regarded as acting in the course of his employment at the time of this accident, and so Goat & Sheep Ltd are unlikely to be held vicariously liable for his negligence.

Liability of Alf

It is just possible that Alf might have been negligent in leaving the bottles on top of the cabinet, especially with seating in the vicinity. However, liability is much less likely to arise in Alf's case for the following reasons.

a) A duty of care is less likely to exist in that injuries to those in the recreation room are less foreseeable in the circumstances – unless Alf is aware that people play frisbee there, or the bottles are left in such a position that they might easily be knocked off the cabinet causing injury. It is also less likely that a court would think it fair, just and reasonable to impose a duty.

b) Novus actus interveniens arising from the independent and unreasonable actions of the claimants in playing frisbee indoors is more likely to be relevant here, breaking the chain of causation and relieving Alf of liability for Clive and Des's injuries.

c) Once again, Goat & Sheep Ltd are unlikely to be held vicariously liable for any negligence on the part of Alf. The leaving of the bottles of wine in the recreation room could hardly be described as taking place in the course of Alf's employment.

Employers' liability of Goat & Sheep Ltd

Whilst employers owe certain non-delegable duties to their staff, such as the duty to provide competent fellow employees and a safe system of working, it is submitted that it is highly unlikely that Goat & Sheep Ltd could be in breach of any of these requirements as they are, no doubt, unaware of their employees activities in the recreation room.

QUESTION FOUR

Richard worked as a gardener with the Peony District Council. He was planting out a bed of rose bushes which the council had purchased from the Floribunda Nurseries. The bushes had been treated with a spray to repel greenfly. It is known that a number of people react to the spray for some days after it has been applied. Richard began to feel breathless, but, before anyone could come to his assistance, he had collapsed. It appears that he is abnormally allergic to the spray. He has suffered permanent brain damage. He is happy and in no physical pain but is unable to look after himself, to work or to pursue his hobby of darts. His mother Stella has given up her job in a supermarket to look after him, but she is quite elderly and it is expected that Richard will eventually have to go into a home.

Advise Richard (a) as to any claims he may have in tort and (b) as to the assessment of damages.

University of London LLB Examination
(for External Students) Law of Tort June 1998 Q6

General Comment

It is important for candidates to note the ambiguity in the facts of this question. It is not made clear whether it was the council or the nursery who were responsible for the spraying of the rosebushes, and the precise nature of liability would have varied accordingly. Candidates could have chosen to deal with employers' liability first, although it might have been more logical initially to consider Floribunda's liability for the possible supply of a defective product. This is because an employer's vicarious liability for the provision of defective equipment depends upon the fault of the third party who supplied it.

Skeleton Solution

Product liability – examine Floribunda's potential liability under the Consumer Protection Act 1987 – is a rosebush a 'product' within the meaning of the Act? – discuss the possibility of liability at common law under the narrow rule in *Donoghue* v *Stevenson* – employers' liability – is Peony vicariously liable for providing Richard with defective equipment under the Employers' Liability (Defective Equipment) Act 1969? – is a rosebush 'equipment' within the meaning of the Act? – if Peony was responsible for the spraying of the rosebush, are they in breach of their non-delegable duty to provide a safe system of working? – the assessment of damages – identify the aim of damages in tort and explain the heads of loss relevant to Richard's circumstances, under which damages will be awarded – make particular reference to future loss of earnings, the provision of care by a relative and loss of amenity.

Suggested Solution

a) *Claims in tort: liability for defective products – Floribunda Nurseries*

If, as seems likely, Florinbunda were themselves responsible for growing the rose bushes and for spraying them with the greenfly repellent, the question arises as to Floribunda's liability as producers of a defective product. Section 2(1) Consumer Protection Act 1987 provides that 'where any damage is caused wholly or partly by a defect in a product, every person to whom subsection (2) … applies shall be liable for the damage'. Section 2(2) lists a number of potential defendants, including the producer of the product, further defined in s1(2)(c) as including a person who carried out (for example in relation to agricultural products) an industrial or other process.

An immediate problem for Richard here is that agricultural products, defined in s1(2) as including 'any produce of the soil' are excluded from the provisions of the Act unless they have undergone an 'industrial process' before supply. The definition is aimed at the processing of raw foodstuffs so that, for example, the processing of meet into beef burgers would be caught by the provisions of the Act. It is submitted that the mere spraying of agricultural produce would not be regarded as an industrial process, and so the rosebushes are not 'products' for the purposes of the Act. If the spraying of crops were to be regarded as an industrial process, the exemption of agricultural produce from the provisions of the Act would be meaningless and ineffective.

Common law

The so-called narrow rule laid down by Lord Atkin in *Donoghue* v *Stevenson* [1932] AC 562 imposes a duty on manufacturers of products to the ultimate consumer in certain circumstances:

> '… a manufacturer of products, which he sells in such a form as to show that he intends them to reach the ultimate consumer in the form in which they left him, with no reasonable possibility of intermediate examination, and with the knowledge that

the absence of reasonable care in the preparation or putting up of the products will result in an injury to the consumer's life or property, owes a duty to the consumer to take that reasonable care.'

The duty as originally defined has been extended in many respects, and could apply to Richard's circumstances for the following reasons.

i) Whilst the grower of plants might not be regarded as a 'manufacturer' in the traditional sense, the duty has been extended to cover a range of persons who create dangers in relation to products, such as repairers, erectors and builders. It is submitted that growers would also fall within the scope of the duty.

ii) The duty, whilst originally relating to food and drink, has been held to apply to a range of products, eg tombstones and cars, so rosebushes are presumably covered.

iii) The duty extends to the ultimate user of the product as well as those within close proximity of it. It is submitted that Richard, as a gardener who plants the product, is within sufficiently close proximity to come within the scope of the duty.

iv) The possibility of an 'intermediate examination' of the rosebushes by Richard is unlikely to exonerate the nursery. The presence of a chemical residue on a plant could not be discovered by a reasonable examination, unless a specific warning had been provided: *Andrews v Hopkinson* [1957] 1 QB 229.

v) It will be for Richard to prove that the nursery failed to take reasonable care by spraying the rosebushes with a dangerous insect repellent. This should not cause any great difficulty. If it can be shown that the Council were not responsible for the spraying, then on the balance of probabilities, it must have been Floribunda who did so. In view of the known risks associated with this particular insect repellent, a finding of breach of duty appears likely.

vi) Richard's abnormal sensitivity to the spray does not render the serious physical injuries he sustained too remote from any negligence on the part of Floribunda. A tortfeasor takes his victim as he finds him. So long as physical injury was foreseeable (there were known risks of adverse reactions to this chemical spray lasting some days after application) the claimant can recover damages, even if the extent of those injuries could not have been foreseen: *Smith v Leech, Brain & Co* [1962] 2 QB 405.

It would appear that Richard's claim in respect of a defective product would therefore lie in common law negligence, rather than under the Consumer Protection Act 1987, due to the exclusion of agricultural products from the scope of the latter.

Liability of Peony District Council as employers

Peony District Council's liability to Richard as his employer will depend upon who was responsible for the application of the insect repellent. If the nursery were responsible for the spraying, then Peony may be vicariously liable for the supply of defective 'equipment' attributable to the fault of a third party under s1(1) Employers' Liability (Defective Equipment) Act 1969. If the spray was applied by the Council, then it would be more appropriate to consider whether Peony were in breach of their non-delegable common law duty to provide a safe system of work.

Employers' Liability (Defective Equipment) Act 1969

Section 1(1) states that:

> 'Where …
>
> (a) an employee suffers personal injury in the course of his employment in consequence of a defect in equipment provided by his employer for the purposes of his employer's business; and
>
> (b) the defect is attributable wholly or partly to the fault of a third party (whether identified or not),
>
> the injury shall be deemed to be also attributable to negligence on the part of the employer.'

In other words, the Council will be vicariously liable for defective equipment supplied to Richard for the purposes of his job, if the defect arose through the fault of Floribunda Nurseries.

The main issue here is whether a rosebush could be said to be 'equipment' within the meaning of the Act. Section 1(3) defines 'equipment' as 'any plant and machinery, vehicle, aircraft and clothing'. In fact, the courts have adopted a wide, purposive approach to the interpretation of this section. For example, in *Knowles* v *Liverpool City Council* [1993] 4 All ER 321 the House of Lords held that a flagstone, which broke whilst being handled by an employee, causing personal injury, should be regarded as equipment even though it was, in fact, 'material upon which the employee used the equipment'. Thus it is clearly arguable that a rosebush, which will have been planted with the use of gardening tools, should be regarded as 'equipment' within the meaning of the Act. If Richard can show that the spray residue caused his injury and that there must, on the balance of probabilities, have been negligence on the part of Floribunda Nurseries (see above), then the Council as well as Floribunda will be liable to him, even though the Council were not to blame.

Safe system of work

If Peony District Council was responsible for the application of the greenfly repellent, then there is likely to have been a breach of their duty as employers to take reasonable care in devising and operating a safe system of work. Such a breach of duty would arise from the use of a known allergen to spray the bushes rather than some safer alternative, and the failure to provide adequate warnings, instructions and personal protective equipment to those employees handling the plants which have been sprayed with the substance. As explained above, Richard's abnormal sensitivity to the spray residue will not render the serious physical injuries he sustained too remote from any negligence on the part of his employer.

b) *The assessment of damages*

Any award of damages will be payable as a lump sum, unless the parties were to agree to a structured settlement. The aim of such an award will be to restore Richard, in so far as money will allow, to the position he was in before the tort(s) took place. An award of damages is usually considered in two parts: 'special damages' covering precisely calculable losses, normally arising pre-trial, and 'general damages', which are not capable of precise mathematical calculation and normally arise post-trial. It is also customary to classify losses sustained as being either pecuniary or non-pecuniary in nature.

Pecuniary losses: loss of earnings

This will include any loss of Richard's earnings both before and after trial. The large part of the award will be for loss of salary post-trial, as Richard is now unemployable on a long-term basis. Any award will include prospective earnings during any 'lost years' due to a reduced life expectancy and loss of pension rights associated with a future loss of salary.

The court will award Richard a lump sum which, when invested, will be sufficient to produce an income equal to the loss of his future salary. The calculation is approached in two stages. The court will first assess Richard's net annual loss, by taking his gross earnings at the date of the accident, but also making an allowance for the possibility of an increase in pay or for promotion. Once this sum has been calculated, a deduction will be made for the income tax and social security contributions he would have paid on his earnings.

The court will then select a multiplier based upon the likely duration of the disability. However, this will not be the same as the number of years Richard would have worked before retirement, because the courts apply a reduction to take account of the possibility that future events might have cut his working life short, eg early death or unemployment. A reduction is also applied to take account of the fact that a lump sum payment will produce an investment income of its own.

Medical expenses reasonably incurred

This includes the cost of nursing care and travel expenses to and from hospital. The cost of nursing care provided by Stella can be recovered by Richard himself: *Hunt* v *Severs* [1994] 2 All ER 385. In *Housecroft* v *Burnett* [1986] 1 All ER 332 it was decided that where a relative gives up work to look after the claimant, the court will award reasonable recompense to the carer, but the ceiling on such an award is the commercial rate for providing such care. It is unlikely that Stella would be paid more than her existing salary whilst she is still able to look after Richard, if her current salary is less than the commercial rate of remuneration for professional nursing care. However, a full commercial rate ought to be recoverable for the years during which Richard will have to spend in a home. The damages awarded in respect of the carer will be held on trust for Stella by Richard: *Cunningham* v *Harrison*

[1973] QB 942. Further deductions will be made to reflect any social security benefits that Richard has received as a result of his injuries since the accident.

Non-pecuniary losses

Richard's non-pecuniary losses include his loss of amenity, ie the loss of capacity to engage in activities which he enjoyed before trial (playing darts) and compensation for his actual injuries. The amounts awarded under these heads are usually assessed by reference to past cases. An award would usually be made for any pain and suffering endured by the claimant; however, Richard appears to be perfectly happy and in no pain, and so damages are unlikely to be awarded under this head.

Finally, Richard will receive interest on the lump sum payment reflecting the lapse in time between the accident and the trial.

QUESTION FIVE

Statutory regulations impose upon employers and employees in the chemical manufacturing industry an obligation to ensure that prescribed protective equipment (including special gloves) are worn when workers are handling chemicals. The regulations apply to the premises of Stinks Ltd. George, Hamish and John, who are all employed there, were engaged in loading chemicals on to a lorry and were all wearing the prescribed clothing. George and Hamish were passing casks containing chemicals up to John who was standing on the back of the lorry. A fly went into John's eye suddenly and he removed his glove to wipe it away. George did not notice and passed a cask up to him. John was unable to hold it. Some of the chemical spilled over his hand. He screamed in agony and clung on to Hamish in desperation.

John suffered serious burns to his hand. He will be permanently disfigured and will not be able to obtain manual employment. Hamish has suffered from severe depression since the incident and has not been able to return to work.

University of London LLB Examination
(for External Students) Law of Tort June 1994 Q7

General Comment

This question is specifically addressed as a possible breach of statutory duty, although it could be argued that the employer owed a like duty in the tort of negligence. The importance of the dual heads of liability is that the statutory duty could be pitched at a higher level than the duty of care in negligence. The question does not indicate the level of duty imposed by the regulations, but suggests that the duty is one of 'strict liability'. Similarly, the question does not actually specify what is required of the student, and this answer is based on the presumption that John and Hamish require advice on liability and assessment of damages.

Skeleton Solution

The concept of employers' liability – statutory duty and strict liability – distinction between strict liability and liability for negligent acts or omissions – method of assessment of damages in personal injuries cases.

Suggested Solution

If John and Hamish are to rely on the tort of negligence as the basis of their claim against their employer, they face an onerous task.

An employer owes certain duties to his employees. Those duties are derived from both common law and statutory sources. For many years an employer was not liable for injury negligently inflicted by another employee on the ground that the employee had consented to the risks involved in his employment: *Bartonshill Coal Co* v *Reid* (1858) 3 Macq 266. This doctrine was finally abolished by s1 of the Law Reform (Personal Injuries) Act 1948.

The employer may now be vicariously liable for the negligence of his employee committed in the course of his employment or for breach of his own non-delegable duty.

In the question set, any negligence appears to be limited to (a) John removing his glove; (b) George failing to notice and passing him a cask; and (c) John clinging on to Hamish in desperation. The question does not specifically ask, but it must be presumed that John wishes to claim damages for his burns injury, and Hamish for his depression and loss of earnings.

I will first address John's potential claim. As against his employer, a claim would lie for the negligence, if any, of George, for which the employer would be vicariously liable, and for the primary negligence of the employer for failing to provide a safe system of work: see *General Cleaning Contractors* v *Christmas* [1953] AC 180.

John will be in great difficulty if he is to claim negligence in respect of either of these heads of allegedly negligent acts. There is nothing to suggest that George was negligent in passing the cask up in circumstances where he and Hamish were engaged in an ongoing process of 'passing casks' to John. That is a matter open to argument on the facts.

Similarly, the employer appears to have discharged his duty to provide a safe system of work by providing gloves.

However, John may have a claim for breach of statutory duty, namely the regulations cited in the question. The duty imposed was an 'obligation to ensure that prescribed protective clothing (including special gloves) are worn when workers are handling chemicals'. If that duty is strict, it matters not that the act of a fly causing John to suddenly remove his glove to wipe his eye was in no way the fault of the employer.

It will be left to the court to determine whether these regulations afford a remedy to an individual employee who suffers injury as a result of breach: *Cutler* v *Wandsworth Stadium Ltd* [1949] AC 398. The court will look to see if the regulations specifically provide for a remedy, and if not, will determine whether the regulations are directed at protecting a class of persons as opposed to society as a whole.

In this case, the effect of the regulation is to provide protection to employees in John's position, and it is highly likely that the court would find that he is entitled to a personal remedy, namely compensation, if the employer breached the duty: *John Summers & Sons Ltd* v *Frost* [1955] AC 740.

Volenti is not a defence to breach of an employer's statutory duty. However, the defence that the employer did all that was reasonably practicable is often provided in regulations: see *Larner* v *British Steel plc* [1993] 1 All ER 102.

There is no information in the question as to whether such a defence is provided in the regulations in issue. If not, it will be assumed that the liability is strict. In view of the unexpected way in which John came to remove his gloves, nothing short of strict liability will assist him. I do not think he has a claim in negligence, nor for breach of statutory duty if the employer's liability is limited to doing what is reasonably practicable.

It should be noted that a person who is the subject of a statutory duty cannot generally discharge that duty by entrusting it to someone else.

Presuming that the duty is strict, it is clear that the breach of duty (ie not ensuring that the gloves were worn for that short period during which John suffered the injury) caused John's injury, and he would therefore be able to claim damages.

The issue of contributory negligence arises, and would go to reduce the employer's liability in a negligence claim, and arguably a breach of statutory duty claim. Although the courts are very reluctant to find contributory negligence in employer/employee cases, as the regulations are designed to protect the employees (see *Caswell* v *Powell Duffryn Associated Collieries Ltd* [1940] AC 152), they will do so if the employee has himself been very foolish or fails himself to comply with the regulations, as in *Bux* v *Slough Metals Ltd* [1974] 1 All ER 262 where an employee removed protective goggles which were misted up.

John's reason for removing his gloves is apparently more legitimate, and verging as it does on an 'emergency' or instinctive situation (see eg *Jones* v *Boyce* (1816) 1 Stark 493), it is unlikely that there would be any finding of contributory negligence.

Hamish's claim is in some respects similar to John's, in that he will only have a claim if the duty is a strict one. He has an added difficulty in that he has to prove that the breach of statutory duty regarding John wearing gloves caused his loss, and that the loss suffered is a recoverable loss.

In terms of causation, the employer will perhaps argue that John's act of grabbing Hamish was a 'novus actus', breaking the chain of causation instituted by the initial breach. The court may well take the view that injury by chemicals, and specifically, by shock brought about by seeing the effects of a chemicals-related injury, was foreseeable, so not too remote. Lord Reid in *Hughes* v *Lord Advocate* [1963] AC 837 said:

> '... a defendant is liable, although the damage may be a good deal greater in extent that was foreseeable. He can only escape liability if the damage can be regarded as differing in kind from what was foreseeable.'

Finally, for Hamish to succeed his 'depression' must fall into the recognised category of 'nervous shock', in that it must be more than simply grief and sorrow and must be a pathological nervous injury: see *Brice* v *Brown* [1984] 1 All ER 997.

If the extent of his depression is of a clinical nature, he will be able to recover if he falls into the category of persons whose relationship to the primary injured person is sufficiently close to justify the imposition of liability on the tortfeasor. The test of proximity has been recognised in several cases, and it is submitted that a worker whose co-employee grabs hold of him whilst the two are engaged in a joint task is sufficiently proximate for his nervous shock to be foreseeable.

In conclusion, the cases of John and Hamish hinge on the degree of liability attaching to the regulations. If strict, their claims have a good chance of success. If there is a statutory defence within the particular regulations of 'reasonable practicability', I feel that their respective claims will fail.

Chapter 10

Product Liability

10.1 Introduction

10.2 Key points

10.3 Key cases and statute

10.4 Questions and suggested solutions

10.1 Introduction

Liability in law for defective products has undergone two major changes: the first was in 1932 when *Donoghue* v *Stevenson* exploded the 'contract fallacy' and the second was the passing of the Consumer Protection Act 1987.

10.2 Key points

Common law position

The Consumer Protection Act 1987 has not repealed the common law rules on defective products which must still be considered.

a) Note the explosion of the 'contract fallacy' in *Donoghue* v *Stevenson* [1932] AC 562 and Lord Atkin's statement: 'A manufacturer of products, which he sells in such a form as to show that he intends them to reach the ultimate consumer in the form in which they left him with no reasonable possibility of intermediate examination, and with the knowledge that the absence of reasonable care in the preparation, or putting up of the products will result in an injury to the consumer's life or property, owes a duty to the consumer to take reasonable care.'

b) The statement has been extended from manufacturers to any supplier who is under a duty to inspect the goods.

c) Note the wide meaning attributed to 'products' and 'consumers' and the meaning of 'reasonable probability of intermediate examination': *Grant* v *Australian Knitting Mills* [1936] AC 85.

d) An express warning of the danger will discharge the manufacturer's duty: *Kubach* v *Hollands* [1937] 3 All ER 907.

e) Since *Aswan Engineering Establishment* v *Lupdine* [1987] 1 All ER 135 it is clear that the damage covered is that to other property of the consumer; if the defect only renders the goods less valuable then any claim is in contract (see Chapter 5).

f) The manufacturer's duty is to take reasonable care, and the claimant usually proves lack of care by showing that the defect arose in manufacture because nothing that happened to the product after it left the manufacturer could have caused the defect: *Mason* v *Williams & Williams* [1955] 1 WLR 549. However, if the product has been handled and used for some time this may be difficult: *Evans* v *Triplex Safety Glass* [1936] 1 All ER 283.

Statutory position

a) The general principle of the Consumer Protection Act 1987 is found in s2: 'Where any damage is caused wholly or partly by a defect in a product, every person to whom subsection (2) applies shall be liable for the damage'.

Subsection (2) applies to the producer, the importer into the European Community and sometimes the supplier of the goods.

Note the extended definition of producer, and those situations in which the supplier may be held liable.

b) By s3(1) a defective product is one in which the safety of the product is not such as persons generally are entitled to expect. Obviously any product is capable of being misused in an unsafe manner (eg a kitchen knife), so note the guidelines in s3(2) as to what matters shall be taken into account.

c) The Act allows various defences in s4. The most important are that the defect did not exist in the product at the relevant time and the 'state of the art defence' ie 'that the state of scientific and technical knowledge at the relevant time was not such that a producer of products of the same description as the product in question might be expected to have discovered the defect if it had existed in his products while they were under his control'. In *EC Commission* v *United Kingdom (Re Product Liability Directive)* Case C–300/95 [1997] 3 CMLR 923, the ECJ dealt with this defence of 'development risks'.

This defence is likely to be very important with, for example, drug manufacturers and side effects. The defendant must prove this defence, ie he must prove that the defect was not one a producer might be expected to discover. Thus the manufacturer will only be liable if he knew or reasonably ought to have known of the defect which is just what the claimants would have to prove in negligence. The only practical difference is that under s4 the burden of proof lies on the defendant while in negligence it would lie on the claimant. (Note the state of the art defence in s4(2)(e) is much wider than that allowed in the original EC Directive 85/374/EEC art 7(a), and there is still debate between the UK government and the European Commission as to whether or not the UK has validly enacted the Directive, which could give rise to problems as to which state of the art defence a defendant could actually rely on.)

d) The claimant must still prove causation, although there is no requirement of foreseeability.

e) By s5 the damage covered is death or personal injury to the claimant or damage to his private property other than the product itself.

f) The Act does not apply to damage below £275, and liability under s2(1) cannot be excluded or restricted.

10.3 Key cases and statute

- *Donoghue* v *Stevenson* [1932] AC 562
  Producers owe a duty of care to the ultimate consumer

- *EC Commission* v *United Kingdom (Re Product Liability Directive)* Case C–300/95 [1997] 3 CMLR 923
  The Commission dealt with the technical defence of 'development risks'

- *Grant* v *Australian Knitting Mills Ltd* [1936] AC 85
  The duty of care is subject to qualifications

- *Kubach* v *Hollands* [1937] 3 All ER 907
  A warning on the product may in circumstances discharge the manufacturers' duty of care

- Consumer Protection Act 1987 – sets out the definitive framework in relation to consumer protection and manufacturers' liability

10.4 Questions and suggested solutions

QUESTION ONE

Discuss the following cases.

a) A supermarket chain sells many lines under its own brand name 'Salmonella'. Peggy buys a packet, labelled 'Salmonella sliced apples. Produce of England. Vacuum packed. Suitable for home freezing. Freeze immediately on purchase. Eat within three months.' Peggy puts them in her home freezer as soon as she gets home two hours after she has purchased them. She uses them two months later. She and her daughter Queenie suffer severe food poisoning which is traced to the apple slices.

b) Ruth buys in England some marker pens manufactured by Ecoli GmbH in Germany. Her teenage son Simon uses the red and white pens to paint a St George's Cross on his face before he joins the spectators at an international soccer match. The red pen contains a pigment which causes a severe rash and itching on Simon's face, which persists for several months.

University of London LLB Examination
(for External Students) Law of Tort June 1997 Q5

General Comment

The question is clearly concerned with processed or manufactured products which have caused personal injury to persons who could be described as 'consumers'. Some analysis of the terms of the Consumer Protection Act (CPA) 1987 is called for and, perhaps, some comment on the improved situation under the CPA 1987 as against the common law.

Skeleton Solution

Scope of the Act and incidence of liability, type of product – producers, suppliers and liability to person supplied and others – nature of the damage and 'defects'; range of recoverable damage – defences.

Suggested Solution

a) Peggy and Queenie have both suffered personal injury as a result of eating apple slices which, by reason of having been machine sliced and packaged, could be said to be a 'product'. This is very important because it brings the matter within the general sphere of product liability as compared with untreated, unprocessed, agricultural produce which is governed by an altogether looser regime imposed by the law of sale of goods and the common law. The Consumer Protection Act (CPA) 1987 provides a very comprehensive and effective type of strict liability where damage has been caused by a 'defect' in a product in a 'consumer' situation. Section 2(4) implies that agricultural produce which has 'undergone an industrial process' is within the ambit of the Act.

The incidence of liability is set out in s2(2) and (3) and it clearly attaches to the 'producer' (s2(2)(a)) and others who hold themselves, by brand or mark, out as the producer (s2(2)(b)), thus catching the supermarket chain. The chain will also be caught as a 'supplier' within s2(3) regardless of the fact that they did not supply the goods direct to Queenie. This express inclusion of suppliers goes a long way towards remedying the severe limitations on the liability of suppliers which were imposed by the common law and only partly remedied by the 'manufacturer's role' in *Donoghue* v *Stevenson* [1932] AC 562.

Section 2(3) also shows that the basis of liability is damage 'caused wholly or partly by a defect in a product'. Clearly, there is no room for foreseeability here and the damage, once causation has been established, is strict so it is obvious that one great drawback with the foreseeability-based common law approach has been removed; the problem from *Evans* v *Triplex Safety Glass Co Ltd* [1936] 1 All ER 283 has disappeared. A 'defect' is defined by s3(1) as meaning that 'the safety of the product is not such as persons generally are entitled to expect', with s3(2) going on to highlight particular circumstances which need to be taken into account in considering what 'persons generally are entitled to expect'.

The instructions on the package (s3(2)(a)) may be adequate, but it is a question of fact whether there is enough information about the need to maintain the vacuum or otherwise for the safety of the consumer. Apart from that, there is the possibility that a two-hour delay, particularly if temperatures were high during the two hours, might have affected matters. But a one- to two-hour delay ought, perhaps, to be anticipated by a producer. In all other respects, the food has been used in accordance with the instructions and there are strong indications of a defect. The range of recoverable damages clearly contemplates personal injury (ss3(1) and 5(3)), but not loss in respect of the product itself (s5(2)), and the liability cannot be ousted by disclaimers, notice etc: s7.

The liability is strict, but not absolute, so the statutory defences within s4 must be considered. The vitally important point about s4 is that the legal burden of proof of the defence is placed upon the defendant producer/supplier by s4(1). The only defence that seems able to be run by the defendant in this case is that in s4(1)(d), ie 'that the object did not exist in the product at the relevant time', the relevant time here being the time of supply. This will be a heavy burden for the chain to discharge in the circumstances.

b) The marker pen is clearly a 'product' and the incidence of liability will apply to the 'producer', Ecoli GmbH: s2(2)(a). This provision is likely to apply to the UK supplier if it fails, on request for information about the manufacturer by Simon as the person who suffers damage, to supply details: s2(3)(b). If the supplier were liable, the liability of producer and supplier would be joint and several. As outlined above, the supply to a person other than the damaged person does not matter provided that there was a supply 'to another' (s4(1)(b)) and that it was a normal business supply: s4(1)(c).

There could be some real difficulties in establishing that there is a 'defect' within s3 in that it is highly likely that the marker pens carried some sort of warning against using on skin. If they did not, there is likely to be an argument that there should be a warning unless Simon has a highly sensitive skin. The express requirement under s3(2)(b) to consider 'what might reasonably be expected to be done with or in relation to the product' would seem to indicate against there being a defect.

The type of damage is within the range of the Act, but if the evidence showed that appropriate medical testing had failed to indicate such a reaction, ie Simon was hypersensitive, the 'development risks' defence within s4(1)(e) might well be relied upon. The Act seems to be working very well in that there is almost a complete absence of case law on the 'defects' provisions, so closer analysis of high-sensitivity complainants must necessarily await judicial examination of the Act.

Neither (a) nor (b) above seem to fall outside the Act so it is not necessary to consider the residual common law jurisdiction which will now mainly apply to non-consumer situations.

QUESTION TWO

Geoffrey, a student, took a holiday job last summer as a gardener at Barsetshire Hall, a stately home owned by Lord Trollope. He was working one day using a rake which had been manufactured by Dudtools plc and recently purchased by Lord Trollope from a reputable supplier. When he had finished work, he discovered that the door of the toolshed had stuck. As he was in a hurry, he tried to pull it open using the prongs of the rake. After a few moments the shaft of the rake split and a large splinter pierced the palm of his hand. Because of a rare blood condition (of which he had until then been unaware), he suffered very severe poisoning and lost a year before he could return to his university studies.

Advise Geoffrey as to any causes of action in tort (a) against Dudtools plc and (b) against Lord Trollope.

How (if at all) would it affect your answer if Geoffrey had known of the blood condition and had told Lord Trollope at the time he took the job?

University of London LLB Examination
(for External Students) Law of Tort June 1996 Q4

General Comment

The question raises issues of Lord Trollope's liability as an employer and also issues of manufacturer's liability for defective products. The final part of the question requires consideration on issues of contributory negligence and volenti.

Skeleton Solution

Dudtools' liability: under the Consumer Protection Act 1987 and at common law; defences – Lord Trollope's liability: safe plant and equipment; volenti and contributory negligence.

Suggested Solution

Geoffrey will wish to show that Dudtools plc are liable for the defective rake. One should first look to the Consumer Protection Act (CPA) 1987 to see if Geoffrey is afforded any statutory protection by it. The rake is clearly a product or 'goods' for the purposes of s1(2) of the Act, and the loss suffered, personal injury, is also covered under s5(1) of the Act. Geoffrey will then have to establish that the damage was caused wholly or partly by a defect in the rake. The standard laid down in s3 of the Act is that the safety of the product must be such as 'persons generally are entitled to expect'. One of the relevant factors in assessing whether the product has achieved this standard is 'what might reasonably be expected to be done with ... the product'. It is here that Geoffrey may experience some difficulties, for it would seem that the rake was not manufactured for the purpose of opening jammed doors. It is arguable, however, that the rake might be expected to be robust enough to cope with general wear and tear of work in the garden. A lot would depend here on the individual facts of the case, eg whether the rake was a plastic garden rake or a heavier hay rake. In any case Geoffrey will have to establish that his injuries are a result of a particular defect in the rake, and not his application of too much force on the rake.

Assuming Geoffrey would be able to establish this, we will consider the defences available to Dudtools. Section 4 of the Act lays down a number of statutory defences to an action for defective products. None of these defences seems to be applicable here. The development risks defence laid down in s4(1) has regard to the state of scientific knowledge at the time of manufacture, but this relates to the defect in the rake, not to Geoffrey's condition, and would be irrelevant unless the defect was caused by something very obscure and untraceable. The defence of volenti would also be inapplicable – as Geoffrey was not aware of the extent of the risk of poisoning, he could not have consented to it. The key issue here is what caused the injury: was it Geoffrey's carelessness, or a defect in the rake? Were it to be the former, Geoffrey would not recover, and were it to be the latter Dudtools would have no defence. The evidence points to a conclusion half way between these positions, ie that the injuries were caused by some defect in the rake, coupled with some fault or carelessness on Geoffrey's part. I would advise, then, that Geoffrey would recover a reduced amount of damages in an action against Dudtools, by virtue of the Law Reform (Contributory Negligence) Act 1945. There is also a possibility of a common law action against Dudtools on *Donoghue v Stevenson* [1932] AC 562 principles. However, if anything the standard of care required at common law from a manufacturer is lower than that required under the CPA 1987 (hence the raison d'être of the Act itself) and so Geoffrey's case would be no stronger. Had Geoffrey known of his condition I would submit that this would have the effect of weakening his claim against Dudtools, as he should have taken more care in the circumstances.

Geoffrey's claim against Lord Trollope will be governed by the duty of care owed by an employer to his employee. The extent of this duty was defined most notably in *Wilsons & Clyde Coal v English* [1938] AC 57. One aspect of this is the duty to provide adequate plant and equipment. Geoffrey will argue that there has been a breach here in that both the shed door and the rake constitute defective plant and equipment. The standard of care required of an employer is the same as that in negligence, ie he is required to take reasonable care, effectively therefore Lord Trollope is obliged to inspect and check the equipment thoroughly enough to spot a defect: *Murphy v Phillips* (1876) 35 LT 477. It may be the case that the defects would not have been discoverable even on a thorough investigation, in which case Lord Trollope would not be liable – this argument would seem stronger in relation to the rake than to the door. Again much will depend on the circumstances surrounding the injury, but there is an arguable case that the equipment is defective.

Assuming Lord Trollope has been in breach of the duty outlined above, the question arises as to whether the loss sustained is too remote a consequence of the breach, as the blood condition is unknown to Lord Trollope. Although Lord Trollope could not have predicted the extent of the injuries caused, due to his ignorance of Geoffrey's condition, the so-called 'eggshell skull rule' will apply here. The rule dictates that as long as some damage to the person is a foreseeable consequence of negligence it generally does not matter that the precise nature and extent of the damage were unforeseeable: *Dulieu* v *White & Sons* [1901] 2 KB 669. A narrower approach was taken in *Tremain* v *Pike* [1969] 1 WLR 1556 where the claimant contracted Weil's disease while employed by the defendants. The disease is very rare and caused when human beings come into contact with rats' urine. There was no evidence that the defendants were aware of the possibility of the disease being contracted and it was held that the defendants were not liable as the damage suffered was 'entirely different in kind' from that which could have been foreseen by the defendants. The Court of Appeal has more recently disapproved this decision in the similar (contract) case of *H Parsons Ltd* v *Uttley Ingham & Co* [1978] QB 791. Lord Denning stated in *Parsons* that the issue of foreseeability applied equally in contract and tort, so this case would imply that the damage suffered by Geoffrey would not be considered too remote in that some injury would be a foreseeable consequence of the provision of a defective door or rake, if it can be established that Lord Trollope failed to inspect the equipment adequately.

As with Geoffrey's potential claim against Dudtools, the court may choose to reduce damages because of Geoffrey's partial fault under the Law Reform (Contributory Negligence) Act 1945, and will reduce the amount according to the relative fault of Geoffrey, although the courts apply this provision reluctantly in employment cases: *Caswell* v *Powell Duffryn Associated Collieries* [1940] AC 152, which indicates that Geoffrey may fare better in his action against Lord Trollope than against Dudtools in this respect. Finally, had Geoffrey known about his condition this would work against him only as regards the defence of volenti. Had he not known of the disease, the defence cannot be established, as he could not consent to a risk he knew nothing about. Where he knew about the condition it is arguable that he knew of the risk and therefore assumed it. This presumes, however, that Geoffrey's knowledge of his blood condition extends to the knowledge that a splinter would cause him such severe poisoning, which would seem unlikely. Furthermore the courts are reluctant to allow the defence of volenti in employment cases (*Smith* v *Baker & Sons* [1891] AC 325) as employees may be under understandable pressures to accept risks at work which they would not normally accept in other situations. This would make it less likely that Lord Trollope could establish a defence of volenti, although Geoffrey's knowledge could increase the court's assessment of fault on his part, and thereby reduce the damages.

QUESTION THREE

Fanny and Gordon were married last year. They received a very expensive record player and stereo system manufactured by Botchit Ltd as a wedding present from Henry, a business associate of Fanny's father. For the first few weeks the equipment caused much trouble. There were unexplained surges of power and the equipment would cut out. The service engineer reported (correctly) that the motor was faulty and could not be repaired. They had to buy a new motor unit at considerable expense.

Two months later smoke started to pour from the turntable. It seems that the original surges of power had damaged the turntable drive, which had now started to overheat when in use. Fanny and Gordon had to buy a new turntable and had to buy new curtains and redecorate the room as the smoke had destroyed the original curtains and decorations.

Fanny and Gordon do not know where Harry bought the equipment and do not want to tell him that his present has caused such trouble. Advise them whether they have a remedy against Botchit Ltd.

University of London LLB Examination
(for External Students) Law of Tort June 1993 Q2

General Comment

This question concerns liability for defective products and is a fairly straightforward problem. Much of the question concerns the Consumer Protection Act 1987 but it is also necessary to consider the position at common law.

Skeleton Solution

Consumer Protection Act 1987: who is a producer?; what is a product?; what is a defect?; what damage is covered?; are there any defences? – position at common law.

Suggested Solution

This problem concerns a defective product manufactured by Botchit Ltd, the potential defendants. The claimants are put to expense in mending the product and then replacing it, as well as in repairing the damage it causes to their property.

One should first look to the Consumer Protection Act 1987 to see if Fanny and Gordon are afforded statutory protection. The stereo system is a product covered by the Act, since s1 defines product as meaning any goods. Under s2(2) of the Act, the producer of the product is liable for the damage caused by a defect in the product. Botchit Ltd, we are told, manufactured the system and are therefore producers covered by this section. F and G do not know the name of the supplier and do not want to ask H where he bought it. While the supplier can also be held liable under s2(3) of the Act, this would be where the supplier fails, upon request being made within a reasonable period after the damage occurs, to identify the producer. Therefore F and G are unaffected by their lack of knowledge of the supplier.

The next question that F and G need to consider is whether there has been a defect within the meaning of the Act. A defect exists, under s3, 'if the safety of the product is not such as persons generally are entitled to expect'. 'Safety' is construed widely and includes safety in the context of risks of damage to property. The problems that occurred in this case arose from the faulty motor, both before and after it was replaced, and meant that the system was not of the safety that one would reasonably expect in a new product. Therefore, the defect falls within the definition of the Act.

Next, the claimants must consider the damage. Unfortunately for them, the Act restricts recovery for property damage in that there is no liability in respect of loss of or damage to the product itself: s5(2). Therefore they cannot recover under the Act for the defective motor unit and turntable. They can only recover for the damage the product causes to their property. Presumably this damage is quite extensive and, in any case, is above the £275 threshold demanded by the Act.

It does not appear that any of the defences provided by s4 of the Act will apply, unless this is a 'state-of-the-art' stereo and Botchit can claim that 'the state of scientific and technical knowledge at the time was not such that a producer of products of the same description as the product in question might be expected to have discovered the defect if it had existed in his products while they were under his control': s4(1)(e). This is the so-called 'development risks' defence.

Therefore Fanny and Gordon can recover under the Act for the damage to their property but not for their outlay on repairing and then replacing the stereo. The next question, then, is whether that expense can be recovered. Obviously there is no contract between claimants and defendants and Fanny and Gordon do not want to involve Henry, who was a party to the contract. So any remedy must lie in tort.

Liability at common law for defective products was most famously stated in *Donoghue* v *Stevenson* [1932] AC 562. However, it applies where the product causes damage to other property than the product itself. There is no general liability at common law for loss to the product. This is despite the House of Lords' decision in *Junior Books* v *The Veitchi Co Ltd* [1983] 1 AC 520 which purported to allow such liability but which has since been disapproved. This is properly the sphere of contract law and I would advise the claimants that they will not recover for damage to the property itself in tort.

QUESTION FOUR

'The provisions of Part I of the Consumer Protection Act 1987 are to be welcomed, but there is scope for the role of fault in the law of tort to be further diminished.'

Discuss.

University of London LLB Examination
(for External Students) Law of Tort June 1988 Q5

General Comment

An essay question that requires an analysis of the provisions of Part I of the Consumer Protection Act 1987 which essentially deals with establishing liability for defective products. A thorough understanding of the 'offences' and 'defences' within the Act is therefore fundamental.

Skeleton Solution

Consumer Protection Act 1987 – strict liability – who is liable – defective – defences –

damage – is Act welcome? – other examples of strict liability – *Rylands*, animals, fire, vicarious liability, nuisance? res ipsa loquitur? – other extensions? – causation and *Wilsher* – replacement of present system by comprehensive no-fault accident compensation scheme.

Suggested Solution

The provisions of Part I of the Consumer Protection Act (CPA) 1987 were introduced to implement the provisions of an EEC Directive relating to product liability. The CPA 1987 purports to introduce a regime of strict liability in the sphere of product liability. Before considering whether or not the Act is to be welcomed it is necessary to outline the principal provisions of the Act.

The main provision of the Act is contained in s2(1) which states that where any damage is caused wholly or partly by a defect in a product then certain persons shall be liable for the damage which is occasioned. The persons who may be liable are the producer of the goods, any person who holds himself out as being a producer of the goods, the importer of the goods into the EEC and, in certain circumstances, the supplier of the product. The liability of the supplier is, however, a secondary liability; that is to say that the supplier may discharge liability by identifying the producer of the goods and it is only where he fails to so this that he will be liable. A product is defined in s1(2) as any 'goods or electricity' and goods is further defined in s45.

The consumer is left with a problem, however, in establishing that the product was defective. A product is defective where the 'safety of the product is not such as persons generally are entitled to expect': s3(2). Thus the product must in some way be unsafe; it will not generally suffice to say that the goods simply did not live up to expectations. A court is to have regard to all the circumstances of the case in considering whether a product is defective but relevant factors include the marketing of the product, any warnings contained on the product and the use to which the product might reasonably be put.

The Act contains a number of defences, the most important of which is the 'state of the art' defence contained in s4(1)(e) which states that it is a defence to show that the state of scientific knowledge at the relevant time was not such that a producer of products of the same description might be expected to have discovered the defect. The presence of this defence makes it difficult to say that the role of fault has been completely eliminated under the CPA because the factors to which a court will have regard in considering whether the state of the art defence has been established are similar to the factors which a court will have regard to in a negligence action.

Finally it should be noted that only certain types of losses are recoverable under the Act. Damages are recoverable for personal injury and death and in relation to damage to private property (provided that it exceeds £275) but damages are not recoverable for the defect in the product itself: s5.

The provisions of the Act are generally to be welcomed in that they improve the position of the consumer who suffers injury as a result of a defective product. But difficulties will remain due to the presence of the state of the art defence which may be invoked by many manufacturers, particularly in relation to the manufacture of drugs. Difficulties will also remain in showing that the product was defective and where the goods themselves are defective and do not cause any other injury no remedy will lie under the Act and the remedy (if any) will be in contract.

These provisions of the CPA are not, however, the only example of liability without fault in English law. Other examples of strict liability in English law are the rule in *Rylands* v *Fletcher* (1868) LR 3 HL 330, vicarious liability (as the employer does not commit a tort), liability under the Animals Act 1971 and liability for the escape of fire. More debatable examples of strict liability are nuisance (although the role of fault within this tort is unclear: see Lord Reid in *The Wagon Mound (No 2)* [1967] 1 AC 617) and res ipsa loquitur. Another source of strict liability is contractual liability, particularly in relation to the satisfactory quality provisions of the Sale of Goods Act 1979. Liability depends on proof that the goods are unmerchantable and not on proof that the vendor was in some way at fault.

Despite the fact that there are a number of areas in which English law recognises liability without fault there is no general principle in English law of liability without fault and there is still room for the extension of no fault liability as can be seen from the case of *Wilsher* v *Essex Area Health Authority* [1988] AC 1074; [1988] 1 All ER 871. The House of Lords held that the claimant must in all cases prove on a balance of probabilities that the negligence of the defendant was the cause of the loss to the claimant. This is likely to cause problems for claimants in medical negligence cases such as *Wilsher* where it is uncertain which of a number of competing causes was the cause of the damage to the claimant. If the claimant can surmount the problems of proof he can recover for all his losses; if he cannot surmount this hurdle he will recover nothing. It seems rather arbitrary that enormous sums of money should hinge on such difficult evidential questions. Large amounts of time and money have so far been spent on research seeking to show that the defendant's fault was the cause of the damage to the claimant. The Pearson Committee discovered that the cost of operating the tort system accounted for some 85 per cent of the sums paid to accident victims.

Similarly it is questionable whether the presence of fault should make such a difference to the claimant in *Wilsher*. His needs are the same whether the negligence of the defendants was the cause of his loss or not. It is difficult to justify a system in which he recovers extremely large sums of money if he can prove the necessary causal link but nothing if he fails. It may be said that the presence of fault is the differentiating factor but in cases such as *Nettleship* v *Weston* [1971] 2 QB 691 the role of personal fault in a negligence action appears to have almost entirely disappeared.

Dissatisfaction with the tort system in New Zealand was such that the tort action has been abolished in relation to personal injury cases and replaced by a comprehensive no-fault accident compensation scheme which covers all accidental injury, except diseases (other than occupational diseases) and is financed by a levy on motor vehicles, employers and employees and out of general taxation.

Such a scheme is likely to ensure a greater extent of equality as between different victims of misfortune in society. It is true that such a system would be expensive to operate but at least more of the money would get to the claimants and not be tied up in administration as in the present fault based system. It is therefore suggested that there is scope for the extension of no-fault liability in English law and that serious consideration should now be given to implementing a comprehensive no-fault accident compensation scheme.

QUESTION FIVE

Critically examine the provisions of Part I of the Consumer Protection Act 1987 relating to product liability. To what extent do these provisions constitute an improvement upon the common law rules?

Written by the Author

General Comment

This question requires a discussion of the main principles establishing liability for defective products under Part I of the Consumer Protection Act 1987. Some discussion of strict liability and available defences is necessary.

Skeleton Solution

Consumer Protection Act 1987 – strict liability – product – who is liable? – defect – defences – common law – fault – state of the art defence – causation – liability of supplier – losses recoverable.

Suggested Solution

The provisions of Part I of the Consumer Protection Act (CPA) 1987 were introduced to implement the provisions of an EEC Directive relating to product liability. The CPA 1987 purports to introduce a regime of strict liability in the sphere of product liability. The main provision of the Act is contained in s2(1) which states that where any damage is caused wholly or partly by a defect in a product then certain persons shall be liable for the damage which is occasioned. The persons who may be liable are the producer of the goods, any person who holds himself out as being a producer of the goods, the importer of the goods into the EEC and, in certain circumstances, the supplier of the product. The liability of the supplier is, however, a secondary liability; that is to say that the supplier may discharge liability by identifying the producer of the goods and it is only where he fails to do this that he will be liable. A product is defined in s1(2) as any 'goods or electricity' and goods is further defined in s45. The consumer is left with a problem, however, in establishing that the product was defective. A product is defective where the 'safety of the product is not such as persons generally are entitled to expect': s3(2). Thus the product must in some way be unsafe; it will not generally suffice to say that the goods simply did not live up to expectations. The Act contains a number of defences, the most important of which is the 'state of the art' defence contained in s4(1)(e) which states that it is a defence to show that the state of scientific and technical knowledge at the relevant time was not such that a producer of products of the same description might be expected to have discovered the defect.

In subjecting these provisions to critical analysis it is necessary to give a brief consideration to the defects in the common law which prompted the enactment of the 1987 Act. The common law was based upon *Donoghue* v *Stevenson* [1932] AC 562, according to which a manufacturer could be liable to a consumer where he had failed to take reasonable care in the preparation of the goods with the result that injury was caused to the consumer's life or property. It is only by understanding the deficiencies in the common law that we can begin to engage in a critical appraisal of the Act. There were a number of defects in the common law which led to the enactment of the 1987 Act. We shall consider each deficiency and the response of the Act to the particular problem.

The first problem at common law was the difficulty which was experienced in showing that the manufacturer was at fault in relation to the defect in the product. The manufacturer was only required to take reasonable care and could argue, for example, that the state of human knowledge did not enable him to discover the defect. This defect has been dealt with to some extent because the Act purports to introduce a regime of strict liability. But it is likely to remain a problem due to the width of the state of the art defence. Indeed the inclusion of the state of the art defence and the width of that defence is the most controversial aspect of the Act.

Secondly, at common law, it could be difficult for a consumer to show that the defect arose during the manufacturing process. In *Evans* v *Triplex Safety Glass Ltd* [1936] 1 All ER 283 the claimant was unable to show that the defect in the windscreen of the car which he purchased was present when the car left the manufacturing process and that it did not materialise during the intervening year when he was using the car. This difficulty has not been dealt with by the Act because there is no provision in the Act which deals with causation, apart from s2(1) which states that the damage must be caused 'wholly or partly' by a defect in the product. Thus causation is likely to remain a problem in such cases as actions against drug manufacturers.

Thirdly, at common law, it was difficult for a consumer to succeed against a supplier in tort. It is true that in many cases the consumer had an action in contract against the supplier but this was of no use to the person who was injured when he received the product as a gift because then there was obviously no contractual relationship between the supplier and the injured party. This difficulty has been resolved by the Act because, although the liability of a supplier is only secondary, if the supplier can identify his supplier the claimant will take an action against that person and if the original supplier cannot identify his supplier then the original supplier himself will be liable. Thus either way the claimant will have a remedy.

Finally at common law there was a difficulty where the goods were simply less valuable, in the sense that they were not as good as the purchaser thought they were. Again the existence of a contract would protect most persons but problems arose when there was no contractual relationship because, unless the case fell within the narrow confines of *Junior Books* v *The Veitchi Co Ltd* [1983] AC 520, there was no remedy available in tort. The Act does not resolve this problem because damages are recoverable under the Act only in respect of 'death or personal injury or any loss of or damage to property': s5(1). But crucially s5(2) provides that a defendant shall not be liable in respect of the 'loss of or damage to the product itself or for the loss of or any damage to the whole or any part of the product which has been supplied with the product in question comprised in it'. Also the Act does not protect disappointed expectations, unless it can be shown that the safety of the product was not such as persons generally are entitled to expect.

The CPA does constitute an improvement upon the common law but it cannot claim to be a wholly satisfactory piece of legislative reform. It remains to be seen how the courts will interpret this legislation, but the width of the state of the art defence means that the Act cannot be said to remedy the deficiencies of the common law completely.

Chapter 11

Occupiers' Liability

11.1   Introduction

11.2   Key points

11.3   Key cases and statutes

11.4   Questions and suggested solutions

11.1 Introduction

Occupiers' liability is a specialised aspect of the tort of negligence, but rather than being covered by common law it is subject to statute, namely the Occupiers' Liability Act 1957 and the Occupiers' Liability Act 1984. Thus in this area close attention must be paid to the exact words of the relevant statute while still being aware of the common law concepts such as breach of duty, etc.

11.2 Key points

Occupiers' Liability Act 1957

Under this Act the occupier of premises owes a duty of care to his visitors.

a) Occupier was defined in *Wheat* v *Lacon* [1966] AC 552: 'Wherever a person has a sufficient degree of control over premises that he ought to realise that any failure on his part to take care may result in injury to a person coming lawfully there, then he is an "occupier" and the person coming lawfully there is his "visitor"'.

Note Lord Denning's four categories of occupier in *Wheat* and the fact that these categories are not exhaustive: *Harris* v *Birkenhead Corporation* [1976] 1 WLR 279.

b) Visitors include invitees and licensees. As regards implied licences see *Robson* v *Hallett* [1967] 2 QB 393 concerning callers, and the restrictive approach to implied licences involving children in *Edwards* v *Railway Executive* [1952] AC 737. The occupier may limit the permission he gives to a visitor to enter the premises as regards space: *The Calgarth* [1927] P 93; *Gould* v *McAuliffe* [1941] 2 All ER 527; purpose of visit: *R* v *Smith & Jones* [1976] 1 WLR 672 and time: *Stone* v *Taffe* [1974] 1 WLR 1575.

c) Premises are widely defined by s1(3)(a).

d) Duty

The duty owed by the occupier is the common duty of care, s2(1), which he may extend, restrict, modify or exclude in so far as he is free to.

By s2(2) the occupier must 'take such care as in all the circumstances of the case is reasonable to see that the visitor will be reasonably safe in using the premises for the purposes for which he is invited or permitted by the occupier to be there'. The House of Lords in *Jolley v Sutton London Borough Council* [2000] 3 All ER 409 held that if damage is foreseeable then there is liability even if the way in which it is caused is not foreseeable. Whether this decision extends the duty of care of the occupier is unknown, but it seems a logical conclusion to be inferred. See also *Fairchild v Glenhaven Funeral Services Ltd; Waddingtons plc v Leeds City Council* [2003] 1 AC 32 on the extent of duty owed by an occupier to an employee of an independent contractor. It is the visitor, not the premises, which must be reasonably safe, and the duty is clearly similar to that in negligence. Note *Hogg v Historic Buildings Commission* [1989] CLY 2573; *Cunningham v Reading Football Club* [1992] PIQR P141; *Gitsham v Pearce* [1992] PIQR 57 and compare *Murphy v Bradford Metropolitan Council* [1992] PIQR 68. Additionally, the 1957 Act provides for four specific situations.

i) Children

Section 2(3)(a) provides that 'an occupier must be prepared for children to be less careful than adults': see *Latham v Johnson & Nephew* [1913] 1 KB 398; *Glasgow Corporation v Taylor* [1922] 1 AC 44 and compare with *Liddle v Yorks (North Riding) CC* [1934] 2 KB 101. As regards very young children anything can be a danger, but occupiers and guardians are each entitled to assume that the other will act reasonably: *Phipps v Rochester Corporation* [1955] 1 QB 450.

ii) Common calling

Section 2(3)(b) of the 1957 Act provides that an occupier may expect that a person, in the exercise of his calling, will appreciate and guard against special risks ordinarily incident to it. The fact that a visitor possesses a special skill does not, of itself, discharge the duty owed: *Salmon v Seafarer Restaurants* [1983] 3 All ER 729; *Ogwo v Taylor* [1987] 2 WLR 988, and note the interpretation of 'ordinarily incident' in *Bird v King Line* [1970] 1 Lloyd's Rep 349.

iii) Warning of danger

Section 2(4)(a) provides that a warning may discharge the duty of care providing that in all the circumstances of the case it is enough to enable the visitor to be reasonably safe: see *Roles v Nathan* [1963] 1 WLR 1117; *Rae v Mars UK* [1990] 03 EG 80. Note, however, that no warning is necessary for an obvious danger: *Staples v West Dorset District Council* [1995] PIQR P439.

iv) Independent contractors

Section 2(4)(b) provides that the occupier is not liable for the fault of an independent contractor if he acted reasonably in entrusting the work to an independent contractor and took reasonable steps to see that the contractor was competent and the work properly done. As to what steps (if any) the occupier need take to check the work compare *Haseldine* v *Daw* [1941] 2 KB 343 with *Woodward* v *Mayor of Hastings* [1945] KB 174.

e) Defences

Both volenti, s2(5), and contributory negligence, s2(3) can apply: see *Simms* v *Leigh Rugby FC* [1969] 2 All ER 923; *Stone* v *Taffe* (above).

Non-visitors

a) Governed by the Occupiers' Liability Act 1984. For the definition of a trespasser see *Robert Addie* v *Dumbreck* [1929] AC 358 and note the House of Lords' decision in *British Railways Board* v *Herrington* [1972] AC 877 which was the common law precursor of the 1984 Act.

b) It is vital to note the conditions that have to be satisfied under s1(3) 1984 Act for the duty to arise, namely:

i) the occupier is aware of the danger or has reasonable grounds to believe that it exists;

ii) the occupier knows or has reasonable grounds to believe that the non-visitor is in the vicinity of the danger or may come into the vicinity of the danger; see *White* v *St Albans City & District Council* (1990) The Times 12 March. This fact was revisited recently in *Donoghue* v *Folkestone Properties Ltd* [2003] 3 All ER 1101 and *Tomlinson* v *Congleton Borough Council and Another* [2004] 1 AC 46; and

iii) the risk is one against which in all the circumstances the occupier may reasonably be expected to offer the non-visitor some protection.

c) The duty, when it arises, is defined by s1(4) 1984 Act as a duty 'to take such care as is reasonable in all the circumstances to see that the non-visitor does not suffer injury on the premises by reason of the danger concerned. See *Revill* v *Newbury* [1996] 2 WLR 239 for a discussion of this duty.

This duty may be discharged by a warning or by discouraging persons from incurring the risk: s1(5). Volenti is preserved as a defence by s1(b): see *Scott and Swainger* v *Associated British Ports and British Railways Board* (1999) QBD 18.

Exclusion of occupiers' duty

Occupiers' Liability Act 1957

Section 2(1) 1957 Act allows the occupier to extend, restrict, modify or exclude his duty in so far as he is free to do so. The major restriction on the occupier's freedom to exclude his duty lies in the Unfair Contract Terms Act 1977, as the duty of care under the 1957 Act is expressly covered by the Unfair Contract Terms Act 1977. However, the 1977 Act, by s1(3) only applies to business liability, so an occupier is free to exclude his non-business liability. For business liability the effect of s2 1977 Act is to render void an attempt to exclude or restrict liability for death or personal injury, and for other loss or damage to make the restriction subject to the requirements of reasonableness.

Occupiers' Liability Act 1984

Although the point is undecided, note the arguments which claim that the duty owed under the 1984 Act cannot be excluded.

11.3 Key cases and statutes

- *Addie (Robert) v Dumbreck* [1929] AC 358
  Defines who a 'trespasser' is for the purposes of an occupier's liability

- *Donoghue v Folkestone Properties Ltd* [2003] 3 All ER 1101
  Was the claimant foreseeable within s1 of the OLA 1984?

- *Glasgow Corporation v Taylor* [1922] 1 AC 44
  Children are presumed to be less careful than adults

- *Harris v Birkenhead Corporation* [1976] 1 WLR 279
  Four categories of occupiers were identified

- *Haseldine v Daw* [1941] 2 KB 343
  An occupier who dishcarges reasonable care in delegating work to independent contractors may not be liable to a visitor

- *Jolley v Sutton London Borough Council* [2000] 3 All ER 409
  Some damage must have been foreseeable for there to be liability

- *Ogwo v Taylor* [1987] 2 WLR 988
  The fact that a visitor may be skilled does not discharge an occupier's duty to him or her

- *Robson v Hallett* [1967] 2 QB 393
  Visitors are deemed to have either express or implied permission to enter the premises

- *Roles v Nathan* [1963] 1 WR 1117
  A warning of any inherent or potential danger may in certain circumstances discharge the occupier's liability

- *Tomlinson v Congleton Borough Council and Another* [2004] 1 AC 46
  Was there a duty of care owed to the claimant?

- *Waddingtons plc* v *Leeds City Council* [2003] 1 AC 32
  Gives an illustration of the extent of duty owed by an occupier to an employee of an independent contractor

- *Wheat* v *Lacon* [1966] AC 552
  Defines who an 'occupier' is

- *White* v *St Albans City & District Council* (1990) The Times 12 March
  Provides a test to decide if the occupier owes a duty of care to the trespasser

- Defective Premises Act 1972 – imposes liability on owners and occupiers of defective premises

- Occupiers' Liability Act 1957 – sets out the framework of liability in respect of visitors

- Occupiers' Liability Act 1984 – sets out the framework of liability in respect of trespassers

11.4 Questions and suggested solutions

QUESTION ONE

Satanic Industries occupy factory premises. They engaged Demon Constructors to carry out substantial construction work on the ground floor, including the reception area. Satanic erected notices at the entrance saying: 'Please take care. Construction work in progress'. Lily, a sales representative, visited the reception area: she had her pet dog, Boxer, with her. While she was talking to Satanic's purchasing officer, Boxer wandered off and fell through a thin sheet of plywood covering a hole in the floor and down a shaft. Lily was unable to reach him, but Matthew, who was an apprentice employed by Demon Constructors and was of very slim build, tried to lean down while Lily held on to his leg. More of the floor gave way and both Lily and Matthew fell into the shaft and were badly hurt. Boxer was so badly injured that he had to be destroyed.

Advise Lily and Matthew as to any claims in tort.

University of London LLB Examination
(for External Students) Law of Tort June 2001 Q5

General Comment

Primarily the issues raised by this question revolve around occupiers' liability. There might possibly be some confusion caused by Boxer, the dog. Boxer is Lily's property and much will depend therefore on Lily's status in relation to her claim for physical injury and property damage. Matthew's situation deserves consideration from two perspectives: as an employee and also as a rescuer.

Skeleton Solution

Lily: is she a visitor for the purpose of the Occupiers' Liability Act 1957?; Boxer's status; the efficacy of the warning – liability of independent contractors – the occupier's liability – Matthew's status: against whom does his claim lie?

Suggested Solution

In a question on occupiers' liability, certain preliminary issues must first be determined. First, the question of who the occupier is; second, whether the claimant can properly be defined as a visitor; and third, the requirement of premises.

There is no problem with establishing who the occupier is from the facts of the question. We are informed that Satanic Industries occupy the factory premises. Therefore, on the basis of *Wheat v E Lacon & Co Ltd* [1966] AC 552, Satanic Industries may properly be described as the occupier. The factory premises would obviously satisfy s1(3)(a) Occupiers' Liability Act (OLA) 1957, which defines what is meant by premises. Finally, the issue of the visitor, which in this case is Lily and her pet dog Boxer. Can they be properly identified as visitors?

The question states that Lily is a sales representative and is therefore at the premises of Satanic Industries in the course of her employment. Hence, Lily would be a visitor for the purposes of the Occupiers' Liability Act (OLA) 1957, but what about her pet dog, Boxer? As Boxer is Lily's property in law, her status would obviously be relevant in relation to Boxer. On this basis, Boxer's presence at Satanic Industries is justified on the premise that as Lily is lawfully a visitor, her property also attains the same status. The next issue is to determine liability.

The duty owed by the occupier is the common duty of care as per s2(1) OLA 1957, which he may extend, restrict, modify or exclude insofar as he is free to. By virtue of s2(2) OLA 1957, the occupier must 'take such care as is reasonable in all the circumstances of the case to ensure that the visitor will be reasonably safe in using the premises for the purposes for which he is invited or permitted by the occupier to be there'. It must be noted that the emphasis is on the visitor, who must be reasonably safe, and not the premises. The duty in this respect is therefore similar to that in negligence.

Whilst Lily was engaged in a conversation with Satanic's purchasing officer, Boxer, her dog, wandered off and fell through a thin sheet of plywood covering a hole in the floor and down a shaft. In trying to rescue the dog, both Lily and Matthew, an apprentice employed by Demon Constructors, also fell into the shaft and were badly hurt. Boxer's injury was so bad that he had to be destroyed.

Is Satanic Industries responsible or could the blame be directed towards the independent contractors, namely Demon Constructors? Have Satanic Industries satisfied the requirements of s2(2) OLA 1957?

First, the issue of whether the notices erected at the entrance sufficiently warned visitors of any risk or danger must be determined. The notice itself does not say much except to say that construction work is in progress and that care should be taken. Section 2(4)(a) OLA 1957 provides that a warning may discharge the duty of care, providing that in all the circumstances of the case it is enough to enable the visitor to be reasonably safe: *Rae v Mars* [1990] 03 EG 801 and *Roles v Nathan* [1963] 1 WLR 1117. If the danger is so obvious, then there is no need for a warning: *Staples v West Dorset District Council* [1995] PIQR P439.

It is certainly possible that the notice was insufficient to enable a human visitor to be reasonably safe, if there was construction work in the area being visited. It is arguable that the warning could have been more strongly worded. Second, the purchasing officer never stopped Lily or her dog Boxer, or reinforced the warning notices in any way. Lily could also find herself contributorily negligent for not realising that there might be a risk to the dog and not keeping it out of mischief.

Section 2(4)(b) OLA 1957 provides that the occupier is not liable for the fault of an independent contractor if he acted reasonably in entrusting the work to an independent contractor and took reasonable steps to see that the contractor was competent and the work was properly done. *Haseldine v Daw* [1941] 2 KB 343 provides a useful illustration of what steps need to be taken by the occupier to ensure that s2(4)(b) OLA 1957 is properly discharged. Since Demon Constructors have been contracted to carry out substantial construction work on the ground floor, obviously Satanic Industries may lack the technical expertise to ensure that the work is competently done, but surely minimal supervision is possible to ensure that the premises is left reasonably safe for the passage of visitors. On this basis, Satanic Industries would remain liable to Lily for her personal injury and for the loss of her property, Boxer. However, assuming Satanic Industries have discharged the duty as to supervision, then liability might lie directly with Demon Constructors.

In any event, both Satanic Industries and/or Demon Constructors may adduce the personal defence of contributory negligence on the part of Lily in allowing Boxer to roam in a potentially dangerous area.

As Matthew is an apprentice employed by Demon Constructors, surely the standard of care imposed by s2(3)(b) OLA 1957 cannot be applied. An apprentice does not, arguably, possess any special skill so that he may be expected to guard against special risks ordinarily incidental to the exercise of his calling: *Salmon v Seafarer Restaurants Ltd* [1983] 3 All ER 729. On this basis, his employers, Demon Constructors, may be liable under employers' liability principles in failing to provide a safe place of work and a safe system of work for Matthew: *Latimer v AEC Ltd* [1953] AC 643. There is also the possibility of a claim against Satanic Industries, as well as Lily for creating the dangerous situation that has consequently been the cause of Matthew's injury. Whilst he may be entitled to name all three parties as potential defendants, ultimately the court may apportion liability as they see fit as per the Civil Liability (Contribution) Act 1978.

However, in trying to rescue the dog Boxer, Matthew becomes a rescuer, but was he negligent in the manner in which he tried to rescue Boxer? When dealing with emergencies, the court normally does not expect the same standard of care expected of reasonable, prudent people: *Ng Chun Pui* v *Lee Chuen Tat* [1988] RTR 298. Therefore, under the circumstances Matthew will be able to recover damages for his injuries.

QUESTION TWO

Until June 1999 Jeff worked as an engineer at Megabyte, manufacturers of electrical equipment. He is now a sales representative for another firm. In March 2000 he had to visit Megabyte's factory in the course of his new job. He waved to the receptionist and went through the door behind her into the workshop to speak to some of his old friends. There is a notice on the door leading into the workshop which states: 'Workshop employees only. No admittance to visitors'. As he chatted, Jeff leant against a piece of heavy equipment, which toppled over on top of him. Kevin, the engineer to whom he was talking, tried to lift the equipment but was unable to hold it and had to let it fall back. Jeff suffered serious crushing injuries. Kevin damaged his back permanently and has had to seek a lighter job.

Megabyte had had the equipment inspected regularly by a specialist firm, which had failed to notice that it had come loose from its moorings.

Advise Megabyte as to its possible liability.

University of London LLB Examination
(for External Students) Law of Tort June 2000 Q4

General Comment

This is a question that requires consideration of the principles relating to occupiers' liability and not just the general principles of the tort of negligence. Issues concerning employers' liability are also relevant: therefore, the student should not merely discuss negligence.

Skeleton Solution

The position of Jeff: is he a visitor or a trespasser?; Occupiers' Liability Act (OLA) 1957 if he is a visitor; Occupiers' Liability Act 1984 if he is a trespasser – was there an implied permission to enter into the workshop? – s2(4)(b) OLA 1957 independent contractors – the position of Kevin: principles of employers' liability in relation to rescuers; the role of independent contractors.

Suggested Solution

Although touching on the area of negligence, this question is primarily concerned with the principles of occupiers' liability. Occupiers' liability is a specialised aspect of common law negligence. The primary distinction is that it is wholly governed by statute, ie the Occupiers' Liability Act (OLA) 1957, which concerns the liability of an occupier of premises to his or her visitors, and the Occupiers' Liability Act 1984, which concerns an occupier's liability to trespassers. As the issues are governed wholly by statute, it is necessary to give close attention to the exact words used by Parliament, simply because they will set out the limits to the ambit of liability.

Before considering the positions of Jeff and Kevin in relation to Megabyte individually, some common issues may be addressed. First, does Megabyte qualify as an occupier? In *Wheat v E Lacon & Co Ltd* [1966] AC 552 an occupier was defined as: 'a person who exercises a sufficient degree of control over premises that he/she ought to realise that any failure on their part to take care may result in injury to a person coming lawfully there'. On this premise, Megabyte is an occupier. Second, the issue of premises must be addressed, which is covered by s1(3)(a) OLA 1957, which in turn states that 'any fixed or moveable structure' will be deemed to be premises: *Wheeler v Copas* [1981] 3 All ER 405. Third, the issue of whether Jeff and Kevin were lawful visitors must be analysed. Visitors include invitees and licensees. This is stated by s1(2) OLA 1957, which requires such a person to have had the occupier's express or implied permission to come on to the premises, and includes those exercising a contractual right of entry. There is no problem with Kevin, who is an employee of Megabyte. He is clearly a visitor. Moreover, Megabyte will also be responsible on the basis of the principles of employers' liability. However, there might be a small problem with Jeff.

Jeff is a former employee of Megabyte but now works as a sales representative for another firm. On the particular day, he had visited Megabyte officially in the course of his new job. This may raise the issue of implied permission. However, it must be borne in mind that the occupier may limit the permission he gives to a visitor to enter the premises as regards space (*The Calgarth* [1927] P 93), or the purpose of the visitor's visit (*R v Smith and Jones* [1976] 1 WLR 672), or as regards the time of the visit (*Stone v Taffe* [1974] 1 WLR 1575). Jeff went into the workshop notwithstanding the notice on the door leading into the workshop. The notice read: 'Workshop employees only. No admittance to visitors'. This notice clearly prohibits visitors from entering the workshop. Be that as it may, did Jeff go into the workshop in pursuance of his job? This is unlikely, given the fact that the question states that he went into the workshop to speak to some of his old friends. This would clearly subject Jeff to the notice. However, Jeff had waved to the receptionist and only then had he gone through the door behind her into the workshop. Therefore, as the receptionist was placed before the door, and as she had allowed Jeff to go into the workshop, was there acquiescence on her part? It would appear that there was an implied permission, as Jeff was not prevented from entering into the workshop. Clearly, the receptionist had authority to stop Jeff and she did not. Also, it is quite common for employers generally to allow former employees some liberty to move around the premises. On this basis, it is submitted that Jeff was a lawful visitor.

Was Megabyte in breach of its duty of care? By virtue of s2(1) OLA 1957, the duty owed by the occupier is the common law duty of care in respect of all visitors on their premises. Section 2(2) OLA 1957 states that the occupier must: 'take such care as is reasonable in all the circumstances of the case to see if the visitor will be reasonably safe in using the premises for the purposes for which he is invited or permitted by the occupier to be there'. This means that the premises must be in good order or safe keep so as to ensure the visitor's safety. Fairly recently in *Jolley v Sutton London Borough Council* [2000] 3 All ER 409 the House of Lords held that if damage is foreseeable, then there is liability, even if the way in which it is caused is not foreseeable. Clearly, the heavy equipment had not been safely secured to the ground. Thus it topples over on top of Jeff, who had leant against it. It could have been any employee in Jeff's position. Surely, on this basis, Megabyte ought to be responsible or liable for Jeff's injury. Perhaps if Megabyte had put up a warning, as required by s2(4)(a) OLA 1957, to warn the visitor of any possible danger, then Megabyte may have discharged the duty of care: *Roles v Nathan* [1963] 1 WLR 1117. Megabyte had not put up any such warning. There is also the possibility that Megabyte may find itself falling foul of s28(1) Factories Act 1961, which imposes a duty to keep the premises safe so far as is reasonably practicable. The important issue here is whether Megabyte could escape liability on the basis that there was a specialist firm of independent contractors who were contracted to regularly inspect the machinery. It is evident that the firm concerned had failed to notice that the machine had come loose from its moorings. This clearly shows negligence on their part.

Section 2(4)(b) OLA 1957 provides that an occupier is not liable for the fault of an independent contractor if he had acted reasonably in entrusting the work to an independent contractor, and took reasonable steps to check that the contractor was competent and that the work was properly executed. Megabyte had clearly employed the services of a specialist firm. Therefore, they have discharged their duty under s2(4)(b) OLA 1957. But is there any failure of supervision on the part of Megabyte? Could they have discovered that the machine had come loose from its moorings on a reasonable, plain and non-technical inspection? If the answer is yes, then Megabyte are liable on the basis of *Woodward v Mayor of Hastings* [1945] KB 174. If, on the other hand, the defect could not have been discovered on a reasonable inspection, then Megabyte are not liable to Jeff, but the independent contractors would be on the basis of *Haseldine v Daw* [1941] 2 KB 343.

As far as Kevin is concerned, an employer owes certain common law duties to an employee, such as the provision of a safe place of work, a safe system of work, proper plant and equipment and competent staff. These duties also overlap under a number of statutes, such as the Factories Act 1961 and the Employers' Liability (Defective Equipment) Act 1969. The issue here is whether or not there was properly maintained plant and equipment: *Smith v Baker* [1891] AC 325. This in turn raises the question of a safe place of work: *Latimer v AEC Ltd* [1953] AC 643. The duty on the employer is not absolute, but merely to take reasonable steps to provide a safe place of work. Again, by entrusting maintenance to a competent firm of specialists, Megabyte has arguably discharged their common law duties. Similar arguments to those used in Jeff's case with regard to the independent contractors may be adduced here. Whilst the employer's duty to his employees is personal and non-delegable, certain special or technical duties may be delegated, in which case the employer will not be held responsible for the negligent performance of those duties, particularly where independent contractors are involved: *Wilsons and Clyde Coal Co* v *English* [1938] AC 57. On this basis, Kevin would be advised to pursue an action against the firm of independent contractors for negligence.

QUESTION THREE

Veronique works as an au pair with the Brown family. One evening when the Browns are out, she invites her friend Lucille to visit her. Lucille works as an au pair with another family. Lucille mentions that she has been unable to find a spare part for her old motor scooter. Veronique says that she is sure Mr Brown may have something in his workshop in the garden and that he will not mind if she has a look. Veronique takes Lucille out to the workshop. A substantial quantity of oil has been spilled on the floor of the workshop and Lucille falls over and cuts her arm very badly. Veronique takes Lucille to the local hospital in her car. On the way there is an accident caused by the negligent driving of Giles. Lucille suffers serious leg injuries. The arm injury does not respond to treatment and it has to be amputated. এই ছবি ।

Advise Lucille.

University of London LLB Examination
(for External Students) Law of Tort June 1999 Q9

General Comment

This question concerns the liability of an occupier of defective premises for loss or injury sustained by those who come onto those premises. Any such case should be dealt with as a statutory claim under the Occupiers' Liability Acts, rather than in common law negligence. Always consider whether the person suffering loss/injury was a visitor or a trespasser at the time of the accident and in the specific part of the premises on which the accident occurred. Occupiers' liability is a specialised aspect of common law negligence, and so it is relevant to consider the concepts of causation and remoteness of damages as they would apply to mainstream negligence claims where they are in issue.

Skeleton Solution

Explain and identify who is the 'occupier' of the premises concerned – discuss whether Lucille is a visitor or trespasser when she enters the garden workshop – identify the relevant Occupiers' Liability Act – discuss whether the occupier owed Lucille a duty of care, and if so, whether such a duty was broken – are Lucille's injuries too remote to recover damages for as against the occupier?

Suggested Solution

The question concerns the liability of an occupier of premises for damage done to those who come onto the premises. The law relating to such liability is largely to be found in the Occupiers' Liability Act (OLA) 1957 as regards visitors, and the Occupiers' Liability Act (OLA) 1984 as regards non-visitors, ie trespassers.

The occupier of the premises

It is vital in all cases to correctly identify the occupier, as it is against this person or persons that a claim for loss/damage arises. Under s1(2) OLA 1957 and s1(2) OLA 1984 the definition of 'occupier' remains the same as at common law. The current test is to be found in the judgement of Lord Denning in the House of Lords case *Wheat* v *E Lacon and Co Ltd* [1966] AC 552 which defines the occupier as a person who 'has a sufficient degree of control over premises that he ought to realise that any failure on his part to use care may result in injury'. *definition of occupier*

In this case it is clear that the Browns are the occupiers of the premises, as it is they who exercise sufficient control over the garden workshop in which the accident occurred. Veronique, as an au pair, cannot be said to be an occupier of either the garden workshop or the whole house, although it is possible that she has the necessary degree of control to be regarded as the occupier of her own room.

Is Lucille a visitor or trespasser when she enters the garden workshop?

It is necessary to decide whether Lucille enters the garden workshop as visitor or non-visitor in relation to the Browns in order to determine which Occupiers' Liability Act to apply to her circumstances. This is important, because the existence and scope of any duty owed by the occupier varies according to the status of the person who comes onto the premises.

Section 1(2) OLA 1957 states that a lawful visitor is, for the purposes of the Act, either an invitee or a licensee. This requires such a person to have had the occupier's express or implied permission to come onto the premises. On the other hand, the term 'trespasser' was defined by Lord Dunedin in *Addie (Robert) and Sons (Collieries) Ltd* v *Dumbreck* [1929] AC 358 as a person 'who goes onto the land without invitation of any sort and whose presence is either unknown to the proprietor or, if known, is practically objected to'.

It is clear that Lucille lacks the Browns' express permission to enter the garden workshop, the invitation coming instead from Veronique. The question as to whether Lucille had the Browns' implied permission to enter seems to depend upon whether Veronique, as the au pair, had the Browns' actual or apparent (ostensible) authority to invite a private guest into the workshop in their absence. On this point, see *Ferguson* v *Welsh* [1987] 3 All ER 777, an analogous case on multiple occupation in which the majority of the House of Lords held that a contractor licensed to enter the occupier's premises to do work was clothed with ostensible authority to invite a subcontractor and their employees onto the land.

Ultimately, each case turns on its particular facts; however, it seems reasonable to expect that Veronique may have been permitted to receive guests in the house, but highly unlikely that such permission would have extended to a search in the workshop for spare parts to a motor scooter. Such an activity surely would have required Mr Brown's express permission. It is therefore submitted that Lucille was a trespasser when she entered the garden workshop, and that any duty owed to her by the Browns would be defined according to the requirements of OLA 1984.

Did the Browns owe Lucille a duty of care under OLA 1984 and, if so, was such a duty broken?

Under s1(3) OLA 1984 the occupier will owe the non-visitor a duty of care provided the following apply.

a) He is aware of the danger or has reasonable grounds to believe it exists. Provided, as seems likely, that Mr Brown was aware of the oil spillage, it follows that at the very least, he must have had reasonable grounds to believe that someone might slip and fall over.

b) He knows or has reasonable grounds to believe that the other (Lucille) is in the vicinity of the danger concerned, or that he may come into the vicinity of the danger (in either case, whether the other has lawful authority for being in that vicinity or not). This requirement is clearly much more difficult to satisfy in the circumstances described, as there is nothing to suggest that Mr Brown might have anticipated that anyone would enter the workshop other than himself. However, it might be argued that if Mr Brown knows that Veronique is to receive a private guest with an interest in mechanics, he might reasonably infer that the guest might be tempted to take a look in the workshop. In this context, the recent cases of *Donoghue* v *Folkestone Properties Ltd* [2003] 3 All ER 110 and *Tomlinson* v *Congleton Borough Council* [2004] 1 AC 46 lend support for this proposition.

c) The risk is one against which, in all the circumstances of the case, he may reasonably be expected to offer the other some protection. A substantial spillage of oil could reasonably be expected to be cleaned up, or alternatively, the door to the garden workshop might easily have been locked (if applicable) and the key removed. These observations also support the argument that, provided a duty is owed by the Browns to Lucille, the duty has been broken. Section 1(4) OLA 1984 provides that the duty is 'to take such care as is reasonable in all the circumstances of the case to see that [the non-visitor] does not suffer injury on the premises by reason of the danger concerned'.

Lucille's main problem will be in establishing that a duty of care is owed to her under OLA 1984, particularly under part (b) of the three part-test above.

Assuming the Browns are in breach of a duty of care owed under OLA 1984 can they be said to have caused the loss suffered by Lucille, namely the amputated arm and the serious injuries to her leg?

Provided that Lucille satisfies the requirements of OLA 1984, she will be able to recover damages for personal injury (s1(9) OLA 1984), but not in respect of loss or damage to property; eg ripped or oil-stained clothing: s1(8) OLA 1984.

It is well established that injury to the person resulting from a breach of duty is recoverable in tort. This remains the position, even though the extent of the damage and the precise manner of its occurrence may not have been foreseeable: *Hughes* v *Lord Advocate* [1963] AC 837. Physical injury is entirely foreseeable where surfaces are slippery, and Lucille will be able to recover compensation for the loss of her arm.

The final question is whether Lucille could claim against the Browns for the injuries to her leg. A defendant is not liable unless the claimant's loss has been caused by the negligence of the defendant, both in fact and in law. The injuries to Lucille's leg have resulted, albeit indirectly, from the original injury to her arm: 'but for' the accident in the workshop, Lucille would not have been in Veronique's car when the second accident occurred: *Barnett* v *Chelsea and Kensington Hospital Management Committee* [1969] 1 QB 428. However, it is suggested that Giles's negligent driving amounts to a new and independent intervening act by a third party (novus actus interveniens), making the leg injury too remote a consequence of any breach of OLA 1984 on the part of the Browns. In other words, it was the act of a third party (Giles) which was the true cause of the injury subsequently suffered by Lucille, an event which was completely independent of the defendant's negligence. In the words of Lord Wright in *The Oropesa* [1943] p32 the second accident was 'a new cause which disturbs the sequence of events, something which can be described as either unreasonable or extraneous or extrinsic'.

QUESTION FOUR

Belinda went to Mugshots, a firm of photographers, to obtain passport photographs. She was accompanied by her six-year-old son Craig, who is very deaf. Mugshots was having new shelving installed by Derek in a room adjoining the waiting area. Derek worked for the local council, but was doing the work for Mugshots in his own time in the evenings and at weekends. There was a swing door through from the waiting area to the area where Derek was working. Belinda was called into the booth to have her photographs taken, and told Craig to wait reading his comic. Craig however wandered off and pushed the swing doors. Ethel, the receptionist, shouted to him to come back, but he did not hear and went through the door. Derek had left a stepladder leaning against some half-finished shelving. Craig knocked against the ladder. The shelving fell on him, causing him a broken arm and leg. Belinda went running to him when she heard his screams. She has suffered from severe depression since the incident.

Advise Belinda and Craig.

University of London LLB Examination
(for External Students) Law of Tort June 1998 Q4

General Comment

This is a question involving loss or injury to someone who comes onto another person's premises, resulting from a defect in the premises. Any such case should be dealt with as a statutory claim under the Occupiers' Liability Acts, rather than in common law negligence. The suggested solution given below is a very full answer to this question, and in an examination it would be permissible to deal only very briefly with the elements of occupiers' liability which are not really in issue eg 'occupier', 'premises' and Craig's status as a visitor.

Skeleton Solution

Explain and identify the 'occupier' of the premises concerned – discuss whether Craig is a visitor or trespasser when he enters the room adjacent to the waiting area – identify the relevant Occupiers' Liability Act – discuss whether the occupier owed Craig a duty of care, and if so, whether such a duty was broken – did Mugshots discharge their duty to Craig by providing a sufficient warning, or by the proper selection and supervision of an independent contractor? – can Belinda claim for her 'nervous shock' as a secondary victim of the accident?

Suggested Solution

The question concerns the liability of an occupier of premises for damage done to those who come onto the premises. The law relating to such liability is largely to be found in the Occupiers' Liability Act (OLA) 1957 as regards visitors to premises.

The occupier of the premises

Under s1(2) OLA 1957 the definition of 'occupier' remains the same as at common law. In this scenario, the occupier of the building in which the accident occurred is clearly Mugshots, as it is they who had a 'sufficient degree of control over the premises' and 'ought to have realised that any failure on their part to use care may result in injury': *Wheat* v *E Lacon and Co Ltd* [1966] AC 552.

However, it is possible for there to be more than one occupier of premises at the same time. Multiple occupation was contemplated as a possibility by Lord Denning in *Wheat* (above) and was held to exist in *AMF International Ltd* v *Magnet Bowling Ltd* [1968] 1 WLR 1028. The question may arise as to whether Derek could be regarded as an occupier of the room adjoining the waiting area: even though he is not present during normal opening hours, he presumably has some ongoing control over the work area and the state in which it is left. Whilst every case turns upon its own facts, it was held in *Page* v *Read* [1984] 134 NLJ 723 that the degree of control associated with the presence and activities of a decorator painting a house was insufficient to give rise to a duty as an occupier. It is therefore submitted that the sole occupier(s) of the business premises in this scenario are likely to be the partners of Mugshots.

This does not prevent Derek from being held liable for Craig's injuries as a non-occupier under ordinary negligence principles, and it has been noted that there is little difference between the standards of care required in ordinary common law negligence compared to those required under OLA 1957. However, ultimately Craig would be best advised to pursue the defendant with the deepest pockets, and this will require a claim against Mugshots under OLA 1957, who are the most likely defendant to carry public liability insurance.

Premises

The room adjacent to the waiting area and the shelving are clearly premises within the meaning of OLA 1957, with s1(3)(a) of the Act referring to 'any fixed or moveable structure'. Even a ladder could be regarded as 'premises' provided it remains in control of the occupier when the accident occurs: *Wheeler* v *Copas* [1981] 3 All ER 405.

Is Craig a visitor or trespasser?

Section 1(2) OLA 1957 states that a lawful visitor is, for the purposes of the Act, either an invitee or a licensee. This requires such a person to have had the occupier's express or implied permission to come on to the premises. Craig is a visitor to Mugshots' premises: his presence is known to the occupier (or its agents) and this presence is not objected to.

A limitation on the permission of visitors to enter some parts of the premises and not others can render the entrant a trespasser upon entry to the restricted area, provided proper steps have been taken to bring the limitation to the visitor's attention: *Gould* v *McAuliffe* [1941] 2 All ER 527. However, it is submitted that the shouting of a warning to 'come back' directed at a deaf child was insufficient to achieve any such limitation, and therefore Craig should be regarded as a visitor when he enters the room adjoining the waiting area.

Are Mugshots in breach of the 'common duty of care'?

Section 2(1) OLA 1957 imposes a common duty of care on occupiers in respect of all visitors to their premises. Section 2(2) states that the duty is:

> 'To take such care as in all the circumstances of the case is reasonable to see that the visitor will be reasonably safe in using the premises for the purposes for which he is invited or permitted by the occupier to be there.'

In deciding how much care Mugshots should reasonably have taken to ensure that Craig was reasonably safe on their premises, a number of factors will be taken into account, such as the nature of the danger, the steps necessary to remove it and the likelihood of injury resulting. In addition, s2(3)(a) OLA 1957 expressly provides that 'an occupier must be prepared for children to be less careful than adults'.

In order to exercise a reasonable degree of care in supervising Derek, it could be argued that Mugshots should have supervised Derek more carefully, ensuring that the shelving was properly secured whilst Derek was absent from the premises. Mugshots might also have closed off the work area by rendering the swing doors inoperable, assuming access to the room could have been avoided during normal business hours. It could be further argued that the oral warning was not enough to allow Craig to be reasonably safe (under s2(4)(a) OLA 1957), in that it failed to identify a specific danger in a specific place, and because Mugshots either knew, or ought to have realised (on the basis of what they had seen of Belinda and Craig) that Craig was deaf. It is possible that shouting a warning to a small boy is inadequate in any event.

Mugshots will undoubtedly attempt to argue that their warning (via their 'agent' employee, Ethel) was enough, in all the circumstances, to enable Craig to be reasonably safe (s2(4)(a) OLA 1957), and that their duty towards him was thereby discharged. In addition, Mugshots might argue that they were entitled to assume that a reasonable mother would not permit her very young child to be allowed to remain in the waiting area alone, especially if very deaf. At the very least, Belinda could have asked the receptionist to supervise her child, and in addition, warned her of Craig's deafness. Alternatively, Belinda might reasonably have been expected to satisfy herself that there were no immediate dangers facing Craig whilst she left him to have her photograph taken. In short, Mugshots would argue that they could not have foreseen that the unsecured shelving in the work area would be a danger to Craig, given Belinda's responsibility for her child's safety. On this point see *Phipps* v *Rochester Corporation* [1955] 1 QB 450, a case in which the occupier of land was held not to have broken any duty of care in respect of a child of five years of age who was not accompanied by an adult.

If this last argument were to succeed, the view appears to be that Belinda herself would be liable as a joint tortfeasor to Craig in common law negligence. Mugshots would primarily be fully liable to Craig, but would have a right to recover a contribution from Belinda under the Civil Liability (Contribution) Act 1978: see Winfield and Jolowicz, *Tort* (16th edn, 2002) at p301.

Have Mugshots discharged their duty to take reasonable care by adequate selection and supervision of an independent contractor under s2(4)(b) OLA 1957?

Mugshots will not be answerable to Craig under this provision if the following criteria are all satisfied.

a) There must have been 'faulty execution of any work of construction … by an independent contractor employed by the occupier'. In practice, these words are given a broad and purposeful construction and it is submitted that they are wide enough to cover dangerously unguarded and unsecured work-in-progress, such as the shelving in the instant case.

b) Mugshots must have acted reasonably in entrusting the work to an independent contractor. It is submitted that it is most probably common commercial practice to engage an independent contractor to put up shelving, even if the job could probably have been undertaken by anyone in the firm with basic DIY skills. Thus, it is probably the case that Mugshots acted reasonably in hiring someone to carry out the work for them.

c) Mugshots must have taken reasonable care to ensure that Derek was competent to carry out the work. This will depend upon the reasons why Mugshots selected Derek to do the work in the first place, and whether they took steps to satisfy themselves that he had sufficient experience to do the job properly. It is clearly relevant to know whether Derek's job on the council involves work of a similar nature.

d) Mugshots must have taken reasonable care to check, if appropriate, that the 'work had been properly done'. Mugshots clearly failed to check that the shelving had been properly secured. Given that the work was not of a particularly technical nature, it is submitted that it would have been reasonable for them to have done so.

Thus it would appear from (d) above that Mugshots may remain answerable to Craig under OLA 1957, assuming that they are in breach of their common duty of care.

Liability in respect of Belinda's 'nervous shock'.

Assuming that Mugshots are liable to Craig under OLA 1957, or that Derek is liable as a non-occupier in negligence, Belinda may be able to claim as a secondary victim, ie one who was not personally involved in the accident nor placed in fear of suffering injury, but nonetheless perceived the consequences of a tort, suffering psychiatric illness as a result.

Two initial requirements which are immediately satisfied on the facts are as follows:

a) Belinda suffered a medically recognised psychiatric illness, ie severe depression: *Chadwick* v *British Transport Commission* [1967] 2 All ER 945; and

b) the illness resulted from a sudden shock.

There are a number of criteria which must be met if Belinda is to succeed in her claim. These criteria were first established by the House of Lords in *McLoughlin* v *O'Brian* [1983] 1 AC 410 and subsequently refined in *Alcock* v *Chief Constable of South Yorkshire* [1992] 1 AC 310. These criteria all seem to apply to Belinda, and can be summarised as follows.

a) It was reasonably foreseeable that Belinda would suffer psychiatric illness, as her relationship with the primary victim (Craig) was sufficiently close. In *McLoughlin* it was held that the relationship between parent and child was sufficiently proximate to recover.

b) Belinda's proximity to the accident or its 'immediate aftermath' was sufficiently close in both space and time. Belinda was in the same building as Craig when the accident occurred and she immediately ran to him when she heard his screams.

c) Belinda suffered psychiatric illness through hearing the accident and seeing its immediate aftermath.

It must be remembered that Belinda may be held partly responsible for Craig's accident and, if so, she may suffer a reduction in compensation on a finding that she was contributory negligent under the Law Reform (Contributory Negligence) Act 1945.

QUESTION FIVE

Sally, aged 10 and a very promising pianist, went to the Grungetown funfair with her mother. She took a ride on the children's chair-o'-plane. While she was on the ride, some pieces of metal broke off. Sally was struck in the arm. The ride was stopped immediately by an automatic safety mechanism and Sally was left trapped in her chair at the top of the ride. Tom, a visitor to the funfair, told staff that he was a steel erector and accustomed to working at heights, and that he was therefore willing to climb up and attend to Sally before the emergency services arrived. Tom had almost reached Sally when he lost his footing and fell to the ground. Sally was released after half an hour, but her arm was permanently disabled. Tom broke his back in the fall and is permanently paralysed and unable to find work.

Advise Sally and Tom as to their entitlement to damages and the principles on which any damages are assessed.

University of London LLB Examination
(for External Students) Law of Tort June 1997 Q3

General Comment

This question raises a wide range of issues so the planning of the answers is vital. Some attempt must be made to deal with Sally's cause(s) of action arising from the original impact and the delay in reaching safety and receiving attention; and the causative effects of the safety mechanism as well as the legal basis and extent of her recovery should be discussed. As for Tom, it will be necessary to consider his position both as visitor and as rescuer, possible defences based upon volenti non fit injuria and contributory negligence, and the basis and extent of his recovery.

Skeleton Solution

Sally's possible causes of action: negligence, under Occupiers' Liability Act 1957; *Rylands* v *Fletcher*; breach of statutory duty – the automatic safety device; the half-hour delay; possible multiple causation and possible novus actus interveniens – Sally's basis of recovery; loss of amenity and her musical prospects; remoteness of damage – Tom as visitor: possible defences – Tom as rescuer: possible defences – Tom's basis of recovery.

Suggested Solution

We are not told the precise cause of the metal fracture. The evidence on this may affect the causes of action relied upon by Sally, but the various possibilities that suggest themselves are: negligence simplicitor based on a failure to maintain or inspect; breach of the common duty of care owed to lawful visitors by the funfair as occupiers under the Occupiers' Liability Act (OLA) 1957; and there might be an 'escape' within the meaning attached to that phrase under the principle in *Rylands* v *Fletcher* (1868) LR 3 HL 330; there might, indeed, be a breach of statutory duty involved as a great deal of fairground machinery is affected by such duties, particularly where safety fencing of moving machinery is involved.

To examine possible difficulties within such a range of potential causes of action is not possible in the time available so, for present purposes, it is assumed that the damage was reasonably foreseeable and that Sally will have a good cause of action based on common law negligence and under the OLA 1957. The next question is whether Sally's injury was in any way affected by the half-hour delay caused by the automatic safety mechanism. If there is no particular additional damage caused by the delay, the situation between Sally and the funfair remains unchanged; if there was reasonable foreseeability of the metal fracture there was also likely to be reasonable foreseeability of the delay in reaching the ground. If, by contrast, the delay has caused some identifiable increase in damage, such as might occur with splintered bones or severed nerves, there is a possible defence argument that the automatic safety system has interfered with the causative process as a possible novus actus interveniens. This would be a complex argument and would probably turn on the question of how foreseeable the consequence was, and how practicable it was to get emergency access and egress. If there were real problems with causation, the court would adopt a commonsense approach: *Yorkshire Dale Steamship Co Ltd* v *Minister of War Transport* [1942] AC 691.

Sally's recovery for her personal injuries will be along conventional lines, in that she would receive special damages for provable losses to the date of trial, such as damaged clothes, wasted school fees or tuition fees, extra travelling costs, etc. She will also recover for general damages under several heads. She would be able to recover for pecuniary loss in respect of future loss of earning potential, which would be likely to be estimated on an annual percentage sum below the national adult average earnings at the time of trial (the 'multiplicand') multiplied by a number of 'years purchase' representing her working lifetime (the 'multiplier'), which would be considerably reduced to allow for 'accelerated receipt'. The effect of taxation and national insurance contributions on earnings would be allowed for: *British Transport Commission* v *Gourley* [1956] AC 185. Any additional prospective expenses, such as adaptation of home or chattels, might be claimed for, as well as prospective medical expenses. Sally will also, under general damages, recover for pain, suffering and loss of amenity in line with similar injury awards as evidenced by works such as Kemp and Kemp, but there may be a very considerable argument as to whether she will be able to recover for the devastating loss of amenity in being unable to pursue her musical interests and, possibly, a career. The speculative aspects of much of this with a claimant aged ten may well restrict recovery to something nearer to what a healthy non-musician might have recovered. Much will turn on the evidence as to her promise as a musician; the process is analogous to remoteness of damage considerations.

Tom might claim as a visitor under the OLA 1957, on the basis that the funfair staff permitted him to attempt a rescue. He may well fare better under this if there is any defence claim of unnecessary rescue or volenti than if he claims under common law as a rescuer. The fairground will be unable to raise the 'special risks, ordinary incident' defence in s2(3)(b) OLA 1957 because he is not exercising his calling but, instead, is there as their permitted rescuer, although they may raise a volenti non fit injuria defence against him under s2(5). If volenti is raised, the same principles will apply as if Tom proceeded as a rescuer of Sally on ordinary negligence grounds. He is unlikely to be seen as volenti (*Baker* v *T E Hopkins and Sons Ltd* [1959] 1 WLR 966) unless the rescue was seen to be 'wanton' as in *Cutler* v *United Dairies Ltd* [1933] 2 KB 297.

Tom's basis of recovery is similar to that of Sally, except that his loss of earning capacity will be much easier quantified, and there will be heavy existing and prospective costs for attendance and nursing care, again worked out on a multiplicand/multiplier basis.

QUESTION SIX

Vick's hobby was jogging. He went for a long jog in the Essex countryside. He did not take a detailed map with him and as a result he got lost. He saw a road in the distance and, to get to it, he climbed over a locked farm gate and started to cross a farm field. There was a notice on the gate which stated: 'Private Property – No Trespassers. Warning: the farmland is dangerous. No liability accepted for any injuries.' Halfway across the field, Vick fell into a five-foot deep hole which was hidden by grass and branches. The owner of the farm, Cedric, had dug this hole two years ago when he was thinking of building a silo. Cedric had abandoned the silo project but forgotten to close the hole. Vick broke his back in the fall.

Advise Vick if he has any rights against Cedric.

Written by the Author

General Comment

Whilst there is a general theme relating to occupiers' liability, the facts clearly incline specifically towards the Occupiers' Liability Act 1984. Hence, discussion should focus on the liability of an occupier towards trespassers and not visitors, although a brief reference to the 1957 Act is useful to bring out the distinctions between the two statutes. Of relevance also is the Unfair Contract Terms Act 1977 and its non-application to the 1984 Act.

Skeleton Solution

Occupiers' Liability Act 1984: duties owed by an occupier towards trespassers; the application of s1(3) and its subsections; the exclusion of liability and the effect of s1(5) – a brief comparison with the Occupiers' Liability Act 1957 and the questionable applicability of Unfair Contract Terms Act 1977 – defence of volenti and contributory negligence, if any.

Suggested Solution

Clearly, the main issue is whether Vick can sue Cedric for compensation for breach of the occupier's statutory duty of care owed to a trespasser. Under the Occupiers' Liability Act (OLA) 1984 the liability of an occupier towards trespassers is defined by s1(3) which states that for a duty of care to arise:

a) the occupier is aware of the danger or has reasonable grounds to believe that it exists;

b) the occupier knows or has reasonable grounds to believe that the non-visitor is in the vicinity of the danger or may come into the vicinity of the danger; and

c) the risk is one against which, in all the circumstances, the occupier may reasonably be expected to offer the non-visitor some protection.

In the present problem the danger was a five-foot deep hole which Cedric himself had dug two years ago and which he had forgotten to fill in or close. Consequently, it would be difficult for Cedric to deny knowledge of this hazard. Further, he must have been aware of the risk of trespass because he had put up a notice discouraging it. Since no effective security measures were taken to prevent trespass (such as an electric fence), the possibility that a trespasser might ignore Cedric's notice and come onto the land within the vicinity of the hole is one that cannot be excluded, and Cedric should have been aware of it. Also, from a practical point of view, since it would take comparatively little effort and resources to fill in the hole or to fence it adequately, Cedric would have been expected to provide such protection against this particular danger, and one which posed a serious threat of injury to any potential trespasser.

Hence, it would appear that all three elements required for the imposition of liability on an occupier under s1(3) of the 1984 Act are present, despite the fact that Vick clearly falls within the definition of a trespasser as provided in *Addie v Dumbreck* [1929] AC 358 and subsequently reaffirmed by the House of Lords in *British Railways Board v Herrington* [1972] AC 877.

Under the OLA 1984, s1(5) permits an occupier to be excluded from his duty by giving adequate warning of the danger to the trespasser, or by otherwise discouraging trespassers from incurring risk. It would appear that the warning need not be such as to make the place reasonably safe for the trespasser to enter, in contrast to the duty owed by the occupier to visitors under s2(4)(a) of the OLA 1957, as illustrated by *Roles v Nathan* [1963] 1 WLR 1117. Hence, it is arguable that Cedric's general warning notice on the gate may be sufficient to exempt him from liability, although the court will have regard to all the circumstances of the case. It is noteworthy that because the hole was a potential risk to Cedric's visitors (despite the warning which was general in nature), the warning may be seen as inadequate to exonerate Cedric from liability. For a more recent decision on the effect of 'warnings', see the House of Lords' case of *Tomlinson v Congleton Borough Council and Another* [2004] 1 AC 46. Here, the warning provided by the occupier was held to be sufficient in order to indemnify the occupier of any liability towards potential trespassers.

Be that as it may, it also appears that although Cedric's liability is clear on the basis of the test laid down in *White v St Albans City and District Council* (1990) The Times 12 March, the OLA 1984 may not be subject to the provisions of the Unfair Contract Terms Act 1977 which specifically applies to the tort of negligence and the duty of care owed under the OLA 1957. Hence, it is open to Cedric to exclude liability for personal injury sustained by trespassers on his land, despite the injury being one which satisfies the remoteness test, as illustrated in *Jolley* v *Sutton London Borough Council* [2000] 3 All ER 409.

The defence of volenti as provided by s1(6) OLA 1984 would not be available to Cedric because although Vick voluntarily entered the land which knew, by virtue of the notice, might be dangerous, he was acting under the pressure of being lost and the need to find the nearest road; in a sense he was rescuing himself and hence could not have been truly consenting to run the risk of injury. The defence of contributory negligence under the Law Reform (Contributory Negligence) Act 1945 would not be of any use to Cedric because the fact that Vick was to blame for getting himself lost in the first place is not sufficiently proximate to the incident of falling down into the hole to be regarded as contributory negligence. However, Vick's decision to ignore the warning notice might count as contributory negligence so as to justify a reduction in the award of damages by the court.

Chapter 12

Private and Public Nuisance

12.1 Introduction

12.2 Key points

12.3 Key cases and statutes

12.4 Questions and suggested solutions

12.1 Introduction

Nuisance, especially private nuisance, can be a complex and confusing topic. This confusion arises because there are few hard and fast rules as to what is a nuisance; rather there are a number of guidelines or factors which the courts may or may not decide are relevant in determining whether an activity amounts to a nuisance. (When we refer to nuisance we mean private nuisance – public nuisance will always be referred to by its full name.)

12.2 Key points

Private nuisance

Definition

Nuisance is an unreasonable interference with a person's use or enjoyment of land, or of some right over, or in connection with it.

Claimants

As nuisance is connected with a person's use or enjoyment of land, the traditional view was that only persons with an interest in land could sue: *Malone* v *Laskey* [1907] 2 KB 141. The necessity for this interest was removed in *Khorasandjian* v *Bush* [1993] 3 WLR 476, where a daughter who lived with her parents was allowed to sue in nuisance. In *Hunter* v *Canary Wharf Ltd* [1996] 1 All ER 482 it was held that a substantial link between the person and the land was necessary, such as occupation of the property as a house. See also *Crown River Cruises Ltd* v *Kimbolton Fireworks Ltd* [1996] 2 Lloyd's Rep 533. Interestingly, in *Pemberton* v *Southwark London Borough Council* [2000] 3 All ER 924, the Court of Appeal held that a 'tolerated trespasser' was able to sue.

Type of harm covered

It is not possible to classify each and every possible activity that may be actionable in nuisance, but three main groups may be identified.

a) Encroachment, ie physical objects actually interfering with the claimant's land, eg tree roots: see *Davey* v *Harrow Corporation* [1958] 1 QB 60. The House of Lords held that a change of ownership of a property does not break the chain of continuity of a nuisance: see *Delaware Mansions Ltd* v *Westminster City Council* [2001] 4 All ER 737 for a relevant (tree-roots) example.

Also includes landslides onto land: *Leakey* v *National Trust* [1980] QB 485.

b) Physical damage to land, eg overflow of water (*Sedleigh-Denfield* v *O'Callaghan* [1940] AC 880) and vibrations: *Hoare* v *McAlpine* [1923] 1 Ch 167.

In *Holbeck Hall Hotel* v *Scarborough Borough Council* [2000] 2 WLR 1396 the court held that the defendant was under a duty to take reasonable steps to provide weatherproofing for the wall once it was exposed to the elements as a result of demolition of the adjoining property. This decision was subsequently affirmed in *Rees* v *Skerrett* [2001] 1 WLR 1541.

c) Interference with enjoyment of property, eg noise (*Tetley* v *Chitty* [1986] 1 All ER 663), smell (*Adams* v *Ursell* [1913] 1 Ch 269) and sex shop in residential area: *Laws* v *Florinplace* [1981] 1 All ER 659.

Unreasonable interference: factors

Not all interferences give rise to liability; there must be give and take between neighbours and the interference must be substantial and not fanciful: *Walter* v *Selfe* (1851) 20 LJ Ch 433. This fact was reaffirmed by the House of Lords in *Southwark London Borough Council* v *Mills; Baxter* v *Camden London Borough Council* [1999] 1 All ER 449. Some factors that the courts taken into account include the following.

a) Duration of the interference

The shorter the duration of the interference the less likely it is to be found unreasonable: *Harrison* v *Southwark & Vauxhall Water Co* [1891] 2 Ch 409.

In *Bolton* v *Stone* [1951] AC 850 it was said that an isolated happening could not constitute a nuisance – what is required is a wrongful state of affairs, even if only temporary: see *Midwood* v *Mayor of Manchester* [1905] 2 KB 597.

b) Sensitivity of the claimant

No account is taken of abnormal sensitivity of persons or property: *Robinson* v *Kilvert* (1884) 41 Ch D 88; *Heath* v *Mayor of Brighton* (1908) 98 LT 718. So if the only reason for the damage is such an abnormal sensitivity the claimant will be without a remedy.

c) Character of the neighbourhood

This is a relevant factor where interference is with health and comfort: *Bamford* v *Turnley* (1860) 3 B & S 62, but not where physical damage to property has been caused: *St Helens Smelting Co* v *Tipping* (1865) 11 HL 642. Note the dictum in *Sturges* v *Bridgman* (1879) 11 Ch D 852: 'what would be a nuisance in Belgrave Square would not necessarily be so in Bermondsey'. Note also that if planning consent has been given for a development, the character of the neighbourhood must be decided by reference to that development and not as it was previously: *Gillingham Borough Council* v *Medway (Chatham) Dock Co* [1992] 3 WLR 449. However, see also *Wheeler* v *Saunders* [1995] 3 WLR 466.

d) Utility of the defendant's conduct

This may be particularly relevant as regards certain activities, eg construction works. However, it is only a factor and may be overriden by other factors in the case: *Bellew* v *Cement Co* [1948] Ir R 61; *Adams* v *Ursell* [1913] 1 Ch 269.

e) Malice

Malice is not a necessary ingredient of nuisance, but its presence may make an otherwise non-actionable act actionable: *Hollywood Silver Fox Farm* v *Emmett* [1936] 2 KB 468.

f) Fault by the defendant

Negligence is not an essential ingredient of nuisance, although it may be present, and it is no defence to nuisance to show that the defendant took all reasonable, or even all possible, care.

Note that the defendant's carelessness in allowing an annoyance to become excessive may make him liable in nuisance: *Andreae* v *Selfridge* [1938] Ch 1.

Defendants

a) Creator of nuisance

The creator of the nuisance by misfeasance rather than non-feasance may be sued even if he no longer occupies the land from which the nuisance emanates: *Southport Corporation* v *Esso Petroleum* [1956] AC 218; [1954] QB 182; [1953] 3 WLR 773.

b) Occupier of the land

The occupier is liable if he creates the nuisance: he is also liable if an independent contractor creates the nuisance following the occupier's instructions and such nuisance was foreseeable.

In *Sedleigh-Denfield* v *O'Callaghan* (above) it was held that an occupier would be liable for a nuisance created by a trespasser where he continued or adopted the nuisance. The occupier is also liable for a nuisance arising out of the natural condition of his land if he knows of the risk and fails to take appropriate action: *Goldman* v *Hargrave* [1967] 1 AC 645; *Leakey* v *National Trust* [1980] QB 485. In other decisions – *Marcic* v *Thames Water Utilities Ltd* [2001] 3 All ER 698 (QBD) and *Marcic* v *Thames Water Utilities Ltd (No 2)* [2001] 1 All ER (D) 111 – it was held that nuisance resulting from the breach of the defendants' duty to take such care as is reasonable under the circumstances was actionable. Conversely, see *Marcic* v *Thames Water Utilities Ltd* [2004] 1 All ER 135 where the House of Lords held that an occupier was not liable purely by virtue of that occupation.

See also the relevance of art 8 of the European Convention on Human Rights and s6 Human Rights Act 1998 in this context.

Landlords

Generally a landlord who has leased premises is not liable for any nuisance subsequently arising therefrom, unless:

a) the nuisance existed prior to the granting of the lease and the landlord knew this;

b) the landlord granted the lease for a purpose which constitutes a nuisance: *Tetley* v *Chitty* (above);

c) the landlord has reserved the right to enter and repair (the landlord is liable whether or not he knows of the defect that gives rise to the nuisance: *Wringe* v *Cohen* [1940] 1 KB 229); or

d) an independent third party, over whom the landlord has no control whatsoever, causes a nuisance. See *Hussain* v *Lancaster City Council* [1999] 4 All ER 125, in which the Court of Appeal distinguished its earlier decision in *Lippiatt* v *South Gloucestershire Council* [1999] 4 All ER 149.

Defences

a) Prescription

Continuing a nuisance for 20 years will legalise it by prescription. Time does not begin to run until the claimant is aware that the nuisance exists: *Sturges* v *Bridgman* (above).

b) Statutory authority

If statute permits, either expressly or by implication, interference with the claimant's rights, no action will lie. See *Allen* v *Gulf Oil Refining* [1981] AC 1001 as regards implied authorisation. This defence will only operate where the interference is an inevitable result of the authorised act: *Corporation of Manchester* v *Farnworth* [1930] AC 171.

c) Other defences

Volenti, contributory negligence, act of God or a stranger and ignorance, where the nuisance is caused 'by a secret and unobservable operation of nature': *Noble* v *Harrison* [1926] 2 KB 332.

Invalid defences

There are a number of defences to nuisance that are not valid.

a) That the claimant came to the nuisance

The ineffectiveness of this defence is shown by *Sturges* v *Bridgman* (above). Note the anomalous dicta in the Court of Appeal in *Miller* v *Jackson* [1977] QB 966 which have not been followed in later cases.

b) Usefulness of the defendant's activity

For example, *Adams* v *Ursell* (above); *Bellew* v *Cement Co* (above).

c) Defendant one of many

It is no defence that the nuisance was caused by a number of persons acting together and the defendant's actions, by themselves, would not have amounted to a nuisance: *Lambton* v *Mellish* [1894] 3 Ch 163.

Remedies

a) Injunction

i) Discretionary remedy that will only be granted where damages are not an adequate remedy.

ii) Note private interests prevailed over public interests in *Pride of Derby* v *British Celanese* [1953] Ch 149 and in *Kennaway* v *Thompson* [1981] QB 88, and that *Miller* v *Jackson* (above) is anomalous in giving priority to public interests.

b) Abatement

Allowed subject to three conditions:

i) notice to defendant;

ii) no unnecessary damage;

iii) least cost to defendant.

See *Burton* v *Winters* [1993] 1 WLR 1077.

c) Damages

i) Usually sought for past nuisance or where property damage has occurred.

ii) Whether damages can be recovered for personal injuries is an undecided point: *Malone* v *Laskey* [1907] 2 KB 141 suggests yes; *Cunard* v *Antifyre* [1933] 1 KB 551 suggests no. However, the tenor of the House of Lords' decision in *Cambridge*

Water Co v *Eastern Counties Leather plc* [1994] 2 WLR 53 strongly suggests, albeit obiter, that no recovery is possible.

iii) It is also uncertain whether pure economic loss is recoverable, although *British Celanese* v *Hunt* [1969] 1 WLR 959 suggests that it is.

iv) The test for remoteness of damage is reasonable foreseeability: *The Wagon Mound (No 2)* [1967] AC 617.

v) The court may award damages in lieu of an injunction: s50 Supreme Court Act 1981. This power is sparingly used according to the principles in *Shelfer* v *City of London Electric Lighting Co* [1895] 1 Ch 287, ie only if: the injury is small; it is capable of being estimated in money; damage can be compensated by a small money payment; and it would be oppressive to the defendant to grant the injunction.

Public nuisance

Public nuisance is a crime as well as a tort. Similar to private nuisance except in public nuisance it is well established that there is no need to have an interest in the land affected and prescription is not a defence. However, the claimant must prove the following.

a) The persons affected by the nuisance are the public or a section of the public: *Attorney-General* v *PYA Quarries* [1957] 2 QB 169; *R* v *Johnson (Anthony Thomas)* [1997] 1 WLR 367.

b) He has suffered damage in excess of annoyance suffered by public at large: *Rose* v *Miles* (1815) 4 M & S 101.

c) Special rules cover public nuisance and the highway.

i) Unreasonable obstruction of the highway constitutes a public nuisance: *Dymond* v *Pearce* [1972] 1 QB 497, even if the obstruction is temporary: *Barber* v *Penley* [1893] 2 Ch 447.

ii) A danger on the highway, eg a pile of rubble, is a public nuisance: *Clark* v *Chambers* (1878) 3 QBD 327.

iii) A danger close to the highway is a public nuisance, so an occupier of premises close to the highway must keep his premises in repair: *Tarry* v *Ashton* (1876) 1 QBD 314 whether or not he is aware of the danger: *Wringe* v *Cohen* [1940] 1 KB 229. There is an exception where the damage arose from a secret and unobservable operation of nature: see *British Road Services* v *Slater* [1964] 1 WLR 498.

iv) Condition of the highway. Section 41 Highways Act 1980 places a duty on highway authorities to maintain highways and s58 provides the defence that reasonable care was taken: see the decision of the House of Lords in *Goodes* v *East Sussex County Council* [2000] 3 All ER 603 for an example.

The Court of Appeal recently upheld the decision of the trial judge that the owner of the property from which pigeon droppings fell was not liable in public nuisance: see *Wandsworth London Borough Council v Railtrack plc* [2001] 1 WLR 368.

12.3 Key cases and statutes

- *Delaware Mansions Ltd v Westminster City Council* [2001] 4 All ER 737
  House of Lords held that a change of ownership does not break the chain of continuity

- *Goodes v East Sussex County Council* [2000] 3 All ER 603
  Makes available the defence of reasonable care having been taken

- *Holbeck Hall Hotel v Scarborough Borough Council* [2000] 2 WLR 1396
  Illustrates the fact that there is a positive duty to take reasonable steps to prevent nuisance

- *Hunter v Canary Wharf Ltd* [1996] 1 All ER 482
  There must be a substantial link between the person and the land for there to be a right of action

- *Hussain v Lancaster County Council* [1999] 4 All ER 125
  The landlord is not liable for the acts of nuisance of third parties over whom the landlord has no control

- *Khorasandjian v Bush* [1993] 3 WLR 476
  The necessity for an 'interest' in land in order to sue was removed

- *Malone v Laskey* [1907] 2 KB 141
  Only those with interest in land could sue in nuisance

- *Marcic v Thames Water Utilities Ltd* [2001] 3 All ER 698
  Nuisance relating from the defendant's breach of duty is actionable

- *Marcic v Thames Water Utilities Ltd* [2004] 1 All ER 135
  Mere occupation does not attract liability in nuisance

- *Pemberton v Southwark London Borough Council* [2000] 3 All ER 924
  A 'tolerated trespasser' was held to be able to sue

- *Rees v Skerrett* [2001] 1 WLR 1541
  Illustrates the fact that there is a positive duty to take reasonable steps to prevent nuisance

- *Southwark London Borough Council v Mills; Baxter v Camden London Borough Council* [1999] 1 All ER 449
  Court held that not all types of interferences give rise to liability automatically

- *Wandsworth London Borough Council* v *Railtrack plc* [2001] 1 WLR 368
  Owner of property could not sue council in public nuisance for pigeon droppings onto his property

- Defective Premises Act 1972 – imposes liability on owners/occupiers of defective premises in negligence, occupiers' liability as well as in nuisance

- Highways Act 1980 – imposed liability on local authorities in public nuisance for the condition of motorways and roads under their care

12.4 Questions and suggested solutions

QUESTION ONE

'Originally in private nuisance only the person who by himself or his servant or agent created the nuisance on his land which interfered with the use and enjoyment of his neighbour's land was liable. The position was different in public nuisance where once the existence of a nuisance on his land comes to the knowledge of the occupier it is his duty to abate it or endeavour to do so.' (*Holbeck Hall Hotel Ltd* v *Scarborough Borough Council*, per Stuart-Smith LJ.)

Discuss the scope and purpose of the tort of nuisance in the light of this quotation.

University of London LLB Examination
(for External Students) Law of Tort June 2001 Q4

General Comment

An essay question should not be used as an excuse to write a general appraisal of the relevant area of law raised by the question, which in this case is private nuisance. The question refers to a specific observation by a judge in a case, and thus calls for critical appreciation within the context of that observation.

Skeleton Solution

Determining liability in private nuisance – the essential elements – a brief analysis of the *Holbeck Hall Hotel* case – the scope and purpose of the tort of nuisance – trespassers and acts of nature: are they valid defences? – distinction from public nuisance.

Suggested Solution

Private nuisance has been defined by Winfield and Jolowicz (Winfield and Jolowicz, *Law of Tort* (16th edn, 2002) (Chapter 14)) as: 'an unlawful interference with a person's use or enjoyment of land, or some right over, or in connection with it'. The House of Lords confirmed in *Hunter* v *Canary Wharf Ltd* [1997] 2 All ER 426 that private nuisance is a tort which attaches to land, and so only those with a proprietorial interest in the land affected may bring an action.

There are many categories of nuisance, but in determining whether the nuisance is actionable the courts must balance the reasonableness of the defendant's activity (which created the nuisance) against the reasonable needs of the claimant to use and enjoy his property. In *St Helens Smelting Co v Tipping* (1865) 11 HL 642, the House of Lords held that there was a distinction between nuisances which cause damage to property and those which cause personal discomfort in the use or enjoyment of land. However, the point raised by the question at hand is not the basis of liability, but rather who the appropriate defendant should be.

Nuisance is essentially a tort of strict liability in the sense that it will be no defence to show that the nuisance was not created intentionally, or even that the defendant used all reasonable care. The leading case that illustrates this point is *Cambridge Water Company v Eastern Counties Leather plc* [1994] 2 WLR 53. This case is also significant as it contains a comprehensive restatement of the scope of liability in nuisance and of the relationship between orthodox private nuisance and public nuisance.

In *Holbeck Hall Hotel Ltd* v *Scarborough Borough Council* [2000] 2 All ER 705, a cliff belonging to the defendant council gave way, and as a consequence a hotel on neighbouring land belonging to the claimant was destroyed. The case was particularly difficult because while the defendant ought to have foreseen some minor slips causing damage to the claimant's rose garden and lawn, there was no reason why it ought to have foreseen the massive slip which destroyed the hotel. In these circumstances, the Court of Appeal held that an occupier that failed to meet the measured duty to take reasonable steps to prevent a nuisance occurring on its land should only be liable to the extent of the damage that ought to have been foreseen. This, it is submitted, is thought to run counter with the usual rule of remoteness of damage: that a defendant is liable for all damage of the same type as ought to have been foreseen, regardless of the extent: *Overseas Tankship (UK) Ltd v Miller Steamship Co Pty Ltd, The Wagon Mound (No 2)* [1967] 1 AC 617.

However, in *Holbeck* the Court of Appeal further suggested that in the circumstances, where the hazard was a result of the forces of nature and the defendant would have gained little benefit from preserving its own land against the hazard, the defendant might well have fulfilled the duty to act reasonably by informing the claimants of the risk and sharing any information relating to it.

Given that the question of whether an occupier will be liable for consequences resulting from a state of affairs he did not create is answered by considering whether the occupier has fulfilled a measured duty of care, it is sometimes suggested that this group of cases should be considered as falling within the tort of negligence. This then raises the question of whether damages can be obtained when a state of affairs only reduces the amenity value of neighbouring land, for example, where an occupier fails to deal with a regular, noisy trespasser, or with smelly rotting rubbish tipped onto his land by trespassers.

In *Southport Corporation* v *Esso Petroleum Co* [1954] QB 182, it was held that the creator of the nuisance by misfeasance rather than non-feasance may be sued even if he no longer occupies the land from which the nuisance emanates. In *Sedleigh-Denfield* v *O'Callaghan* [1940] AC 880, it was held that an occupier would be liable for a nuisance created by a trespasser where he continued, or adopted, or in any way authorised or continued to authorise the nuisance. Likewise in *Leakey* v *National Trust* [1980] QB 485, the court held that the occupier would also be liable for a nuisance arising out of a condition of his land if he knows of the risk and fails to take appropriate action. This arguably also attracts liability under the Defective Premises Act 1972, which imposes a positive duty on the owner/occupier of a property to ensure that his/her property is in good keep and order. Recently, in *Marcic* v *Thames Water Utilities Ltd* [2001] 3 All ER 698, it was held that a nuisance resulting from the breach of the defendant's duty to take such care as is reasonable under the circumstances was actionable. This decision was subsequently reversed in the House of Lords, *Marcic* v *Thames Water Utilities Ltd* [2004] 1 All ER 135, wherein their lordships held that mere occupation does not attract liability in nuisance. There must be evidence of commission or ommission. This must, of course, be contrasted with the decision of the Court of Appeal in *Hussain* v *Lancaster City Council* [1999] 4 All ER 125, where it was held that a landlord is not liable in nuisance if an independent third party or a trespasser, over whom the landlord has no control whatsoever, causes a nuisance. This seems to be the view within the ambit of public nuisance.

With public nuisance, there is the availability of the defence of all such care as is reasonable under the circumstances having been discharged, as illustrated in *Goodes* v *East Sussex County Council* [2000] 3 All ER 603. This decision was given support by the case of *Southwark London Borough Council* v *Mills* [1999] 1 All ER 449, where the court held that not all types of interferences would give rise to liability automatically. This contention received further approval in *Wandsworth London Borough Council* v *Railtrack plc* [2001] 1 WLR 368, where the court held that an owner of property could not sue the council in public nuisance because pigeon droppings were falling onto his property.

Perhaps the distinction between private and public nuisance (as observed by Stuart-Smith LJ) is that in public nuisance the owner or occupier has a positive duty to abate or take steps to negative the nuisance. This positive duty, however, is subject to the defence of secret and unobservable operations of nature, as illustrated by *British Road Services* v *Slater* [1964] 1 WLR 498.

Public nuisance, unlike private nuisance, is also a crime as well as a tort. Hence it is deserving of more consideration prior to the imposition of liability in any case.

QUESTION TWO

Benison District Council own an inner city site which has been cleared for future development. On the site there is a small gymnasium which has not been demolished. The Council has allowed St Christopher's Church to use the gymnasium each weekday afternoon as a 'drop-in centre' for young homeless people. The church provides a games room, tea and cakes and advice about health and welfare problems. The centre proves very popular, is well attended and often attracts some very rowdy youngsters who are not homeless but hang around the hall all afternoon.

Fenella runs a woman's health club in an adjoining street. She complains that a number of youngsters from the centre are constantly peering through the windows of the club and some of them come in and try to chat to the members of the club. Some of the members have told her that, because they feel uncomfortable and are sometimes frightened to leave the club in the early evening, they have decided not to renew their membership. Every Friday Geoffrey, who occupies the premises next to Fenella, holds meditation sessions for business people afflicted by stress, and complains that the noise from the gymnasium interferes with these sessions.

Discuss whether Fenella or Geoffrey would have a cause of action in nuisance.

University of London LLB Examination
(for External Students) Law of Tort June 2000 Q5

General Comment

Though this appears to be a standard question on private nuisance, attention is drawn to the fact that there are potentially two defendants, the Council and the church. Thus the issue of liability in nuisance should be properly addressed.

Skeleton Solution

Introduction – categories of nuisance – Fenella's claim of nuisance (annoyance): factors or principles of nuisance relevant to establishing liability; who is liable (Council or church)? – Geoffrey's claim of nuisance (noise): factors or principles of nuisance relevant to establishing liability; who is liable (Council or church)? – remedies – possible defences.

Suggested Solution

Nuisance, particularly private nuisance, can be a complex and confusing area of tort. This confusion arises because there are few hard and fast rules as to what amounts to a nuisance: rather, there are a number of guidelines or factors which the court may, or may not, consider as being relevant in determining whether an activity amounts to a nuisance. Private nuisance regulates unreasonable interference with an occupier's use or enjoyment of his rights over land. The law seeks to find a balance between the legitimate, but conflicting, interests of landowners – the right of an occupier to use his land as he chooses – and the right of his neighbour not to have his use of land interfered with. The litigants in these actions are usually neighbours in the popular sense of the word. It is no wonder that an academic, Dean Prosser, (1989) CLJ 55 remarked: 'There is perhaps no more impenetrable jungle in the law than that which surrounds the word "nuisance"'.

As the question concerns the rights of two individuals, Fenella and Geoffrey, each will be dealt with in turn.

Fenella

Fenella's complaint is that there are a number of rowdy youngsters, from the centre run by the church on the premises owned by the Council, who peer through the windows of her health club and have tried to 'chat up' the members of the club, causing fear as well as annoyance. As a result of this, some of the members have informed her that they will not be renewing their membership with the health club.

Clearly, the interference here relates to the enjoyment of the property free from any annoyance. Whilst it is not possible to classify each and every possible activity that may be actionable in nuisance, the three main groups may be identified as the following: cases involving encroachment, as in *Davey v Harrow Corporation* [1958] 1 QB 60; cases involving physical damage to land or property, as in *Sedleigh-Denfield v O'Callaghan* [1940] AC 880; and finally cases involving interference with enjoyment of property, as in *Tetley v Chitty* [1986] 1 All ER 663. Fenella's case would clearly fall within the third category.

It must be pointed out that not all interferences give rise to liability: there must be give and take between neighbours and the interference must be substantial and not fanciful, as stated in *Walter v Selfe* (1851) 20 LJ Ch 433. This fact was reaffirmed in *Baxter v Camden London Borough Council* [1999] 1 All ER 449, by the House of Lords. Fenella is not complaining about noise but rather annoyance in the form of harassment from rowdy youngsters, which seems to be scaring away her members. Two cases deserve consideration on this point. In *Hussain v Lancaster City Council* [1999] 4 All ER 125, the claimants were subjected to a campaign of harassment by people who lived as tenants on a council estate owned by the defendant council. This disrupted the claimant's business. An action for nuisance against the council failed (apart from on grounds concerning policy issues) on the basis that the claim was in essence related to the claimants' right to be free from racial harassment, as opposed to the right in relation to the use of their land or property. Conversely, in *Lippiatt v South Gloucestershire Council* [1999] 4 All ER 149, a group of travellers allegedly set up camp on land belonging to the council and used the camp as a 'launching pad' for a series of damaging invasions on a neighbouring farmer's property. In this case, the Court of Appeal held that the council was arguably liable for the nuisance resulting from the state of affairs on its land.

In Fenella's case, the annoyance created by the rowdy youngsters does in fact interfere with her rights to use her land and property free from interference. Presumably the church is aware of this and has not done anything to address the issue. Thus Fenella could arguably succeed in an action for nuisance against the church. The church would prove to be a better defendant because they can be said to have created, authorised, adopted or allowed to continue the nuisance. It is likely that the council has knowledge of these matters and hence cannot be implicated for not taking reasonable steps to eliminate the problem. The church is the basis of the cause of the nuisance, and it is them who must be held liable. Fenella must also establish the following conditions in order to be successful. First, that the duration of the interference is continuous and unreasonable: *Harrison* v *Southwark & Vauxhall Water Co* [1891] 2 Ch 409. Second, that there is no abnormal sensitivity on her part: *Heath* v *Mayor of Brighton* (1908) 98 LT 718. Third, that the character of the neighbourhood is such that the annoyance or interference is unjustified: *Bamford* v *Turnley* (1860) 3 B & S 62. Fourth, the utility of the defendant's conduct in relation to the nuisance concerned: *Bellew* v *Cement Co* [1948] Ir R 61. Finally, the issue of malice or fault on the part of the defendant must also be considered: *Andreae* v *Selfridge* [1938] Ch 1.

The church has clearly been careless in allowing the annoyance to become excessive and this exposes them to liability in private nuisance. Fenella might apply for an injunction plus damages for the loss that she has suffered. On the facts, the church has no valid defence on which it can rely.

Geoffrey

Geoffrey's complaint is essentially concerned with noise, which is clearly recognised as a category of nuisance, as in *Tetley* v *Chitty* [1986] 1 All ER 663. However, Geoffrey only holds meditation sessions on Friday's and is thus affected only when he holds these sessions. Geoffrey must also prove all the above elements (as discussed under Fenella) in relation to the duration of the interference, abnormal sensitivity, character of the neighbourhood, utility of the defendant's conduct and malice or fault. Geoffrey may have a problem with proving that he (as well as his clients) are not abnormally sensitive (to noise, in this instance). This would be problematic on the basis that they are all involved in meditation sessions. Are the premises appropriate or useful for such an activity to be conducted in? It is submitted that they are not, on the basis of the decision in *Robinson* v *Kilvert* (1884) 41 Ch D 88. Also, given the fact that the whole area might be subject to future development by the Council, this might arguably change the character of the neighbourhood, which would then prove unsuitable for Geoffrey's activity. If Geoffrey is successful in overcoming the 'abnormal sensitivity' hurdle, then his action would be against the church, which is the sole cause of the nuisance (they have created, adopted or authorised it). As in Fenella's case, the church appear to have no valid defence.

QUESTION THREE

'The word "nuisance" is difficult to define precisely. It has been said to be protean when questions are raised as to the conduct which may give rise to liability. But the underlying principles, which distinguish the tort of nuisance from the tort of negligence for example, are, I think, capable of reasonably precise definition in the light of the authorities.' (*Hunter* v *Canary Wharf Ltd* (1997), per Lord Hope of Craighead.)

Discuss.

University of London LLB Examination
(for External Students) Law of Tort June 1998 Q1

General Comment

Recent developments in tort are always likely to form the basis of examination questions, especially important decisions of the House of Lords. Those candidates who have carefully studied the judgment in *Hunter* and its wider implications will have been well placed to answer this question. As ever, a more detailed analysis and comment on the case is expected of candidates, as a compromise to predictability.

Skeleton Solution

Introduce the tort of private nuisance in relation to the *Hunter* case – describe why the tort may be said to be 'protean' in nature, given its application to a wide range of scenarios – what are the distinguishing features of nuisance and negligence (as identified by their Lordships)? – why were these important in the *Hunter* case? – describe the court's decision regarding standing, damages and the applicability of the tort to interference with TV reception (including Lord Cooke's dissent) – conclude by saying something about the importance of the decision in *Hunter* and possible future activity in this area.

Suggested Solution

The case of *Hunter* v *Canary Wharf Limited* [1997] 2 All ER 426 raised important questions as to the scope of the tort of private nuisance. The tort itself is concerned with unreasonable interference with a person's use or enjoyment of his land, or some right over or in connection with his land. The House of Lords in *Hunter* explained the tort as falling within three main categories: nuisance by encroachment on a neighbour's land; nuisance by direct physical injury to a neighbour's land; and nuisance by interference with a neighbour's quiet enjoyment of his land.

These categories are extremely wide in that they cover a large variety of potential claims and factual scenarios. For example, under the third category, interference might be caused by dirt, dust, noise, smoke, smell and vibrations arising from a huge range of activites. In *Thompson-Schwab* v *Costaki* [1956] 1 WLR 335 the sight of prostitutes and their clients entering and leaving neighbouring premises amounted to a private nuisance. In *Khorasandjian* v *Bush* [1993] 3 WLR 476 the Court of Appeal even went so far as to grant an injunction in favour of a young girl against the defendant, who had embarked on a course of harassment against her at the parental home. In *Hunter*, one of the questions before the Lords was whether interference with TV reception suffered by local residents following the construction of the Canary Wharf tower (a building which is almost 250 metres high, over 50 metres square, and clad in stainless steel) could amount to a private nuisance. A second, more fundamental, question related to who had the right to bring an action in nuisance for the interference caused to TV reception, and, in a separate action, for dust caused by the construction of a link road to the Docklands area.

It was this question which prompted the majority of the Lords to comment upon the distinguishing features of actions in nuisance and negligence, and it is this aspect of the *Hunter* case which will be dealt with first.

The distinguishing factors of negligence and nuisance

Lord Hoffmann, quoting from Lord Simonds in *Read v Lyons Ltd* [1947] AC 156, noted that nuisance only protects interests in land, and that it is a tort of strict liability ie it is no defence for a defendant to say that he took all reasonable steps to prevent it. Negligence, on the other hand, is fault-based (breach of a duty to take reasonable care) and protects interests of many kinds, not just those in land. Lord Cooke noted that in nuisance, damages may be recovered for interference with the use and enjoyment of land, whereas there is no remedy for discomfort or distress (not resulting in bodily or psychiatric injury) in negligence. Lord Hope, in examining the scope of each tort, noted that the function of nuisance is to control the activities of an owner/occupier of property within the boundaries of his own land which may harm the owner/occupier of neighbouring land. In other words, the duty is owed to owners and occupiers. In negligence, however, the duty extends to those who are foreseeably closely and directly affected by the defendant's act or omission: *Donoghue v Stevenson* [1932] AC 562. In appropriate circumstances, this might include persons on neighbouring land who are neither owners nor occupiers. It should be noted that in some situations, the two torts overlap and may provide concurrent remedies.

The right to sue in private nuisance

The decision of the majority flowed from the proposition that nuisance is a tort which attaches to land ie is directed against the claimant's enjoyment of the land affected. On this basis, an action in nuisance can only be brought by a person who has an interest in such land. These persons might include one who has actual possession, such as a freeholder, tenant in possession or a licensee with exclusive possession, or a reversioner, where the nuisance is sufficiently permanent in character to damage the reversion itself.

The Lords impliedly accepted the decision of the Court of Appeal in *Foster v Warblington UDC* [1906] 1 KB 648 which upheld the right, in exceptional cases, of someone who has exclusive possession of land (even though he cannot prove title) to sue in private nuisance. Lord Lloyd stated that the first two categories of private nuisance involve damage to land and therefore only a person who has a proprietary interest in that land can sue. By implication, therefore this must also be true of the third category. Lord Hoffmann agreed that the third category did not constitute a separate tort.

In a powerful dissent, Lord Cooke argued that whilst the decision of the majority achieves symmetry and uniformity in the law of nuisance (the rules being the same for each of the three categories), their approach does not give adequate weight to current perceptions of the rights and status of spouses, de facto partners and children living at home. In relation to children in particular, he noted the recognition given to the interests of children by international convention. Article 16 of the UN Convention on the Rights of the Child 1989 protects children from unlawful interference with their home. Article 8 of the European Convention for the Protection of Human Rights and Fundamental Freedoms recognises the right to respect for private and family life, aimed in part at protecting the home. Jurisprudence of the European Court of Human Rights shows that the protection of the home extends to protection from nuisance, even though children clearly have no proprietary rights over the family home.

Lord Cooke therefore considered the Court of Appeal decision of *Khorasandjian* to have been correctly decided and regarded the fact of 'occupation of property as a home' to be an acceptable basis from which to bring an action in nuisance. He felt that other resident members of the family, de facto partners and lodgers, could as a matter of policy be allowed to claim in private nuisance if they had suffered a 'truly serious interference with domestic amenities'.

However, the majority of their Lordships overruled *Khorasandjian*, Lords Goff and Lloyd stating that the Court of Appeal had simply exploited the tort of nuisance in order to introduce, by the back door, a tort of harassment out of sympathy with the claimant. They noted that a tort of harassment had since received statutory protection under the Protection from Harassment Act 1997, and a remedy was no longer needed at common law. The approach taken in *Khorasandjian* was to transform the tort of nuisance to one which attaches to the person rather than to land. The effect would be to allow a claimant to recover for loss less severe than personal injury upon criteria relating only to the balancing of the interests of neighbours, rather than negligence.

Damages

The proposition that the tort of nuisance attaches to land only also formed the basis of the decision of the majority as to the correct measure of damages recoverable in nuisance. Under the first two categories of nuisance involving damage to land, compensation will be assessed according to the diminution in value of the property. This will normally be the cost of remedial work and repair. However, where a nuisance simply affects the enjoyment of land, then damages will be assessed according to the loss of the amenity value of the land, assuming the nuisance does not affect the overall market value. This would be a relatively low single payment to the proprietor(s) of the land, and will not depend upon the overall number of people who were affected.

Although not necessary for the actual decision in *Hunter*, considerable doubt was cast upon the question of whether damages for personal injury are recoverable in private nuisance. Lord Goff stated that the correct action for the recovery of such loss is negligence. Lord Hoffmann drew attention to the anomalous outcome of compensation for personal injury being easier to recover if suffered at home rather than at work.

TV reception

It was agreed unanimously that interference to TV reception in the circumstances did not amount to a private nuisance. The Lords held that a building, which by its mere presence prevents something from reaching the claimant's land, is not a nuisance. The tort must take the form of something emanating from the defendant's land, or, occasionally, from some offensive conduct of neighbours. The blocking of TV reception was comparable by analogy with the loss of a view, which is not actionable in private nuisance. Lords Goff and Hoffmann agreed that at common law, people are entitled to build freely on their land unless restricted by a covenant or an easement. It was further doubted whether an easement could exist against the interruption of TV/radio signals.

A common theme of the majority of their Lordships' judgments related to the unpredictability of building developments causing interference with TV reception, and the large number of potential claimants involved in such a situation. Lords Goff and Hoffmann pointed out that the most appropriate time to raise an objection to possible TV interference would have been at the stage of application for planning permission to the local planning authority, although it was noted that this course of action would not have been open to the residents in this case. Lord Cooke preferred to approach the question according to the reasonable user test, holding that Canary Wharf Tower had been a reasonable development in all the circumstances.

Conclusion

The decision in *Hunter* is an important one, because it preserves the distinction between nuisance and negligence as two separate torts subject to different rules. It settled the question of who can sue in private nuisance and the basis for awarding damages for loss of the use and enjoyment of land. It might be argued that Lord Cooke's approach to the question of standing should achieve favour in the future, as the courts are now under an obligation to decide a case's compatibility with Convention rights (unless prevented from doing so by primary legislation), and to take into account the jurisprudence of the European Court of Human Rights in doing so: Human Rights Act 1998. The protection of the home, as an aspect of the right to respect for private and family life, contained in art 8 of the Convention, seems to require protection to be given to all members of the household against nuisances.

Important questions have yet to be answered following *Hunter*; for example, whether damages for personal injury are available in nuisance and whether interference with TV reception caused by something emanating from the defendant's land can form the basis of an action. Further judicial activity in this area can be anticipated. For the time being, the House of Lords appear to have applied the brakes to the development of the tort of nuisance to cover novel situations.

QUESTION FOUR

Maisie and Nigel live next door to each other in a row of terraced houses. Nigel works on night shifts and is studying for an Open University degree. He spends most days sleeping, studying or watching Open University programmes on television. Maisie has been licensed by the local council under statutory powers as a child minder and is permitted to look after up to ten children under five during the daytime from Monday to Friday. Nigel finds the noise of the children in Maisie's house and garden very distracting; it keeps him awake and makes it difficult to concentrate on the television programmes. He has taken to singing obscene songs in a loud voice. Some of the young children have picked up the words and the parents are threatening to remove them from Maisie's care.

Advise Maisie and Nigel.

University of London LLB Examination
(for External Students) Law of Tort June 1996 Q1

General Comment

This is a classic private nuisance problem involving two neighbours whose uses of their property are mutually incompatible. The question involves analysing the strengths of each side's potential claim in nuisance and the remedies available to each.

Skeleton Solution

Nigels's claim in nuisance: reasonableness, statutory authority, social utility; remedies; Maisie's claim in nuisance: reasonableness, malice; remedies.

Suggested Solution

Assuming Nigel has the necessary proprietary interest there is a prima facie argument against Maisie. Noise is a type of disruption which is capable of amounting to nuisance: *Halsey* v *Esso Petroleum Co Ltd* [1961] 1 WLR 683. Nigel will need to establish that Maisie's conduct is unreasonable; however arguments that Maisie's conduct is socially useful, and that it has been authorised or licensed by statute will mitigate against this.

Considering the social utility of Maisie's conduct first, although this does not strictly speaking amount to a defence to a nuisance action (*Bellew* v *Cement Ltd* [1948] Ir R 61 and *Adams* v *Ursell* [1913] 1 Ch 269) it will be taken into account when assessing whether or not Maisie's conduct has been unreasonable, and so a nuisance. Certainly the balance of utility here would seem to be against Nigel, as his study habits and requirements are a purely personal preference, whereas Maisie's conduct is of use to the community at large. Further, Nigel's wish to sleep during the day is idiosyncratic, and the law of nuisance will not protect an abnormally sensitive claimant: *Robinson* v *Kilvert* (1889) 41 Ch 88. On balance I would advise that on the face of it Nigel cannot complain that Maisie's conduct is unreasonable. This is of course subject to evidence about the noise levels, which may in fact be abnormally loud.

In addition to this, Masie may be able to rely on the fact that she has statutory licence to carry on her activities. The House of Lords case of *Allen* v *Gulf Oil Refining Co Ltd* [1981] AC 1001 is the leading authority on this defence. In the *Allen* case villagers sued in nuisance for disruption caused by the construction of an oil refinery near their village. The construction had been authorised by statute. Although the statute contained no direct authorisation for the noise levels etc involved, the House of Lords held that this disruption was a natural consequence of the authorised act and held against the villagers. According to this authority, were Nigel to win on the reasonableness point Maisie would have to show that the noise levels were a natural consequence of the authorised act, ie childminding for up to ten children up to five years old. I would submit that Maisie would have no difficulty establishing this (subject again to the levels not being abnormally high for this size of a group of children) and for these reasons Nigel's claim would be unlikely to succeed.

Turning to Maisie's case, again noise is the problem and this is capable of being a nuisance (*Halsey*), and again Maisie will have to show that Nigel has been unreasonable in his conduct: *Miller* v *Jackson* [1977] QB 966.

In *Christie* v *Davey* [1893] 1 Ch 316 the defendant was so annoyed by the claimant's singing lessons next door that he was provoked into disrupting these by making noise. The deliberate nature of the defendant's conduct made it actionable in nuisance. Similarly in *Hollywood Silver Fox Farm Ltd* v *Emmett* [1936] 2 KB 468 the defendant's malicious conduct in firing his gun to interfere with the breeding of his neighbour's foxes was held to be a nuisance. The contrasting case of *Bradford Corporation* v *Pickles* [1895] AC 587 has been distinguished, and it is submitted that the fact that Nigel is aware of the presence of small children and the fact that his language is obscene point to the conclusion that his conduct is both deliberate and malicious. I would advise Maisie that she has a strong claim against Nigel in nuisance.

There is no direct authority as to whether Maisie can recover damages for loss of business in nuisance, although there are dicta to suggest that loss flowing as a natural consequence of a nuisance may be recoverable: *Ryeford Homes* v *Sevenoaks District Council* (1989) 16 Con LR 75. Since no business has yet been lost I would advise that Maisie seek an injunction against Nigel.

QUESTION FIVE

Last year Whelk acquired a country estate at the edge of a village. There is a large field which is next to Lady Oyster's house. Whelk often hires out the field on Saturdays and Sundays to his friend Mussel who works for a charity which arranged outings and funfairs for children who have been taken into care or who live in deprived inner city areas. Sometimes up to 200 children attend a party. Lady Oyster dislikes the noise and is also upset that many of the children are allowed to run around naked and sometimes make obscene gestures at Lady Oyster and her guests in her garden.

Mussel also sometimes allows his friend Limpet to operate his hamburger and hot dog stall at the entrance to the field. A long queue sometimes forms which blocks the entrance to Lady Oyster's drive. Last week ladies arriving for a bridge party at Lady Oyster's could not turn into her drive because of the queue. Lady Oyster went out to clear a way; she slipped on a hot dog which had been dropped just outside her gate and broke her leg. When she had been taken to hospital, some children from the funfair went into her garden, dug up some of her plants and scratched their names on the paintwork of her car.

Advise Lady Oyster.

University of London LLB Examination
(for External Students) Law of Tort June 1992 Q3

General Comment

This is a nuisance question which covers private and public nuisance. It is important to decide who can be sued in order to advise, but it is otherwise a standard and fairly straightforward nuisance question.

Skeleton Solution

Introduction – private nuisance – factors to consider – who can be sued – infringement of right of way – public nuisance – trespass – conclusion.

Suggested Solution

This question primarily concerns nuisance, which can be defined as the unreasonable interference with a person's use and enjoyment of his land. This tort concerns the protection of property rights; in this case, Lady Oyster's right to enjoy her property without interference.

Lady Oyster has an interest in the land, in that it is her property that is affected, and this gives her the right to sue in nuisance : *Malone* v *Laskey* [1907] 2 KB 141. It means that her house guests do not have such a right.

Firstly, Mussel arranges parties for up to 200 deprived children who offend Lady Oyster in a number of ways. Is this a nuisance? In *St Helens Smelting Co* v *Tipping* (1865) 11 HL 642 a distinction was made between nuisance causing material damage and nuisance affecting use and enjoyment. We are dealing with the latter, which allows us to consider various factors.

The duration of the nuisance is one such factor and we are told it happens every weekend. In *Bolton* v *Stone* [1949] 1 All ER 237 Oliver J said that a nuisance must 'be a state of affairs, however temporary, and not merely an isolated happening'. Another factor is the character of the neighbourhood. Lady Oliver would no doubt echo Thesiger LJ's dictum in *Sturges* v *Bridgman* (1879) 11 Ch D 852 that 'what would be a nuisance in Belgrave Square would not necessarily be so in Bermondsey'. These children may be acting in what is to them an acceptable way, but one which the gentility of the village makes unacceptable.

Noise is prima facie actionable (*Halsey* v *Esso Petroleum Co* [1961] 1 WLR 683), but one might wonder if Lady Oyster is being abnormally sensitive about the nakedness and the gestures, in which case these would not be actionable: *Heath* v *Mayor of Brighton* (1908)

98 LT 718. Also, Mussel will point to the utility of his conduct in helping these deprived children.

In balance, one might argue that Lady Oyster can certainly sue for the noise. The number of children, the frequency and the location outweigh any social utility. However, their offensive nakedness and arguably their gestures are not a sufficient interference.

Therefore the next question is: whom does she sue? The immediate creators of the nuisance – the children – may be sued, but there is little point suing them for damages. However, the remedy Lady Oyster will probably seek will be an injunction. Whelk owns the land which is hired out to Mussel who is employed by the charity. If Whelk had relinquished possession and control of the field to Mussel, then he would not be liable. However, if he had let the field for the express purpose of holding parties then he would be liable: *Tetley* v *Chitty* [1986] 1 All ER 663. Since the word 'hire' is used, we can presume that Mussel has no proprietary interest and therefore Lady Oyster could sue Whelk as occupier of the land as well as Mussel and vicariously his employers as creators of the nuisance.

One can deal with the rest of the question more briefly. Limpet's hamburger stall causes the entrance to Lady Oyster's drive to be blocked. This is an infringement of a right of way and if Lady Oyster can prove the interference, other factors – such as the benefit of the activity – are not relevant: *Colls* v *Home and Colonial Stores Ltd* [1904] AC 179. Lady Oyster can sue Whelk and the creators of the nuisance. Again, she will probably seek an injunction.

Lady Oyster goes out and slips on a hot dog, breaking her leg. This amounts to a public nuisance, in that Lady Oyster is injured in a particular way, suffering damage over and above the inconvenience being caused generally by the hot dog stand: *Rose* v *Miles* (1815) 4 M & S 101. Lady Oyster may also sue in negligence in that Whelk, Mussel and Limpet have failed to exercise reasonable care. Her remedy for her injuries will be in damages.

Finally, some children go into the garden and cause damage. It is tempting to consider this under the rule in *Rylands* v *Fletcher* (1868) LR 3 HL 330, in that the children collected on Whelk's land are certainly likely to do mischief if they escape! However, this is not the use of the land the courts have in mind when applying the rule.

Lady Oyster will sue for the trespass to her land. Again, her ownership creates the right to sue. The children have entered the land and – since trespass is actionable per se – no damage is required. The difficulty with this in terms of an action in nuisance is that the trespass of the children is a 'one-off' rather than a state of affairs, although one could argue that the state of affairs is the regular presence of the children and this is simply an escape of that nuisance (*Bolton* v *Stone*). She may also have an action in negligence.

Therefore, I would advise Lady Oyster to sue Whelk, Mussel and the charity and seek an injunction to prevent the various nuisances. She should recover damages from Limpet and the other parties for her broken leg and should sue in trespass and negligence for her property damage.

QUESTION SIX

The Mudborough Council have maintained a children's playground on one particular site for some 50 years. It is used by children from all over Mudborough, mainly by children under five during school terms, but also by older children during the holidays. Three years ago a private developer built a number of houses on land adjoining the playground. The purchasers of two of these houses, whose gardens back on to the playground are now complaining of interference from the playground.

One, James, complains that the noise the children make prevents him sleeping in the afternoon. He has to do so as he works on night shifts. The other, Keith, complains that the older children climb on his garden fence so that he and his family have no privacy in their back garden. He also complains that children often come into his garden to retrieve balls which have come over the fence.

Both James and Keith want to get the playground closed. Advise them of their legal rights.

Written by the Author

General Comment

Another common question examining the liability of a local authority in private nuisance and, possibly, negligence. The availability of the equitable remedy of injunction and possible defences must also be discussed.

Skeleton Solution

Private nuisance – definition – interference – unreasonableness – character of neighbourhood – loss of enjoyment/damages – defence of prescription – availability of damages/injunction as a remedy.

Suggested Solution

James and Keith would be advised to bring an action in private nuisance and will seek the remedy of a mandatory injunction against the Council so that the playground may be closed.

The essence of the tort of nuisance is unreasonable interference with another's enjoyment of his land. Private nuisance has been defined as being committed when a person is held responsible for an act indirectly causing physical injury to land or substantially interfering with the use or enjoyment of land or of an interest in land, where in the light of all the surrounding circumstances, this injury or interference is held to be unreasonable. The claimant's case will be based on the fact that there has been a substantial and unreasonable interference with their enjoyment of their property: see *Walter* v *Selfe* (1851) 4 De G & S 315.

'Substantial interference' will exclude any interference which is trivial, and although the loss of one night's sleep has been held not to be trivial (*Andreae* v *Selfridge* [1938]

Ch 1), the interference suffered by James and Keith must generally not be an isolated incident and it may, however, be a 'state of affairs, however temporary': per Oliver J in *Bolton v Stone* [1950] 1 KB 201; [1951] AC 850. The House of Lords' decision in *Southwark London Borough Council v Mills; Baxter v Camden London Borough Council* [1999] 4 All ER 449 lends support to this contention.

James claims that he is unable to sleep not at night but in the afternoons and therefore it may be argued that he is an abnormally sensitive claimant. However, those cases concerning abnormal sensitivity suggest that the sensitivity lies in the use to which the house is put, rather than personal sensitivity on the part of the claimant himself: *Robinson v Kilvert* (1884) 41 Ch D 88.

Unreasonable interference concerns several factors which will apply to both James's and Keith's cases. As the House of Lords in *Sedleigh-Denfield v O'Callaghan* [1940] AC 880 pointed out: 'A balance has to be maintained between the right of the occupier to do what he likes with his own land and the right of the neighbour not to be interfered with. It is impossible to give any precise or universal formula but it may broadly be said that a useful test is perhaps what is reasonable according to the ordinary usages of mankind living in society.'

The character of the neighbourhood is taken into account in assessing what is reasonable (*Bamford v Turnley* (1860) 3 B & S 62), save in cases involving physical damage: *St Helen's Smelting Co v Tipping* (1865) 11 HL Cas 642. At this point, it must be said that in this case, both claimants have come to the nuisance; the nuisance has not come into existence after they have moved in. The playground has been run for 50 years; the houses were built only three years ago. The court would therefore expect greater tolerance by the claimants since they have chosen to live near the playground and may have had some idea of the problems they might have to face. If, however, the nuisance is sufficiently great, the case may be actionable regardless of the locality: *Halsey v Esso Petroleum* [1961] 1 WLR 683; [1961] 2 All ER 145. Applying the test used in *Halsey* by Veale J the standard is that of the ordinary and reasonable man who lives in the vicinity of the playground. It is submitted that noise will be expected during the daytime and in school holidays, so that James's claim may fail under this head, although Keith's claim in relation to children climbing over the fence should not be affected by this consideration.

The Council may attempt to set up the defence of prescription (as in *Miller v Jackson* [1977] QB 966; [1977] 3 WLR 20) by claiming that they have a right to commit the alleged private nuisance over a period of at least 20 years with continual use and that the claimants (or their predecessors in title) knew of the nuisance. The defence was raised in *Sturges v Bridgman* (1879) 11 Ch D 852 but the court held that the defence must fail since the time ran from when the nuisance became apparent. Applying that decision to the facts of the case, the nuisance has only existed for a maximum of three years, so that this defence must fail.

James's claim is arguably doubtful but Keith should have an arguable case. In deciding whether to grant the injunction, the court will have regard to the public interest as opposed to the infringement of the individual's rights. In *Miller* v *Jackson* (above), the public interest suggested that an injunction should be refused where to hold otherwise would have meant that the playing of cricket would be prevented although this approach was not followed in *Kennaway* v *Thompson* [1981] QB 88; [1980] 3 WLR 361.

Keith may have an alternative action in trespass which involves the 'intentional or negligent entering on or remaining on, or directly causing any physical matter to come into contact with land in the possession of another'. The children have entered Keith's garden clearly without his permission or consent, but the problem here is whom to sue. It would be extremely difficult to bring in the Council as defendants and it may not be worthwhile to bring such an action. Although trespass is actionable per se, many trivial trespassers where no damage is caused to the land are ignored, and this may well be one of those cases.

Chapter 13

The Rule in *Rylands* v *Fletcher* and Fire

13.1   **Introduction**

13.2   **Key points**

13.3   **Key cases and statutes**

13.4   **Questions and suggested solutions**

13.1 Introduction

This rule imposes strict, but not absolute, liability on a defendant and was formulated thus by Blackburn J:

> '... a person who for his own purposes brings on to his lands and collects and keeps there anything likely to do mischief if it escapes, must keep it in at his peril, and, if he does not do so, he is prima facie answerable for all the damage which is the natural consequence of its escape: *R* v *F* (1866) 1 LR 1 Ex 265.'

This statement was approved by the House of Lords with the addition that the defendant had made a 'non-natural' use of his land: *Rylands* v *Fletcher* (1868) LR 3 HL 330.

13.2 Key points

Rylands v Fletcher

For his own purposes

If the thing is brought onto the land for the purpose of someone else the rule does not apply: *Rainham Chemical Works* v *Belvedere Fish Guano Co* [1921] 2 AC 465.

Brings on to his lands

a) The rule applies to things brought on to the land, not to things which are naturally on the land (see *Ellison* v *Ministry of Defence* (1997) 81 BLR 101), and include such things as thistles (*Giles* v *Walker* (1890) 24 QBD 656) and rainwater: *Smith* v *Kenrick* (1849) 7 CB 515.

b) It is an undecided point as to whether the defendant must be in occupation of the land from which the thing escaped, or whether control of the land is sufficient.

Dangerous things

The rule applies to 'anything likely to do mischief if it escapes'. However, almost anything can do mischief if it escapes, so nowadays there is no requirement that the thing which escapes is dangerous (see *Read* v *Lyons* [1947] AC 156) but the more dangerous a thing is the more likely it will be a non-natural use of land.

Escape

The thing must escape: *Read* v *Lyons* (above).

Non-natural user

a) In *Rylands* v *Fletcher* (above) 'natural' meant something naturally on the land or there by nature.

b) Later cases eg *Rickards* v *Lothian* [1913] AC 263 have used 'natural' to mean ordinary or usual, and in *Rickards* it was said that to bring *Rylands* into effect there had to be a special use of land bringing increased danger to others and not ordinary use of land or such use as is proper for the general benefit of the community. However, in *Cambridge Water Co* v *Eastern Counties Leather plc* [1994] 2 WLR 53 this criterion was criticised and the meaning 'something that was there by nature' was preferred. This point was revisited by the House of Lords in *Transco plc* v *Stockport Metropolitan Borough Council* [2004] 1 All ER 589.

c) In *Mason* v *Levy Auto Parts* [1967] 2 QB 530 special use and increased danger were equated with negligence.

d) In *British Celanese* v *Hunt* [1969] 1 WLR 959 it was held that the manufacturing of electrical components on an industrial estate was not a non-natural user of land as that was the very purpose for which the land was designed. However, in *Cambridge Water* (above) the storage of substantial quantities of chemicals on industrial premises was said (obiter) to be a 'classic case of non-natural use'. It thus seems that the original meaning of this phrase is to be preferred.

Foreseeability of damage

In *Cambridge Water* (above), after an extensive survey of the rule it was held that foreseeability of damage was an essential ingredient of *Rylands*.

Protected interests

a) A landowner who suffers property damage on his land can claim: *Rylands* v *Fletcher* (above); *Hunter* v *Canary Wharf Ltd* [1997] AC 655.

b) A landowner who suffers property damage while his property is not on his land (eg car parked on a public road) has been allowed to recover: *Halsey* v *Esso Petroleum* [1961] 1 WLR 683.

c) Landowners' personal injuries

Recovery was allowed in *Hale* v *Jennings* [1938] 1 All ER 579, but doubted in *Read* v *Lyons* (above). Again in *Cambridge Water* (above) it was doubted that the rule applies to personal injuries. This was confirmed in *Hunter* v *Canary Wharf Ltd* [1997] AC 655.

d) Non-landowners' personal injuries

Held that *Rylands* applied to this category in *Halsey* v *Esso Petroleum* (above) and *Perry* v *Kendrick's Transport* [1956] 1 WLR 85, although *Read* is against recovery. However, all these cases must be reviewed in the light of *Cambridge Water* (above).

e) Economic loss

An undecided point, although *Weller* v *Foot & Mouth Disease Research Institute* [1966] 1 QB 569 is against. See also *Cambridge Water* (above) where the claim for economic loss was dismissed.

Defences

a) Act of God

See the definition in *Tennant* v *Earl of Glasgow* (1864) 2 M (HL) 22, and note the only case where it has been successfully pleaded, namely *Nichols* v *Marsland* (1876) 2 Ex D 1.

b) Fault of the claimant

See, for example, *Ponting* v *Noakes* [1894] 2 QB 281.

c) Claimant's consent

Express or implied consent by the claimant to the thing being brought onto the defendant's land is a defence: *Kiddle* v *City Business Premises* [1942] 2 All ER 216; *Peters* v *Prince of Wales Theatre* [1943] KB 73.

d) Common benefit

Where the thing is maintained for the common benefit of both claimant and defendant, the defendant is not liable in the absence of negligence: *Kiddle* v *City Business Premises* (above); *Dunne* v *North West Gas Board* [1964] 2 QB 806.

e) Act of third party

If an independent act of a third party causes the damage, and this act is not foreseeable, the defendant is not liable: *Rickards* v *Lothian* (above); *Perry* v *Kendrick's Transport* (above).

f) Statutory authority

If the thing is maintained under statutory authority, no liability will arise in the absence of negligence: *Green* v *Chelsea Waterworks* (1894) 70 LT 547.

Be that as it may, many areas concerning hazards are now covered by statute. The statute may at times impose liability as well as provide a defence in certain circumstances.

Fire

There are three situations at common law in which liability for fires may arise.

a) In nuisance where the fire interferes with the use or enjoyment of land: *Goldman* v *Hargrave* [1967] 1 AC 645.

b) In negligence where the defendant failed to take reasonable care: *Musgrove* v *Pandelis* [1919] 2 KB 43; *Ogwo* v *Taylor* [1987] 2 WLR 988. The case of *Ribbee* v *Norrie* [2001] PIQR P8 provides a useful example of this.

c) In an action for fire. In *Mason* v *Levy Auto Parts* (above) it was held that the claimant must show:

   i) the defendant brought on to his land things likely to catch fire and kept them there in such conditions that if they did ignite the fire would be likely to spread to the claimant's land;

   ii) this was done in the course of some non-natural use;

   iii) the things ignited and the fire spread.

   Note the similarity to *Rylands*.

Common law defences

Act of a stranger

Act of God

Default of claimant

Consent of the claimant

Statutory authority

Refer back to the relevant discussions under *Rylands*.

Statutory position

a) Section 86 Fires Prevention (Metropolis) Act 1774 provides a defendant is not liable for fires which begin accidentally. Accidentally means caused by 'mere chance' or 'incapable of being traced to any cause' – it does not cover negligence: *Filliter* v *Phippard* (1847) 11 QB 347. A fire which is negligently allowed to spread, having been started accidentally, is treated as a separate fire not within the Act: *Musgrove* v *Pandelis* (above); *Goldman* v *Hargrave* (above); *Sochaki* v *Sas* [1947] 1 All ER 344.

b) Railway statutes

The Railway Fires Acts 1905 and 1923 create and limit liability for fire damage caused by sparks from engines.

13.4 Key cases and statutes

- *Cambridge Water Co* v *Eastern Counties Leather plc* [1994] 2 WLR 53
  The storage of substantial quantities of chemicals was said to be non-natural – illustrates that foreseeability of damage is an essential ingredient of *Rylands*

- *Hunter* v *Canary Wharf* [1997] AC 655
  Landowner suffering property damage may sue in *Rylands*

- *Read* v *Lyons* [1947] AC 156
  There is no requirement that the thing that escapes must be dangerous

- *Ribbee* v *Norrie* [2001] PIQR P8
  Liability may arise under *Rylands* where there is evidence of negligence

- *Rickards* v *Lothian* [1913] AC 263
  Natural use means ordinary or usual use

- *Rylands* v *Fletcher* (1868) LR 3 HL 330
  Imposes a strict liability on defendants who make a non-natural use of their land

- *Transco plc* v *Stockport Metropolitan Borough Council* [2004] 1 All ER 589
  Whether use of land was one of non-natural

- Fires Prevention (Metropolis) Act 1774 – no liability for fires caused accidentally

- Railway Fires Acts 1905 and 1923 – create and limit liability for fires caused by sparks from engines

13.5 Questions and suggested solutions

QUESTION ONE

Ronald leased a small country house from Percival. With Percival's consent, he assigned the unexpired two years of the lease to Stewart in 1998. A shed in the garden contained a considerable amount of rubbish including some paint tins. Stewart did not want to use the shed, did not ask Ronald to remove the rubbish and did not investigate what was there. The paint tins had in fact been used to store a highly corrosive chemical. It has now destroyed the containers and seeped into the adjoining property of Terence. It has made it impossible to grow flowers in a large part of Terence's garden and has destroyed his prize sunflowers. Stewart has disposed of the paint tins but says that he cannot do anything about the chemical which has seeped into the soil. Terence knows that Stewart always likes to watch the 'Newsnight' programme at 10.30 each evening on television and Terence always uses electrical equipment at the time in order to interfere with reception. Ronald's present whereabouts are unknown.

Advise the parties.

University of London LLB Examination
(for External Students) Law of Tort June 1999 Q8

General Comment

Students who were well aware of the recent House of Lords decisions in *Hunter* v *Canary Wharf* and to a lesser extent *Cambridge Water* would have been well placed to answer this question. A thorough knowledge of the rules would have been necessary to have made some observations on the question of whether Percival might be liable to Terence in respect of the escaped chemicals.

Skeleton Solution

Terence – action in private nuisance for the escaped chemicals – does Terence have sufficient standing to bring a claim? – can a single event give rise to liability in private nuisance? – who can Terence sue? – measure of damages – alternative action in *Rylands* v *Fletcher* – whether the storage of the chemicals was a non-natural use of the land – who can Terence sue? – Stewart – whether interference with TV reception can form the basis of an action in private nuisance – whether nuisance is actionable (noting the relevance of malice) – brief mention of remedies.

Suggested Solution

Damages for the clean up costs of Terence's land and the destroyed flowers are potentially recoverable in both the tort of private nuisance and under the rule in *Rylands* v *Fletcher* (1868) LR 3 HL 330.

Private nuisance

Private nuisance has been defined by Winfield and Jolowicz (16th edn, 2002) as 'an unlawful interference with a person's use or enjoyment of land, or some right over, or in connection with it'. The House of Lords in *Hunter* v *Canary Wharf Ltd* [1997] 2 All ER 426 confirmed that private nuisance is a tort which attaches to land, and so only those with a proprietorial interest in the land affected may bring an action. Terence must therefore be a freeholder, a tenant in possession or a licensee with exclusive possession of the neighbouring premises in order to have sufficient standing to bring a claim.

Generally, nuisances may take three different forms: encroachment on a neighbour's land, direct physical injury to a neighbour's land or interference with a neighbour's quiet enjoyment of the land. Whilst Terence's land has suffered direct physical damage, there is some uncertainty as to whether an isolated or a single escape can constitute a nuisance. The position appears to be that if damage resulted from a pre-existing state of affairs, it will constitute a nuisance: see *Midwood* v *Mayor of Manchester* [1905] 2 KB 597 in which a gas explosion was held to be an actionable nuisance as it followed a build-up of gas in the main. It is clearly arguable that the migrating chemical which caused damage to Terence's land resulted from their storage and gradual escape from the shed next door over a period of time, and it is therefore submitted that this amounted to a pre-existing state of affairs giving rise to a nuisance.

Who can Terence sue?

Ronald's whereabouts are unknown and so Terence's potential claims are against Percival (the reversioner) and Stewart (the tenant). It is not clear whether it was Ronald or Percival who accumulated the paint tins. Stewart was not responsible for their presence. If Percival was responsible for the storage of the chemical, he may be held liable as a previous occupier of the premises, because he knew, or ought to have known, of the hazardous state of affairs: *St Anne's Well Brewery Co* v *Roberts* (1928) 140 LT 1.

As for Stewart, there is authority to suggest that he will be liable as an occupying tenant of the premises: *Montana Hotels* v *Fasson Pty* (1986) 69 ALR 258. Stewart's liability, notwithstanding his ignorance of the hazard, would seem to be consistent with the notion of strict liability in the tort of private nuisance.

Was this an actionable nuisance?

In determining whether the nuisance is actionable, the courts balance the reasonableness of the defendant's activity (which created the nuisance) against the reasonable needs of the claimant to use and enjoy his property. However, in *St Helens Smelting Co* v *Tipping* (1865) 11 HL Cas 642, the House of Lords held that there was a distinction between nuisances which cause damage to property and those which cause personal discomfort in the use or enjoyment of land. It is easier to establish nuisance in the former case, as the courts do not take into account the character of the area as a relevant factor. We have already seen that single escapes of the type which occurred in this case can amount to actionable nuisances, and it is submitted that the fact of physical damage to Terence's land in the circumstances will allow him to claim. There appear to be no problems as to whether damage of the kind that took place in this case was foreseeable, given the highly corrosive nature of the chemical being stored: *Cambridge Water Co* v *Eastern Counties Leather plc* [1994] 2 WLR 53.

Damages

Terence will be able to claim compensation according to the diminution in value of his land. This is likely to be equal to the cost of re-instatement, ie the clean up costs. Terence ought to be able to claim, in addition, compensation for the cost of the plants and flowers destroyed. There seems to be no English authority on the question of whether Terence could claim for any economic losses flowing from prizes he might have won in respect of the sunflowers.

Rylands *v* Fletcher

Since the *Cambridge Water* case, it is clear that this tort is nothing more than a specific application of the law of private nuisance in relation to isolated escapes. For liability to attach under this rule, it must be proved that:

a) the defendant brought something onto his land in the course of some non-natural use of it;

b) there has been an escape of that thing from the defendant's land to the claimant's land;

c) damage has resulted to the claimant's property; and

d) it must have been foreseeable that damage of the kind that took place would occur.

The only issue here is whether the corrosive chemical amounted to a non-natural use of the land. This concept receives no precise definition in the authorities, although Lord Goff in the *Cambridge Water* case stated: 'The storage of substantial quantities of chemicals on industrial premises should be regarded as an almost classic case of non-natural use'. Whether the storage of some paint tins containing a highly corrosive chemical on residential premises would be regarded as a non-natural use is uncertain. It might be argued that if the storage of chemicals is a non-natural use of industrial premises, it certainly ought to be so regarded on residential premises, even if the quantities involved are less. In general, the more dangerous a thing is, the more likely it is to constitute a non-natural use. This fact was raised in the case of *Transco plc* v *Stockport Metropolitan Borough Council* [2004] 1 All ER 589.

Who can Terence sue?

In *Rylands* v *Fletcher* Blackburn J spoke of a person who 'for his own purposes' brings things onto his land. This would appear to rule out Stewart as a potential defendant, liability thus depending upon whether it was Percival or Ronald who was responsible for the storage of the paint tins. However, in *Cambridge Water*, the rule in *Rylands* v *Fletcher* was held to be an offshoot of the tort of private nuisance. In view of this, it is might be argued that the same rules should apply in relation to potential defendants as were discussed for private nuisance.

Is Terence liable to Stewart for the interference with TV reception?

Stewart, as a tenant, has a proprietorial interest in the land affected by Terence's activities and therefore has sufficient standing to mount an action in private nuisance. The first issue is whether interference with TV reception can amount to a private nuisance. Comments made by Buckley J in the case of *Bridlington Relay Ltd* v *Yorkshire Electricity Board* [1965] Ch 436 suggested that, at the time of that case, TV reception could not be regarded as such an important part of an ordinary householder's enjoyment of his property so as to amount to a legal nuisance. However, later cases in other common law jurisdictions have held that TV viewing is an important incident of the ordinary enjoyment of property and should be protected. In *Hunter*, the House of

Lords held that interference with TV reception caused by the blocking of such transmissions by the erection of a building did not constitute a nuisance. However, obiter comments of Lords Hoffmann and Cooke suggest that interference with TV reception could, in some circumstances, amount to a nuisance. In the light of the decision in *Hunter*, it is submitted that where such interference is caused by something emanating from the defendant's land, such as Terence's use of electrical equipment, then an action will lie. The point remains to be firmly decided.

Assuming that such interference can form the basis of a claim in nuisance, it must be decided according to the balancing test whether or not there is an actionable nuisance. All the factors in this case point to the resolution of that balancing exercise in favour of Stewart. In the normal course of events, relevant factors would be as follows.

a) The character of the neighbourhood in which the nuisance took place. The facts of the question indicate a residential countryside area, where interference with TV reception is likely to be uncommon and therefore subjectively more disturbing.

b) The fact that the interference took place at night time, when residents are most likely to be viewing TV.

c) The fact that this was a repeated and continuing interference.

Moreover, the fact that Terence was motivated by malice tips the balance very firmly in Stewart's favour (*Christie v Davey* [1893] 1 Ch 316) and it is submitted that the court is likely to be persuaded to grant an injunction restraining or restricting Terence's use of the electrical equipment. Stewart may also be entitled to damages for the loss of amenity value to his property covering the period of intentional interference up to the time of any injunction. Any such award would consist of a relatively low one-off payment.

QUESTION TWO

Cruella Enterprises Ltd manufacture leather garments. They receive a threat from an 'animal rights' organisation that their factory will be occupied by protesters. This is reported to the managing director who decides that it is a hoax and takes no special security measures. Two weeks later a bomb explodes beside a drum of acid which the company uses in its manufacturing processes. The acid pours into the adjoining premises of DeVile Ltd where a large number of used car tyres are stored. Thousands of pounds worth of damage is done to the tyres and the reaction with the acid unexpectedly produces toxic vapours. Neighbouring factories have to close down for several days until the vapours have dispersed.

Advise Cruella Enterprises and DeVile.

University of London LLB Examination
(for External Students) Law of Tort June 1997 Q4

General Comment

Students should be prepared to deal with the general question of whether a duty exists to prevent the acts of third parties and how far such a duty might extend. The question also requires a consideration of the law of nuisance and *Rylands* v *Fletcher*. The nature of the damage will also require some discussion of unlikely or remote consequences, and pure and consequential economic loss. The vicarious liability of the company for the torts of its managing director should be discussed.

Skeleton Solution

Whether there is a duty to prevent the acts of third parties: *Smith* v *Littlewoods* – the claim by DeVile Ltd: negligence, nuisance and *Rylands* v *Fletcher* – the claims brought by the neighbouring factories against Cruella Enterprises Ltd and DeVile Ltd – the unexpected consequences; *Cambridge Water* v *Eastern Counties Leather*; remoteness of damage – the range of recovery; consequential economic loss; pure economic loss – vicarious liability.

Suggested Solution

The original source of the damage in this situation is the unlawful bombing of Cruella's factory and, if it were possible to find the miscreants, they could be held to account. But, as this result is unlikely, Cruella will be probably forced back upon their insurers for their own property damage. The real question is to what extent, if at all, will Cruella be liable for damage to others. The complaint that will be levelled against the company and its managing director is that they failed to prevent the act of the 'animal rights' third party. This directly raises the question whether, and in what circumstances, such a duty arises. The leading case is now *Smith* v *Littlewoods Organisation Ltd* [1987] AC 241, from which it is clear that no such operational duty exists but that within certain exceptional situations, Lord Goff illustrating four, a duty may arise.

In Cruella's situation, some of the exceptional features may be present. Lord Goff pointed to the case where a landowner allows or knows that a source of danger on his land is being created by a third party as a situation where a duty might arise; similarly, a duty may arise where a person has created or tolerated a potential danger which only needs the agency of a third party to 'trigger off' a risk to others as in *Haynes* v *Harwood* [1935] 1 KB 146. It is assumed for present purposes that such a duty is owed by Cruella and, in the absence of evidence of how secure the site and acid storage is under normal circumstances, that the duty is breached. This duty will be owed, at least, to adjoining owners such as DeVile Ltd under conventional 'neighbour' principles: per Lord Atkin in *Donoghue* v *Stevenson* [1932] AC 562.

The claim by DeVile Ltd may, as outlined above, be brought on ordinary negligence principles. If, however, it were found that Cruella's security was such that no special measures were needed or, perhaps, practicable, this cause of action would disappear. It would then be necessary to consider alternatives, and the ones that suggest themselves are nuisance and/or *Rylands v Fletcher* (1868) LR 3 HL 330 liability. A claim might be brought in private nuisance, even for an isolated escape, if there is evidence of a generally insecure site with an underlying, unsatisfactory state of affairs as in *British Celanese v A H Hunt Ltd* [1969] 1 WLR 959, but this sort of claim would fail in the circumstance of a reasonably secure site and storage as with the claim in negligence. It might, however, succeed if the overall site security was good (preventing a negligence claim) but the storage of acid left something to be desired. A more promising probability would be under *Rylands v Fletcher* on the basis that Cruella had brought a substance onto their premises which was likely to do harm if it escaped. This use of their land would, undoubtedly, be a 'non-natural' use and this is the very type of situation for which the remedy is intended. The acid has simply escaped under gravity, but there is a defence to *Rylands*, that of the act of a stranger as in *Perry v Kendrick's Transport Ltd* [1956] 1 WLR 85. However, as Cruella knew that there was a possibility of sabotage, this might not be a defence here. Liability under *Rylands v Fletcher* depends very much upon reasonable foreseeability, both of the escape and of the consequences of the escape: *Cambridge Water Co v Eastern Counties Leather plc* [1994] 2 WLR 53. This principle was reitereated in the case of *Transco plc v Stockport Metropolitan Borough Council* [2004] 1 All ER 589.

The neighbouring factories, if they claim against Cruella, may have some difficulties whatever cause of action they rely upon. The problem is that the rules of remoteness of damage laid down in *The Wagon Mound (No 1)* [1961] AC 388 show that property damage of a type that is not reasonably foreseeable is unrecoverable. This would seem to bar a negligence action based on toxic vapours, and a very similar result obtains in nuisance and *Rylands v Fletcher* since the *Cambridge Water* case. This would not, of course, prevent a claim by DeVile Ltd against Cruella for direct acid damage to the tyres.

An even more formidable obstacle for the neighbouring factories is that most of their loss appears to be in the form of lost production. There are two possibilities here. First, that there may be stock or material which has been damaged or rendered useless by the closures and, second, that the loss is pure economic loss in the form of lost productivity and continuing overhead costs. If the factories can get a claim going against Cruella (perhaps on the basis that the vapours are of the general acidic nature), they may be able to recover for the first head of the loss as that can be seen to be consequential economic loss. They will be unable to recover for the pure economic loss in negligence or *Rylands*: *Spartan Steel and Alloys Ltd v Martin & Co (Contractors) Ltd* [1973] QB 27. The question whether such a loss is recoverable in nuisance is unclear but, as the interference is with the enjoyment of land as manufactures, there seems no reason in principle why such loss should not be recoverable.

There would be little doubt that any negligence by the managing director would be 'within the course of his employment' so as to bring down vicarious liability on Cruella.

There is the possibility that the neighbouring factories may wish to claim against DeVile for the escape of fumes from their premises under *Rylands v Fletcher*. This could probably be met by a defence of lack of reasonable foreseeability under *Cambridge Water v Eastern Counties Leather plc* or possibly act of a stranger as in *Perry v Kendrick's Transport Ltd*.

QUESTION THREE

'I incline to the opinion that, as a general rule, it is more appropriate for strict liability in respect of operations of high risk to be imposed by Parliament, than by the courts. If such liability is imposed by statute, the relevant activities can be identified, and those concerned can know where they stand.' (*Cambridge Water Co v Eastern Counties Leather plc* (1994), per Lord Goff of Chieveley.)

a) What is the significance of this case?

b) Do you agree with Lord Goff's view about the respective roles of the courts and Parliament?

University of London LLB Examination
(for External Students) Law of Tort June 1994 Q1

General Comment

This involves discussing a quotation from a judgment in relation to both its context in that judgment, and on a wider, more practical basis. The scope for moving outside the confines of the question is great, but should obviously be avoided.

Skeleton Solution

a) Nuisance – *Rylands* v *Fletcher* – damage/harm – foreseeability – natural v non-natural use.

b) Strict liability – statute v common law – parliamentary supremacy/separation of powers – rule of law.

Suggested Solution

a) The most significant aspect of the *Cambridge Water* [1994] 2 AC 264 decision appears to relate both to nuisance and to the rule under *Rylands* v *Fletcher* (1866) LR 1 Ex 265, and to a consideration of whether foreseeability of a particular type of harm was necessary in determining an award of damages. The case also involved an attempt to clarify the issue regarding the assessment of the use of land as either natural or non-natural. The latter, subsidiary point was only considered briefly as the main decision of the court rendered fuller discussion irrelevant. The House of Lords appears to have concluded that foreseeability of harm of the relevant type by the defendant was a prerequisite for the recovery of damages, in both nuisance and under *Rylands* v *Fletcher*.

The *Cambridge Water* case revolved around an almost typical nuisance/*Rylands* v

Fletcher scenario. The defendant was using and storing a chlorinated solvent, a mile from a borehole belonging to and used by the claimant for the abstraction of water for domestic use. The solvent, over a period of time, seeped into the water supply and, as a result of a European Commission ruling, the water was classed as being unfit for human consumption. As a result, the claimant claimed damages in, alternatively, negligence, nuisance and under the rule in *Rylands* v *Fletcher*. The case made a steady progression through the court hierarchy, until it fell for the House of Lords to decide upon the issues raised. The Court of Appeal had declined to determine the case on the basis of the rule in *Rylands* v *Fletcher*, but instead held that there was a parallel rule of strict liability in nuisance. The House of Lords felt unable to agree with the stand taken by the inferior court and considered that this was not a case in which extending the bounds of nuisance was proper and appropriate. In reviewing this whole area, their Lordships turned firstly to the question of foreseeability of damage in nuisance. Although the appearance of the liability is strict, in that the fact that the defendant has taken all reasonable care will not exonerate him from liability, the principle of 'reasonable user' acts as a form of control mechanism. Within this area of law no suggestion is made, however, that the defendant should be held liable for damage of a type which he could not reasonably foresee. This appears to have been the view of the Privy Council in *Overseas Tankship (UK) Ltd* v *Miller Steamship Co Pty, The Wagon Mound (No 2)* [1967] 1 AC 617. In that case, Lord Reid felt unable to discriminate 'between different cases of nuisance, so as to make foreseeability a necessary element in determining liability' (p460).

It was against this general background that Lord Goff turned to the rule in *Rylands* v *Fletcher* and, in particular, the judgment of Blackburn J. It was possible to discern a view that foreseeability of the risk was a prerequisite to the recovery of damages. His Lordship considered some of the authorities that had been presented as offering an opposite perception. However, it was felt that the undeniable connection between the rule in *Rylands* v *Fletcher* and nuisance meant that it was merely a logical step to afford the same test for both types of claim. This was not to say that the rule in *Rylands* v *Fletcher* was, as the examination of the point by the House of Lords in *Read* v *J Lyons & Co Ltd* [1947] AC 156 revealed, to be the development of a test of strict liability. It appeared that the House of Lords was concerned to have the *Rylands* v *Fletcher* rule considered as an extension of the law of nuisance to cases of isolated escapes from land. As the quotation suggests, Lord Goff did not consider that is was for the judiciary to take the law down that particular path.

The second point, that was mentioned only for the sake of completeness, related to the discussion of whether storing of solvent on land was a natural or non-natural use of land. In the original action, the trial judge had attempted to label it a natural use and thereby allow the exception to come into play. However, the House of Lords felt bound to decide that the storing of such chemicals was a non-natural use.

b) Looking at the respective roles of the courts and Parliament involves considering their places within the constitution of this country. At its most basic, Parliament makes the law, and it is left to the courts to interpret that law, in accordance with general presumptions and both internal and external aids to construction. There is a whole wealth of issues pertaining to the separation of powers within constitutional law, to which this question could relate. However, it is the extent to which the courts should take their role of interpreters of the law which appears to have been behind Lord Goff's consideration, and correct assessment, of these issues.

In general, it seems that those producing legislation are doing so in a way that is both carefully structured and well-informed. This being so, it means that the need for the courts to try and achieve the same ends via the use of the common law is reduced. This can only be of benefit as the common law is, and can only be, of general application. The 'system' is called upon to operate in so many differing environments that it cannot be too specific. Therefore, it would be unfair to expect the common law to accommodate areas of law that are overly technical. It must be left to the agency that can afford to meet those technical challenges head on and, as Lord Goff goes on to say, '… statute can where appropriate lay down precise criteria establishing the incidence and scope of such [strict] liability'.

The inherent dangers in allowing the courts to take a more active role in the defining of such controversial issues are a price too high to pay just to answer the courts' fears of a reluctant legislature. There may well come a time, and probably a judiciary, when the failure of Parliament to meet the challenges set by areas such as environmental pollution will lead to the redefining of roles. This would be a great shame and could lead to the judiciary's 'floodgate' fears acting in their favour, but against the general rule of law.

The imposition of liability in a haphazard and general way on the basis of 'no fault' may have quite a dramatic effect on the commercial ability of some businesses to survive. If, in relation to 'strict liability', Parliament is reluctant to create such a duty, it cannot really be for the courts to do it on Parliament's behalf. It seems that until the legislature can develop a fair and sophisticated system of compensation, then the courts' hands will be, and must remain, tied.

QUESTION FOUR

Andrew, Basil and Clive each leases premises on an industrial estate. Andrew has recently greatly increased the use of his premises and often overloads the drains and sewage system. There is frequently an unpleasant smell hanging over the other workshops and both Basil and Clive find that there is sometimes a flow back of sewage into their systems.

Basil uses his premises for his photography business. He has chemicals stored in his basement. These are kept in accordance with the manufacturers' instructions. However water has seeped into the basement from Andrew's overflowing sewage system and this results one evening in a violent explosion. Bricks and glass shower down on Clive's premises damaging some goods stored there and Daphne, who was walking past in the street, was showered with broken glass.

Discuss the issues of liability in tort raised by these facts.

University of London LLB Examination
(for External Students) Law of Tort June 1993 Q8

General Comment

The question requires an analysis of the law relating to private and public nuisance as well as *Rylands* v *Fletcher*. In addition, it also raises the possibility of negligence which requires a discussiion of the concepts of foreseeability and remoteness.

Skeleton Solution

Private nuisance: factors to consider – public nuisance – the elements of *Rylands* v *Fletcher* – negligence and the question of remoteness.

Suggested Solution

This question is concerned with property being used in such a way that it annoys or damages other people. It is therefore concerned with the torts of private and public nuisance and the rule in *Rylands* v *Fletcher* (1866) LR 1 Ex 265 as well as with negligence.

The first problem to deal with is the smell hanging over other workshops owing to A overloading the drains and sewage system. Any action would be in private nuisance, which can be defined as unlawful interference with a person's use and enjoyment of land. An unpleasant smell is sufficient to constitute a nuisance: eg *Rapier v London Tramways Co* [1893] 2 Ch 588.

B and C are both leaseholders and therefore have sufficient interest in the land to sue in nuisance: *Inchbald* v *Robinson* (1869) LR 4 Ch 388. They can sue A because presumably he or his servants or agents created the nuisance. The damage is not tangible and has not caused material damage, therefore one has to consider a number of factors to decide whether or not A acted unreasonably and created a smell which constitutes a nuisance.

One of these factors is the nature of the locality. As was memorably stated by Thesiger LJ in *Sturges v Bridgman* (1879) 11 Ch D 852, 'What would be a nuisance in Belgrave Square would not necessarily be so in Bermondsey'. A, B and C all lease properties on an industrial estate, therefore it might be felt that unpleasant smells are a hazard of such places. However, it is submitted that the fact the smell emanates from overloading the drains and sewage systems, rather than from the proper use of the premises, makes the nature of the location less relevant. Smells from drains are equally unpleasant everywhere.

It may be that A is involved in some activity of general benefit, which would be a factor in his favour, although in the Irish case of *Bellew* v *Cement Co* [1948] Ir R 61 the court forbade a nuisance even though it meant closing the only cement factory in Ireland. In A's case, whatever the activity, he has overloaded the system which would surely negate the mitigating effect of social utility.

The court would not take account of any abnormal sensitivity on the part of A or B: eg *Heath* v *Mayor of Brighton* (1908) 98 LT 718. On the other hand, the fact that the smell is frequent is important for the success of the action, since a temporary or occasional smell would probably be insufficient: eg *Bolton* v *Stone* [1951] AC 850.

These are the issues of liability with regard to the smell and, on the facts, it seems likely that B & C's action in private nuisance would succeed. The remedy they would be seeking would be an injunction to bring the nuisance to an end.

What has been said about the smell will also apply to the flow back of sewage into B and C's systems with regard to an action in private nuisance, although if the flowback has caused material damage, the additional factors become less relevant, since the nuisance is tangible. The remedy would be in damages.

Is there an action in public nuisance? The smell is a nuisance which materially affect the reasonable comfort and convenience of a class of Her Majesty's subjects, namely the occupants of the industrial estate. It arises from A overloading the drains and sewage system. B and C have also suffered additional, particular damage – the flow back of sewage – beyond the general inconvenience caused by A's behaviour. Therefore they could sue in public nuisance also.

Turning to B, he has brought chemicals onto his premises. Since these have been kept in accordance with manufacturers' instructions, it does not appear that he has acted negligently, unless it could be argued that it was negligent to keep them there in the first place. Nevertheless, they have come into contact with water and exploded, causing damage to C's premises and personal injury to D. The action that one is looking at here is under the rule in *Rylands* v *Fletcher*.

The rule as stated by Blackburn J is this: a person who for his own purposes brings on his lands and collects and keeps there anything likely to do mischief if it escapes, must keep it at his peril, and, if he does not do so, is prima facie answerable for all the damage which is the natural consequence of its escape. This rule was somewhat tempered by Lord Cairns LC in the House of Lords when he relied upon the 'non-natural use' of the land to uphold the decision. Subsequent case law has similarly relied upon this additional element, which has weakened the strict liability that would otherwise apply. (Indeed, were this not the case, then B and C might have been helped by one of Blackburn J's examples, that of the person whose cellar is invaded by the filth of his neighbour's privy!)

Applying the rule to the facts of this case: the rule in *Rylands* v *Fletcher* has been applied to explosions: *Miles* v *Forest Rock Co* (1918) 34 TLR 500. The chemicals have been accumulated on B's land for his own purposes, in other words for his own benefit.

There has been an escape, in that the explosion has extended beyond B's land: see the House of Lords' decision in *Read* v *Lyons* [1947] AC 156. Keeping combustible chemicals carries with it inherent risks and it is submitted that this is non-natural use of the land. The dicta of Lord Goff in *Cambridge Water Co* v *Eastern Counties Leather plc* [1994] 2 WLR 53 bears relevance here. See also *Transco plc* v *Stockport Metropolitan Borough Council* [2004] 1 All ER 582 on the same point.

The risk is B's and, subject to any defences, he is therefore liable under the rule. While C could certainly recover damages for property damage, there has been some uncertainty over recovery for personal injury. Although the House of Lords in *Read* v *Lyons* doubted whether there could be recovery for personal injury, given the context of the original decision in *Rylands* v *Fletcher*, there have been decisions in which damages for personal injuries were allowed (eg *Perry* v *Kendrick's Transport Ltd* [1956] 1 WLR 85), although such recovery was doubted in *Cambridge Water*.

B will argue, in his defence, that the explosion was caused not by him, but by A and that A's act was an unforeseeable one. He will say that he has followed the manufacturers' instructions and has not been negligent and, if he can prove this and that the seeping water was unforeseeable, he has a defence to the claim. From the facts, this may seem to be the case.

Finally, there is the issue of A's negligence. He owes a duty of care to B and C as well as to D, the passer-by, not to injure them by his negligent acts. He has breached this duty by unreasonably unloading the drains and sewage system. This breach may have caused damage to B and C's sewage systems, in which case they can sue him for damages. It has also caused the damage to C's premises and to D, since 'but for' A's negligence, the explosion would not have occurred: *Barnett* v *Chelsea and Kensington Hospital Management Committee* [1969] 1 QB 428.

However, it is arguable whether it is foreseeable that overloading one's drains will lead to an explosion and therefore A will argue that the damage to C and D is too remote. The test of foreseeability is contained in *The Wagon Mound (No 1)* [1961] AC 388, namely that the damage is too remote if a reasonable man would not have foreseen the consequences.

QUESTION FIVE

Giles has a very large oil storage tank on his farm. He uses the oil to run the central heating system in his farmhouse, in his glasshouses in which he grows vegetables and in the building in which he houses a thousand battery chickens. Giles allows his barn to be used each week by the local Boy Scout troop. One evening a scout wanders away from the barn and accidentally turns the drain tap of the tank. The oil spills out and on to the land of Giles's neighbour, Ham, where it destroys his crop of brussels sprouts which were at a very delicate stage of development. While rushing to attempt to stop the oil after he has seen it cover his sprouts Ham slips on the oil, falls and cuts open his head.

Advise Ham.

Written by the Author

General Comment

A specific question on *Rylands* v *Fletcher* but with the possibility of liability under private nuisance and/or negligence. The law must be analysed in respect of both personal injuries as well as property damage.

Skeleton Solution

Rylands v *Fletcher* definition – non-natural use – escape – causing loss/damage – remedies – private nuisance principles establishing liability – recoverability of damages – action under negligence – *Donoghue* principles – damages.

Suggested Solution

In this problem, there are several causes of action on which Ham may base his claim, and they are *Rylands* v *Fletcher*, private nuisance and negligence in respect of the damage to his property and his personal injury respectively.

The rule in *Rylands* v *Fletcher* (1868) LR 3 HL 330 imposes strict liability on a defendant for the escape from land under his control of things brought on to his land in the course of a non-natural user of the land, where those things are such that they are 'likely to do damage if they escape' and damage is foreseeable: *Cambridge Water Co* v *Eastern Counties Leather plc* [1994] 2 WLR 53. The first question is therefore whether the large oil storage tank which Giles has on his land constitutes a 'non-natural user'. 'Non-natural' was considered in *Transco plc* v *Stockport Metropolitan Borough Council* [2004] 1 All ER 589.

'Non-natural' for this purpose does not simply mean artificial, but imparts some element of risk or danger: *Read* v *Lyons* [1947] AC 156. In *Mason* v *Levy Auto Parts of England Ltd* [1967] 2 QB 530, MacKenna J considered that the relevant factors were:

a) the quantities of material (in *Mason*, combustible material) which the defendants brought onto the land:

b) the way in which they were stored;

c) the character of the neighbourhood.

Lord Moulton in *Rickards* v *Lothian* [1913] AC 263 said that the use must not merely be the ordinary use of the land or such a use as is proper for the general benefit of the community. This classic formulation of the test was criticised by the House of Lords in *Cambridge Water* where the simple test 'there by nature' was preferred, and by this criterion there has been a non-natural user of the land.

While it may be argued that since Giles has chosen oil central heating, he should be allowed to store the oil on his own land, the fact remains that the oil has escaped from his land to the land of another. Similar substances which have been held to be non-natural user have been gas (*North Western Utilities Ltd* v *London Guarantee & Accident Co* [1936] AC 108), electricity (*National Telephone Co* v *Baker* (1933)) and petrol (*Musgrove* v *Pandelis* [1919] 2 KB 43, although this decision is doubtful).

On the facts of this case, the large quantity of oil stored on Giles' land, suggests a non-natural user; this is re-inforced by the fact that the neighbourhood is predominantly rural, rather than industrial.

Giles must have brought the oil on to the land for his own use, which he has, and the oil has escaped. The oil is dangerous because of its flammability, and, as in this case, because of its contaminating qualities giving rise to foreseeable damage.

On this analysis there is a prima facie case against Giles and he will be liable for the damage suffered by Ham unless he can plead as a defence that the escape was caused by the act of a stranger. This act must be independent in the sense that Giles must have had no control over the boy scout (*Perry* v *Kendrick's Transport Ltd* [1956] 1 WLR 85; [1956] 1 All ER 154), and it must be such that Giles could not reasonably have foreseen it and therefore guarded against it.

Giles, it is submitted, clearly has some degree of control over the boy scouts since he has permitted them to be on his land and presumably he has the right to ask them to leave at any time. In addition to this, he allows them to use the barn each week and it is reasonably foreseeable that some of them may wander about the farm. He should, therefore, take precautions by making any potentially dangerous structure or substance on the farm inaccessible to them. This he has clearly failed to do, and should therefore be liable.

Under the rule in *Rylands* v *Fletcher*, compensation for damage to property has always been recoverable, so that Ham will be entitled to damages for the loss of his brussels sprouts and, if applicable, their loss of profit. There is some doubt as to whether personal injuries damages are recoverable under the rule because its origins are in nuisance and trespass to land where only property damage is recoverable: *Read* v *Lyons* [1947] AC 156; [1946] 2 All ER 471.

Certain authorities do allow recovery for personal injuries: one such case is *Hale* v *Jennings Bros* [1938] 1 All ER 579, where the successful claimant was a bare licensee who did not have an interest in land. The Court of Appeal in *Perry* v *Kendrick's* left the point open, but did not rule out the possibility of the recovery of damages for personal injury, and damages were also awarded in *Schiffman* v *Order of St John* [1936] 1 All ER 557. The House of Lords in *Read* v *Lyons* seemed to suggest such damages were irrecoverable, as they did in the *Cambridge Water* case.

He may also have a claim in private nuisance, for which he must have an interest in land, which he seems to have on the facts. He must show an interference by Giles with

Ham's use of his land or his enjoyment of that land. It is not impossible for a nuisance consisting of one event to be actionable, despite Oliver J's dictum in *Bolton* v *Stone* [1951] AC 850; [1951] 1 All ER 1078 that a nuisance must be 'a state of affairs, however temporary and not merely an isolated happening'. In *Midwood* v *Mayor of Manchester* [1905] 2 KB 597 the claimant succeeded in a nuisance action where a gas main exploded on the grounds that the nuisance consisted not only of the explosion but also of the pre-existing state of affairs during which the gas was accumulating on the defendant's premises. This reasoning may be applied to Ham's case to render Giles' interference with Ham's land unreasonable.

Against, there is some uncertainty in the law of nuisance as to whether damages for personal injury are recoverable since the tort is designed to protect property rather than the person. *Malone* v *Laskey* [1907] 2 KB 141 suggests that such damages are recoverable.

The better course of action may be for Ham to rely on negligence in relation to his personal injury claim. Under Lord Atkin's neighbour principle in *Donoghue* v *Stevenson* [1932] AC 562, Giles, as a neighbouring landowner should reasonably foresee that by his negligent acts or omissions he may cause harm or injury to Ham, therefore, he owes him a duty of care. Although the damage is caused by a third party, he has a right of control over the boy scout (*Home Office* v *Dorset Yacht Co* [1970] AC 1004; [1970] 2 WLR 1140) and a reasonable man would, in the circumstances have guarded against interference with the oil storage tank. Certainly, the damage to Ham's land is reasonably foreseeable and Ham stands a good chance of recovering damages in negligence.

Chapter 14

Animals

14.1   Introduction

14.2   Key points

14.3   Key cases and statutes

14.5   Questions and suggested solutions

14.1 Introduction

Liability for animals exists at both common law and under statute, particularly the Animals Act 1971. Section 2 of this Act is particularly important and its contents should be studied and understood, together with s6, before any question on animals is attempted.

14.2 Key points

Common law position

Liability may arise under normal tortious principles for acts done through the agency of an animal. Note the following examples.

Nuisance

a) Allowing an animal to block the highway: *Cunningham* v *Whelan* (1917) 52 Ir LT 67.

b) Noisy animals: *Leeman* v *Montague* [1936] 2 All ER 1677.

Battery

Setting a dog on another.

Trespass

Allowing an animal to trespass: *League Against Cruel Sports* v *Scott* [1985] 2 All ER 489.

Negligence

Failure to prevent dogs escaping: *Draper* v *Hodder* [1972] 2 QB 556.

Animals Act 1971

Dangerous animals

By s2(1) Animals Act 1971 'where any damage is caused by an animal which belongs to a dangerous species, any person who is a keeper of the animal is liable for the damages, except as otherwise provided by this Act'.

Note:

a) The definition of keeper in s6(3).

b) The definition of dangerous species: s6(2) 'not commonly domesticated in the British Islands and whose fully grown animals normally have such characteristics that they are likely, unless restrained, to cause severe damage or that any damage that they may cause is likely to be severe'.

c) It is the species which must be dangerous and not the particular animal, so it is no defence to show that the animal in question was tame.

See the decision of *Flack v Hudson* [2001] QB 698, in which the Court of Appeal held that one keeper could successfully bring an action against another keeper within the 1971 Act.

Non-dangerous animals

Note the complex wording of s2(2):

'Where damage is caused by an animal which does not belong to a dangerous species, a keeper of the animal is liable for the damage … if –
(a) the damage is of a kind which the animal, unless restrained, was likely to cause or which, if caused by the animal, was likely to be severe; and
(b) the likelihood of the damage or of its being severe was due to characteristics of the animal which are not normally found in animals of the same species or are not normally so found except at particular times or in particular circumstances; and
(c) those characteristics were known to that keeper …'

a) Regarding s2(2)(b) in *Wallace v Newton* [1982] 1 WLR 375 it was held that the animal need not have a vicious tendency to attack others, merely that it possessed characteristics not normally found in that species. This fact was given support by the House of Lords in the case of *Mirvahedy v Henley* [2003] 2 All ER 401.

b) See *Kite v Napp* (1982) The Times 1 June; *Cummings v Grainger* [1977] QB 397 and *Curtis v Betts* [1990] 1 All ER 769 for examples of such characteristics, and note that the comparison is with animals of the same breed rather than with animals of that type generally: *Hunt v Wallis* [1994] PIQR P128.

c) See *Curtis v Betts* (above) for the correct interpretation of s2(2)(b) and *Smith v Ainger* [1991] CLY 1416 for the correct interpretation of s2(2)(a).

d) See *Cummings* v *Grainger* (above) and *Curtis* v *Betts* (above) for examples of all the requirements of s2(2) being met.

e) See *Smith* v *Ainger* (above) for a wide interpretation of s2(2)(a).

Note that there has to be a causal link between s2 and the damage: *Jaundrill* v *Gillett* (1996) The Times 30 January.

Defences

See s5 1971 Act.

a) Damage wholly due to the fault of the claimant: s5(1).

b) Volenti: s5(2) (but not for an employee of the keeper – s6(5)).

c) Against trespassers if:

  i) the animal was not kept for the protection of persons or property; or

  ii) if it was then keeping it for that purpose was reasonable: s5(3).

Note in *Cummings* v *Grainger* (above) although the claimant made out a case under s2(2), she failed because the defendant could rely on s5(2) and s5(3).

Finally, note that neither an act of God nor an act of a stranger is a defence to s2.

Straying livestock

Section 4 1971 Act imposes liability for animals which stray on to another's land and cause damage or expense, and s7 allows an occupier onto whose land livestock has strayed to sell the livestock to recover for damage to his property and expenses caused, subject to the closely defined conditions in s7(3).

By s5(5) there is no liability where the livestock stray from a lawful use of the highway: *Tillet* v *Ward* (1882) 10 QBD 17; *Matthews* v *Wicks* (1987) The Times 25 May.

Animals straying on to the highway

Liability arises if animals stray on to the highway: s8(1), but note the defence in s8(2).

Protection of livestock against dogs

Section 3 imposes strict liability when dogs kill or injure livestock, and s9 allows a defendant to kill or injure a dog to protect livestock.

Guard Dogs Act 1975

Section 1 of this Act provides that a person shall not use, or permit the use of, a guard dog on any premises unless a competent handler is present and a warning notice is exhibited at the entrance to the premises. However, breach of s1 is a criminal offence only, and s5(1) of this Act expressly provides that breach shall not confer a civil right of action.

14.3 Key cases and statutes

- *Cunningham* v *Whelan* (1917) 52 Ir LT 67
  Allowing an animal to block the highway could amount to nuisance

- *Flack* v *Hudson* [2001] QB 698
  One keeper could sue another keeper of animal within the Animals Act 1971

- *Jaundrill* v *Gillett* (1996) The Times 30 January
  Causation must be established in order to recover damages

- *League Against Cruel Sports Ltd* v *Scott* [1985] 2 All ER 489
  Animals can also commit trespass

- *Leeman* v *Montague* [1936] 2 All ER 1677
  Keeping noisy animals could be a nuisance

- *Matthews* v *Wicks* (1987) The Times 25 May
  No liability where the livestock stray from a lawful use of the highway

- *Mirvahedy* v *Henley* [2003] 2 All ER 401
  Section 2(2)(b) of the A A 1971 must be contextually interpreted

- Animals Act 1971 – sets out the parameters of liability and available defences

- Guard Dogs Act 1975 – sets out the law on the keeping and use of guard dogs

14.4 Questions and suggested solutions

QUESTION ONE

Adam is an amateur biologist. In order to house his very large collection of rats and mice, he built a series of cages in his garden. These were built on top of a disused trench whose existence had been forgotten and was not discovered while the cages were being built. A few weeks later the trench gave way under the weight of the cages and large numbers of rats and mice escaped. Many of them made their way into Brian's house next door where they frightened his wife and children. A colony of the rats have established themselves in an overgrown garden belonging to Cecil, an elderly recluse. These attract cats to Cecil's garden which adjoins Brian's where their howling during the night keeps Brian and his family awake. Brian has started retaliating by using electrical equipment at times when he knows that it will interfere with the reception of wild life television programmes which Adam likes to watch.

Discuss the rights and liabilities of the parties in tort.

University of London LLB Examination
(for External Students) Law of Tort June 1988 Q3

General Comment

This question raises discussion of the Animals Act 1971 and how liability is measured thereunder. It also requires consideration of *Rylands* v *Fletcher* as well as nuisance itself as a possibility. The discussion should also include issues of foreseeability, remoteness and available defences, if any.

Skeleton Solution

Animals Act 1971 – s2(2)(b) – damage – fright – *Rylands* – does it apply to animals? – defences – nuisance – who is liable? – remoteness – *Sedleigh-Denfield* – malice – television and recreational interests.

Suggested Solution

This question raises a number of issues. The basic problem is identifying the cause of action. The first issue relates to the escape of the rats and mice from Adam's garden. The rats and mice have escaped and frightened Brian's wife and children. The first possibility is a cause of action under the Animals Act 1971 but such an action would experience considerable difficulties. Rats and mice are not dangerous animals (s2(1)) but they may be non-dangerous animals under s2(2) of the Act. The damage which a rat or a mouse may cause by a bite is arguably likely to be severe but the problem is that the likelihood of the damage being severe must be due to characteristics of the rats or the mice which are not normally found in rats or mice or are not normally found except at particular times or in particular circumstances. This requirement does not appear to have been met here unless the rats or mice are being used by Adam, who is an amateur biologist, for some unusual purposes and this characteristic has caused them to escape and do damage. If, however, it is held that the rats and mice are covered by s2(2) then Adam, as the keeper of the rats and mice, will be liable for the damage which they cause. Damage is defined in s11 as including injury to any person, which for this purpose includes impairment of a mental condition. Therefore Brian's wife and children may not be able to recover if they have suffered mere fright; they must show that some mental condition of theirs has been impaired. Liability under the 1971 Act is strict and there do not seem to be any other defences which Adam could invoke under the Act.

There could also be liability under the rule in *Rylands* v *Fletcher* (1868) LR 3 HL 330 if collecting rats in his house is held to be a non-natural user of land. The test to be applied is whether there is some special use of the land by Adam bringing with it increased danger to others: *Rickards* v *Lothian* [1931] AC 263. There is certainly an accumulation as the rats and mice appear to have been brought on to the land and there has also been an escape. The most difficult question here is whether the rule in *Rylands* applies to the escape of animals. In *Behrens* v *Bertram Mills Circus Ltd* [1957] 2 QB 1 it was held that it was possible that such an action could be taken under the rule in *Rylands*, but an example given of the type of case in which it was thought it might be applicable was the escape of a tiger, and rats and mice are nowhere near as dangerous as tigers. On the other hand if one asks the question whether rats and mice are likely to do mischief if they escape the answer might well be 'yes' so as to bring them within the scope of the rule. Once again it is unclear whether Brian's wife and children will be able to recover in respect of their fright. It depends on whether or not their 'fright' is a medically recognised psychiatric illness. An additional problem is created by the dicta of Lord MacMillan in *Read* v *Lyons* [1947] AC 156 that damages in a *Rylands* action are not recoverable for personal injury. Recovery was allowed in *Perry* v *Kendrick's Transport Ltd* [1956] 1 WLR 85 and *Hale* v *Jennings* [1938] 1 All ER 579, but the tenor of the judgment is *Cambridge Water Co* v *Eastern Counties Leather plc* [1994] 2 WLR 53 is against recovery. Adam may rely upon the defence of act of a stranger or an act of God by suggesting that the cause of the damage was the collapse of the trench which enabled the rats to escape. The difficulty here is that the weight of the cages is a factor which contributes towards the collapse and it is unlikely that he will be able to establish either of these defences.

Alternatively the entrance of the rats on to the land of Brian and Cecil may constitute the tort of trespass to land. The claimant in a trespass to land case must show that he has possession of the land and that there has been interference with his possession. Trespass can be committed where an animal belonging to the defendant trespasses on the claimant's land. Trespass is a tort of intention in the sense that the defendant must have intended to enter upon the land where the trespass was committed. It remains unclear whether trespass to land can be committed negligently and this issue is crucial here because the trespass of the rats is not intentional. A useful case here is *League Against Cruel Sports Ltd* v *Scott* [1985] 2 All ER 489. The claimants, who were opposed to blood sports, owned a sanctuary for wild deer and refused the defendant permission to come on their land during a local hunt. Despite this fact the hunt strayed on to the claimants' land on seven occasions and the master of the hunt was held to be liable in trespass if he knew that there was a real risk of hounds entering on to the claimants' land and if he intentionally or negligently permitted the hounds to enter the claimants' land. An application of this reasoning here would lead to the conclusion that Adam may be liable to Brian and Cecil in the tort of trespass to land if it can be shown that he was negligent in permitting the rats to escape and this will turn on whether he should have known of the existence of the trench under his garden.

The howling of the cats during the night may constitute a nuisance. Nuisance may be defined as the unlawful interference with a person's use or enjoyment of his land. Formerly only persons having an interest in land could sue in private nuisance: *Malone* v *Laskey* [1907] 2 KB 141, but this rule was recetly relaxed by the Court of Appeal who held that members of a houseowner's family had a cause of action in nuisance: *Khorasandjian* v *Bush* [1993] 3 WLR 476. Hence, following *Khorasandjian* both Brian and the members of his family may sue in private nuisance. In considering whether the howling constitutes a nuisance the court will have regard to the duration of the nuisance, the fact that it is at night, the character of the locality (apparently residential), the utility of the defendant's conduct (none) and any abnormal sensitivity of the claimant (trying to get some sleep at night could not be described as abnormally sensitive use).

Thus the howling appears to be a nuisance but the problem arises as to who is liable for the nuisance. The howling of the cats at night is likely to be too remote a consequence of any tort committed by Adam. The nuisance takes place on Cecil's land. It is clear that the occupier of the land may be liable where he has created the nuisance but Cecil has not created the nuisance. However in *Sedleigh-Denfield* v *O'Callaghan* [1940] AC 880 the House of Lords held that the occupier could be liable for the nuisance of a trespasser if he continued or adopted the nuisance. Here it is submitted that the presence of the cats is analogous to the position of the trespassers. Here it cannot be said that Cecil has adopted the nuisance but he could have continued it. A person continues a nuisance if, with knowledge or presumed knowledge of the existence of the nuisance, he fails to take reasonable means to bring it to an end, although he had ample time to do so. Cecil is an elderly recluse but we are not told that he is deaf so he must have knowledge of the howling and the only question is: has he failed to take reasonable steps to bring it to an end? Much here depends on the standard which is expected of an elderly recluse.

Adam may have a cause of action against Brian in nuisance in respect of the interference with his television programmes. Two particular points are relevant here. The first is that Brian is actuated by malice and his activities are similar to those of the defendant in *Christie* v *Davey* [1893] 1 Ch 316 where the defendant resorted to beating on trays, whistling and shrieking in an effort to disrupt the piano lessons which the claimant was giving next door. It was held that the defendant had committed the tort of nuisance. This would suggest that Brian is committing the tort of nuisance and that Adam may be entitled to an injunction to restrain the nuisance. In *Bridlington Relay Ltd* v *Yorkshire Electricity Board* [1965] Ch 436 Buckley J refused to grant an injunction to the claimants when the defendants' power line interfered with the reception on the claimants' television broadcasting system. However, in the more recent case of *Hunter* v *Canary Wharf Ltd* [1997] AC 655 it was held that such interference could constitute an actionable nuisance. So it is submitted that the tort of nuisance has been committed by Brian and that Adam will be entitled to an injunction restraining the commission of the nuisance.

QUESTION TWO

Plum was exercising his alsatian dog, Terror, in the park when he saw Grape trying to steal the handbag of a young woman wheeling a pram. Plum released the dog from its lead and said, 'Get him, Terror.' Terror pounced on Grape and brought him to the ground. Grape hurt his back when he fell and was also bitten in the face. Grape was a drug addict and therefore could not be given the normal treatment for the bite and for his other injuries. As a result his treatment was delayed and he was in hospital for six months. At the time of his injury he had just been asked to join a new pop group, the

Soft Fruits, which has now had a number of successful concerts. Grape's place was taken by another instrumentalist and he is now unemployed.

Advise Grape.

University of London LLB Examination
(for External Students) Law of Tort June 1987 Q7

General Comment

This question requires analysis of liability under the Animals Act 1971 as well as negligence and possibly trespass. Causation, remoteness and available defences should also be discussed within context.

Skeleton Solution

Plum – sets Terror on Grape – Animals Act 1971 – dangerous or non-dangerous species – *Cummings* – negligence – trespass to the person – assault by words – battery – remoteness in intentional torts – causation – ex turpi causa – effect of defence.

Suggested Solution

Grape may have a remedy against Plum under the Animals Act 1971 and at common law for the torts of negligence, assault and battery. In all cases, however, Plum may have available to him the defence of ex turpi causa.

Dealing firstly with Grape's claim under the Animals Act 1971, Plum is clearly the keeper of Terror under s6(3) of the Act because he owns Terror and so will be liable for the acts of Terror if they fall within the ambit of the Act. After the case of *Flack* v *Hudson* [2001] QB 698, it was held by the Court of Appeal that the 1971 Act did not prevent one keeper from initiating an action against another keeper. The 1971 Act draws a distinction between dangerous and non-dangerous species and so it is important to consider the category, if any, into which Terror falls. The position of alsatian dogs was considered by the Court of Appeal in *Cummings* v *Grainger* [1977] QB 397. To constitute a dangerous species it must be shown under s6(2) that an alsatian dog is not commonly domesticated in the British Islands (which is not the case here) and that a fully grown alsatian dog normally has such characteristics that it is likely, unless restrained, to cause severe damage or that any damage which it may cause is likely to be severe. Hence an alsatian is not a member of a dangerous species and Plum is liable for its acts under s2(2) of the Act. Three conditions must be satisfied before Plum can be held liable under s2(2). In the first place it must be shown that the alsatian dog was likely, unless restrained, to cause damage or that, if it caused damage, that damage was likely to be severe. The damage done by a bite from an alsatian dog is likely to be severe. Secondly it must be shown that the likelihood of damage or of its being severe was due to characteristics which are not normally found in alsatians or are not normally found except at particular times or in particular circumstances. This hurdle was overcome in *Cummings* because it was held that alsatian dogs were not normally vicious except in the 'particular circumstances' of their being kept as guard dogs. Here it could be argued that the attack by Terror was simply a normal characteristic of an alsatian when it is released in such circumstances by its owner. If this was the case then Grape could not proceed against Plum under s2(2). Lastly it must be shown that these characteristics were known to the keeper. Here it could be shown that Plum was aware of the characteristics because he told Terror to get Grape, showing that he was aware of Terror's potential to attack people.

If Grape was unable to satisfy the second of these conditions then he may have to resort to a common law negligence action. If the damage done by Terror was a foreseeable consequence of the release of Terror then Plum may be liable in the tort of negligence: see *Draper* v *Hodder* [1972] 2 QB 556.

Plum may however have a defence to Grape's action under the 1971 Act. He may argue that, under s5(1), the damage was caused 'wholly by the fault of the person suffering the damage', namely Grape. This, however, involves a rather strained construction of s5(1) in that it requires the court to hold that in attempting to steal the woman's handbag Grape had, by that act, brought about the attack by Terror. It is submitted that a court would not accept such a strained construction of the section. Difficulty would also be caused in relation to s5(1) by the fact that it was Plum's exhortation which was the factor which was the immediate cause of the attack by Terror.

A more likely defence is the defence of ex turpi causa. This defence is essentially one based upon public policy so that a cause of action in tort may be denied to a person who was committing a criminal act at the time at which the tort was alleged to have been committed. See the House of Lords' decision in *Tinsley* v *Milligan* [1993] 3 WLR 126 for a discussion of the scope and basis for this defence. It must be shown that there is a causal connection between the offence and the damage which the claimant has suffered (see *Ashton* v *Turner* [1981] QB 137). Thus in *Cummings* v *Grainger* (above) Lord Denning stated that a burglar who was bitten by a guard dog may be met by a plea of ex turpi causa. Therefore it can be argued that, as Grape was in the course of a criminal act, Plum's response was a legitimate one and that therefore Grape will be unable to recover from Plum.

Alternatively Grape may argue that Plum has committed the torts of assault and battery. An assault is committed where the defendant by his threat puts the claimant in a state of reasonable apprehension of immediate physical contact with his person. Here an assault would appear to have been committed when Plum shouted 'Get him, Terror' and released the dog from its lead. This would certainly put Grape in reasonable apprehension of immediate contact with his person. Once again, however, Plum may have available to him the defence of ex turpi causa.

The attack by Terror at the instigation of Plum could constitute the tort of battery. A battery consists of a direct act of the defendant which has the effect of causing contact with the person of the claimant, without the latter's consent. The difficulty here may lie in establishing whether the attack by Terror was a 'direct act of the defendant'.

However, it does not seem to matter that Plum used an animate object to injure Grape. In *Dodwell v Burford* (1670) 1 Mod 24 the defendant smacked the claimant's horse causing it to bolt and throw and injure the claimant. It was held that a battery had been committed. It is likely that here the act of Plum is a direct one because there is no intervening act between him releasing Terror and Terror's attack on Grape. Once again, however, Grape may be met with the defence of ex turpi causa. The defence was invoked in the case of *Murphy v Culhane* [1977] QB 94, where the claimant's husband was killed by the defendant during the course of criminal conduct instigated by the claimant's husband. Lord Denning held that the deceased would have been unable to maintain an action in battery because of the defence of ex turpi causa. Lord Denning did, however, hold that the defence would not be applicable where the act of the defendant was out of all proportion to the occasion. It is unlikely to be the case here that Plum's action was out of all proportion to the occasion as he was simply attempting to prevent Grape from escaping with the proceeds of the theft.

Assuming, however, that the defence of ex turpi causa was not made out and that Grape was entitled to recover damages, a difficult issue then arises as to the damage which Grape has suffered. Grape has suffered both personal injury and consequential loss of earnings. Grape's physical injuries have been made worse by the fact that he is a drug addict and so cannot have the normal treatment for the bites. However, the rule in tort is that you must take your victim as you find him: see *Smith v Leech, Brain* [1962] 2 QB 405. It is not the case here that Grape has unreasonably refused to undergo treatment; it is simply the case that by virtue of the fact that he is a drug addict that he is unable to undergo the treatment. This, therefore, is the classic type of case to which the eggshell skull rule is applicable and it is submitted that Plum would be liable for the damage suffered by Grape.

The loss of earnings as a pop group instrumentalist poses more difficulty. It is well settled that loss of earnings caused by negligently inflicted personal injury are recoverable, but here there is difficulty over the issues of remoteness and causation. Once again it is clear that the fact that the tortfeasor injures a high income earner is no defence to an action in tort and so the loss is not too remote. However, it is possible to argue, relying upon the decision of the Court of Appeal in *The Arpad* [1934] P 189, that a musician may not be able to recover for the losses which he suffers as a result of being disabled by the defendant from being able to perform particular contracts. However, it is submitted that this is incorrect and that there is no reason why Grape should not be able to recover for his loss of earnings. The fact that he earns his income by performing contracts to play music should not bar him from recovering in respect of his loss of earnings.

One further problem remains, however, and that is that Grape had not accepted the offer to join the group at the time of the accident. Thus, he may find it difficult to prove that the attack by Terror caused him any loss. For example, Plum might argue that the pop group could have withdrawn the offer or that Grape might not have joined the group anyway. However, it is submitted that Plum would have to prove that one of these two possibilities was what would, in fact, have happened. Having caused the loss it would not lie in the mouth of Plum to argue that Grape would not have joined the group. So it is submitted that, unless Plum was able to prove one of these two points, Grape would be able to recover for his loss of earnings, subject to a deduction for the unemployment benefits received to the date of trial.

QUESTION THREE

Sally, an animal lover, lives in a home with a garden on the outskirts of a village. She keeps a large number of animals and also is in the habit of looking after sick and wounded wild animals which are brought to her. Other residents in the village complain of the noise and smell, particularly Tracey, who lives next door to Sally, and is frightened of all animals.

Una, a village girl who helps out at Sally's house, allowed a ferret which Sally was treating to escape from its cage. It ran into Tracey's garden where Victor, her two-year old son, was playing. Victor thought it was a cat and tried to play with it, but the ferret bit him. Tracey heard his screams and struggling to overcome her fears beat away the ferret. Victor was not seriously hurt, but the strain on Tracey was such that she has been suffering from nervous illness ever since.

Discuss the rights and liabilities of the parties in tort.

> University of London LLB Examination
> (for External Students) Law of Tort June 1985 Q6

General Comment

A question that overlaps a number of torts, such as nuisance, *Rylands* v *Fletcher*, negligence and liability under the Animals Act 1971. Defences must also be raised where relevant and applicable.

Skeleton Solution

Private and public nuisance – Animals Act 1971, liability and defences – *Rylands* v *Fletcher* – negligence.

Suggested Solution

This problem concerns potential liability for a number of torts. The residents and Tracey may consider bringing an action in nuisance against Sally for the noise and smell of the animals. If sufficient members of the community (*Attorney-General* v *PYA Quarries* [1957] 2 QB 169) are affected, then an action may be brought in public nuisance, either by the Attorney-General as a relator action or by Tracey as a member of the community who has suffered damage over and above the rest. Otherwise Tracey and any other residents affected may bring an action in private nuisance by showing that Sally has interfered with the use and enjoyment of their land, here by way of personal inconvenience rather than actual damage, and since the decision of the Court of Appeal in *Khorasandjian* v *Bush* [1993] 3 WLR 476 it will not be necessary for any potential claimants to have an interest in land and so all the residents could sue in private nuisance.

The law expects give and take between neighbours and, to strike a balance between a claimant's quiet enjoyment of his land as against the defendant's right to do what he likes on his land, the defendant must be acting unreasonably. In cases involving inconvenience, the nature of the locality is taken into account (*St Helen's Smelting Co* v *Tipping* (1865) 11 HLC Cas 642; *Sturges* v *Bridgman* (1879) 11 Ch D 852), and the courts have also taken the view that the inconvenience must not be trifling (*Halsey* v *Esso Petroleum* [1961] 1 WLR 683). It must generally be a continuing state of affairs, rather than an isolated event (*Bolton* v *Stone* [1951] AC 850). Compensation has been awarded for smells from animals (*Bone* v *Seale* [1975] 1 All ER 787), and, as long as the inconvenience is more trifling, it is submitted that on the facts of this case, the above criteria are satisfied. However, abnormal sensitivity on the part of the claimants may destroy their claim (*Robinson* v *Kilvert* (1884) 41 Ch D 88; *Whycer* v *Urry* [1956] JPL 365), and while the courts may have some regard to the social utility of the defendant's conduct, it is by no means conclusive if, as here, the defendant is doing something which may indirectly benefit the community: *Adams* v *Ursell* [1913] 1 Ch 269.

On balance, therefore, if the inconvenience is sufficiently grave, there is an actionable nuisance against Sally by the residents and possibly also by Tracey, as her fear would not then constitute abnormal sensitivity.

As far as the escape of the ferret is concerned, there may be liability under the Animals Act 1971. The first point to consider is whether a ferret is a dangerous or non-dangerous species. Under s6(2), a dangerous species is one which is not commonly domesticated in the British Isles and whose fully grown animals normally have such characteristics that they are likely, unless restrained, to cause severe damage or that any damage they cause is likely to be severe (liability under this section is strict). Alternatively, under s2(2) there are three criteria for liability for non-dangerous animals. It is submitted that the latter is the category into which the ferret would fall since it does not fit within the ambit of s6(2).

Before considering s2(2) in detail, the keeper must be ascertained; by virtue of s6(3), a person is the keeper if he owns the animal or has it in his possession or if he is the head of a household of which a member under the age of sixteen owns the animal. From this definition, Sally will be the keeper as opposed to Una, since the animal is in Sally's overall possession or control, although s6(4) states that where an animal is in a person's possession in order to restore it to its owner, that person is not the keeper; however, as the ferret here is a wild animal one assumes it will not be restored to its owner as such. The present position is reflected in the Court of Appeal's decision in *Flack* v *Hudson* [2001] QB 698 where it was held that one keeper could sue another keeper under the 1971 Act.

Under s2(2) Sally will be liable for the injury to Victor if it is the kind of damage which the animal unless restrained is likely to cause or which if caused by the animal is likely to be severe. Injury by biting is, it is submitted, damage which ferrets are likely to cause. Section 2(2)(b) is more difficult to ascertain; possibly it may be argued that the likelihood of the damage only occurs at particular times or in particular circumstances in ferrets (perhaps expert evidence is needed here), and those characteristics must be known to Sally, or Una as the keeper's servant. None of the defences under s5 apply in this case, and it must be pointed out that Tracey's nervous illness is possibly not a likely type of damage under s2(2)(a).

An alternative cause of action for both Tracey and Victor in view of the uncertainties outlined above is negligence, which may be brought against Sally and possibly Una. Sally may be liable for insufficient fencing around the garden, and Una for her lack of care in allowing the ferret to escape (subject to her age). Tracey will wish to recover for nervous shock, defined as mental injury or psychiatric illness (*Brice* v *Brown* [1984] 1 All ER 997), but in order to do so, she must prove that Sally or Una owed her a duty of care. The question here is whether nervous shock is a reasonably foreseeable consequence of Sally's negligence in not establishing adequate fencing etc, or of Una's negligence in allowing the animal to escape. It is submitted that both parties will owe a duty of care to neighbouring householders not to allow animals to escape since injury of some kind is reasonably foreseeable. As regards Tracey's nevous shock, Tracy would appear to be able to satisfy the criteria required by *Alcock* v *Chief Constable of South Yorkshire Police* [1991] 4 All ER 907 is that Tracey's relationship to the primary victim (Victor) is sufficiently close that it is reasonably foreseeable that Tracey might suffer nervous shock; Tracey's proximity to the accident is sufficiently proximate in both time and space; and Tracey suffered nervous shock through seeing and hearing the accident. In the absence of further details, it would appear from the facts that both Sally and Una are in breach of duty from which damage has resulted both to Victor and to Tracey.

Tracey and Victor may also consider an action in *Rylands* v *Fletcher* (1868) LR 3 HL 330, so long as the rule could extend to the escape of an animal; by analogy, *Rylands* has been held applicable to the escape of people (*Attorney-General* v *Corke* [1933] Ch 82) but this case has met considerable criticism. Otherwise, there has been an escape of an animal that is dangerous but one must question whether this constitutes a non-natural user of land. Sally's use of the land may be a special use if there is a sufficiently large number of animals on it. Personal injuries have been held to be actionable under *Rylands* (*Perry* v *Kendrick's* [1956] 1 WLR 85; *Hale* v *Jennings* [1938] 1 All ER 579), although this is currently an area of considerable doubt: *Read* v *Lyons* [1947] AC 156; *Cambridge Water Co* v *Eastern Counties Leather plc* [1994] 2 WLR 53. And there do not appear to be any defences appropriate to Sally's case; she could not plead that Tracey has impliedly consented to the source of the danger since it may well be that Sally has acted negligently: *Attorney-General* v *Cory Bros* [1921] 1 AC 521. There is unlikely to be an action in nuisance for the escape of the ferret, since it is an isolated event, and as such is not actionable unless it has been preceded by such a state of affairs as existed in

Midwood v *Mayor of Manchester* [1905] 2 KB 597, or unless the damage is sufficiently serious, which it is submitted is not the case here.

In conclusion, therefore, the villagers and Tracey may have an action against Sally in nuisance and possibly in *Rylands* v *Fletcher* (see above); Tracey and Victor will have a case in negligence against Sally and Una; and Victor may have an arguable case under the Animals Act 1971.

QUESTION FOUR

'The enactment of the Animals Act 1971 was a job half done. Its provisions are inadequate as a statutory basis for liability in respect of damage done by animals.'

Discuss.

Written by the Author

General Comment

Essay questions on the Animals Act 1971 are rarely set in examinations, but for the sake of good practice one is incorporated here. The question requires a thorough understanding of both the 1971 Act and the Guard Dogs Act 1975.

Skeleton Solution

Background to Act – distinction between dangerous and non-dangerous animals drafting of s2(2) – not comprehensive – Guard Dogs Act 1975 – strict liability – s4 – suitability of tort law for statutory regulation.

Suggested Solution

The law of tort has always made separate provision for the liability of animals. Prior to the Animals Act 1971 there was an old form of action which was specifically applicable to damage caused by animals. This was an action on the case for damage done by a savage or dangerous animal and was known as the 'scienter' action. To establish liability the claimant had to show that the defendant, who was the keeper of the animal, knew or ought to have known that the animal was of a dangerous character. For this purpose a distinction was drawn between two different types of animals; dangerous animals (ferae naturae) and non-dangerous animals (mansuetae naturae). Once it was shown that the animal belonged to one or other category the liability which was imposed on the defendant was strict.

The Animals Act 1971 was introduced in an effort to codify the law relating to the liability for the acts of animals and to bring it up to date. The Act was introduced after extensive consideration of the law by the Law Commission but has nevertheless been subjected to considerable criticism. This is, however, mitigated by the willingness of the House of Lords to make decisions which reflect the need for the judiciary to take account of changes that affect society in many ways. One such decision is the judgment by the Court of Appeal in *Flack v Hudson* [2001] QB 698.

The Act abolishes the old scienter action and replaces it with a statutory code enacted in s2. The abolition of the old form of action was a useful step to take because one of the problems which is sometimes caused by legislation in the area of tort law is that the old forms of action are retained and the legislation is superimposed on the existing common law. This can cause problems in seeking to marry together the common law and the statute. However, the Act is not an exhaustive statement of the range of liability for damage caused by animals. A claimant may elect to bring an action in negligence, trespass to the person or defamation where the damage, defamatory statement or attack is carried out by an animal belonging to the defendant. Thus a problem still remains in ascertaining the relationship between the common law and statute law because a claimant can still try to use the common law to evade the statutory restrictions. Even the statutory provisions are not complete because in 1975 the Guard Dogs Act was enacted to make further provision for the use of guard dogs. Thus the Act may be said to be a job half-done because it is not a complete statement of the liability for damage done by animals because a considerable body of law still lies outside the ambit of the Act in the common law.

Section 2 of the 1971 Act retains a distinction between dangerous and non-dangerous species. A dangerous species is a species which is not commonly domesticated in the British Islands and whose fully grown animals normally have such characteristics that they are likely, unless restrained, to cause severe damage or that any damage which they may cause is likely to be severe: s6(2). The keeper (defined in s6(3)) of such a dangerous species is liable, subject to certain defences, for the damage caused by the animal: s2(1). In relation to non-dangerous species the keeper of an animal is liable where the damage is of a kind which the animal, unless restrained, was likely to cause or which, if caused by the animal, was likely to be severe (s2(2)(a)), the likelihood of the damage or of its being severe was due to characteristics of the animal which are not normally so found in animals of the same species or are not normally found except at particular times or in particular circumstances (s2(2)(b)) and these characteristics were known to the keeper: s2(2)(c). The drafting of s2(2) is not entirely satisfactory. Difficulties arise in giving a meaning to s2(2)(b) because it is not entirely clear what was meant by the phrase 'characteristics of the animal which are not normally so found in animals of the same species'. In *Kite v Napp* (1982) The Times 1 June it was held that a dog was caught by s2(2)(b) because it had a propensity to attack people carrying bags. But, had it not been for such an unusual propensity, it is doubtful whether the dog would have been caught by the Act. See *Hunt v Wallis* [1994] PIQR P128 where it was held that in deciding whether a dog had characteristics not normally found in animals of the same species, the relevant comparison was with dogs of the same breed rather than with dogs generally. This would appear to admit the defence that all members of that species are bad-tempered. In an Act which was supposed to clarify the law one could have hoped for better drafting than this. The drafting of s2(2)(b) was subjected to criticism by the Court of Appeal in *Cummings v Grainger* [1977] QB 397. It is also submitted that the retention of the distinction between dangerous and non-dangerous animals was less than satisfactory because animals come in many different shapes and sizes and it is not clear what useful purpose is served by trying to compress them within two groups.

The Act is also unsatisfactory in that it makes no provision for a test for remoteness of damage. Is the test established in *Wagon Mound (No 1)* [1961] AC 388 to be applied or the directness test applied in *Rylands* v *Fletcher* (1868) LR 3 HL 330? Once again one would have thought that the Act would have some provision for this situation.

Section 4 of the Act makes provision for the liability for damage caused by straying livestock. The section is badly drafted because it is not entirely clear whether it applies to personal injury. But it appears that the intention was to provide a remedy for property damage only and it is submitted that the omission of protection for personal injury is rather unusual because the law of tort usually accords greater protection to a person's interest in his personal security than in his property.

However, it is submitted that the Animals Act 1971 is generally a satisfactory piece of legislation. It has a number of defects which we have noted, principally the fact that it is not comprehensive and the rather poor drafting of s2(2)(b). But it is suggested that it would be going too far to suggest that the Act was 'a job half-done'. Rather the Act underlines the difficulty of legislating in the area of tort law. Tort law, by its very nature, is open textured and it is difficult to tie liability down within precise boundaries. The same problem can be seen in both the Occupiers' Liability Acts. Seen in this light, the Animals Act 1971 does not appear inadequate as a piece of legislation, but it is an open question whether it would have been preferable to refuse to legislate and to allow the courts to develop the common law in a more flexible manner.

From time to time however the courts do, as may be necessary, give decisions that reflect the current position of society. For instance, the presumption that one keeper could not sue another keeper under the Animals Act of 1971 was rebutted by the Court of Appeal in *Flack* v *Hudson* (see above).

Chapter 15

Defamation

15.1   Introduction

15.2   Key points

15.3   Key cases and statutes

15.4   Questions and suggested solutions

15.1 Introduction

Defamation is a major topic in tort, and students must not only have a good grasp of the elements of liability (which are relatively straightforward), but also of the defences, especially those of qualified privilege and fair comment. A knowledge of the Defamation Act 1996 is also required.

Note also that by virtue of the Defamation Act 1996 (Commencement No 2) Order 2000, the remaining provisions of the Defamation Act 1996 came into force on 28 February 2000, with the exception only of the repeal of the Broadcasting Act 1990, Schedule 20, para 3.

15.2 Key points

Libel and slander

a)   A defendant's statement in permanent form is libel.

b)   Television and radio broadcasts are treated as libel: ss1 and 16 Defamation Act 1952, as are theatre performances: s4 Theatres Act 1968.

c)   A defendant's statement in transient form is slander.

d)   A statement can include pictures, cartoons or a wax effigy: *Monson* v *Tussaud's* [1894] 1 QB 671

e)   Libel is actionable per se; slander requires proof of special damage.

f)   However, slander is actionable per se where it:

i)   imputes a crime punishable by imprisonment;

ii)   imputes certain contagious and infectious diseases, eg VD, plague, leprosy;

iii) imputes unchastity in a woman (Slander of Women Act 1891);

iv) is calculated to disparage the claimant in any office, profession, calling, trade or business held or carried on by him at the time of the publication: s2 Defamation Act 1952.

Claimant

Only a living person may sue in defamation. This includes companies: *Metropolitan Saloon Omnibus v Hawkins* (1859) 4 H & N 87, but not trade unions: *EETPU v Times Newspapers* [1980] QB 585. In *Derbyshire County Council v Times Newspapers* [1993] 2 WLR 449 the House of Lords held that a local authority could not sue for libel in respect of its governmental and administrative functions.

Elements of defamation

The claimant must prove:

a) a defamatory statement;

b) which refers to the claimant; and

c) which was published to a third party.

Defamatory statement

a) The test is: does the statement tend to lower the claimant in the estimation of right thinking members of society generally (*Sim v Stretch* [1936] 2 All ER 1237), or expose the claimant to hatred, ridicule or contempt (*Parmiter v Coupland* (1840) 6 M & W 105)? In *Berkoff v Burchill* [1996] 4 All ER 1008 it was held that a statement which held up the claimant to contempt, scorn or ridicule or tended to exclude him from society could be defamatory even though it did not impute disgraceful conduct or lack of professional skill.

b) The standard is objective – what would right thinking members of society think, not the claimant's friends (*Byrne v Deane* [1937] 1 KB 818)?

In *Hartt v Newspaper Publishing plc* (1989) The Times 9 November the Court of Appeal held that in determining the meaning of the words the approach adopted should be that of the hypothetical ordinary reader who was neither naïve nor unduly suspicious, but who might read between the lines and be capable of loose thinking.

In *Charleston v News Group Newspapers* [1995] 2 WLR 450 the House of Lords re-emphasised that the statement or article must be considered in its entirety.

c) For slander only, note the special rule that abuse or insult is not defamation: *Parkins v Scott* (1862) 1 H & C 153; *Lane v Holloway* [1968] 1 QB 379.

d) If the statement is not prima facie defamatory, but only by implication, the claimant will have to plead an innuendo.

e) A true innuendo involves the existence of extraneous facts which the claimant must prove: *Tolley v Fry* [1931] AC 333; *Cassidy v Daily Mirror* [1929] 2 KB 331.

f) A false innuendo arises where the words have a secondary meaning, either because the words have several meanings or a slang meaning: *Allsop v Church of England Newspaper* [1972] 2 QB 161; *Winyard v Tatler Publishing* (1991) The Independent 16 August.

Reference to the claimant

a) The statement must reasonably be understood to refer to the claimant (judge to decide) and be so understood by reasonable people (jury to decide).

b) The defendant need not intend to refer to the claimant: *Hulton v Jones* [1910] AC 20; *Cassidy v Daily Mirror* (above).

c) It is no defence that the defendant intended to refer to another person: *Newstead v London Express Newspapers* [1940] 1 KB 377.

d) There is no requirement that the defendant expressly refer to the claimant: *Morgan v Odhams Press* [1971] 1 WLR 1239; *Cassidy v Daily Mirror* (above).

e) Statements regarding a class will not be taken to refer to an individual member of that class unless the class is so small that the statement must necessarily refer to each member of it, or the words point particularly to the claimant: *Knupffer v London Express Newspapers* [1944] AC 116.

Publication

a) This means the act of making the statement known to someone other than the claimant. This does not create an automatic right to sue – see *Jameel and Another v Wall Street Journal Europe SPRL* [2004] 2 All ER 92.

b) Publication to the defendant's spouse is insufficient (*Wennhak v Morgan* (1888) 20 QBD 635) but to the claimant's spouse is sufficient: *Wenman v Ash* (1853) 13 CB 836.

c) Publication must be made to a person who understands the defamatory nature of the statement and its reference to the claimant: *Sadgrove v Hole* [1901] 2 KB 1.

d) Publication need not be intentional – negligent publication is enough: *Theaker v Richardson* [1962] 1 WLR 151.

e) Each repetition of the statement constitutes a fresh publication, and a fresh cause of action arises: *Cutler v McPhail* [1962] 2 QB 292.

See also *Slipper v BBC* [1991] 1 All ER 165 on liability for republication.

In *Godfrey* v *Demon Internet Ltd* [1999] 4 All ER 342 the High Court held that an internet service provider had, within the definition of publication, satisfied the criteria required for an action of defamation to succeed.

Note: This was the first defamation action involving the Internet. Actions of this sort are, however, more common in the United States.

Fast track procedure

A summary procedure was introduced by ss8 and 9 Defamation Act 1996 to dispose of straightforward cases. Damages are assessed by a judge and cannot exceed £10,000. The procedure is available to both claimants and defendants and applies where either side's case has no realistic prospect of success.

Note that under the new procedural rules, defamation cases which are of a value of less than £10,000 are automatically tried through the fast track procedure for which there is no jury: Civil Procedure Act 1997. See also the relevance of this under the Access to Justice Act 1999.

Defences

Consent

For example: *Chapman* v *Lord Ellesmere* [1932] 2 KB 431.

Innocent dissemination

Under s1 Defamation Act 1996, it is a defence for a person to show:

a) he was not the author, editor or publisher of the statement;

b) he took reasonable care regarding its publication;

c) he did not know, and had no reason to believe, that what he did caused or contributed to the publication.

Justification or truth

a) The defendant must prove that the statement is true in substance rather than in each and every respect: *Alexander* v *North Eastern Railway* (1865) 6 B & S 340.

By s5 Defamation Act 1952, if the words contain two or more distinct charges, a defence of justification will not fail merely because the truth of every charge is not proved if the words not proved to be true do not materially affect the claimant's reputation, having regard to the true charges.

b) By s13 Civil Evidence Act 1968 a conviction in a criminal court is conclusive proof that the convicted person committed the crime.

c) By s8 Rehabilitation of Offenders Act 1974, a spent conviction may be used for justification, fair comment or qualified privilege in the absence of malice.

d) The defendant may plead a less defamatory meaning than that alleged by the claimant and that in this lesser sense the statement is true. The defendant may also widen the meaning of the words by arguing that they impute general dishonesty rather than dishonesty in a particular matter: *Williams* v *Reason* [1988] 1 All ER 262, and he may plead justification of any alternative meaning of the words: *Prager* v *Times Newspapers* [1988] 1 All ER 300.

e) The defendant must particularise the meaning of the words he alleges are justified: *Lucas-Box* v *News Group Newspapers* [1986] 1 WLR 147, and this must be done clearly so that the claimant and the court are aware of precisely what meaning the defendant intends to justify: *Morrell* v *International Thomson Publishing* [1989] 3 All ER 733.

Fair comment

That is, the statement is fair comment based on true facts made in good faith on a matter of public interest.

a) Public interest is interpreted widely: see Lord Denning's comments in *London Artists* v *Littler* [1969] 2 QB 375.

b) The comment must be based on true facts which must be either stated in the comment or be capable of being inferred from the comment: *Kemsley* v *Foot* [1952] AC 345. If not all the facts are true note the effect of s6 Defamation Act 1952. If the fair comment is based on an untrue statement made on a privileged occasion note that the report of the statement must be fair and accurate: *Brent Walker Group* v *Time Out* [1991] 2 WLR 772.

c) The statement must be one of opinion and not of fact, although it may be difficult to distinguish between these: *Dakhyl* v *Labouchere* [1908] 2 KB 325.

d) By fair is meant that the defendant must have honestly believed the opinion expressed: *Slim* v *Daily Telegraph* [1968] 2 QB 157, and not that a reasonable person would agree with the opinion: *Silkin* v *Beaverbrook Newspapers* [1958] 1 WLR 743.

Note the situation where the allegation is that the claimant had a corrupt or dishonest motive: *Campbell* v *Spottiswoode* (1863) 3 B & S 769.

e) The defence may be rebutted by showing the defendant was acting out of malice, ie spite, ill-will or improper motive: *Thomas* v *Bradbury, Agnew & Co Ltd* [1906] 2 KB 627. Note that the claimant must prove malice: *Telnikoff* v *Matusevich* [1991] 3 WLR 952. However, if the author of the statement acts maliciously and the publisher does not, the publisher is not tainted with the author's malice: *Lyon* v *Daily Telegraph* [1943] KB 746.

Absolute privilege

No action will lie for any defamatory statement, no matter how false or malicious, made in:

a) parliamentary proceedings, although MPs and peers can waive this privilege to pursue a defamation action (s13 Defamation Act 1996);

b) official reports of parliamentary proceedings;

c) state communications;

d) judicial proceedings;

e) fair, accurate and contemporaneous reports of judicial proceedings in the UK and Europe (s14 Defamation Act 1996);

f) reports of the Parliamentary Commissioner;

g) husband and wife communications.

To this extent, the case of *Mahon v Rahn (No 2)* [2000] 4 All ER 41 provides a useful example of this defence. See also *Gray v Avadis* (2003) 100 (36) LSG 43.

Qualified privilege

The defence can be destroyed by showing that the defendant was actuated by malice. Malice means the defendant had no honest belief in the truth of his statement: *Horrocks v Lowe* [1975] AC 135.

The defence applies to:

a) Fair and accurate reports of judicial and parliamentary proceedings (no need to be contemporaneous or in a newspaper): *Turkington and Others v Times Newspapers* [2000] 3 WLR 1670.

b) Certain reports covered by s15 Defamation Act 1996. Note those which are privileged unless published with malice and those privileged subject to the right of explanation or contradiction.

c) Statements made under a duty, ie a statement made by A to B concerning C where:

   i) A is under a legal, social or moral duty to make the statement to B and B has a corresponding interest to receive it: *Watt v Longsden* [1930] 1 KB 130.

   ii) A has an interest to be protected and B is under a duty to protect that interest: *Osborne v Boulter* [1930] 2 KB 226.

   iii) A and B have a common interest in the statement: *Watt v Longsden* (above); *Bryanston Finance v De Vries* [1975] QB 703.

Note that it is possible to sidestep the defence of qualified privilege by framing an action in negligent misstatement. *Lawton v BOC Transhield* [1987] 2 All ER 608; *Spring* v *Guardian Assurance* [1994] 3 WLR 354 which held that the writer of a reference owed a duty of care to the subject of the reference.

The case of *Loutchansky* v *Times Newspapers* [2001] 4 All ER 115 illustrates how the Court of Appeal dealt with this defence. In *Baldwin* v *Rusbridger* [2001] EMLR 47 the Court of Appeal felt that this defence should not be extended to journalists in most circumstances.

The House of Lords shared this view in *Reynolds* v *Times Newspapers Ltd* [1999] 4 All ER 609 by stating that the media do not have an unfettered right to publish what they believe to be in the public interest.

In *Grobbelaar* v *News Group Newspapers Ltd* [2002] 1 WLR 3024 the House of Lords upheld the defence of qualified privilege. Interestingly, in *Kearns* v *General Council of the Bar* [2003] 2 All ER 534 the Court of Appeal held that the Bar Council could not rely on this defence.

Apology

A newspaper or periodical may plead apology as a defence if the statement was published without malice and without gross negligence, and an apology was published as soon as possible; a payment into court by way of amends must also be made: Libel Acts 1843 and 1845.

Offer to make amends

This has replaced s4 Defamation Act 1952. The offer must be to make and publish a suitable correction and apology and to pay compensation. If the parties cannot agree compensation it may be decided by the court. If the offer is accepted, proceedings end; if not accepted, it is a defence. However, it will not be a defence if the offeror knew that the statement could refer to the claimant and was both false and defamatory.

Remedies

Usually damages, decided by a jury. In *Rantzen* v *Mirror Group Newspapers* [1993] NLJ 507 the Court of Appeal held that the test of whether damages awarded are excessive is whether a reasonable jury could have thought that the award was necessary to compensate the claimant and to re-establish her reputation. If not the Court of Appeal may order a new trial under s8(1) Courts and Legal Services Act 1990 or substitute a sum under s8(2) of the 1990 Act. A jury may be referred to previous such awards by the Court of Appeal, but not to previous jury awards. In the meantime juries should be told to consider the purchasing power of any award, as in *Sutcliffe* v *Pressdram* [1990] 1 All ER 269.

The claimant may seek an interlocutory injunction, but this is rarely granted where the defence is one of justification, fair comment or qualified privilege: *Bestobell Paints* v *Bigg* (1975) 119 SJ 678.

The limitation period for defamation is now one year: s24A Limitation Act 1980 as modified by s5 Defamation Act 1996.

15.3 Key cases and statutes

- *Baldwin* v *Rusbridger* [2001] EMLR 47
  Defence of qualified privilege

- *Branson* v *Bower* [2002] 2 WLR 452
  Illustrates how the defence of fair comment operates

- *Charleston* v *News Group Newspapers* [1995] 2 WLR 450
  Court emphasised that the whole statement must be considered in its entirety

- *Derbyshire County Council* v *Times Newspapers* [1993] 2 WLR 449
  Public bodies are accountable and therefore cannot sue in libel in respect of their governmental and administrative functions

- *Godfrey* v *Demon Internet* [1999] 4 All ER 342
  Publication is possible through the internet

- *Gray* v *Avadis* (2003) 100 (36) LSG 43
  Exemplifies the defence of absolute privilege

- *Grobbelaar* v *News Group Newspapers Ltd* [2002] 1 WLR 3024
  Defence of qualified privilege was upheld

- *Hamilton* v *Al Fayed* [2001] 1 AC 395
  Examines the defence of privilege and the right to waive it

- *Jameel and Another* v *Wall Street Journal Europe SprL* [2004] 2 All ER 92
  Publication does not create an automatic right to sue

- *Kearns* v *General Council of the Bar* [2003] 2 All ER 534
  Illustrates the operation of the defence of qualified privilege

- *Loutchansky* v *Times Newspapers* [2002] EWHC 2490
  Defence of qualified privilege not available as of right to newspapers

- *Mahon* v *Rahn (No 2)* [2000] 4 All ER 41
  Provides a useful example of the defence of absolute privilege

- *Metropolitan Saloon Omnibus Co* v *Hawkins* (1859) 4 H & N 87
  Only a living person may sue in defamation

- *Monson* v *Tussaud's* [1894] 1 QB 671
  A wax effigy could amount to a libel

- *Morgan* v *Odhams Press Ltd* [1971] 1 WLR 1239
  The statement must reasonably be understood to refer to the claimant

- *Reynolds* v *Times Newspapers Ltd* [1999] 4 All ER 609
  Defence of qualified privilege .

- *Sim* v *Stretch* [1936] 2 All ER 1237
  Provides a definition of what amounts to defamation

- *Slim* v *Daily Telegraph* [1968] 2 QB 157
  Characterises the elements of the defence of fair comment

- *Taylor* v *Serious Fraud Office* [1998] 4 All ER 801
  Witnesses in judicial proceedings have absolute immunity

- *Telnikoff* v *Matusevitch* [1991] 3 WLR 952
  Defence of fair comment may be rebutted by proving malice

- *Theaker* v *Richardson* [1962] 1 WLR 151
  Publication need not be intentional – negligent publication is enough

- *Tolley* v *J S Fry & Sons Ltd* [1931] AC 333
  A true innuendo involves the existence of extraneous facts

- *Totalise plc* v *Motley Fool Ltd & Another* [2002] 1 WLR 1233
  Illustrates the relationship between pre-action disclosure and date protection in conjunction with actions in defamation

- *Turkington and Others* v *Times Newspapers* [2000] 3 WLR 1670
  Illustrates the defence of qualified privilege

- Civil Procedure Act 1997 and the Access to Justice Act 1999 – created a new fast-track procedure without a jury for defamation cases with less than £10,000

- Courts and Legal Services Act 1990 – the Court of Appeal has power to slash the awards made by a jury if it is felt that the award was excessive or unjustified

- Defamation Acts 1952 and 1996 – set out the framework within which liability is assessed, as well as making available certain defences

- Libel Act 1843 – makes available the defence of apology and amends

- Slander of Women Act 1891 – outlines the different types of action which are actionable per se

- Theatres Act 1968 – theatre performances could be construed as a form of libel

15.4 Questions and suggested solutions

QUESTION ONE

'My conclusion is that the established common law approach to misstatements of fact remains essentially sound ... The elasticity of the common law principle enables interference with freedom of speech to be confined to what is necessary in the circumstances of the case. This elasticity enables the court to give appropriate weight, in today's conditions, to the importance of freedom of expression by the media on all matters of public concern.' (*Reynolds* v *Times Newspapers Ltd*, per Lord Nicholls of Birkenhead.)

Discuss.

University of London LLB Examination
(for External Students) Law of Tort June 2001 Q1

General Comment

This question deserves careful reading, as the hasty candidate may find himself discussing the law on negligent misstatements instead of the specific issues within the law of defamation on which the question focuses. The question also raises the issue of whether the law of defamation draws a balance with freedom of expression.

Skeleton Solution

The general principle required for establishing an action for defamation – the need to protect an individual's reputation – the need for freedom of expression – is there a balance between the two? – was this issue addressed in *Reynolds* v *Times Newspapers Ltd*? – the defence of privilege; justification – final analysis.

Suggested Solution

Essentially the question raises an analysis of two moral rights, ie protection of privacy and protection of reputation. There is certainly a link in practice between the right to privacy and the right to reputation, although this link is not recognised by English law in any formal sense. In French law, for example, there are distinct categories of 'préjudice matériel' and 'préjudice morale' to cover those harms which respectively can and cannot be reduced to mere financial loss. In the UK, however, both the freedom of speech and the protection of reputation have developed separately. Hence the unawareness that each right does in fact protect an aspect of personal integrity and dignity. An examination of this distinct and yet overlapping feature is thus necessary. Perhaps this is what Lord Nicholls meant by the elasticity of common law in *Reynolds* v *Times Newspapers Ltd* [1999] 4 All ER 609.

Defamation occurs where the defendant publishes a statement about the claimant which reflects on the claimant's reputation so as to lower him in the estimation of right thinking members of society, or which tends to cause the claimant to be shunned or avoided (Jones, *Torts* (8th edn, 2002)).

Freedom of expression, on the other hand, is a public law concept that has developed as a form of residual right, insofar as civil liberties are concerned, alongside the right to assemble and associate. As to whether there is a balance between these two conflicting rights, it is a subjective issue which requires an objective assessment. Certainly, the advent of the Human Rights Act 1998 has undoubtedly affected the balance by introducing both a positive right to privacy (art 8 of the European Convention on Human Rights) and a right to freedom of expression (art 10 of the European Convention on Human Rights). In Europe considerable weight is given to the latter, especially, but not only, in relation to political and public affairs, including criticism of those in the public domain. This is also evident from the decisions and attitude of the European Court of Human Rights. Comparatively speaking, our existing strong bias towards the protection of a claimant's reputation may not adequately protect freedom of speech.

In *Reynolds* v *Times Newspapers Ltd* [1999] 4 All ER 609 Lord Nicholls underlined the importance of personal reputation and commented:

> 'It is in the public interest that the reputation of public figures should not be debased falsely. In the political field, in order to make an informed choice, the electorate needs to be able to identify the good as well as the bad.'

In providing a right of redress to those who have unjustifiably suffered damage to their reputations by the publication of defamatory material, the law does, however, seek to balance individual interests against the general interests of a democratic society by ensuring free speech. The law achieves such a balance in two ways. First, by preventing some types of potential claimant from bringing actions in defamation, as was the case in *Derbyshire County Council* v *Times Newspapers Ltd* [1992] QB 770, where the House of Lords held that local authorities, as democratically elected government bodies, and actual government departments which are statutory corporations, must be open to uninhibited public criticism, and are therefore not entitled to bring a claim in defamation. This decision clearly upholds the principle of freedom of expression as regards actions (or the lack of action) taken by local authorities and central government departments.

Second, a balance is struck by the law by providing a range of defences to those who are alleged to have published defamatory material. These defences are, first, justification, second, fair comment, and third, privilege which is categorised into two: absolute and qualified. Each of these will now be briefly dealt with. Defences have also been developed at common law which allow for honest opinions to be expressed on matters of public interest.

Justification is a full defence and if the defendant can prove that the substance of the defamatory statement is true, then he has defeated the claimant's action. This is so even if the defendant was acting spitefully in publishing the statement: *Alexander* v *North Eastern Railway Co* (1865) 6 B & S 340.

The defence of fair comment is frequently invoked by the courts, especially by the press, and along with qualified privilege is one of the defences which is important in establishing the limits of free speech in this country. Indeed, Lord Nicholls in *Reynolds* [1999] 4 All ER 609 stated that: 'the freedom of expression protected by this defence has long been regarded by the common law as a basic right, long before the emergence of the human rights Convention'. The defendant must show that the matter to which the statement referred was one of public interest, that his comment was an opinion based upon true facts (which were impliedly or expressly identified in the publication), that the comment was fair and that it was free of malice. In *London Artists Ltd* v *Littler* [1969] 2 QB 375 Lord Denning defined public interest as: '… that which is such so as to affect people at large, so that they may legitimately be interested in, or concerned with, what is going on; or what may happen to them or others'. Public interest therefore is a question of fact that the court has to determine.

In the case of *Mahon* v *Rahn (No 2)* [2000] 4 All ER 41, the Court of Appeal reaffirmed that no action will lie for any defamatory statement, no matter how false or malicious, made in the following instances as a result of the defence of absolute privilege:

a) parliamentary proceedings, although MPs and peers can waive this privilege to pursue a defamation action (s13 Defamation Act 1996);

b) official reports in parliamentary proceedings;

c) matters of state communications;

d) judicial proceedings;

e) fair, accurate and contemporaneous reports of judicial proceedings in the UK and Europe (s14 Defamation Act 1996);

f) reports of the Parliamentary Commissioner;

g) communications between husband and wife.

This defence therefore recognises that, in certain circumstances, it is particularly important to encourage the free and uninhibited communication of particular information from particular sources. The court in *Adam* v *Ward* [1917] AC 309 stated that the categories of privileged occasions are never closed.

The occasions on which a qualified privilege may arise are potentially wide, such as the fair and accurate reports of judicial and parliamentary proceedings, and there will be freedom of expression in these circumstances unless the publisher of the statement was actuated by malice. The burden of proof falls upon the claimant on these occasions to prove that the defendant was malicious. Such a burden will be difficult to discharge, and will involve proving that the defendant had no honest belief in the truth of his statement, or that the defendant used the occasion for some reason other than that for which the privilege existed: *Horrocks* v *Lowe* [1975] AC 135.

Some common law jurisdictions have gone so far as to recognise a generic category of qualified privilege in respect of political discussion. Such recognition tips the balance in favour of the freedom of expression, as there is no initial presumption of defamation in the case of a politician who has been the subject of a widespread or adverse comment in the media.

In conclusion, it is submitted that the decision of the House of Lords in *Reynolds* [1999] 4 All ER 609 is consistent with s12 Human Rights Act 1998, which requires the court to pay particular regard to the importance of freedom of expression. Indeed, the common law shows an elasticity to put both these rights on a scale which is just, fair and equitable.

QUESTION TWO

A parliamentary by-election is taking place soon in the constituency of Barsetshire North. The *Barsetshire Chronicle* carried the following item on its front page about the candidates: 'What a motley crew are on offer for the good voters of Barsetshire North! First there's Maisie Mazda. Like all politicians, she likes to pass herself off as something she is not. She may look the glamourous granny, but we know it's not nature but the surgeon's knife which gave her the face and figure she always seems so anxious to flaunt. Then there's Tom Toyota. No orator he! His hackneyed phrases and turgid delivery must make him a prime candidate for "most boring politician of 2000". And if you don't like them, you're left with Horace Honda. Just what is Horace whispering into the ear of the lovely girl who calls him "daddy" but isn't his daughter (see photo left). For full by-election coverage, see page seven'.

Maisie Mazda had once had cosmetic surgery to remove a small mole from her cheek. The coverage on page seven explains that the girl in the photograph is Horace's niece, Jackie, whom he and his wife brought up after her parents were killed in an air crash when she was aged eight.

Advise as to any possible claims in defamation.

University of London LLB Examination
(for External Students) Law of Tort June 2000 Q3

General Comment

This is a relatively straightforward question requiring specific application of the principles of defamation to the given scenario. Students should be vigilant not to merely provide a general survey of the rules governing defamation.

Skeleton Solution

In respect of each party named, Maisie, Tom and Horace: analyse whether the statements are defamatory; does the statement refer to the party named?; publication; are there any defences available?; what is the position of Jackie?

Suggested Solution

The principal aim of the law of defamation is the protection of individual reputation. Defamation occurs, therefore, where the defendant publishes a statement about the claimant which reflects on the claimant's reputation so as to lower him in the estimation of right thinking members of society, or which tends to cause the claimant to be shunned or avoided. The central problem is how to reconcile this purpose with the conflicting demands of free speech. It is undeniable that both are highly valued in our society, the one as perhaps the most dearly prized attribute of civilised man, the other the very foundation of a democratic community.

This question involves the publication of certain statements in relation to three candidates, Maisie, Tom and Horace, by the *Barsetshire Chronicle* in respect of a parliamentary by-election. Defamation can occur in one of two ways. The first amounts to libel and the second amounts to slander. Libel is usually written. It is material in a permanent form or nature and is visible to the naked eye: *Monson* v *Tussauds* [1894] 1 QB 671. Therefore, the statement published by the *Barsetshire Chronicle* clearly amounts to libel. Libel is actionable per se and involves the following elements which must be proven by the claimant. First, the statement is defamatory; second, the statement referred to the claimant; and third, the statement was published to a third party. We will now examine the position of Maisie, Tom and Horace individually to see if an action for defamation is sustainable on the facts.

Maisie Mazda and the Barsetshire Chronicle

a) Is there a defamatory statement?

There are two statements which are relevant to Maisie. One is the fact that she likes to pass herself off as something she is not, and the other is that she has had cosmetic surgery to make her look glamourous. The issue here is: are these statements defamatory in nature? The test is: do these statements tend to lower the claimant in the estimation of right thinking members of society generally (*Sim* v *Stretch* [1936] 2 All ER 1237), or do they expose the claimant (Maisie) to hatred, ridicule or contempt (*Parmiter* v *Coupland and Another* (1840) 6 M & W 105)? In *Berkoff* v *Burchill* [1996] 4 All ER 1008, the court held that a statement which left the claimant subject to contempt, scorn or ridicule, or tended to exclude him from society, could be defamatory even though it did not impute disgraceful conduct or lack of professional skill. The standard here is objective, ie what would right thinking members of society think, and not the claimant's friends: *Byrne* v *Deane* [1937] 1 KB 818.

On the face of it, the statements made by the *Barsetshire Chronicle* do appear to be defamatory in nature, as they imply that, if Maisie has not disclosed that she has had cosmetic surgery, she may be inclined not to disclose other matters too, thus implying a characteristic lack of candour.

b) Do the statements refer to Maisie?

The statement in question must be a direct reference to the claimant (this is decided by the judge), and be understood as being a direct reference to the claimant by reasonable people (this is decided by the jury). Be that as it may, in *Morgan* v *Odhams Press Ltd* [1971] 1 WLR 1239 the court made it clear that there is no requirement that the defendant expressly refer to the claimant. On the facts, Maisie would have no problems establishing that the statements expressly referred to her.

c) Has there been a publication to a third party?

No problem here, as the statements were published in a newspaper: *Sodgrove* v *Hole* [1901] 2 KB 1. Maisie, therefore, has a sufficiently strong case in defamation. The issue now is whether the *Barsetshire Chronicle* are entitled to rely on any defences.

d) Defence of justification?

As the statements are assertions of fact, they have to be justified in substance, and the fact that Maisie did have cosmetic surgery to remove a small mole from her cheek would not sufficiently meet the charge: *Lucas-Box* v *News Group Newspapers Ltd* [1986] 1 WLR 147.

e) Defence of qualified privilege?

This defence applies to fair and accurate reports of judicial or parliamentary proceedings: *Turkington and Others* v *Times Newspapers* [2000] 3 WLR 1670. This defence has also been raised within the context of public interest. Since the statements made by the *Barsetshire Chronicle* are matters of opinion based on a substratum of fact, there is argument for the defence of qualified privilege to apply as the public are entitled to know facts about people whom they might elect as their representatives. However, this must be balanced with the decision in *Baldwin* v *Rushbridger* [2001] EMLR 47, wherein the Court of Appeal stated that this defence should not be extended to journalists. This follows the view taken by the House of Lords in *Reynolds* v *Times Newspapers Ltd* [1999] 4 All ER 609 where their Lordships felt that the media does not have an unfettered right to publish what they believe to be in public interest.

Tom Toyota and the Barsetshire Chronicle

a) Is there a defamatory statement?

The newspaper called him 'the most boring politician of 2000' and said that his hackneyed phrases and turgid delivery make him a poor orator (a qualification which is essential for politicians). In *Hartt* v *Newspaper Publishing plc* (1989) The Times 9 November, the Court of Appeal held that in determining the meaning of the words, the approach adopted should be that of a hypothetical ordinary reader who was neither naïve nor unduly suspicious, but who might read between the lines and be capable of loose thinking. On this basis, the statement might influence the voters (and others!) to conclude that Tom does not possess the requisite qualifications and character of a politician, which may influence their decision to vote, or not vote, for him in the election. So, it does amount to a defamatory statement.

b) Does the statement refer to Tom?

Yes, undoubtedly, Tom has been clearly identified by the article: *Cassidy* v *Daily Mirror Newspapers Ltd* [1929] 2 KB 331.

c) Has there been a publication to a third party?

Yes, the newspaper article!

d) Defence of fair comment?

There may be the defence of fair comment. That is, the statement is fair comment based on true facts made in good faith on a matter of public interest. On the basis of *Derbyshire County Council* v *Times Newspapers* [1993] 2 WLR 449, it is accepted that politicians must be subjected to some scrutiny or criticism in the public interest. So long as the defendant is not actuated by any malice and honestly believed in the opinion expressed, the defence would be available: *Slim* v *Daily Telegraph Ltd* [1968] 2 QB 157.

e) Defence of qualified privilege?

Again, similar arguments as those put forward in Maisie's case (above) might be relevant.

Horace Honda and the Barsetshire Chronicle

a) Is there a defamatory statement?

There is no doubt that the comments in the newspaper would lead all its readers to imply that Horace is having an affair with a young woman. If the statement is not prima facie defamatory, but only by implication, then the claimant will have to plead an innuendo. Whilst a true innuendo involves the existence of extraneous facts which the claimant must prove: *Tolley* v *JS Fry & Sons Ltd* [1931] AC 333, a false innuendo arises where the words have a secondary meaning, either because the words have several meanings or a slang meaning: *Allsop* v *Church of England Newspaper* [1972] 2 QB 161.

Therefore, Horace would be judged as having an affair, but only by those who merely read the headlines and not the full coverage. On the basis of *Charleston* v *News Group Newspapers* [1995] 2 WLR 450, whether the statement would amount to defamation deserves closer scrutiny. In *Charleston*, a case which bore similar facts, the House of Lords held that the statement or article must be considered in its entirety, and not by simply looking at the part of the article (the headlines) instead of the whole article (ie the full coverage on page seven). The full coverage does explain the true position. I am inclined to believe that the court will follow the rationale of *Charleston* and will thus find that the statement relating to Horace Honda is not sufficiently defamatory.

Could Jackie sue for defamation?

If Jackie succeeds in establishing the elements of defamation then she might possibly have a case against the *Barsetshire Chronicle*, but on the basis that there was/were no defamatory statements (only her photo was published, and the full coverage on page seven provided an explanation), she would be unsuccessful. The *Charleston* arguments would once again prevail.

QUESTION THREE

'We do not for an instant doubt that the common convenience and welfare of a modern plural democracy such as ours are best served by an ample flow of information to the public concerning, and by vigorous public discussion of, matters of public interest to the community.' (*Reynolds* v *Times Newspapers* (1999).)

Discuss. To what extent is the English law of defamation consistent with that view?

University of London LLB Examination
(for External Students) Law of Tort June 1999 Q1

General Comment

Candidates should avoid a general discussion of the elements of defamation in this question, instead concentrating on the conflict between the need for freedom of expression and the need for the law to protect individual reputations. Discussion concerning the extent to which the law of defamation protects free speech should concentrate on the defences to an action in defamation, including that of qualified privilege which was the subject of the appeal in the *Reynolds* case. Since this question was set, *Reynolds* has been the subject of a further appeal to the House of Lords, and it is that judgement which is subject to analysis and comment below. The judgment of Lord Nicholls in particular is essential reading for candidates in this area.

Skeleton Solution

Explain that the question is about the conflicting interests of free expression and the need to protect individual reputations – briefly discuss the tort of defamation as a prima facie restriction on the freedom of expression – explain how the law seeks to redress the balance, ie by placing restrictions upon those who can sue and the defences available in a defamation action, those being justification, fair comment and privilege (explain the defences with particular reference to the promotion of free speech) – explain the approach adopted in other jurisdictions to whether political discussion enjoys qualified privilege – discuss the *Reynolds* case and the extent to which the decision upholds freedom of expression, making reference to the position under the European Convention on Human Rights and the Human Rights Act 1998.

Suggested Solution

The quote refers to the need for freedom of expression, and in the context of the House of Lord's decision in *Reynolds* v *Times Newspapers Ltd* [1999] 4 All ER 609 it was the expression and communication of information concerning political matters which was in issue.

The tort of defamation represents a restriction on the freedom of expression by recognising the need to protect individual reputations in certain circumstances. The publication of a statement which adversely affects a person's reputation is a defamation, and may be subject to civil proceedings. The claimant need not prove that the allegations were false. Nor must he prove that he suffered damage, provided that the publication was in written or permanent form. However, it should not be supposed that the need to protect individual reputations is a matter of merely personal interest. In *Reynolds*, Lord Nicholls underlined the importance of personal reputation and commented:

> 'It is in the public interest that the reputation of public figures should not be debased falsely. In the political field, in order to make an informed choice, the electorate needs to be able to identify the good as well as the bad.'

In providing a right of redress to those who have unjustifiably suffered damage to their reputations by the publication of defamatory material, the law does, however, seek to balance individual interests against the general interests of a democratic society by ensuring free speech. The law achieves such a balance in two ways: by preventing some types of potential claimant from bringing actions in defamation, and by providing a range of defences to those who are alleged to have published defamatory material. Each of these will be dealt with in turn.

Restrictions upon those who may bring actions in defamation

In *Derbyshire County Council* v *Times Newspapers Ltd* [1993] 2 WLR 449 the House of Lords held that local authorities, as democratically elected government bodies, and central government departments, which are statutory corporations, must be open to uninhibited public criticism, and are therefore not entitled to bring a claim in defamation. Individual councillors who have been defamed may bring actions in their own name, but the only legitimate response of a local council which is subject to public criticism is to defend itself by public utterances and by debate in the local council chamber.

This decision clearly upholds the principle of freedom of expression as regards actions (or lack of action) taken by local authorities and central government departments.

Defences

A range of defences exist to protect defendants from defamation actions in certain circumstances, thus in theory upholding and encouraging the principle of freedom of expression. The defendant may, of course, establish that the allegations were true. However, this alone is not enough to encourage free speech: the difficulties of proving the truth of every allegation, and the fear and uncertainty of expensive litigation, would have a chilling effect, discouraging the publication of potentially important material. Thus, defences have also been developed at common law which allow for honest opinions to be expressed on matters of public interest, and for statements to be made on privileged occasions, even though honest factual mistakes were made.

Justification

If the defendant can prove that the substance of the statement was true, then he has a complete defence (*Alexander* v *North Eastern Railway Co* (1865) 6 B & S 340), even if he was acting spitefully in publishing the statement.

Fair comment

The defence of fair comment is frequently invoked by the courts, especially by the press, and along with qualified privilege is one of the defences which is important in establishing the limits of free speech in this country. Indeed, Lord Nicholls in *Reynolds* stated that 'the freedom of expression protected by this defence has long been regarded by the common law as a basic right, long before the emergence of human rights Conventions'. The defendant must show that the matter to which the statement referred was one of public interest, that his comment was an opinion based upon true facts (which were explicitly or implicitly identified in the publication, at least in general terms), that the comment was fair and that it was made without malice.

That freedom of expression is promoted by this defence may be illustrated by reference to the broad manner in which some of the elements are defined. A matter is said to be in the public interest whenever it 'is such as to affect people at large, so that they may legitimately be interested in, or concerned at, what is going on; or what may happen to them or others': *London Artists Ltd* v *Littler* [1969] 2 QB 375 per Lord Denning.

As to whether the comment is 'fair' Lord Nicholls in *Reynolds* stated:

> 'Judges have emphasised the latitude to be applied in interpreting this standard. So much so that the time has come to recognise that in this context the epithet "fair" is now meaningless and misleading ... the basis of our public life is that the crank, the enthusiast, may say what he honestly thinks as much as the reasonable person who sits on a jury. The true test is whether the opinion, however exaggerated, obstinate or prejudiced, was honestly held by the person expressing it.'

Privilege

This defence recognises that, in certain circumstances, it is particularly important to encourage the free and uninhibited communication of particular information from particular sources. This is achieved either by providing a blanket immunity from things published on particular occasions (absolute privilege), eg statements made in Parliament, or by judges, counsel, parties or witnesses during judicial proceedings, or by protecting what is published from liability unless the claimant can prove that the defendant was actuated by malice (qualified privilege). This fact was clearly illustrated in *Gray* v *Avadis* (2003) 100 (36) LSG 43.

A number of occasions benefiting from qualified privilege have been identified by the courts and by Parliament. For example, fair and accurate reporting of the public proceedings of legislatures, courts and public enquiries worldwide are subject to qualified privilege under the Defamation Act 1996.

However, the courts do not regard these categories of 'occasions' as being closed. In *Adam* v *Ward* [1917] AC 309 Lord Atkinson stated:

> '... a privileged occasion is ... an occasion where the person who makes a communication has an interest or a duty, legal, social or moral, to make it to the person to whom it is made, and the person to whom it is made has a corresponding interest or duty to receive it. This reciprocity is essential.'

The occasions on which a qualified privilege may arise are therefore potentially wide, and there will be freedom of expression in these circumstances unless the publisher of the statement was actuated by malice. The burden of proof falls upon the claimant on these occasions to prove that the defendant was malicious. Such a burden will often be difficult to discharge, and will involve proving that the defendant had no honest belief in the truth of his statement, or that the defendant used the occasion for some reason other than that for which the privileged existed: *Horrocks* v *Lowe* [1975] AC 135.

Qualified privilege and the publication of political discussion in the media

Some common law jurisdictions have gone so far as to recognise a generic category of qualified privilege in respect of political discussion. Such recognition tips the balance in favour of the freedom of expression, as there is no initial presumption of defamation in the case of a politician who has been the subject of adverse comment in the media. This might be thought unfair given that the widespread dissemination of defamatory material is potentially extremely damaging to those in the public eye. For instance, this defence failed in the case of *Kearns* v *General Council of the Bar* [2003] 2 All ER 534.

In the United States, recognition of a 'public figure' defence occurred in the case of *New York Times Co* v *Sullivan* (1964) 376 US 254. A public official cannot recover damages for defamation relating to his official conduct unless he proves that the statement was knowingly false or made with reckless disregard as to its accuracy. A claimant is entitled to a pre-trial inquiry into a newspaper's sources and the editorial decision-making process.

In Australia, the High Court in *Lange* v *Australian Broadcasting Corporation* (1997) 145 ALR 96 held that qualified privilege automatically exists in respect of the dissemination of information, opinions and arguments concerning government and political matters, subject only to a requirement of due care. Precise guidelines were laid down as to the steps required of publishers to satisfy the requirements of due care. A publisher must not only believe that the imputation was true, but must also take reasonable steps to verify the accuracy of the information and must seek and publish a response from the individual defamed, where practicable.

Reynolds *v* Times Newspapers Ltd

This case was brought by the former Irish Prime Minister, Albert Reynolds, following his resignation on the collapse of the coalition government in 1994. An article in the *Sunday Times* alleged that he had lied to the Irish Parliament and to his coalition colleagues. The story was of interest to a British readership, as Reynolds had been one of the chief architects of the Northern Ireland peace agreement. The article proved to be factually false even though it had been honestly made. The main issue before the House of Lords was whether the newspaper were entitled to rely on the defence of qualified privilege. Counsel for Times Newspapers invited the House to consider developing a new category of qualified privilege to cover the publication of political information, in line with the approach adopted in Australia.

Consequences for the protection of personal reputation

The leading judgment was that of Lord Nicholls, who underlined the importance of personal reputation:

> 'Reputation is an integral and important part of the dignity of the individual. It also forms the basis of many decisions in a democratic society which are fundamental to its well-being: whom to employ or work for, whom to promote, whom to do business with or to vote for. Once besmirched by an unfounded allegation in a national newspaper, a reputation can be damaged forever, especially if there is no opportunity to vindicate one's reputation.'

Their Lordships refused to establish a new generic category of qualified privilege based upon the publication of political information, as it was thought that this would not provide adequate protection for the reputation of politicians: it would be extremely difficult for a political figure to prove malice without discovering the newspaper's sources, which are largely protected by s10 Contempt of Court Act 1981. Contrast this with the position in the US, where a public figure is entitled to a pre-trial enquiry to discover sources and details of the editorial decision-making process. Their Lordships also pointed out that it was inconsistent to provide protection as regards political discussion but not in respect of other matters of serious public concern, given that certain non-political public figures exercise great practical influence.

A recurring theme throughout the judgements was the suspicion that any blanket privilege would be subject to abuse by the press given the commercial pressures to publish scoops and the temptation to exaggerate or distort facts to excite the interest of readers. Lord Nicholls in particular noted that the self-regulation of the press had not always been a success.

Lord Nicholls upheld the traditional duty/interest test outlined in *Adam* v *Ward*, stating that the question of whether the public were entitled to know political or other information was a question to be determined by a judge considering all the circumstances of the publication. He put forward ten non-inclusive factors which might be considered when determining whether the duty/interest test would be satisfied, including the seriousness of the allegation, the nature and source of the information, the steps taken to verify it, whether comment was sought from the claimant and whether the article contained the gist of the claimant's version of events. An approach to determining the existence of qualified privilege which involves balancing the competing interests of the parties on a case-by-case basis according to the individual facts would accord with the approach and jurisprudence of the European Court of Human Rights.

On the facts, Times Newspapers were unable to establish the defence of qualified privilege, as their failure to seek or to publish Mr Reynold's explanation of events meant that the public had no right to know the information concerned.

Consequences for the protection of freedom of expression

We have seen that the defences available to an action in defamation go some way towards protecting the rights of those who engage in honest political reporting and discussion, at least where the subject matter can be said to relate to the public interest. The decision in *Reynolds* relating to qualified privilege seems to uphold the interests of individual reputations at the expense of freedom of expression. However, this is far from being the true effect of their Lordships' decision. Freedom of expression is now the starting point for the consideration of any claim for qualified privilege by the media, and the courts are instructed to pay particular regard to the vital functions discharged by the press in acting as both 'bloodhound' and 'watchdog'. Lord Nicholls stated that courts should be reluctant to conclude that an article involving political discussion is not in the public interest: any doubts should be resolved in favour of publication. Lord Steyn even suggested at one point that the press have a general duty to inform the public on political matters and that the public has a right to be informed. However, their Lordships ultimately favoured a case-by-case approach to this question. Lord Nicholls affirmed that any unwillingness on the part of newspapers to disclose their sources should not weigh against them when determining the duty/interest test.

The approach of the House is consistent with s12 Human Rights Act 1998 which requires the courts to pay particular regard to the importance of freedom of expression. The law regarding political discussion (and indeed other matters of public concern) has now moved closer to the Australian approach in *Lange*, without the establishment of any new generic category of qualified privilege or precisely defined public interest criteria. It is likely that the courts will, in future, find that qualified privilege exists in cases where reasonable and responsible standards of journalism have been adhered to.

QUESTION FOUR

Chill and Douche, two members of the building inspections team in the Loamshire Fire Brigade, carried out an inspection of the engineering building at Loamshire University. They reported that the notice boards were a fire hazard and that, if notices continued to be displayed anywhere in the corridors and staircases other than in specially constructed glass cases, they would seek a court order closing the building. At a meeting with student representatives a few days later, Flame, the Dean of Engineering, remarked that because of 'the Hitlerite tendency' of the local fire brigade, he had to prohibit students from displaying any notices advertising their societies. The next issue of the Student Union newspaper carried a banner headline reading, '"FIRE INSPECTORS ARE FASCIST SCUM", SAYS DEAN.' Copies of this newspaper are handed out to students on the campus, and are also prominently on sale in local newsagents.

Advise the parties as to any possible claims in defamation.

University of London LLB Examination
(for External Students) Law of Tort June 1998 Q7

General Comment

This should be a relatively straightforward question for candidates who have a sufficient understanding of the principles of defamation and are aware of the changes brought about by the Defamation Act 1996. It is necessary for candidates to clearly organise their answers, by dealing with the separate potential actions disclosed by the facts under different headings.

Skeleton Solution

Action by Chill and Douche against Flame in slander – was this slander actionable per se? – were the words defamatory? – could Chill and Douche claim as individuals in respect of a 'group' slander? – were there any defences available to Flame, eg qualified privilege and fair comment? – action by Chill and Douche against the newspaper and others in libel – were the words defamatory? – could Chill and Douche claim as individuals in respect of a 'group' libel? – defences available, eg offer to make amends? – action by Flame against the newspaper and others in libel – defences available, eg fair comment and offer to make amends.

Suggested Solution

The question involves a number of potential claims in the tort of defamation, arising from untrue statements which have injured the reputation of those concerned.

Action by Chill and Douche against Flame in slander

Spoken statements are not in a permanent form and are therefore classified as slanders. Generally, slanders are only actionable if the claimants can show that they have suffered special damage, ie have suffered a loss which is capable of being estimated in money. However, there are a number of exceptional cases where slanders become actionable per se, such as where the statement imputes unfitness to one's trade or calling.

Flame's description of the 'Hitlerite tendency' of the local fire brigade was clearly calculated to disparage Chill and Douche in their profession or calling, and therefore no proof of special damage will be required on their part: s2 Defamation Act 1952.

There is no single definition of a defamatory statement; however, they have been held to include 'words which tend to lower the ... [claimant] in the estimation of right-thinking members of society generally' (*Sim v Stretch* [1936] 2 All ER 1237), possibly exposing him to 'hatred, contempt or ridicule' (*Parmiter v Coupland and Another* (1840) 6 M & W 105), or causing people to shun him or lose confidence in him: *Youssoupoff v Metro-Goldwyn-Mayer* (1934) 50 TLR 581. Words may be defamatory 'even though they neither impute disgraceful conduct to the ... [claimant] nor any lack of skill or efficiency in the conduct of his trade or business or professional activity, if they hold him up to contempt, scorn or ridicule, or tend to exclude him from society': *Berkoff v Burchill* [1996] 4 All ER 1008. It is submitted that the suggestion that the local fire brigade display 'Hitlerite tendencies' is likely to induce hatred, ridicule and contempt to those at the meeting and even impute disgraceful conduct on the part of the inspectors. On the other hand, Flame might argue that, if the words were uttered in a fit of temper, they should have been understood as amounting to nothing more than vulgar abuse, and therefore not defamatory: *Fields* v *Davis* [1955] CLY 1543.

However, a more fundamental issue here is whether Chill and Douche can claim that they have been defamed as individuals when the comments made related to the local fire brigade as a whole. Generally, where the defamatory statement has been directed at a group or class of persons, no individual belonging to that class may sue, unless there is something in the words or the circumstances in which they were uttered which might identify the claimant in particular: *Knupffer* v *London Express Newspapers Limited* [1944] AC 116. Alternatively, if the group which is alleged to have been defamed is very limited in size, then the statement might be understood as referring to the claimant: *Browne* v *D C Thompson* [1912] SC 359.

It is submitted that Chill and Douche are likely to experience problems establishing that they, as individuals, have been slandered. Flame's comments were directed at the local fire brigade and made to a group of student representatives several days after the inspection took place. If anyone present at the meeting was to have observed Chill and Douche at work in the building, then Flame's comments might have been taken as being directed at them individually. Otherwise, it is likely that the local fire brigade consists of too many individuals for the comments to be taken as referring to any one of them. However, it should be noted that the subsequent repetition of Flame's words indicate that they were understood as referring specifically to fire inspectors.

Defences: qualified privilege

The effect of this defence is to protect the maker of the statement from liability in defamation provided he acted honestly and without malice. It will be for the claimants, Chill and Douche, to prove that Flame was actuated by malice, ie that he had no honest belief in the truth of his statement, or that he used the occasion for a purpose extending beyond that for which the qualified privilege existed: *Horrocks* v *Lowe* [1975] AC 135.

However, only statements made in certain circumstance enjoy a qualified privilege. One set of circumstances is 'where the person who makes a communication has an interest, or a duty, legal, social or moral, to make it to the person to whom it is made, and the person to whom it is made has a corresponding interest or duty to receive it. This reciprocity is essential': *Adam* v *Ward* [1917] AC 309 per Lord Atkinson.

It is clear that Flame has a legal duty (under health and safety legislation) or at the very least a social/moral duty to instruct the students not to display notices given the apparent hazards involved and the possible closure of the building. To this extent the students have an interest in receiving the information. However, Flame's comments regarding 'Hitlerite tendencies' indicate that he has used the occasion for a purpose extending beyond that for which the qualified privilege exists, ie to disparage the inspectors. It is submitted that the claimants could rebut a provisional finding of qualified privilege and prove that Flame was actuated by malice. This was evident in *Kearns* v *General Council of the Bar* [2003] 2 All ER 534.

Fair comment

This defence is relevant where comment is honestly made on a matter of public interest. The defendant must prove four elements.

a) The comments related to a matter of public interest 'such as to effect people at large, so that they may be legitimately interested in, or concerned at, what is going on; or what may happen to them or others': *London Artists Ltd* v *Littler* [1969] 2 QB 375 per Lord Denning. The prohibition of the display of notices affects the students of the faculty and their ability to continue to use the building, and so Flame's comments are clearly in the public interest.

b) The statement was one of opinion, not fact. It is submitted that Flame's comments regarding the inspectors' 'Hitlerite tendencies' were clearly opinion, based upon his experience of their previous conduct.

c) The comments were fair in all the circumstances of the case. This is an objective test based upon whether any fair-minded person could honestly express the opinion in question, even if it was exaggerated, obstinate or prejudiced. It is difficult to apply this test conclusively to the facts. It might be thought that the inspectors had been overzealous in discharging their duties and that Flame had a reasonable basis for his comments, even if he over-exaggerated. On the other hand, it might be thought that Flame's words were so overstated that his motives must have been improper, and consequently his comments would be regarded as unfair.

d) The comments were not inspired by malice, ie spite, ill-will or any other improper motive.

Is Flame liable for the republication of his defamatory words?

A maker of a defamatory statement may also find himself liable for the damage caused by the repetition of the defamatory statement by a third party, at least where that repetition was reasonably foreseeable. An unauthorised repetition of such a statement by an independent third party (here the Student Union Newspaper and the various distributors) may well be regarded as a novus actus interveniens breaking the chain of causation, provided Flame could not reasonably have anticipated the repetition of his slander as a natural and probable consequence of his original comments: *Slipper* v *British Broadcasting Corporation* [1991] 1 QB 283.

Claim by Chill and Douche against the Student Union Newspaper and others for libel

Every time a defamatory statement is repeated, the tort is committed again and a fresh cause of action arises. Anyone who participated in the publication of the Student Union Newspaper or its mechanical distribution is potentially liable, subject to a range of defences. Such persons would include the author of the headline, the editor, the printer, the proprietor of the newspaper, the distributors (on campus) and the newsagents.

The headline is potentially a libel as it exists in a permanent form. The words used in the headline are stronger than those originally uttered by Flame and possibly more defamatory. The newspaper might argue that the headline merely reported vulgar abuse spoken by the Dean, and should not be understood to be defamatory of the inspectors themselves. They would argue that an ordinary hypothetical reader, who was not 'avid for scandal', would not necessary believe in the truth of the statement, simply in the fact that it was said. On the other hand it could be argued that an ordinary reader who is neither 'naïve' nor 'unduly suspicious' might read into it an implication of disgraceful conduct on the part of the inspectors 'more readily than a lawyer' having 'indulged in a certain amount of loose thinking': *Hartt* v *Newspaper Publishing plc* (1989) The Times 9 November. Ultimately, whether the words uttered are reasonably capable of being defamatory is a question of law for the judge before the matter can be put to the jury.

The same problems arise here as to whether Chill and Douche could be said to have been defamed as individuals, given that the statement was aimed at a group of persons. The headline is more specific in that it refers to fire inspectors rather than members of the local fire brigade. Assuming the article goes on to explain the background to the Dean's comments, it is possible that the headline could be taken as inferentially referring to Chill and Douche by those with special local knowledge of the inspectorate: *Morgan* v *Odhams Press Ltd* [1971] 1 WLR 1239.

Defences: offer to make amends

Under s2(4) Defamation Act 1996 it is open to the newspaper to make an offer to make amends by publishing a suitable correction and apology and to pay compensation. If Chill and Douche were to accept such an offer, any proceedings against the paper would be brought to an end, and if the parties were not able to agree on compensation, this amount would be decided by the court. Under s4, if an offer is not accepted, the fact that the offer has been made is a defence to defamation proceedings unless the claimants can prove that the statement referred to them and was both false and defamatory.

A defence of fair comment would be bound to fail in this case, because the introduction of the word 'scum' seems to indicate an improper motive or malice on the part of the author, thus rendering the comment unfair.

Action by Flame against the Student Union Newspaper and others in libel

The essence of such a claim would be that the newspaper exaggerated Flame's comments in a way that affects his professional standing and raises a question as to whether he is discharging his duties in an appropriate manner. The imputation of 'disgraceful conduct' on Flame's part may hold him up to contempt, scorn or ridicule and lower him in the estimation of right-thinking people. The headline refers to Flame personally and so the only question remaining is whether the newspaper can avail itself of a defence.

Defence: fair comment

If this article is simply about the Dean's outburst, then it might be said to be of public interest in that it calls into question Flame's professional conduct and whether he is discharging his duties in an appropriate manner. A bare statement of fact (for example a verbatim report of Flame's comments) cannot found the defence. However, the words 'fascist scum' seem to represent an opinion of the true meaning of Flame's original words.

It would have to be decided whether a fair-minded person could honestly express the opinion that the Dean, in his original comments, had really been suggesting that the inspectors were 'fascist scum'. The addition of the word 'scum' and the fact that the statement is portrayed as a direct quote (which is clearly inaccurate) might indicate some improper motive to portray the Dean in a bad light, and as such the defence would fail. An offer to make amends to the Dean could also apply here.

QUESTION FIVE

Evaluate the changes made by the Defamation Act 1996. Are there any other changes to the law of defamation which you would like to see?

University of London LLB Examination
(for External Students) Law of Tort June 1997 Q6

General Comment

This question requires the student to highlight the perceived improvements upon the former position, rather than an arid description of the provisions of the 1996 Act. Some emphasis is needed on the summary procedures provided and, if possible, some comment on the 1991 Neill Report. There is scope in this question to deal with the perceived problems that the Act does not really address in detail, such as jury damages awards, 'internet' defamations, exemplary damages etc.

Skeleton Solution

Section 1: innocent dissemination – ss2–4: unintentional defamation and offers of amends – s5: limitation periods – ss8–10: summary disposals – s13: parliamentary waivers – damages awards by juries – new techniques of publication – exemplary damages.

Suggested Solution

The Defamation Act 1996 has introduced a wide-ranging series of reforms to the existing law, both by way of clarification and substantive reform. Only time and use will show how effective the legislation is, but any assistance at all in this complex area is welcome. The 1996 Act came about as a result of widespread dissatisfaction with the existing law which led to a Lord Chancellor's Consultation Paper in 1990 and the recommendations of Lord Justice Neal in his 1991 Report, many of which are reflected in the Act.

Section 1 has codified the former common law defence of innocent dissemination and, very helpfully, has defined the scope of the defence by exclusion of 'authors', 'editors' and 'publishers', going on in s1(2) to further define the excluded class, and in s1(3) the included class. As at common law, it will be for the defendant to show that he took 'reasonable care' in respect of a publication and that he did not know, and had no reason to believe, that he was publishing a defamation. This is unlikely to prove too onerous a burden for anyone other than a defendant who habitually operates close to the limit.

Sections 2–4 bring in a greatly improved regime for an unintentional defamation defence of apology and offer of amends. This is quite different from the former regime under s4 Defamaton Act 1952 in that it contemplates that, in the event of failure to agree on either the steps to be taken by way of correction, apology and publication or the amount of compensation in amends, both matters will be determined by the court. This will only be appropriate in the circumstance where the sum offered, or likely to be decided upon, is less than £10,000 because that is the current upper limit for summary disposal by the judge alone: s9(1).

There are other important changes in ss2–4 in that a defendant who intends to rely upon apology and amends as a defence must do so before he puts forward any other defence – it cannot be put forward after service of any other defence (s2(5)) – and once committed to, apology and amends cannot, thereafter, rely upon other defences: s4(4). The defendant can, however, use an offer to try to mitigate damages whether he has relied on it for a defence or not: s4(5). An extremely important change is brought in by s4(3) which raises a statutory presumption that the defendant was innocent of the knowledge of reference to the claimant and of the defamatory effect upon the claimant. This completely reverses the burden of proof on this vital matter and is likely, by itself, to lead to a great increase in using this provision as against its predecessor, s4 Defamation Act 1952.

Section 5 adds new ss4A and 32A to the Limitation Act 1980 so as to reduce limitation periods for defamation and malicious falsehood to one year as against the former three years and six years, subject to a judicial discretion to extend the period on equitable grounds which are wider than the former rules on accrual of knowledge of a right to an action.

Sections 8–10 make very sweeping changes in that they allow a judge to take full control of actions where the claimant has no realistic prospects of success and there is no other reason to try the claim or an application by the claimant for summary disposal, or where matters under ss2–4 are in dispute. In all cases, the disposal is by the single judge and the overall range of matters suitable for summary trial is capped at £10,000 damages. Otherwise than on a claimant 's insistence the judge will not act summarily unless he is satisfied that summary relief will adequately compensate the claimant:

s8(3). This begins to bring defamation proceedings at the lower end of the scale more in line with other types of action, and the intention seems to be that, ultimately, all claims of whatever scale will come before the judge at an interlocutory stage for consideration of the possibility that a summary disposal is possible.

Section 13 brings in, for the first time, a possibility for waiver of the absolute privilege attaching to parliamentary proceedings by persons covered by the privilege so that they may conduct defamation proceedings. This came about as a result of the 'cash for parliamentary questions' issues and is likely to be but sparingly relied upon, although its potential value can be seen.

The Act might have gone further in attempting to deal with the vagaries of awards of damages by juries, perhaps by giving the judge a discretion to remit questionable awards directly to the Court of Appeal for consideration under s8 Courts and Legal Services Act 1990. Time will tell how much such a change is still required or, indeed, whether jury awards should be replaced by the decision of the judges. It may be that the bubble of such awards has been burst by the guidelines in *John v MGN Ltd* [1996] 2 All ER 35.

The Act might, similarly, have gone further in response to information technology developments, although s1(3) has arguably touched on the problem of computerised defamations. Also, the immense sums of money to be gained from deliberate defamations with profit in view might well have provided a reason to expand upon the circumstances in which exemplary damage awards might be made. Perhaps the legislators have retained their confidence in the common law and its ability to cope with such matters. The Act has, at least, moved forward on some fronts.

Chapter 16

Trespass to the Person and to Land

16.1   Introduction

16.2   Key points

16.3   Key cases and statute

16.4   Questions and suggested solutions

16.1 Introduction

Trespass to the person includes the torts of battery, assault and false imprisonment, and like trespass to land it is actionable per se.

16.2 Key points

Battery

Definition

A direct act of the defendant which causes contact with the claimant's body without the claimant's consent.

Elements

a) The act must be direct: see *Scott* v *Shepherd* (1733) 2 W Bl 892 for the effect of intervening acts.

b) The act must be intentional. It is clear that the tort cannot be committed in the absence of intent (*Stanley* v *Powell* [1891] 1 QB 86), and it cannot be committed negligently (*Letang* v *Cooper* [1965] 1 QB 232; *Miller* v *Jackson* [1977] QB 966; *Wilson* v *Pringle* [1987] QB 237), ie there is no overlap between the torts of battery and negligence. See *Stubbings* v *Webb* [1993] 2 WLR 120 where the House of Lords emphasised the distinct and separate nature of these two torts.

c) The act must be hostile: *Wilson* v *Pringle* (above).

d) There must be active contact with the person of the claimant, however slight: *Cole* v *Turner* (1704) 6 Mod 149.

Defences

a) Consent. For example, a medical operation, playing sport in accordance with the rules, but if the defendant steps outside the rules an action in battery may lie: *R v Billinghurst* [1978] Crim LR 553. Note that the rationale of consent for everyday jostlings in *Cole* v *Turner* (above) and *Collins* v *Wilcock* [1984] 3 All ER 374 was rejected by the Court of Appeal in *Wilson* v *Pringle* (above).

b) Self defence. Providing that the steps taken are not out of proportion to the harm threatened: *Lane* v *Holloway* [1968] 1 QB 379. *Participants who voluntarily involve themselves in fights are taken to have consented to the battery. (Lane V Holloway)*

c) Contributory negligence. See *Barnes* v *Nayer* (1986) The Times 19 December. *contributory negligence, volenti and ex turpi cause could be a defence to trespass to the person. (Barnes V Nayer).*

d) Lawful arrest.

e) Parental authority.

Assault

Definition

A threat to apply force to another whereby that other is reasonably put in fear of immediate physical contact.

Elements

a) A threat is sufficient. If actual physical contact occurs the tort of battery is committed.

b) The essence of the tort is fear. It now seems that words alone are sufficient: *R v Wilson* [1955] 1 WLR 493.

c) Words may accompany an act and prevent it from being an assault: *Turberville* v *Savage* (1669) 1 Mod Rep 3.

d) If the defendant is restrained from physical contact by a third party, the tort of assault is still committed because the claimant was in fear of immediate physical contact: *Stephens* v *Myers* (1830) 4 C & P 349.

False imprisonment

Definition   *Unlawful constrain (अर्थात अवैध अड़न)*

The total deprivation of the freedom of another, for any period, however short, without lawful justification.

Elements

a) The restraint may be physical, eg placing the claimant in a locked room, or practical, eg surrounding the claimant by threatening persons.

b) The restraint must be total. If the claimant has a reasonable means of exit no imprisonment has taken place merely because he is inconvenienced: *Bird* v *Jones* (1845) 7 QB 742.

c) The restraint must be unlawful; if a condition or restriction on leaving premises is reasonably imposed and the claimant chooses not to comply with this, there is no false imprisonment: *Robinson* v *Balmain Ferry* [1910] AC 295.

d) There is no obligation to assist another to obtain his freedom: *Herd* v *Weardale Steel Coal & Coke* [1915] AC 67.

e) The tort is committed even if the claimant is unaware of the restriction on his liberty: *Meering* v *Grahame-White Aviation* (1919) 122 LT 44; *Murray* v *Ministry of Defence* [1988] 2 All ER 521, although this may affect the quantum of damages.

f) Note that a prisoner cannot sue for false imprisonment as regards deprivation of his residual liberty (*Weldon* v *Home Office*; *R* v *Deputy Governor of Parkhurst Prison, ex parte Hague* [1991] 3 WLR 341), although in *Pritchard* v *Ministry of Defence* (1995) The Times 27 January it was held that unlawfully requiring a person to serve in the armed forces could constitute false imprisonment.

g) The Court of Appeal held that a failure by the police to review a suspect's detention period could be tantamount to false imprisonment: see *Roberts* v *Chief Constable of the Cheshire Constabulary* [1999] 2 All ER 362.

h) In *R* v *Governor of Brockhill Prison, ex parte Evans (No 2)* [2000] 4 All ER 15 the House of Lords held that miscalculating the prison release date amounted to a false imprisonment for which the governor was found viable.

i) In *Olutu* v *Home Office* [1997] 1 All ER 385 their Lordships felt that art 5 of the European Convention on Human Rights must be borne in mind when deciding the issue of false imprisonment.

Defences

a) Consent

b) Lawful arrest: see ss24 and 25 Police and Criminal Evidence Act 1984 and note the trap in *Walters* v *WH Smith* [1914] 1 KB 595 and its recent application in *R* v *Self* [1992] 1 WLR 657. Note also *Davidson* v *Chief Constable of North Wales* [1994] 2 All ER 597.

c) Lawful imprisonment: see s12(1) Prison Act 1952.

Intentional infliction of nervous shock

It was held in *Wilkinson* v *Downton* [1897] 2 QB 57 that where the defendant wilfully does an act calculated to cause physical damage to the claimant, and has in fact caused harm, a cause of action arises. See also *Janvier* v *Sweeney* [1919] 2 KB 316.

Harassment

A tort created by the Protection from Harassment Act 1997. Section 1(2) provides the test as to whether a course of conduct was one which a reasonable person would think amounted to harassment. In *R* v *Constanza* [1997] Crim LR 576 the Court of Appeal held that the test was an objective one. See also *Thomas* v *News Group Newspapers Ltd* [2002] EMLR 41 for another Court of Appeal decision on this point. Intentional harassment was discussed by the Court of Appeal in *Wong* v *Parkside Health NHS Trust* [2003] 3 All ER 932.

Trespass to land

Definition

A direct interference with the possession of another's land, without lawful justification.

Elements

a) Possession

Possession not ownership gives the right to sue.

i) Thus, a landlord can only sue where damage is to his reversion: *Jones* v *Llanrwst UDC* [1911] 1 Ch 393.

ii) But where a tortfeasor claims possession, the courts are willing to hold that any action by the owner which shows an intent to take possession is sufficient to give the right to sue in trespass: *Ocean Estates* v *Pinder* [1969] 2 AC 19.

b) Interference

Must be direct and immediate, eg entry or placing something on land, including resting a ladder on the claimant's wall: *Westripp* v *Baldock* [1938] 2 All ER 799.

If a person abuses permission to be on land or refuses to leave when asked he becomes a trespasser: *Robson* v *Hallett* [1967] 2 QB 393.

If the trespass is continuing, a new cause of action arises each day the trespass lasts: *Holmes* v *Wilson* (1839) 10 Ad & El 503.

Some interferences have given rise to problems.

i) Highway

Where the highway is used for a purpose which is not reasonably incidental to the purpose of passage, a trespass can be committed against the person in possession of the highway: *Hickman* v *Maisey* [1900] 1 QB 572; *Harrison* v *Duke of Rutland* [1893] 1 QB 142.

ii) Subsoil

Trespass can be committed against the owner of the subsoil: *Cox* v *Moulsey* (1848) 5 CB 533.

iii) Airspace

There is no need for contact with the claimant's land; an intrusion into the claimant's airspace is sufficient: *Kelsen* v *Imperial Tobacco* [1957] 2 QB 334.

However, the intrusion must be at a height which interferes with the property: *Lord Bernstein* v *Skyviews* [1978] QB 479, where it was held that the claimant could not sue in respect of an overflying aircraft. In this respect, see the recent case of *Glen* v *Korean Airlines Co Ltd* [2003] 3 WLR 273, where the principle was upheld.

But in *Anchor Brewhouse Developments* v *Berkley House* [1987] 2 EGLR 173 it was held that *Bernstein* was confined to the specific issue of overflying aircraft, so the claimant could obtain an injunction to prevent the trespass of the boom of a crane into their airspace despite the considerable cost of complying.

iv) Trespass ab initio

Where the defendant enters land with the authority of law (rather than of the claimant) and later abuses that right he becomes a trespasser ab initio: *The Six Carpenters' Case* (1610) 8 Co Rep 146a; *Cinnamond* v *British Airports Authority* [1980] 2 All ER 368.

Intent

The defendant must have intended to enter the land, but need not have intended to trespass. Hence it is no defence to show that the defendant was unaware the land belonged to someone else: *Conway* v *Wimpey* [1951] 2 KB 266, but it is a defence to show he had no intention of entering the land: *Smith* v *Stone* (1647) Style 65.

Defences

a) Licence

There is no trespass where there is express or implied consent; only when the consent is exceeded or revoked can a trespass occur: *Robson* v *Hallett* (above).

b) Lawful authority

For example, police; to abate a nuisance; public right of way.

c) Necessity

It was held in *Rigby* v *Chief Constable of Northamptonshire* [1985] 1 WLR 1242 that necessity was a defence to trespass to land, providing that the defendant had not negligently contributed to the necessity.

Remedies

a) Damages

Only nominal damages will be awarded for a trivial trespass.

If the land is damaged, the measure is the loss in value of the land.

b) Injunction

This is particularly useful where the trespass is continuing or threatened.

c) Re-entry

A person entitled to possession may re-enter and use reasonable force to eject the trespasser: *Hemmings v Stoke Poges Golf Club* [1920] 1 KB 720.

d) Mesne profits

The claimant may sue for profits the defendant has made from his occupation, and for damages for deterioration and costs of obtaining possession.

e) Ejection

The claimant may bring an action for ejectment where he has an immediate right to possession.

f) Distress damage feasant

Where his land is damaged by a chattel, the claimant may retain the chattel until the owner pays compensation. The claimant has no right to sell or use the chattel.

For an interesting comparison, see the Court of Appeal decision in *Vine v Waltham Forest London Borough Council* [2000] 4 All ER 169. The Court of Appeal dealt with the issue of conversion to goods in *Costello v Chief Constable of Derbyshire Constabulary* [2001] 3 All ER 405.

g) Self redress

In clear and simple cases or in an emergency: *Burton v Winters* [1993] 1 WLR 1077.

16.3 Key cases and statute

- *Conway v George Wimpey & Co Ltd* [1951] 2 KB 266
  Intention to enter the land is sufficient for trespass even though there is no intention to trespass

- *Costello v Chief Constable of Derbyshire Constabulary* [2001] 3 All ER 405
  Exemplifies the situation where the tort of conversion may be committed

- *Glen v Korean Airlines Co Ltd* [2003] 3 WLR 273
  No right to sue over damage caused by aircraft

- *Lane* v *Holloway* [1968] 1 QB 379
  Self-defence is a valid defence to battery

- *Murray* v *Ministry of Defence* [1988] 2 All ER 521
  The tort of false imprisonment is committed when a person's liberty is restricted unlawfully

- *Ocean Estates* v *Pinder* [1969] 2 AC 19
  Mere possession will give the right to sue for trespass to land

- *R* v *Billinghurst* [1978] Crim LR 553
  Consent may rebut the presumption of battery

- *R* v *Constanza* [1997] Crim LR 576
  Gives an illustration of what amounts to a tort of harassment

- *R* v *Governor of Brockhill Prison, ex parte Evans (No 2)* [2000] 4 All ER 15
  Miscalculating the release date of a prisoner amounted to a false imprisonment

- *R* v *Wilson* [1955] 1 WLR 493
  Assault is defined as the fear of immediate infliction of personal harm or violence

- *Rigby* v *Chief Constable of Northamptonshire* [1985] 1 WLR 1242
  Necessity may be a defence to trespass to land

- *Robson* v *Hallett* [1967] 2 QB 393
  Visitors may become trespassers if they abuse their permission

- *Scott* v *Shepherd* (1733) 2 W Bl 892
  For battery, the act must be direct

- *Thomas* v *News Group Newspapers Ltd* [2002] EMLR 4
  An illustration of what amounts to a tort of harassment

- *Vine* v *Waltham Forest London Borough Council* [2000] 4 All ER 169
  Illustrates what amounts to unauthorised interference with personal property

- *Webb* v *Chief Constable of Merseyside Police* [2000] 1 All ER 209
  If there is no power to retain goods, the police might be committing the tort of conversion

- *Westripp* v *Baldock* [1938] 2 All ER 799
  The interference or trespass must be direct and immediate

- *Wilkinson* v *Downton* [1897] 2 QB 57
  Wilful acts on the part of the defendant give rise to a cause of action in tort not withstanding the fact that there is no intention to cause injury or damage

- *Wilson* v *Pringle* [1987] QB 237
  For battery, the act must be hostile

- *Wong v Parkside Health NHS Trust* [2003] 3 All ER 932
  The House of Lords affirmed that there was no general common law tort of invasion of privacy

- Protection from Harassment Act 1997 – created a tort of harassment

16.4 Questions and suggested solutions

QUESTION ONE

Gorgon Enterprises were building a new factory. For two weeks they hired a huge crane from Crane Co, together with its driver, Max. One day Max saw a group of boys spraying lorries on the site with paint from aerosol cans. He caught one of the ringleaders, Neil, aged 12, and pulled him down from the lorry. Neil fell heavily and banged his head. A blood clot developed and he suffered severe brain damage. He has still an expectation of life of 30 years but is unlikely ever to find employment.

Advise Neil's parents (a) whether there is a cause of action in tort and, if so, against whom, and (b) how financial compensation should be assessed.

University of London LLB Examination
(for External Students) Law of Tort June 1996 Q8

General Comment

The first question calls for discussion of the tort of battery, and its potential overlap with the tort of negligence, and any defences available. It also requires an examination of the principles of vicarious liability.

The second question asks for a general discussion of the remedy of damages and the various heads of damages available to Neil.

Skeleton Solution

a) Battery – negligence – ex turpi causa non oritur actio – vicarious liability.

b) Damages – general – special.

Suggested Solution

a) At issue here is whether Neil will have a cause of action in battery or negligence against Max, and whether he would also have an action against Gorgon Enterprises and/or Crane Co.

Battery is the direct, intentional (or, possibly, reckless) infliction of unlawful physical force upon another person, who does not consent to such touching: *Letang v Cooper* [1965] 1 QB 232; *Wilson v Pringle* [1987] QB 237. Where the force is inflicted unintentionally, or indirectly, then an action in negligence will lie: *Letang v Cooper*; *Fowler v Lanning* [1959] 1 QB 426.

It is submitted that Max has committed the tort of battery, as the force which he inflicted upon Neil was direct and intentional. In *Polland* v *John Parr & Sons* [1927] 1 KB 236, it was held that employees can use reasonable force in the protection of their employer's property – however, it is argued that the force used by Max in these circumstances was not reasonable, and there is an issue as to whether Max is an employee of Gorgon (see below).

Similarly, s3(1) Criminal Law Act 1967 allows anyone to use reasonable force to prevent the commission of a crime, such as criminal damage, in this case. Again, it is contended that Max has used unreasonable force in these circumstances, and that this statutory defence is therefore not available to him.

Max could try to plead the defence of ex turpi causa non oritur actio, which means that the defendant should not benefit from his guilty act. Thus, in *Pitts* v *Hunt* [1990] 3 WLR 542, a drunken person riding on the handlebars of a motorcycle was held unable to recover in negligence from the driver – his criminal act was held to have caused his injury. In this case, it is submitted that ex turpi would not apply, as the injury was not caused by Neil's unlawful activity, but rather by Max's use of force.

Max will be liable for the full extent of Neil's injuries – it is immaterial that they are more severe than could reasonably have been foreseen.

As Max's financial resources may be limited, Neil's parents may wonder if Gorgon Enterprises or Crane Co could also be sued. The general rule in law is that an employer will be vicariously liable for the torts of his or her employees committed in the course of their duties. There is no question that Max is an employee of Crane Co, but it is not so clear whether he can be considered one of Gorgon. Generally speaking, employers will not be liable for torts of their independent contractors. In *Mersey Docks and Harbour Board* v *Coggins & Griffiths (Liverpool) Ltd* [1947] AC 1 a crane operator and his crane were 'lent' to a firm of stevedores. In the course of the operation, he negligently injured a third party. It was held that though the stevedores had the ability to direct what sort of work should be done, the stevedores did not have the ability to direct how the work would be done. As such, they were not in control of the crane operator and he was therefore not their employee. It is submitted that a similar situation exists here, and that Max is only an employee of Crane Co and not of Gorgon.

For Crane Co to be vicariously liable to Neil, however, it must also be established that Max was acting within the course of his employment. This will be a question of fact, but a good guideline was given by Salmond and Heuston (*Salmond and Heuston on the Law of Torts* (24th ed, 2002), p443) to the effect that a servant will be acting within the course of his employment when he performs a wrongful act authorised by the master, or the act is a wrongful and unauthorised mode of performing an act authorised by the master.

It has been held that an employee acting on his own initiative, as Max appears to have been doing in this case, can be acting within the course of his employment. In

Polland v *Parr*, it was held that an employee could be acting within the scope of his employment where he genuinely believed that his employer's property was in danger, and used force to protect the property. However, in Max's case, the lorries were not his employer's property.

If Crane Co had expressly or impliedly given Max a discretion to act in this manner when the property of others was threatened, then he could be construed as acting within the scope of his employment: *Smith* v *North Metropolitan Tramways Co* (1891) 55 JP 330. Whether or not this is the case is not clear from the facts of the question, and this is doubtful, given that his primary role was to operate the crane. In *Warren* v *Henlys Ltd* [1948] 2 All ER 935, the employer of a petrol station attendant was held not to be vicariously liable when he assaulted a customer in an act of personal vengeance – the garage has given no such discretion to the employee.

It is submitted that in pulling Neil off the lorry, Max acted out of the scope of his employment, and that Crane Co would not be vicariously liable.

Thus, Neil's parents should be advised that Neil would have an action in battery against Max, but not against Gorgon. They would also need to be informed that it is unlikely they would be able to sue Crane Co for Max's tort.

b) Neil's parents should be advised that the function of damages in English law is to compensate the claimant for the pecuniary and non-pecuniary loss which flows from the tort. Neil will be entitled to general and special damages.

General damages are those which are said to flow directly from the tort itself, and which do not need to be specifically pleaded in a case. In general damages, Neil could claim for non-pecuniary loss, including pain and suffering and loss of amenity. Neil will be able to claim damages for any pain and suffering which he has experienced or will experience as a result of the accident, or necessary medical treatment: *Cutler* v *Vauxhall Motors Ltd* [1971] 1 QB 418. He will also be able to claim damages for loss of amenity, which is to say enjoyment of life: *Lim Poh Choo* v *Camden and Islington Area Health Authority* [1980] AC 174.

Such damages will usually be awarded as a single lump sum – the quantum of these damages changes over time, and guides such as Kemp & Kemp's *Quantum of Damages* (Tolley's Practitioner Series, 2003) would need to be consulted for a guide to the general amount.

Special damages refer to the particular damage which results from the unique circumstances of the case, and need to be specifically pleaded. For example, Neil could claim financial losses between the date of the injury and trial, but would need to claim them as special damages (though he is unlikely to have lost any earnings, so the only damages of this kind are likely to be medical expenses).

Other special damages which Neil can claim from Max can be divided into two broad heads.

Future losses resulting from the injury

This means that Neil can be compensated for his loss of earning capacity in the future. This compensation will be assessed based upon a number of factors, including Neil's future employment prospects, his enduring incapacity for the future, and the number of working years which he has lost: *Taylor* v *O'Connor* [1971] AC 115.

To assess an amount for pecuniary damages, the court will derive a figure which is said to represent what Neil's annual earnings would have been in the future – the multiplicand – and will multiply it by the number of working years which he has lost – the multiplier. Deriving the multiplicand for a young boy of Neil's age may be difficult and arbitrary, but a court will still do so with children: *Housecroft* v *Burnett* [1982] 1 WLR 71 (though with older children, on the verge of a career, the multiplicand will be higher). With regard to the multiplier, we are told that Neil has an expectation of life of 30 years, but in reality a court will scale this figure down, to take into consideration such contingencies as unemployment and sickness. Once the figure is received, standard amounts will also be deducted for items such as income tax and other payments Neil would have made to the government such as national insurance contributions. Similarly, certain government payments, such as disability allowances, would need to be deducted (but not payments under private insurance policies). The aim will be to ensure that Neil is compensated, but that he is not overcompensated.

Future medical expenses

These will include payment of any kind of future medical expenses which Neil may have, such as medication, nursing care, etc. He could also claim compensation if members of his family had to give him care: *Croke* v *Wiseman* [1981] 3 All ER 852.

QUESTION TWO

Keith is a lecturer in law at the University of Slumsville. One of his duties is to organise moots and mock trials. He arranged with Lucy, a mathematics student, and Mark, a law student, that they would stage an incident which would be the basis of a mock trial. In accordance with the arrangement, as Lucy walked into a mathematics lecture, Mark seized her from behind, tore her shoulder bag from her and rushed from the room. Lucy collapsed and another student, Noel, sprang from his seat and tackled Mark. In the ensuing scuffle, Mark suffered a dislocated shoulder and Noel lost several teeth.

Lucy suffered from a rare medical condition and the incident caused a spasm which constricted her throat and she died of asphyxiation. Neither Lucy nor anyone else had known that she suffered from this condition, but the evidence now is that she could have died at any time if she suffered severe shock. Mark's shoulder injury did not respond to treatment and he is likely to have a permanent disability. He was so distressed by learning of Lucy's death that he suffered a complete nervous breakdown and is unlikely to be able to resume his studies.

Advise Mark, Noel and Lucy's father as to any possible claims in tort.

University of London LLB Examination
(for External Students) Law of Tort June 1990 Q3

General Comment

A typical question on trespass to persons. Students should be vigilant not to dismiss the criminal liability of the characters. The tortious concept of trespass should be analysed and the availability of defences should also be explored.

Skeleton Solution

Lucy and Mark: trespass; define battery; hostile touching; defence of volenti; defence of consent – Noel and Mark: battery; citizen's arrest; could Mark be a trespasser?; causation; consider the possibility of vicarious liability.

Suggested Solution

As regards the incident between Lucy and Mark and its consequences, as Mark's act is intentional we must consider trespass to the person and in particular the tort of battery which consists of the intentional and direct application of force to another person. In *Letang* v *Cooper* [1965] 1 QB 232 it was held that where the act which caused the damage was intentional the cause of action lies in trespass to the person, and this was accepted by the Court of Appeal in *Wilson* v *Pringle* [1987] QB 237. Thus it would appear that there is no overlap between the torts of trespass to the person and negligence, and this view was accepted by the House of Lords in *Stubbings* v *Webb* [1993] 2 WLR 120.

Clearly Mark's actions constitute an intentional and direct application of force to Lucy. However, Lucy has a problem in establishing liability in that in *Wilson* v *Pringle* it was held that the act of touching the claimant had to be a 'hostile touching'. In view of Lucy's agreement with Mark to stage the incident the touching would appear to be non-hostile. A further problem for Lucy is that she has consented to the physical contact by Mark and volenti would provide a complete defence to Mark. Even if Lucy was unaware of the exact incident, providing she was aware in general terms of what was to happen this would be enough to support the defence of volenti: *Chatterton* v *Gerson* [1980] 3 WLR 1003; [1981] QB 432.

Noel has committed a battery on Mark as Noel's actions were direct and intentional. Noel would seek to raise the defence of acting in support of the law as he thought that Mark had stolen Lucy's property. By s24(4) Police and Criminal Evidence Act 1984 a person may arrest without warrant any person who is, or who he suspects with reasonable cause to be, in the act of committing an arrestable offence. Section 24(5) also allows any person who has reasonable cause to believe that a person is guilty of an arrestable offence to arrest that person without warrant if that arrestable offence has in fact been committed. Thus Noel has fallen foul of the trap in *Walters* v *W H Smith* [1914] 1 KB 595 in that he must prove that an offence has actually been committed, and it is no defence to show there were reasonable grounds for believing the person arrested to be guilty. Hence Noel cannot rely on the defence that he was acting in support of the law and is liable to Mark in battery. Noel will be prima facie liable for the damage to Mark's shoulder and as regards Noel's lost teeth, he will be regarded as the author of his own misfortune.

Noel could also attempt to justify his attack on Mark on the grounds that Mark was a trespasser in so far as Mark is a law student and the lecture was a mathematics lecture. However, as Noel is not the occupier of the lecture theatre he will have to show that he has the authority of the occupier to eject a trespasser, which seems unlikely. Noel would also have to show that Mark was requested to leave the premises, had a reasonable opportunity to do so, and failed to leave. As no request was made for Mark to leave Noel cannot raise this defence.

As regards the injury to Mark's shoulder, as Noel intended to inflict harm on Mark no question of remoteness of damage will arise: *Quinn* v *Leatham* [1901] AC 495; *Doyle* v *Olby (Ironmongers) Ltd* [1969] 2 QB 158 and Noel will be liable for the damage to Mark's shoulder. As regards Mark's nervous breakdown the question of causation arises, ie what event caused the breakdown. We are told that it was caused by Mark's distress at Lucy's death. Turning to Lucy's death we are told Lucy collapsed after Mark removed her shoulder bag and that Noel attacked Mark after this occurrence. I assume that the 'incident' referred to in the problem which caused the spasm was therefore the removal of the bag by Mark. As Mark intended to harm Lucy then again no question of remoteness of damage would arise and Mark would be liable to Lucy's death, but as we have seen Lucy's consent will provide a total defence to Mark's actions.

Thus we should advise Mark that he can sue Noel in respect of his dislocated shoulder, but that he has no remedy for the nervous breakdown he has suffered. We should advise Noel that he is liable to Mark for Mark's shoulder injury, but has no remedy as regards his lost teeth. We should advise Lucy's father that he has no claim.

We could also consider whether Keith is vicariously liable for the actions of Lucy or Mark. Keith is not the employer of Lucy or Mark but we should consider whether an ad hoc agency has arisen as in *Ormrod* v *Crossville Motor Services* [1953] 1 WLR 1120 where Keith is the principal and Lucy and Mark are his agents acting on his behalf. If so, then the University of Slumsville would be liable for Keith's acts as they are his employer, Keith is their employee and Keith was organising the incident in connection with a mock trial and so was acting in the course of his employment. However, this would not affect the liabilities of the parties as described above.

QUESTION THREE

Arthur has agreed with Bertram to use his front room on the day following the Cup Final in order to watch the local team return triumphant or otherwise, with the Cup. He agrees to pay five pounds for this. On the morning of the day in question Arthur arrives with several friends, some of whom appear to be still intoxicated after the celebrations of the previous night, Bertram says: 'The deal's off. Take this mob away.'

Arthur says: 'You can't do this. We agreed. Let me through.'

He pushes Bertram aside and sits down in the room. Bertram fetches his friend Bruce who throws Arthur out onto the road and injures his back. Arthur's friends who have retreated out of the house in some disarray throw bottles through the windows of Bertram's house.

Advise Bertram.

Written by the Author

General Comment

This question requires analysis of the tort of trespass to land as well as the tort of trespass to persons. Though criminal damage is evident, it is sufficient to mention it within context.

Skeleton Solution

Define trespass to land – is there an effective and immediate entry? – any defences available – define trespass to persons – assault – battery – trespasser and criminal damage – any defences?

Suggested Solution

When Arthur agrees with Bertram to use his front room in return for £5, he is given a contractual licence to enter the premises. Arthur's friends, however, are not part of the agreement, and when they walk up Bertram's path to his house, they have merely an implied gratuitous licence.

Both contractual and gratuitous licences are 'bare licences' and should be distinguished from a licence coupled with a grant where the licensee is granted a proprietary interest in the land to which the licence is ancillary to enable the licensee to enjoy the grant. A bare licence can be revoked at will, subject to the payment of compensation in the case of a contractual licence, whereas a licence coupled with a grant cannot be revoked arbitrarily. Therefore, when Bertram says, 'The deal is off. Take this mob away', he is withdrawing Arthur's contractual licence in respect of which Arthur may be able to claim compensation (although it could be an implied term of the agreement that he would be in a condition suitable to entering the premises) and Arthur's friends' gratuitous licence.

When Arthur pushes Bertram aside and enters the house, there is an assault if Bertram apprehended fear of battery, and a battery since Arthur has intentionally applied force to Bertram. The lightest touch of a person is actionable: *Cole* v *Turner* (1704) 6 Mod 149. Both torts are actionable per se, ie without proof of damage although, if no damage is established, Bertram's entitlement is to nominal damages only, ie a few pounds in recognition that the claimant's rights have been infringed.

When Arthur sits down in the front room, he also commits a trespass to land because he has entered without lawful authority or the permission of Bertram, the person in possession. Again, this tort is actionable per se.

When Bertram's friend, Bruce, throws Arthur out of the house and injures his back, he is ejecting a trespasser. If a trespasser enters forcibly the occupier may use reasonable force to eject him without a prior request to leave. Third parties may intervene only as agents of the occupier, and the force used may only be such as is necessary to remove the trespasser; it may not be used as chastisement.

Here Bruce is acting as Bertram's agent, but the force used, if excessive, may be both an assault and a battery and, since injuries were sustained, if Arthur is successful he will recover substantial, as opposed to nominal, damages. The question of whether the force employed was reasonable is a question of fact to be decided by the court in all the circumstances.

Throwing bottles through Bertram's window is an act of criminal damage by Arthur's friends. If Bertram was in the room at the time, it is an assault and battery. The acts also amount to a trespass to land, for this tort can be committed by putting things on to the land: *Turner* v *Thorne and Thorne* (1959) 21 DLR (2d) 29; *Gregory* v *Piper* (1829) 9 B & C 591. This is actionable at the suit of Bertram, the person in possession.

QUESTION FOUR

Minos owns a large detached house in its own grounds. It adjoins a park owned by the Cnossos District Council. Visitors frequently go to the park to fly kites, which often blow at some height over Minos's house and garden and occasionally become entangled in his trees or in parts of the house.

One day Icarus, aged 14, went to the park with his father, Daedalus, to fly his kite. A strong wind was blowing towards Minos's house and the kite was blown out of the park and became fouled on the telephone wires attached to the chimney breast of the house. Icarus rang the front door bell to ask for permission to retrieve his kite but received no reply. He took a ladder which he found in the garden and climbed on to the roof. Minos returned home at that point and, seeing Icarus, lost his temper and removed the ladder, locking it away and telling Icarus that he could stay on the roof all night. Daedalus, who had remained in the park, now came into Minos's garden, advanced threateningly and told him that, if he did not replace the ladder, he would give him a thrashing that he would remember for the rest of his life. Minos tried to strike Daedalus with a spade, but Daedalus was able to avoid it and to punch Minos, leaving him lying winded. He then helped Icarus down and they left. Minos later cut down the kite but refuses to give it back to Icarus.

Advise Minos (i) as to whether he can stop the activities of the kite flyers and (ii) as to his rights and liabilities in respect of the incident involving Icarus and Daedalus.

University of London LLB Examination
(for External Students) Law of Tort June 1986 Q4

General Comment

This question spans the area of nuisance and trespass to land generally. Trespass to person issues also arise and reference to the tort of conversion also seem to surface. Students should show versatility over these areas in order to perform well in this question.

Skeleton Solution

Nuisance in kites flying over Minos's house – injunction appropriate remedy to stop this and should be sought against the Council – availability of such an injunction and factors considered in granting it. Trespass to land – Icarus not trespasser in merely recovering his kite but, quaere, if so when he climbed onto roof of house. Daedalus a trespasser in entering Minos's property in threatening manner. Assault and battery – Minos could sue Daedalus in assault and battery and Daedalus could sue Minos for assault. False imprisonment – Icarus appears to have a good cause of action for this against Minos. Conversion – Icarus may be able to sue for conversion in respect of his kite.

Suggested Solution

If Minos wishes to stop kites flying over his house and garden from the park owned by Cnossos District Council then he must seek an injunction against the Council. In order to obtain this injunction he must show that the Council is liable in nuisance. This is a case of nuisance rather than trespass to land because the activities of kite-flyers are not a direct interference but only a consequential interference with the use or enjoyment of his property. It may be added that whether an interference is direct or consequential is often a matter of judicial opinion and, as the judgments of the Court of Appeal and speeches in the House of Lords in *Southport Corporation* v *Esso Petroleum Co Ltd* [1956] AC 218; [1954] 2 QB 182 indicate these opinions may differ sharply. Further, in order for a case in trespass to succeed it must be shown that there was an intentional interference with the rights of Minos. The facts of this case do not suggest such on the part of the Council. See *Smith* v *Stone* (1647) Style 65.

As regards an action in nuisance, Minos has an interest in the land affected: *Malone* v *Laskey* [1907] 2 KB 141. The Council is the appropriate defendant in this action because it is the occupier of the park and it seems that as a matter of procedure a nuisance action must be brought against the occupier from whose premises the nuisance emanates: see *Smith* v *Scott* [1973] 1 Ch 314. There should be no difficulty in holding the Council liable in nuisance. The case law strongly suggests that where an occupier of land allows a person onto his premises, whose activities he is in a position to regulate or control, and that person commits a nuisance, then the occupier is liable. See *Matania v National Provincial Bank Ltd* [1936] 2 All ER 633. Thus, an occupier is liable for a nuisance committed by an independent contractor whom he invites to his premises and also for the activities of gypsies whom he permits to take up residence on his premises: see *Attorney-General* v *Corke* [1933] Ch 82. Therefore, as the kite-flyers were only visitors to the park whose activities could be regulated or even stopped by the Council, they are accordingly liable for the nuisance caused by them.

The mere fact that a case in nuisance is made out against the Council does not necessarily mean that Minos will get an injunction to prevent kite flying in the future: see *Miller* v *Jackson* [1977] QB 966. This equitable remedy, like all equitable remedies, is discretionary and may only be granted in cases of nuisance, it seems, if on balance the social and other merits of the defendant's conduct are outweighed by claimant's right to an injunction. In *Miller* v *Jackson* the Court of Appeal would not have granted an injunction to stop the playing of cricket, even if a nuisance, because socially it was a good thing and, furthermore, account was taken of the fact that the claimant had come to the nuisance knowing of it, ie purchasing a house in that case which was next to the cricket ground. This decision has caused some difficulty in that it appears to go against earlier decisions such as *Shelfer* v *City of London Electric Lighting Co* [1895] 1 Ch 287 where the defendant's conduct in operating a power station was stopped because it caused vibrations in the claimant's premises even though this was socially useful. The court in that case pointed out that no matter how beneficial a defendant's activity might be if it amounted to a nuisance then, the court would not let him 'buy the right to commit it'. In more recent cases the courts appear to be more inclined to grant an injunction unless it would be unworkable in the circumstances. In *Kennaway* v *Thompson* [1981] QB 88 the claimant got an injunction to restrict power boat racing on a lake next to her house. The fact she came to build her house there knowing that such activities took place on the lake was considered but did not prevent the court granting the injunction so as to restrict the increase in the size, noise and frequency of such boats on the lake. In *Tetley* v *Chitty* [1986] 1 All ER 663 an injunction was granted to prevent go-kart racing near the claimant's house and the social utility of this activity was given little weight.

In the light of these decisions Minos would appear to have a good prospect of obtaining an injunction. Damages would be of little value to him if he is being constantly bothered by kites becoming entangled in his trees or parts of his house and the consequent trespass by kite-flyers to retrieve them. The Council could easily take steps to forbid kite-flying in the park or, alternatively restrict it to areas of the park where such interference with Minos would not occur. But it may be added that if the number of times kites actually fall on Minos's premises is small he may be refused relief. I doubt if a court would grant an injunction to stop mere kite flying over Minos's premises if the kites were so high as not to interfere with ordinary user by Minos. However, much must depend on the facts for it is one thing to expect him to put up with the occasional kite but quite another to expect him to put up with hundreds of them regularly.

In respect of the incident involving Icarus and Daedalus, Minos may bring proceedings on the basis of trespass to land and assault and battery. But he may also be liable to Icarus for false imprisonment, and trespass to goods, and to Daedalus for assault.

Minos may sue for trespass to land in respect of the kite landing on his property, in respect of Icarus's entry to retrieve it especially by climbing on the roof of his house, and in respect of Daedalus's entry to his garden in a threatening manner. As regards the claim concerning the kite, whether this is trespass depends on whether it is regarded as a 'direct' or a 'consequential' interference with Minos's land. As stated earlier there is some difficulty in the case law over this distinction. The decision in *Gregory v Piper* (1829) 9 B & C 591 and some of the judgments in *Southport Corporation v Esso Petroleum* suggested that if the defendant intentionally initiated a force which directly caused the kite to land in Minos's land this would be sufficient. Other judgments in the Esso case suggest that this would not be anything but 'consequential' and not actionable in trespass. If the entry of the kite was a trespass then there would have been a 'continuing trespass' for as long as it remained there. See *Konskier v Goodman* [1928] 1 KB 421. Icarus would have a duty to remove it and for this purpose he would have a licence to enter onto Minos's land to recover it. In doing this he would not be a trespasser, but it may be otherwise regarding his climbing onto the roof of the house. Further, if the entry of the kite was not of itself a trespass, a similar licence would be inferred so no trespass would arise. See *Anthony v Heney* (1832) 8 Bing 186. It may be noted that legal authority on these points is thin and there is little beyond the case cited. So far as Daedalus is concerned his entry onto Minos's land appears to have been made for the purpose of securing the release of Icarus but it was also to threaten Minos. In view of the latter it is difficult to see how Daedalus's entry onto Minos's land could be treated as anything other than an act of trespass. See *Anthony v Heney* (above).

Minos may also bring proceedings against Daedalus for assault and battery. Two incidents are relevant here, first the threats which Daedalus made while advancing towards Minos and, second, the punch Daedalus delivered winding Minos. The first incident amounted to an assault since its object was to create an apprehension of imminent harmful or offensive conduct. The words used would have aroused fear in the mind of a reasonable person in the circumstances: see *Read v Coker* (1853) 13 CB 850. The second incident amounted to a battery only as it does not appear to have been preceded by any threats by Daedalus: see *Cole v Turner* (1704) 6 Mod 149. Daedalus may seek to raise a defence of self-defence in respect of this incident but it is unlikely to succeed if Minos was in no position to hit him with the spade when he delivered his punch. Self-defence only permits the use of such force as is reasonable in the circumstances and, thus, it is also arguable that a punch which left Minos winded was excessive: see *Lane v Holloway* [1968] 1 QB 379.

Icarus may have a claim against Minos in false imprisonment in respect of the removal of the ladder so as to leave him stranded on the roof. It may be that he was a trespasser in going onto the roof to retrieve his kite but this does not permit false imprisonment. This tort consists of restricting a person's freedom through actual confinement or preventing him from leaving a place in which he is: see *Balmain New Ferry* v *Robertson* (1906) 4 CLR 379. If Icarus was stranded on the roof without a reasonable means of escape then the elements of the tort are satisfied, see *Meering* v *Graham-White Aviation* (1919)122 LT 44. It is irrelevant that the roof may be spacious or pleasant since the real issue is whether he was prevented from leaving the place: see *Bird* v *Jones* (1845) 7 QB 742. Whether Minos has any defence here is debatable since he appears to have been aware of the reason for Icarus's presence on the roof. But, matters may have been different if he had reasonably believed him to be a burglar and took the action he did in order to confine him so that he could call the police: see *Alderson* v *Booth* [1969] 2 QB 216.

Icarus may also have a claim against Minos for conversion because of the refusal of the latter to give him back the kite: see *Howard Perry* v *British Railways Board* [1980] 1 WLR 1375. Against this claim Minos may be able to allege distress damage feasant in defence, ie that he is entitled to retain the kite until any damage to his property caused by it is compensated.

Daedalus may have a claim against Minos for assault in respect of the incident where the latter attempted to hit him with the spade. The necessary conditions for assault, referred to above, appear to be satisfied.

QUESTION FIVE

Alan is an old age pensioner living with Brian, his nephew, in Stoketon. Brian treats Alan badly, threatening to punch him if he leaves his room without permission. Alan is too frightened to disobey. Their neighbour, Clive, suspects that Alan is badly treated and tells Diane, the Stoketon social services supervisor. Diane tells Clive that social services will arrange a visit but they fail to do so and simply pass on the information to a local pensioner support group. Edward, a volunteer from the group, calls but fails to recognise the signs of age abuse which would be obvious to a professional. Alan becomes so depressed that he tries to commit suicide by jumping out of his window. He breaks his leg and is taken to Stoketon Hospital where Fiona, an experienced medical student working in casualty, fails to recognise the problems that can be caused by bone fractures in the elderly. As a result, Alan does not receive proper treatment and will always have to walk with the aid of a stick. If Alan had received proper treatment, he would have had a reasonable chance of making a full recovery.

Advise Alan.

University of London LLB Examination
(for External Students) Law of Tort June 1991 Q5

General Comment

This question covers aspects relating to the torts of assault and false imprisonment, as well as general issues concerning negligence. Elements of vicarious liability also arise. Concepts of causation, remoteness and foreseeability are also raised.

Skeleton Solution

Alan v Brian: ingredients of torts of assault and false imprisonment – Alan v Stoketon Council: vicarious liability for Diane; the law on omissions: is there a duty to rescue?; the special rules for public authorities; causation; prevention of suicide attempts; 'novus actus interveniens' – Alan v Edward: standard of care from a volunteer – Alan v Stoketon Hospital: direct and vicarious liability for hospital staff; standard of care; inexperienced staff; causation; balance of probabilities test; is loss of a chance recoverable in tort?

Suggested Solution

A number of possible claims arise out of the facts given and it will be convenient to consider them separately, although in some claims there will be similar or overlapping issues (such as causation).

Alan v Brian (A v B)

A may sue B for assault. Assault is any act (including words) which causes another person to apprehend the infliction of immediate unlawful force: *Wilson v Pringle* [1987] QB 237. B's threat to punch A falls within this definition.

A may also sue B for false imprisonment, which involves the unlawful imposition of constraint on one's freedom of movement from a particular place: *Wilson v Pringle*. B's confinement of A to his room under duress falls within this definition. The recent decision of the Court of Appeal in *Roberts v Chief Constable of the Cheshire Constabulary* [1999] 2 All ER 362 confims this contention.

Both torts are actionable per se.

Alan v Stoketon Council

If Diane was negligent the Council will be vicariously liable as her employer for acts or omissions occurring during the course of her employment.

The first difficulty is in establishing that the Council owed A a duty of care. The failure to arrange the promised visit by the social services department is an example of a pure omission and the law of tort does not impose a positive duty to act (here, effectively, a duty to rescue) unless there is a special relationship between the parties in which one exercises control and the other is dependent on the controlling party.

Mere status does not imply control or duty to rescue; there must be also practical ability to control the particular situation, such as in the case of a lifeguard on the lookout for swimmers in distress: example given by Bowman and Bailey in *Public Law* (1984) P4, 277.

The courts are especially reluctant to impose positive duties on public authorities which may be faced with limited resources and difficult operational decisions, eg it has been held that the police are not under a duty to answer a burglar alarm or 999 emergency call in the absence of a contract or other special relationship with the claimant: *Alexandrou* v *Oxford* [1993] 4 All ER 328; *Hill* v *Chief Constable of West Yorkshire* [1988] 2 All ER 238.

However, in the present problem Diane had promised to investigate A's circumstances and such assumption of responsibility might be enough to give rise to the duty of care. If so, it is advised that the Council were in breach of that duty by 'passing the buck' to an unprofessional organisation.

The next issue is one of causation. If A had suffered further abuse from B as a result of the failure to investigate, there would be little doubt as to the Council's liability. However, A's actual damage is the broken leg caused by a suicide attempt at a time when he was depressed. Although the Council were under a duty to exercise supervision, it would be going too far to suggest that they were under a duty to prevent a suicide attempt, because they did not have sufficient degree of control over Alan's hour-by-hour movements. Even if they had had such control (eg, if A had been transferred into their custody) a suicide attempt would be unforeseeable in the absence of direct knowledge of A's clinical depression and suicidal tendencies.

For those reasons the present facts are distinguishable from *Kirkham* v *Chief Constable of Greater Manchester Police* [1990] 2 WLR 987 where the police had known of such tendencies in a remand prisoner but had failed to alert the hospital wing which would otherwise have taken protective action. The prisoner's widow was successful in suing the police for negligence (defences of 'ex turpi causa', and 'volenti' were rejected, and the plea of contributory negligence was also regarded as unavailable).

Hence, although the Council were in breach of their duty of general supervision, A cannot sue them for the damage to his leg, which was not caused by such breach of duty. The suicide attempt could be described as a 'novus actus interveniens' breaking the chain of causation leading from the breach of duty to the actual damage sustained.

Alan v *Edward (A* v *E)*

On the existence of a duty of care it has been said that if a person undertakes to perform a voluntary act he is liable if he performs it improperly: per Willes J in *Skelton* v *L & NW Ry* (1867) LR 2 CP 631. Hence the issue here is whether Edward was in breach of the duty he undertook to investigate A's circumstances. The standard of care expected from him was that which would be expected from a member of a 'pensioner support group'. Since the objectives of such a group are wide-ranging and involve activities of a political nature rather than medical or quasi-medical the law would not impose on its members the standards expected from a professional social services worker. Since the facts indicate that the signs of A's age abuse were not obvious to a non-professional such as Edward, he was not in breach of his duty to A. Even if there were a breach of the duty of care, E would not be liable because of the causation issue, which would apply in the same way as in A's claim against the Council (above).

A v *Stoketon Hospital*

If Fiona was negligent Stoketon Hospital (SH) would be liable, either directly for failure to provide competent medical staff or vicariously for the individual act of negligence committed by an employee in the course of employment: *Cassidy* v *Ministry of Health* [1951] 1 All ER 574.

On the issue of medical negligence the test will be whether Fiona failed to diagnose a problem which would have been diagnosed by a responsible body of medical practitioners: *Bolam's Case* [1957] 2 All ER 118. On that test Fiona is in breach of her duty of care to A and her inexperience will not affect her liability because a uniform standard of care is required from all those who undertook the practice of medicine in the casualty unit of the hospital, be they doctors of 30 years' experience or, like Fiona, a student 'learning on the job': *Wilsher* v *Essex Area Health Authority* [1988] 1 All ER 871. In the law of tort the duty is tailored to the act being performed and not to the actor performing it: for example, in *Nettleship* v *Weston* [1971] 2 QB 691, it was held that the standard of care owed by a learner-driver is no different to that owed by a qualified, confident driver.

However, even though Fiona was in breach of her duty of care, the issue of causation remains: did her breach cause A's permanent disability? If it can be shown that it was more probable than not that A would have been permanently disabled in any event as a result of the suicide attempt, that will conclude the issue in the hospital's favour, because evidence that D's conduct may have caused or contributed to P's injury will only result in a finding that it did cause that injury if there is no or inadequate evidence of any other causal factor which on the balance of probabilities resulted in the injury: see *Hotson* v *East Berkshire Area Health Authority* [1987] 2 All ER 909 where it was found that there was a 25 per cent chance that the delay in diagnosis contributed to the development of D's condition but a 75 per cent chance that it would have happened anyway as a result of established other causes. It was held that the delay in diagnosis was not a cause of the injury on the civil standard of probabilities and so the hospital escaped liability. It was left open whether a lost chance of recovery which could be proved to result from a breach of duty could be compensated in tort, as it clearly is in contract law (*Chaplin* v *Hicks* [1911] 2 KB 786: see further, article Hill (1991) MLR 511).

In the present case the facts would seem to suggest that it was Fiona's negligence which prevented A's complete recovery and therefore A may have at least an arguable case for compensation on the basis of his lost chance of complete recovery.

Chapter 17

Deceit, Malicious Falsehood, Passing Off

17.1   Introduction

17.2   Key points

17.3   Key cases and statute

17.1 Introduction

These torts cover the infliction of economic harm, but for historical reasons they are not classed with the economic torts (see Chapter 18).

17.2 Key points

Deceit

Definition

The wilful and reckless making of a false statement to another with the intent that the other shall act on reliance upon the statement and that other relies to his injury: *Pasley v Freeman* (1789) 3 TR 51.

Note the similarity and the differences between this tort and the tort of negligent misrepresentation; deceit is, in fact, the tort of fraudulent misrepresentation.

Elements

a) False statement

The representation must be false and there must be a representation either by speech or conduct: *R v Barnard* (1837) 7 C & P 784. Liability may also arise from a failure to speak where:

i)   an initially true representation becomes false to the knowledge of the maker (*With v O'Flanagan* [1936] Ch 575);

ii) the representation is a misleading half-truth (*Nottingham Brick v Butler* (1886) 16 QBD 778);

iii) there is a uberrimae fidei contract;

iv) there is a fiduciary relationship between the parties.

b) Representation of existing fact, not:

   i)   mere puff (*Dimmock* v *Hallett* (1866) LR 2 Ch App 21);

   ii) opinion (*Bisset* v *Wilkinson* [1927] AC 177) unless the maker had special knowledge (*Brown* v *Raphael* [1958] Ch 636) or the statement was not his true opinion (*Smith* v *Land & House Property Corpn* (1884) 28 Ch D 7);

   iii) intention, unless a present intention is misrepresented (*Edgington* v *Fitzmaurice* (1885) 29 Ch D 459);

   iv) law.

c) Knowledge of falsity

The false statement must be made knowingly, or without belief in its truth, or recklessly careless whether it be true or false: *Derry* v *Peek* (1889) 14 App Cas 337.

d) Intention

The defendant must intend that his statement is acted on. No problem arises where the statement is made to the claimant directly, but difficulties can arise where the statement is made to a class of persons; compare *Peek* v *Gurney* (1873) LR 6 HL 377 with *Andrews* v *Mockford* [1896] 1 QB 372.

e) Claimant must act on the statement

But the statement need not be the decisive factor as regards the claimant's decision: *Edgington* v *Fitzmaurice* (above). If the claimant was unaware of the misrepresentation (*Horsfall* v *Thomas* (1862) 1 H & C 90), or regarded it as unimportant (*Smith* v *Chadwick* (1884) 9 App Cas 187), or relied on his own investigations (*Attwood* v *Small* (1838) 6 Cl & Fin 232), reliance will not be present. However, the fact that the claimant could have found that the defendant's statement was false will not negate reliance: *Redgrave* v *Hurd* (1881) 20 Ch D 1.

f) Damage

The claimant must show that he has suffered damage from the statement and can recover for all loss, whether or not it was reasonably foreseeable: *Doyle* v *Olby (Ironmongers) Ltd* [1969] 2 QB 158.

Malicious falsehood (or injurious falsehood)

Definition

The making of a false statement, with malice, to a person other than the claimant which causes damage to the claimant, as in eg *Ratcliffe* v *Evans* [1892] 2 QB 524.

Note the distinctions between deceit, malicious falsehood and defamation, namely: in deceit the false statement must be made to the claimant; in malicious falsehood and defamation it is made to a third party.

Defamation is an attack on the claimant's reputation; malicious falsehood is typically an attack on the claimant's business or property, although there can be an overlap with defamation: *Joyce* v *Sengupta* [1993] 1 WLR 337.

Elements

a) False statement

As in deceit there must be a statement of fact, not puff, opinion, etc. Compare *White* v *Mellin* [1895] AC 154 and *De Beers* v *Electric Co of New York* [1975] 1 WLR 972 for the difference between a trader boosting his own goods and denigrating the claimant's goods. See also the more recent case of *Vodafone Group plc* v *Orange Personal Communications Services Ltd* (1996) The Times 31 August.

b) Malice

That is, an improper motive such as spite or a wish to injure the claimant. If the defendant knows his statement is false, or is reckless whether it be true or false, then malice is present. An honest belief in the truth of the statement, or absence of intent to injure the claimant, shows an absence of malice: *Balden* v *Shorter* [1933] Ch 247.

c) Damage

The claimant must suffer damage from the statement: see *Allason* v *Campbell* (1996) The Times 8 May. Proof of general loss of business is sufficient: *Ratcliffe* v *Evans* (above), and note s3 Defamation Act 1952 and its application in *Kaye* v *Robertson* [1991] FSR 62.

Passing off

Definition

There must be 'a misrepresentation, made by a trader in the course of trade, to a prospective customer of his or ultimate consumer of goods or services supplied to him, which is calculated to injure the business or goodwill of another trader (in the sense that this is a reasonably foreseeable consequence) and which causes actual damage to a business or goodwill of the trader by whom the action is brought or will probably do so' per Lord Diplock in *Erven Warnink* v *Townend* [1979] AC 731.

As the elements are self-explanatory we shall look at the ways in which the tort may be committed.

Methods of passing off

a) Direct statement that goods belonging to the claimant belong to the defendant, as in *Lord Byron* v *Johnson* (1816) 2 Mer 29.

b) Imitating the appearance of the claimant's goods, eg *White Hudson* v *Asian Organisation* [1964] 1 WLR 1466; *Reckitt & Coleman Products* v *Borden Inc* [1990] 1 All

ER 873. Note the extension of this concept to advertising campaigns: *Cadbury-Schweppes* v *Pub Squash* [1981] 1 WLR 193.

c) Using a similar name for goods, eg *Reddaway* v *Banham* [1896] AC 199; *Bollinger* v *Costa Brava Wine* [1960] Ch 262; *Erven Warnick* v *Townend* (above); *Mothercare* v *Penguin Books* [1988] RPC 113; *Taittinger* v *Allbev Ltd* [1994] 4 All ER 75, but note *Harrods Ltd* v *Harrodian School* [1996] RPC 697 and that the claimant cannot protect the name of a class of goods: *British Vacuum Cleaner* v *New Vacuum Cleaner* [1907] 2 Ch 312. A recent illustration is provided by the case of *Inter Lotto (UK) Ltd* v *Camelot Group plc* [2003] 4 All ER 575.

d) Using the claimant's name, ie the use of the claimant's name as opposed to the name of the claimant's goods: *Maxim's Ltd* v *Dye* [1977] 1 WLR 1155.

The High Court held in *Artistic Upholstery Ltd* v *Art Forma (Furniture) Ltd* [1999] 4 All ER 277 that the use of name may amount to a passing off, if it is capable of misleading the public.

e) Using the defendant's name. The defendant may not use his own name if that would mislead the public: *Parker-Knoll* v *Knoll International* [1962] RPC 265.

Note that if the parties are not in the same trade it is more difficult for the claimant to prove that the public will be misled: *Granada* v *Ford Motor Co* [1972] FSR 103; *McCullough* v *May* [1947] 2 All ER 845. Similarly where the product is only bought by professionals who would not be misled by any attempted deception: *Hodgkinson & Corby* v *Wards Mobility Services* [1994] 1 WLR 1564. A false endorsement would also be tantamount to passing off: see *Irvine* v *Talksport Ltd* [2003] 2 All ER 881.

Note also the relevance of the perception of the public and the effect of a disclaimer: *Associated Newspapers* v *Insert Media* [1991] 3 All ER 535. Finally note that the mere copying, however deliberate or provocative, of the name or style which another trader had used for his goods or services is not necessarily sufficient to found an action in passing off: *County Sound* v *Ocean Sound* [1991] FSR 367.

Remedies

Injunction and/or damages or the profits of the passing off.

17.3 Key cases and statute

*   *Artistic Upholstery Ltd* v *Art Forma (Furniture) Ltd* [1999] 4 All ER 277
    An unincorporated association, through one of its members, may sue in passing off

*   *Derry* v *Peek* (1889) 14 App Cas 337
    Maker must know that statement is false

- *Doyle* v *Olby (Ironmongers) Ltd* [1969] 2 QB 158
  False statement must cause loss or damage to claimant

- *Edgington* v *Fitzmaurice* (1885) 29 Ch D 459
  Claimant must act on the statement

- *Erven Warnink BV* v *J Townend & Sons (Hull) Ltd* [1979] AC 731
  Provides a definition of the tort of passing off

- *Gregory* v *Portsmouth City Council* [2000] 1 All ER 560
  The House of Lords considered the limits of the tort of malicious prosecution

- *Inter Lotto (UK) Ltd* v *Camelot Group plc* [2003] 4 All ER 575
  Passing off arise where there is sufficient similarity between two trade marks

- *Irvine* v *Talksport Ltd* [2003] 2 All ER 881
  A false endorsement could also result in a passing-off action

- *Pasley* v *Freeman* (1789) 3 TR 51
  Provides a definition of the tort of deceit

- *Ratcliffe* v *Evans* [1892] 2 QB 524
  The making of a false statement with malice amounts to malicious falsehood

- *With* v *O'Flanagan* [1936] Ch 575
  For deceit, there must be a false representation by speech or conduct

- Defamation Act 1952 – claimant does not have to prove actual loss to claim damages
  in the tort of malicious falsehood

Chapter 18

The Economic Torts

18.1   Introduction

18.2   Key points

18.3   Key cases and statute

18.4   Questions and suggested solutions

18.1 Introduction

Here we are concerned with the intentional, as opposed to negligent, infliction of harm on another. Many of the cases are concerned with industrial action and alleged unlawful competition, and this area is still being developed by the courts. There are, however, limitations to this development as there is no common law requirement that parties must trade fairly: *Associated Newspapers Group plc* v *Insert Media Ltd* [1988] 1 WLR 509. Note that this is not the position in European Community law: in *Akzo Chemie* v *Commission of the European Communities* Case C–62/86 (1991) The Times 7 October the European Court held that art 86 of the Treaty of Rome (now art 82 EC) prohibited a dominant undertaking from eliminating a competitor by means other than competition on merit and that not all price competition was legitimate.

18.2 Key points

Background

In *Mogul Steamship* v *McGregor, Gow & Co* [1892] AC 25 the House of Lords held that conspiracy to injure the claimant was not actionable as the defendant had not committed an unlawful act vis-à-vis the claimant. Similarly, in *Allen* v *Flood* [1898] AC 1 it was again held that the claimant could not sue the defendant in the absence of an unlawful act. But in *Quinn* v *Leatham* [1901] AC 495 it was held that the defendants had conspired unjustifiably to inflict harm on the claimant and so were liable. The difference between *Quinn* and *Mogul* and *Allen* is that in *Quinn* there was more than one defendant, and the rule that a number of persons acting together can make a lawful act actionable is confined to conspiracy to injure and is not to be extended: *Lonrho Ltd* v *Shell Petroleum Co (No 2)* [1982] AC 173.

We shall now consider the various economic torts.

Conspiracy

Definition

The agreement of two or more persons to do an unlawful act or a lawful act by unlawful means: *Mulcahy* v *R* (1868) LR 3 HL 306, 317. The second part of this definition covers the anomalous tort in *Quinn* v *Leatham* (above).

In *Lonrho plc* v *Fayed* [1991] 3 WLR 188; [1991] 3 All ER 303 the House of Lords held that the tort of conspiracy to injure could be established either by showing that an intention to injure the claimant in his business was the predominant purpose, even though the means used were lawful and would not have been actionable if carried out by an individual, or by showing that unlawful means were used. But where there was intent to injure the claimant and unlawful means were used it was no defence to show that their predominant purpose was to protect their own interests; it was sufficient that they had used unlawful means to constitute the tort.

Common elements

a) Two or more persons. Note that a company can conspire with its directors, and a husband and wife can conspire with each other.

b) Parties combine. No contractual agreement is required, merely that the parties combine for a common purpose.

c) Damage to the claimant is required.

Unlawful act conspiracy

This includes conspiracy to commit a crime or tort and probably a breach of contract.

Lawful act by unlawful means conspiracy

Because it is anomalous (see (a) above) the scope of this tort has been restricted. In *Crofter Hand Woven Harris Tweed Co* v *Veitch* [1942] AC 435 it was held that no action would lie where the predominant purpose of the defendants was not to injure the claimant but rather to defend their own interests, providing no unlawful means were used. The defendants may not avail themselves of this defence if they are motivated by spite: *Huntley* v *Thornton* [1957] 1 WLR 321. Recently, the approach taken by the courts in *Yukong Lines Ltd of Korea* v *Rendsburg Investments Corporation of Liberia, The Rialto (No 2)* [1998] 4 All ER 82 seems to support this line of reasoning.

Inducing a breach of contract

This is the most developed of the economic torts and dates back to *Lumley* v *Gye* (1853) 2 El & B1 216.

Forms of the tort

In *Thomson* v *Deakin* [1952] Ch 646, three forms were identified.

a) Direct persuasion to break a contract eg *Lumley* v *Gye* (1853) 2 El & Bl 216.

b) Defendant prevents performance by direct and unlawful means.

c) Defendant induces third party to break his contract with his employer so that the employer is unable to peform his contract with the claimant. For this third form there are four elements: the defendant must have known of the contract between the claimant and the employer; the defendant must have intended to breach this contract; the employees must have broken their contracts of employment; the breach between the employer and the claimant must have been a necessary consequence of the breach by the employees of their contracts of employment. Note the application of these criteria in *Thomson* v *Deakin* (above) and its application in *Middlebrook Mushrooms* v *Transport and General Workers Union* [1993] ICR 612. It may be difficult in particular cases to decide which form of the tort has occurred: *Stratford* v *Lindley* [1965] AC 269.

In *Law Debenture Trust Corpn* v *Ural Caspian Oil Corporation Ltd* [1994] 3 WLR 1221 it was held that the tort did not cover a situation where the right violated was a secondary right to a remedy arising out of the inducement of a breach.

Knowledge and intention

The defendant must have knowledge of the contract broken and have intended to bring about a breach of contract; the tort cannot be committed negligently.

The exact nature of the breach need not be known; in *Merkur Island Shipping* v *Laughton* [1983] 2 AC 570 it was held that trade union officials must be deemed to know that industrial action would lead to a breach of contract. Recklessness is sufficient intent: *Emerald Construction* v *Lowthian* [1966] 1 WLR 691.

Breach

Actual breach is not required; it is sufficient if the performance of the contract is interfered with: *Torquay Hotel Co* v *Cousins* [1969] 2 Ch 106.

Damage

Damage to the claimant is essential, but the courts are willing to infer that a breach of contract has caused damage.

Justification

Self-interest (*South Wales Miners' Federation* v *Glamorgan Coal* [1905] AC 239) or altruistic motives (*Greig* v *Insole* [1978] 1 WLR 302) is not justification. The defence was reviewed in *Edwin Hill* v *First National Finance* [1989] 3 All ER 801 where the possession of an equal or superior right to the claimant was held to constitute justification, as was a moral duty to intervene (*Brimelow* v *Casson* [1924] 1 Ch 302), or the fact that the contract interfered with was inconsistent with a previous contract with the interferer: *Smithies* v *National Association of Operative Plasterers* [1909] 1 KB 310.

Intimidation

The modern law here dates from *Rookes* v *Barnard* [1964] AC 1129.

Definition

Consists of threats by the defendant to a third party that the defendant will use unlawful means against the third party unless the third party does or refrains from some act and the claimant suffers loss as a result.

Elements

a) Threat

The defendant must threaten or put pressure on the third party, and the courts distinguish between a threat and a warning.

b) Unlawful means or act

The threat must be of some unlawful means or act, which includes a crime, tort or breach of contract: *Rookes* v *Barnard* (above).

c) Submission to threat

The third party must submit to the defendant's threat.

d) Damage

The claimant must suffer damage.

e) Justification

It is unclear whether justification exists as a defence.

See *Godwin* v *Uzoigwe* [1993] Fam Law 65 for an example of this tort.

Interference with trade by unlawful means

This has only been recognised as a separate tort in *Merkur Island Shipping* v *Laughton* (above) and *Hadmor Productions* v *Hamilton* [1983] 1 AC 191; [1982] 2 WLR 322.

Unlawful means includes a crime, tort or breach of contract, but in *Lonrho* v *Shell Petroleum Co (No 2)* [1982] AC 173 the defendants were in breach of a penal statute and the breach interfered with the claimant's business, but the claimant could not recover. Also in *Chapman* v *Honig* [1963] 2 QB 502 it was held there was no action in tort in respect of a contempt of court, whereas in *Acrow v Rex Chainbelt* [1971] 1 WLR 1676 a contempt of court was held to be unlawful means when the claimant suffered loss thereby.

In *Lonrho plc v Fayed* [1989] 2 All ER 65 the Court of Appeal held that it was not an essential element that the predominant purpose was to injure the victim rather than to further the defendant's own interest. Nor was it necessary to prove the existence of a complete tort between the tortfeasor and the person against whom the wrong was committed. However, it was necessary to prove that the unlawful act was directed against the claimant or was intended to harm the claimant. In *Associated British Ports* v *Transport and General Workers Union* [1989] 1 WLR 939 it was suggested in the Court of Appeal that the defendant union was liable for causing its members to contravene regulations, even though the breach was not actionable by the employers and the union could not be liable for inducing a breach. It was the presence of an intent to injure the claimant which turned a non-actionable inducement of breach into unlawful means. This is difficult to reconcile with *Lonrho Ltd v Shell Petroleum Co (No 2)* (above), but this tort is still a developing area.

Immunity of statute

Note that many economic tort cases have concerned industrial action, and often there is statutory immunity from action in tort.

18.3 Key cases and statute

- *Crofter Hand Woven Harris Tweed Co Ltd* v *Veitch* [1942] AC 435
  No action would lie if there was no intent to injure the claimant's business

- *Law Debenture Trust Corporation* v *Ural Caspian Oil Corporation Ltd* [1993] 1 WLR 1221
  Provides a useful illustration of the tort of inducing a breach of contract

- *Lonrho Ltd* v *Shell Petroleum Co Ltd (No 2)* [1982] AC 173
  Reaffirmed the line of reasoning adopted in the *Mogul* case

- *Lonrho plc* v *Fayed* [1991] 3 WLR 188
  The tort of conspiracy must establish an intention to injure the claimant's business

- *Middlebrook Mushrooms Ltd* v *Transport and General Workers Union* [1993] ICR 612
  The court has the final say as to whether acts of inducement are tortious or not

- *Mogul Steamship Co Ltd* v *McGregor, Gow & Co* [1892] AC 25
  A conspiracy to injure is not actionable in the absence of an unlawful act

- *Yukong Lines Ltd of Korea* v *Rendsburg Investments Corporation of Liberia, The Rialto (No 2)* [1998] 4 All ER 82
  A lawful act, even if it is done by unlawful means, may not be actionable in tort if there is no intention to injure the claimant's business

- Fair Trading Act 1973 – governs some of the torts relating to unfair trading and anti-competition practices

18.4 Questions and suggested solutions

QUESTION ONE

Discuss the issues of tortious liability which arise in the following situations.

a) Ben and Clive were members of staff of the Downland University and are both keen researchers and have published many books and articles. The Higher Education Funding Council is conducting a research assessment exercise evaluating the research output over the past four years of members of staff in post in universities on 31 March 1996. In November 1995 Upmarket University offered Ben and Clive appointments with substantial financial inducements if they took up appointment there on 1 March. Unusually for a university contract (where the normal period of notice is three months) Ben and Clive had to give six months' notice, but they resigned from Downland and accepted appointments at Upmarket on 1 March. Their research output since 1992 is therefore attributed to Upmarket University, and Downland University has received a low research rating and its funding has been severely reduced.

b) Daphne owns several florists' shops. She obtains many of her supplies from a market garden owned by Edgar. She telephones Edgar each Friday to place her order for the coming week. Freda tells Daphne (correctly) that Edgar has a financial stake in a farm run by his brother, which exports live animals to the European continent. Daphne is very active on behalf of 'animal rights' and immediately notifies Edgar that she will take no more supplies from him.

University of London LLB Examination
(for External Students) Law of Tort June 1996 Q6

General Comment

Both of these questions ask the candidate to address torts within the sphere of unlawful interference with trade, in the context of specific situations. The first one calls for a discussion of the tort of inducing breach of contract, and the second one asks for a more thorough examination of the various component torts in this area.

Skeleton Solution

a) Inducing breach of contract – knowledge of existence of contract and intention to breach – inducement – breach caused loss – damage – justification.

b) Unlawful interference with trade – conspiracy – inducing breach of contract – intimidation.

Suggested Solution

a) At issue is whether Upmarket University, in luring Ben and Clive, has committed the tort of inducing breach of contract, and if so, what remedies are available to Downland University.

The tort of inducing or procuring breach of contract has its origins in the case of *Lumley* v *Gye* (1853) 2 E & B 216. It encompasses situations where the defendant – lacking any justification – persuades or offers inducement to a third party to breach their contract with the claimant, causing damage to the claimant; the defendant must have knowledge of the existence of the contract and intend for the breach to take place: *Merkur Island Shipping Corp* v *Laughton* [1983] 2 AC 570. For Upmarket to have committed the tort, each of these ingredients must be present.

Thus, Upmarket must have known of the existence of Ben and Clive's contracts of employment, and have intended that they be breached: *Merkur Island*. The fact that a contract of employment exists between these two and Downland is obvious; for Upmarket to have intended Ben and Clive to breach the agreement, it is necessary for Upmarket to know of its terms. In businesses where the standard terms of the contract are well known, constructive knowledge of the terms will be imputed to the defendant: per Neill LJ in *Middlebrook Mushrooms Ltd* v *Transport and General Workers Union* [1993] ICR 612 at 612.

We are told here that the customary notice period for an academic is three months, and that Ben and Clive's period of six months is exceptional. It is thus arguable that the only term of which Upmarket will have constructive knowledge is the usual three-month notice period; if Upmarket does not have actual knowledge of Ben and Clive's six-month period, then it will not have committed the tort, as it will not have intended them to breach their contracts.

Clearly, Ben and Clive have breached their contracts with Downland.

If Upmarket did have knowledge of the six-month period, it must next be proven that they used some degree of direct persuasion to convince Ben and Clive to breach their contracts with Downland: *Thomson* v *Deakin* [1952] Ch 646. This component has been manifestly established, given that we are told the two received substantial financial inducements.

Finally, Downland must have suffered damage as a result of the breach of contract for the tort to be made out: *Exchange Telegraph Co* v *Gregory & Co* [1896] 1 QB 147. The loss of funding due to Downland's poor rating, due to Ben and Clive's breach, would be sufficient for this purpose.

If Upmarket has committed the tort of inducing breach of contract, any attempt to raise justification – ie that it has some moral or legal right to procure the breach – as a defence would likely fail. Among the things which the court will assess when considering the applicability of this defence are the relative status of the defendant and claimant, and also the object of inducing the breach: *Glamorgan Coal Co* v *South*

Wales Miners' Federation [1903] 2 KB 545. It is most doubtful that the wealth of Upmarket, combined with its motives in these circumstances would afford them the defence of justification. Downland could thus claim from Upmarket all damages which flow from the breach, which may be higher than those for a simple breach of contract: *Lumley v Gye*. In this case, Downland would be able to recover the funding lost as a result of its poor research rating.

b) At question here is whether Daphne or Freda could be liable for the torts relating to unlawful interference with trade, which is to say the unlawful interference with the economic interests of another, other than by false representation: *Allen v Flood* [1898] AC 1. (We are told that Freda's comment is true, so there can be no grounds for any action based upon the tort of deceit, which deals with misrepresentations.) These include the torts of conspiracy, inducing breach of contract, and intimidation.

The tort of conspiracy involves either an agreement between two or more people to do an unlawful act, or to do a lawful act by unlawful means: *Mulcahy v R* (1868) LR 3 HL 306. The purpose behind such a conspiracy must be to damage the claimant's business: *Crofter Hand Woven Harris Tweed Co v Veitch* [1942] AC 435. In this case, there is no agreement between Daphne and Freda to do anything unlawful, so the tort of conspiracy has not been committed.

The fact that the relationship between Daphne and Edgar is not a contractual one, and that there is no evidence to suggest that Freda intended Daphne to discontinue this relationship, would imply that the tort of inducing breach of contract cannot be established on these facts.

The tort of intimidation involves the existence of an intention to injure the business of the claimant, combined with the existence of an unlawful threat, which could include a crime, tort or breach of contract: *Rookes v Barnard* [1964] AC 1129. While Daphne may have intended to injure Edgar's business by taking her business elsewhere, in the absence of a contract to the contrary this is not unlawful. Thus, she has not committed the tort of intimidation, as she is merely doing what in law she is entitled to do: *Ware and De Freville v Motor Trade Association* [1921] 3 KB 40.

It is therefore submitted that Edgar has no cause of action in tort against either Daphne or Freda.

QUESTION TWO

Conrad owns and manages a private college giving instruction in art and photography. Daisy, who had dropped out of a course at the college, gave a talk to a meeting of the League of Righteous Ladies describing how students had to pose naked and indecently in some of the classes. Emma and Florence who were at this talk resolved to do something about the situation at the college.

A few days after the talk Emma was told by Gordon, who rented rooms in her house, that he had applied to enrol at Conrad's college. Emma said to him, 'If you sign up to go to that college, you'll be out in the street, bag and baggage, before the day is out'. Gordon did not want to have to look for new lodgings and telephoned the college to withdraw his application.

Florence is employed by the education department of the local authority. Her job is to process applications for student grants. When students enquire whether grants are available for courses at Conrad's college, she tells them that the authority has resolved not to make any awards for courses there, although she knows that this is untrue. As a result some students decide not to apply to the college. Two students who had previously had grants for the first year of a course applied for renewal of their grants for the second year. Florence did not put these applications before the appropriate committee, but told the students that they had been turned down. The students had to withdraw from the college.

Advise Conrad whether he had any action in tort in respect of the conduct of Emma and Florence.

University of London LLB Examination
(for External Students) Law of Tort June 1988 Q4

General Comment

This question requires an analysis of the torts within the classification of unlawful interference with trade. Discussion must involve the torts of intimidation, inducement, conspiracy and malicious falsehood. The possible defence of justification should also be raised.

Skeleton Solution

Emma – intimidation – threat– unlawful means – breach of contract? – submission – damage – justification – interference with trade by unlawful means – Florence – malicious falsehood – false statement – malice – conspiracy – lawful or unlawful means? – justification.

Suggested Solution

Conrad may have a cause of action against Emma and Florence arising out of their activities. Although we are asked to advise Conrad whether he has a cause of action, in many cases it would be easier if the college were to be the claimant in any action because the activities of Emma and Florence were aimed against the college rather than against Conrad personally. As each incident raises different issues of legal principle we will deal with them separately.

The first issue relates to the conversation between Emma and Gordon. In threatening to throw Gordon out on the street Emma may have committed one of the economic torts against Conrad. It is unlikely to be the tort of inducing breach of contract (*Lumley* v *Gye* (1853) 2 El & Bl 216) because at the time of the conversation Gordon had only applied to go to the college and so there was no contract between Gordon and the college which Emma could seek to persuade Gordon to break. Nor is there a contract which Emma could interfere with.

Instead Conrad could argue that Emma has committed the tort of intimidation in its three party form. This tort was resurrected from obscurity in *Rookes* v *Barnard* [1964] AC 1129. This tort consists of a threat by the defendant against a third party that the defendant will use some unlawful means against the third party unless the third party does or refrains from doing some act which he is entitled to do and as a result the claimant suffers loss.

The first thing which must be established is that the defendant has threatened the third party. The courts formally distinguish between a threat and a warning; a threat being of an 'or else' kind. Here it seems clear that Emma has threatened Gordon. Secondly the threat must be of some unlawful act or means. Here the most likely unlawful means is breach of contract if Emma is threatening to throw Gordon out on to the street in breach of contract. In *Rookes* v *Barnard* (above) it was held by the House of Lords that breach of contract counts as unlawful means for the purposes of the tort of intimidation. Lord Devlin stated that a threat to breach a contract could be as coercive as a threat of violence and so must count as unlawful means. However if Emma is threatening to terminate Gordon's licence to occupy the premises lawfully then there will be no unlawful means and the tort will not have been committed.

Assuming the existence of unlawful means the third ingredient is submission to the threat by the third party. Again this is satisfied because Gordon has withdrawn his application. Fourthly the claimant must have suffered damage. Damage is the very gist of the action but the courts are generally willing to infer that the defendant's actions have caused loss to the claimant and do not require proof of particular damage. The problem here is that we do not know whether the college would have offered Gordon a place but in general it can be said that if people are dissuaded from applying to the college it must inevitably suffer damage.

Finally there may be a defence of justification. In *Rookes* Lord Devlin left open the question whether such a defence exists, but in *Morgan* v *Fry* [1968] 2 QB 710 Lord Denning suggested that such a defence does exist. Emma may argue that her threat was justified because of the fact that students had to pose naked and indecently in some of the classes and that she was justified in seeking to dissuade people from attending the college. In *Brimelow* v *Casson* [1924] 1 Ch 302, which was a case concerned with the tort of inducing breach of contract, it was held that the defendant union official was justified in inducing actresses to break their contracts of employment with the claimant because their wages were so low that they had to resort to prostitution to supplement their wages. So the court may be prepared to have regard to such moral issues and Emma may be able to succeed with the defence of justification. But it must be noted that we do not know whether these allegations are true because Emma was informed of them by a student who had dropped out of the college and who may have had a grudge against the college. If the allegations are untrue Emma will not be able to rely on the defence of justification.

Second, Conrad could argue that Emma had committed the tort of interference with trade or business by unlawful means. Such a tort has been recognised on a number of occasions; most recently by the House of Lords in *Hadmor Productions* v *Hamilton* [1983] 1 AC 191; [1982] 2 WLR 322 and *Merkur Island Shipping Corp* v *Laughton* [1983] 2 AC 570. See also the Court of Appeal decision in *Lonrho plc* v *Fayed* [1989] 2 All ER 65. It is clear that there has been an interference with Conrad's business because Gordon has been persuaded to withdraw his application to attend the college. The problem is in establishing the existence of unlawful means. Once again the unlawful means could only consist of a threat by Emma to break her contract with Gordon unless he withdraws his application and again it is clear that breach of contract counts as unlawful means.

In relation to Florence it could be said that she has committed the tort of malicious falsehood in telling students that the authority has decided not to make any grant awards for courses there even though she knows that this is untrue. Malicious falsehood (sometimes referred to as injurious falsehood) consists of the making of a false statement, with malice, to a person other than the claimant, with the result that the claimant suffers damage. The false statement must be a statement of fact and this is clearly satisfied here. Conrad will have to prove that Florence made the statement maliciously; that is that she acted out of spite or a desire to injure the claimant. Here Florence knows that the statement is false and she has made the statement in order to inflict injury on the college and so it is submitted that Conrad will be able to prove that Florence was actuated by malice: *Greers Ltd* v *Pearman & Corder Ltd* (1922) 39 RPC 406. Finally Conrad must show that he has suffered damage as a result of Florence's statement and this should be satisfied because we are told that as a result of her information students have not applied to the college. Generally Conrad must show that he has suffered special damage but this can be satisfied by showing that he has suffered a general loss of business as a result of Florence's false statement: *Ratcliffe* v *Evans* [1892] 2 QB 524. Section 3 of the Defamation Act 1952 may apply if Florence has informed the students in writing or other permanent form. The effect of the application of s3 would be to dispense with the need to prove special damage. Alternatively Conrad may wish to use the tort of malicious falsehood as the unlawful means for the purposes of the tort of interference with trade or business by unlawful means.

In relation to the two students who have had to withdraw their applications, if the students were contractually obliged to return to the college then Conrad may have an action against Florence for inducing the students to break their contracts with the college. It could be argued that she has committed the tort by preventing performance of the contract taking place by some other direct and unlawful means (that is other than by persuasion). This is analogous to the example cited by Jenkins LJ in *DC Thomson* v *Deakin* [1952] Ch 646 of a defendant wrongfully taking the contracting party's tools so that he was unable to carry out his contractual obligations. It is essential to note that unlawful means is essential to this branch of the tort and here the unlawful means would have to consist of her failure to put the grant applications before the appropriate committee (this could be unlawful means if the students were contractually or statutorily entitled to have their applications considered).

Finally Conrad may have an action against Emma and Florence in the tort of conspiracy. We are told that they 'resolved to do something about the situation at the college'. To establish the existence of this tort it must be shown that there was a combination between Emma and Florence. This will no doubt arise because of the fact that they have resolved to do something about the situation. So although they carry out the acts separately it is likely that there will be a conspiracy because they have a common aim. The only issue is whether this is lawful means conspiracy or unlawful means conspiracy. In this connection it is important to note that it is unclear whether breach of contract constitutes unlawful means (the point was left open in *Rookes* v *Barnard* (above)), although the malicious falsehood would certainly count as unlawful means: *Sorrell* v *Smith* [1925] AC 700. The distinction is important in this connection because there is a much wider role for the defence of justification in the lawful means conspiracy then there is in unlawful means conspiracy: see *Crofter Hand Woven Harris Tweed Co Ltd* v *Veitch* [1942] AC 435. If it was held to be lawful means conspiracy they would probably be able to justify their acts but if, as is more likely, it is held to be unlawful means conspiracy then the success of the defence will depend upon the issues we considered above in relation to *Brimelow* v *Casson*.

Finally the remedies which may be open to Conrad are injunctions to restrain the commission of these torts in the future and damages for any losses sustained as a result of the torts committed by Emma and Florence.

QUESTION THREE

Catherine runs a highly successful catering business, which has attracted much custom away from older-established businesses run by Dora and Emma. Catherine made an exclusive contract with Fergus under which he was to supply fresh fruit and vegetables to her business as required. Catherine won an important order to provide the lunch for a business convention. She placed orders with Fergus, including one for papaya which the organisers had specifically requested. Dora told Fergus correctly that six South African businessmen were to be attending the lunch and was not surprised that Fergus (who is secretary of a local anti-apartheid group) refused to carry out the order. Dora and Emma also bought up all the available supplies of papaya. Catherine was obliged to make special arrangements at considerable expense to fly in papaya from Malaysia for the luncheon; she was able to procure other fruit and vegetables locally, although some were of inferior quality.

Advise Catherine whether she has any cause of action against Dora or Emma.

University of London LLB Examination
(for External Students) Law of Tort June 1987 Q5

General Comment

A question requiring discussion of unlawful acts of interference with trade. Analysis of the tort of conspiracy by unlawful means is also relevant, as is the defence of justification.

Skeleton Solution

Catherine's initial act fair competition – direct intervention by Dora – direct – breach or interference? – justification – purchase of papaya – indirect form of tort – no unlawful means – conspiracy – justification.

Suggested Solution

Catherine has won customers from Dora and Emma by fair competition and the latter have no lawful cause of complaint arising out of the fact that they have lost customers to Catherine. Catherine has now suffered loss as a result of the refusal of Fergus to deliver the order and because of the fact that Dora and Emma have bought up all the available supplies of papaya. As these two issues raise different legal points we will deal with them separately.

Dora has 'told' Fergus correctly that six South African businessmen would be attending the lunch and as a result Fergus has refused to carry out the order. Catherine may have a cause of action against Dora for the tort of inducing breach of contract. The form of the tort which is alleged to have been committed is the direct form of the tort. The direct form of the tort is committed when a person directly persuades one of the contracting parties to break his contract with the claimant: see *D C Thomson & Co Ltd v Deakin* [1952] Ch 646. Dora may argue that she did not attempt to persuade Fergus but that she merely 'told' him correctly who would be attending the lunch. It is true that the courts do formally draw a distinction between persuasion and the mere giving of advice, but in *Square Grip Reinforcement Co Ltd v MacDonald* 1968 SLT 65 Lord Milligan held that where the party who conveys the information was desperately anxious to achieve a particular result then the court was likely to interpret such a suggestion as constituting persuasion. Applying this test here, Fergus was the secretary of the local anti-apartheid group and so Dora must have known that the likely effect of her telling Fred that South Africans were to be at the lunch would be that he would refuse to carry out the order with Catherine. Given that Dora seems to be intent upon securing revenge against Catherine for taking her customers away, it is likely to be the case that Dora was desperately anxious that Fergus breach his contract with Catherine. So it would appear that the persuasion element is satisfied.

Catherine must also show that Dora acted with the requisite knowledge and intention; that is, she intended that a breach of contract would ensue as a result of her information or that she was reckless as to whether or not a contract would be breached: *Emerald Construction Co v Lowthian* [1966] 1 WLR 691. It is likely that she would intend to breach the contract because she appeared to know that Fergus was supplying the order for the lunch.

Third, Catherine must show that a breach of contract ensued as a result of the persuasion by Dora. Fergus was, however, to supply fruit and vegetables 'as required'. It is therefore unclear what the nature of the relationship was between Fergus and Catherine. It may have been that there was a long term contract between them or it may have been that there was a separate contract between them each time that Catherine ordered the goods. Whatever the precise nature of their contractual relationship, it is submitted that the fact that Catherine had 'placed an order' with Fergus indicates that there was a contractual relationship between them and so there was a breach of contract induced. Had it been the case that there was no breach, but only an interference with the contract, then it would have been difficult for Catherine to succeed with her action because it is uncertain whether the tort of interference with contractual relations extends to the direct form of the tort due to the lack of unlawful means. In *Torquay Hotel Co Ltd* v *Cousins* [1969] 2 Ch 106 Lord Denning did appear to say that the tort of interference with contractual relations could be committed in its direct form, but in *Merkur Island Shipping Corp* v *Laughton* [1983] 2 AC 570 Lord Diplock interpreted Lord Denning's judgment as referring to the indirect form of the tort. It is submitted that the latter interpretation is the one which is generally accepted as being part of English law, so that if it was the case that there had been no breach then it is unlikely that Dora would have committed any tort.

Fourth, Catherine must show that she has suffered damage as a result of the breach. This she clearly has because she was unable to secure her usual supply of vegetables and so she has supplied the diners with vegetables of an inferior quality. However Dora could argue that Catherine has suffered no loss because Fergus would have been unable to perform the contract anyway because she and Emma had bought up all the available supplies of papaya. Although this may be true in relation to the papaya, there is no suggestion that the contract with Fergus was confined to the supply of papaya so that, in so far as Fergus would otherwise have delivered other fruit and vegetables to Catherine, Catherine would be able to show that she had suffered damage. Finally it must be shown that there was no justification for the action of Dora. Dora is likely to argue that her action was justified because apartheid is contrary to public policy as are dinners to which supporters of such a regime are invited. However, the defence of justification is of uncertain ambit in this tort. The only case in which the defence has succeeded is *Brimelow* v *Casson* [1924] 1 Ch 302 where the employees' wages were so low that they were compelled to resort to prostitution to supplement their wages. It was held that this exceptional fact was sufficient to justify the defendant's action in inducing the employees to break their contracts of employment. However in *Greig* v *Insole* [1978] 1 WLR 302 it was held that the pursuit of altruistic goals did not constitute a justification for inducing another to breach his contract. Therefore Catherine may have a cause of action against Dora for inducing a breach of her contract with Fergus.

Catherine may also have a cause of action against Dora and Emma for buying up all the papaya so that Fergus was unable to perform his contract with her. Here two causes of actions may lie. The first is the tort of inducement of breach of contract. In this instance it would be by preventing the performance of the contract taking place by some direct means other than persuading Fergus not to perform the contract. One example given by Jenkins LJ in *Thomson v Deakin* was of a defendant taking the employee's tools so that the employee was unable to carry out his contract with his employer. In this version of the tort it must be shown that the defendants used unlawful means in preventing Fergus from performing his contractual obligations. Dora and Emma achieved their aim by buying up all the available papaya on the market; they achieved their aim by lawful means and so no action would lie against them for the tort of inducing breach of contract.

An action may, however, lie against them in the tort of conspiracy. The tort of conspiracy consists of two distinct branches; conspiracy to commit an unlawful act and conspiracy to do an act which, if done by an individual would not be actionable, but which becomes actionable by virtue of the fact that it is done in combination. Here we are concerned with the second of these two branches. There is a combination between Emma and Dora and Catherine suffers damage as a result of their combination so these elements of the tort are satisfied. To succeed in this form of the tort it must be shown that Dora and Emma acted with the predominant purpose of inflicting damage upon Catherine, *Lonrho plc v Fayed* [1991] 3 All ER 303. In the case of *Crofter Hand Woven Harris Tweed Co Ltd v Veitch* [1942] AC 435 it was held that pursuit of self interest constituted a justification for this form of the tort. The difficulty here is that Dora and Emma do not appear to have acted out of self interest but out of a desire to inflict damage upon Catherine. They could, however, seek to argue that their purpose was the pursuit of self interest in that they were simply buying up products for their own businesses. Alternatively Dora and Emma could argue that their real aim was to protest against apartheid. In *Scala Ballroom (Wolverhampton) Ltd v Ratcliffe* [1958] 1 WLR 1057 it was held that a refusal by union members to play at a ballroom which operated a colour bar was justified. The difficulty for Dora and Emma is, however, to show that their real aim was to protest against apartheid and not to inflict damage upon Catherine. Therefore it is submitted that Dora and Emma have committed the tort of conspiracy for which they will be liable in damages to Catherine.

Therefore Catherine will be able to recover the loss which she has suffered as a result of the torts committed by Dora and Emma. She will be able to recover the expense which she incurred in flying in the papayas because Dora and Emma had bought up all the local supplies. Catherine had been specifically asked to provide papaya for the meal and so it was reasonable for her to fly in papaya from Malaysia. Both Dora and Emma knew that Catherine needed the papaya so they could not argue that the loss was too remote. Catherine can also recover for the loss which she has suffered as a result of the provision of inferior vegetables.

QUESTION FOUR

Anne, Betty, Christine, and David are members of the Blackhill Common committee, whose aim is to prevent the planned building of an American nuclear missile base at

Blackhill Common. Anne, Betty and Christine are morally opposed to the use of nuclear weapons and their presence anywhere in Britain. David is a building contractor in the town of Lymeswold near to an alternative site for the base, who hopes to secure lucrative building contracts if the base cannot be built at Blackhill Common and so is sited near Lymeswold.

The committee learns that Michael has a contract with the Ministry of Defence to carry out building work at Blackhill Common and resolve to disrupt the contract by the following methods.

a) Anne informs Norman who has put in a bid to supply Michael with bricks that, if he does not withdraw the bid, the Committee will ensure that all local authorities opposed to nuclear weapons will be told of his involvement so that they will not deal with him in the future.

b) David offers Oliver, who has been engaged by Michael to survey the Blackhill Common site, a large sum of money if he does not carry out the survey.

Norman withdraws his bid and Oliver agrees not to carry out the survey. As a result Michael is not able to do work on time and the contract is terminated by the Ministry of Defence.

Advise Michael.

Written by the Author

General Comment

This question requires candidates to address torts within the sphere of unlawful interference with trade, particularly the torts of conspiracy, inducing breach of contract and intimidation, as well as conspiracy to injure by unlawful means.

Skeleton Solution

Conspiracy agreement – intention to injure – interference with trade – consequential loss – inducement – is there a contract existing? – interference with trade by unlawful means – intimidation – consequential loss – conspiracy to injure by unlawful means.

Suggested Solution

Michael will bring actions against the various defendants with the area of economic torts.

The committee's resolution to disrupt the contract may involve a conspiracy to injure and here Michael will sue Anne, Betty and Christine and David. He must prove an agreement of two or more persons to do an unlawful act or a lawful act by unlawful means (and one conspirator alone may be found liable in tort). Where unlawful means are not used, the court must consider the motive of the conspirators in order to ascertain whether they desired to injure the claimant, or whether their predominant interest was, for example, to protect their business interests: *Lonrho Ltd v Shell Petroleum Co (No 2)* [1982] AC 173; *Lonrho plc v Fayed* [1991] 3 All ER 303. In *Crofter Hand Woven Harris Tweed v Veitch* [1942] AC 435 there was no conspiracy where trade unionists sought to improve terms and conditions of employment in tweed mills, rather than to injure the claimant.

In Michael's case, the defendants may argue that their predominant purpose was a political and moral one, rather than the desire to cause injury to him. However, the object of the defendants may also be said to be the disruption of Michael's contract, so that the conspiracy becomes one of unlawful means; if injury has, as a result, been caused to Michael, then the tort has been committed. The motive or object of the defendants then becomes irrelevant. It is submitted that this is perhaps the preferable argument since the outcome of the agreement is the decision to interfere with Michael's contract and, as Michael's contract is eventually terminated, he has suffered loss as a result. The four conspirators may then be jointly and severally liable to Michael for the resulting financial loss. The only defence which they could raise may be justification, but this usually only applies to the protection of business interests (*Mogul Steamship Co v MacGregor, Gow & Co* [1892] AC 25) or working conditions, so the defence would be unlikely to succeed.

When Anne succeeds in inducing Norman to withdraw his bid, no contract has as yet been made between Norman and Michael, so that she cannot be liable for inducing a breach of their contract. Michael must therefore rely on the tort of interference with trade by unlawful means, which has received recent support in decisions such as *Merkur Island Shipping v Laughton* [1983] AC 570 and *Hadmor Productions v Hamilton* [1983] 1 AC 191. In *Lonrho plc v Fayed* [1989] 2 All ER 65 the Court of Appeal held that it was not an essential element of this tort that the predominant purpose was to injure the victim rather than further the tortfeasor's interest, nor was it necessary to prove a complete tort between the tortfeasor and the person against whom the tort was committed. The problem in Michael's case is in showing the existence of unlawful means; Anne has used a threat against Norman but it is a threat to pass on true information to local authorities. However, in *Square Grip Reinforcement v MacDonald* 1968 SLT 65, Lord Milligan held that where a person who conveys information was desperately anxious to achieve a particular result hten the court was likely to interpret the conveyancing of this information as persuasion. But even if such persuasion is proved it is merely a threat to interfere with contracts which have not yet been contemplated.

Because of the above difficulties, Michael may wish to bring an action against Anne in intimidation. This involves putting pressure on a person to do something which he would not otherwise do, and it incorporates the idea of an unpleasant sanction. Anne must also have threatened unlawful means such as a criminal or tortious act, or the breach of a contract (*Rookes v Barnard* [1964] AC 1129), and there will be no intimidation if the act threatened is legal and one which the defendant has a right to do. Michael's case is one of three-party intimidation, since Anne has threatened Norman to the detriment of Michael. Again, the problem is in proving the use of unlawful means; since the threat does not involve a breach of an existing contract, and does not involve any other unlawful act, Michael would not have a good case in intimidation, and therefore would not benefit in bringing an action against Anne individually.

Oliver, on the other hand, does have a valid and existing contract with Michael, and David, by offering him money not to carry out the survey, has induced Oliver to breach his contract with Michael. A distinction was drawn by Lord Denning in *Torquay Hotel Co v Cousins* [1969] 2 Ch 106 between direct and indirect interference of contractual relations, and Michael's case involves direct interference since David has induced a breach of contract: *Lumley v Gye* (1853) 2 El & Bl 216. In accordance with other criteria laid down by Slade J in *Greig v Insole* [1978] 1 WLR 302 David must be shown to have knowledge of the contract (though not its exact terms) and the intention to interfere with it. Michael must prove that as a result he has suffered special damage and he must rebut any defence of justification put forward by the defendants; for example, they may rely on the fact that they are ultimately acting out of a moral and political aim. This defence rarely succeeds, and usually applies where the contract itself is unlawful: *De Francesco v Barnum* (1890) LR 45 Ch D 430.

Michael, therefore, has a good case against David and against all four defendants as conspirators to injure him. It should be pointed out, however, that in cases where there is a conspiracy to injure by unlawful means, the claimant gains little benefit from pleading conspiracy and may prefer to concentrate on the substantive tort which has been committed, thus Michael may wish to bring an action against David alone.

QUESTION FIVE

The Outrageous Fellowship is a religious sect. It recruits young people into its missionary work; they are encouraged to cut themselves off from their families and careers. Emily, who is sympathetic to the Fellowship's aims, has sold to its representatives in England an option to purchase for a very low price her country estate in a quiet location as possible headquarters. Emily's nephew, Frank, a road haulier, dislikes the proposed arrangement. Giles lives nearby. His daughter joined the Fellowship six years ago and has not been in touch with her parents since. Frank and Giles are determined that the Fellowship will not establish itself in the locality. They have learned that officials of the Fellowship will soon be visiting from the USA to inspect possible sites.

Advise Frank and Giles on the legality of these possible proposed actions:

a) Giles will visit Emily, tell her about his daughter and try to persuade her to cancel the option;

b) Frank and Giles will arrange that during the inspection they and their friends and Frank's drivers will drive their cars and lorries at high speed along the neighbouring roads, which are subject to a speed limit, in the hope that the Fellowship will have to purchase another estate at the normal market rate.

University of London LLB Examination
(for External Students) Law of Tort June 1992 Q5

General Comment

This question requires an analysis of the torts of unlawful interference with trade and the possible defences.

Skeleton Solution

Introduction – inducing breach of contract – elements of the tort – defences – interfering with business by unlawful means – conspiracy – elements of the tort.

Suggested Solution

This problem concerns the economic torts. Emily has sold an option to purchase her country estate to the Outrageous Fellowship. Giles and Frank wish her to break that contract and they will try to dissuade the Fellowship from taking advantage of the sale.

Firstly, Giles will visit Emily and tell her about his daughter's indoctrination in the hope of persuading her to break the contract. This is the tort of inducing breach of contract, which has its origins in the case of *Lumley* v *Gye* (1853) 2 El & Bl 216. In that case the claimant, a theatre owner, contracted with an opera singer, Johanna Wagner, to perform exclusively in his theatre. The defendant, a rival theatre owner, 'enticed and persuaded' her to break the contract. The aim of the tort is to protect contractual relations.

Will Giles commit the tort? We are told he will try to persuade Emily. In *DC Thomson & Co Ltd* v *Deakin* [1952] Ch 646, it was held that a distinction may be drawn between persuasion and advice in the sense of 'a mere statement of, or drawing of the attention of the party addressed to, the state of facts as they are'; the latter not being actionable. This is a difficult distinction. In Giles's terms, it means that a revelatory statement of facts which causes Emily to recant would not be tortious. However, if the advice is intended to have persuasive effect then it is more than mere advice. Therefore, it seems likely Giles will be liable under that head.

Giles must have knowledge of the contract between Emily and the Fellowship – although he need not know of every detail: *Emerald Construction Co Ltd* v *Lowthian* [1966] 1 WLR 691. There must also be intention to break the contract. It is not a defence for Giles to say his intention is in fact to expose the Fellowship as a sham. While that may be his overriding purpose, his immediate intention is to break Emily's contract (eg *Lonrho plc* v *Fayed* [1989] 2 All ER 65). Giles must, for this tort, interfere with a subsisting contract. However, if Emily, under the contract, had an option to terminate which she exercised, albeit upon Giles's advice given by lawful means, then it is argued that there would be no liability. In *Torquay Hotel Co Ltd* v *Cousins* [1969] 2 Ch 106, Lord Denning MR talked of liability where a 'third person prevents or hinders one party from performing his contract, even though it be not a breach'. The distinction is the use of lawful means. Finally, on this tort, the Fellowship must suffer loss through the breach. Without damage, the action fails.

Giles, if sued, would wish to raise the defence of justification, saying that he was under a moral obligation: *Brimelow* v *Casson* [1924] 1 Ch 302. However, this is not a strong defence, despite Giles's honest intentions.

Second, Frank and Giles plan to drive lorries at high speed along the neighbouring roads and this may give rise to an action for interference with business by unlawful means: *Merkur Island Shipping Corp* v *Laughton* [1983] 2 AC 570 and *Lonrho plc* v *Fayed* (above). We are told of Frank and Giles's intention and also that there is a speed limit on the roads. However, this branch of the economic torts is less well-developed. While it seems logical that a proprietary right – such as the Fellowship has – should be protected, it is not clear if this is covered by this tort.

Their actions could also give rise to an action for conspiracy. A definition of this tort is provided by Willes J in *Mulcahy* v *R* (1868) LR 3 HL 306: 'A conspiracy consists not merely in the intention of two or more, but in the agreement of two or more to do an unlawful act, or to do a lawful act by unlawful means'. Frank and Giles's plan falls into the first category.

They satisfy the three elements of the tort: firstly, there are two of them. Second, there is a 'combination' between them for a common purpose. Thirdly, there must be damage to the claimant – which can be measured by the additional expense the Fellowship will be put to. It is an unlawful means conspiracy, because they intend to break the law (as, for example, *Lonrho Ltd* v *Shell Petroleum Co (No 2)* [1982] AC 173). They may also be trespassing on the highway, and a conspiracy to commit a tort can constitute unlawful means: *Sorrell* v *Smith* [1925] AC 700.

It is suggested, therefore, that both proposed actions could be tortious and could result in Frank and Giles being sued by the Fellowship.

Chapter 19

Remedies

19.1 Introduction

19.2 Key points

19.3 Key cases and statutes

19.4 Questions and suggested solutions

19.1 Introduction

The general remedies available are damages, injunctions and self-help. Of these damages is the most important remedy and we shall concentrate on this. The Damages Act 1996 was passed to give a statutory footing to certain forms of damages.

19.2 Key points

Types of damages

The general principle is to put the claimant in the position he would have been in had the tort not been committed, in so far as this can be done by money, ie it is to compensate the claimant and not to punish the defendant.

Nominal damages

Show that the claimant's rights have been infringed, but that he has suffered no loss.

Contemptuous damages

Usually one penny and show that the action should not have been brought. Often the claimant, despite winning the case, will not get his costs and may even have to pay the defendant's costs.

General damages

Damage which the law presumes to follow from the tort in question, eg pain and suffering following personal injury. Need not be quantified in the statement of claim.

Special damages

Capable of being calculated exactly and must be pleaded, eg loss of earnings.

Special damage

This is the actual loss which must be proved if the tort is not actionable per se.

Aggravated damages

Take into account the claimant's injured feelings, although they should be moderate: *Archer* v *Brown* [1985] QB 401 and are not usually awarded in negligence cases: *Kralj* v *McGrath* [1986] 1 All ER 54; *AB* v *South West Water Services Ltd* [1993] 1 All ER 609.

The case of *Khodaparast* v *Shad* [2000] 1 All ER 545 provides a useful illustration of the award of aggravated damages for malicious falsehood.

Exemplary damages

According to *Rookes* v *Barnard* [1964] AC 1129 and *Cassell* v *Broome* [1972] AC 1027 they are only awarded where:

a) there has been an oppressive, arbitrary or unconstitutional act by a servant of the government (eg *Holden* v *Chief Constable of Lancashire* [1987] QB 380; *Bradford Metropolitan City Council* v *Arora* [1991] 3 All ER 545);

b) the defendant has calculated that he will make a profit despite paying damages (*Cassell* v *Broome* (above));

c) authorised by statute.

Even where these first two criteria are satisfied, exemplary damages are only awarded for torts for which such an award could have been made in 1964: *AB* v *South West Water Services Ltd* (above). The House of Lords in *Kuddus* v *Chief Constable of Leicestershire Constabulary* [2001] 3 All ER 193 awarded exemplary damages for misfeasance in public office.

Prospective damages

Damages must take into account future loss as well as damage already suffered, since only one action may arise from the same cause of action: *Fitter* v *Veal* (1701) 12 Mod 542, and this rule also applies to claims settled out of court: *O'Boyle* v *Leiper* (1990) The Times 26 June. Successive actions will only lie for continuing torts (eg trespass to land) or where the facts do give rise to more than one cause of action: *Brunsden* v *Humphrey* (1884) 14 QBD 141.

Damages for personal injury

These damages fall into two categories – pecuniary loss and non-pecuniary loss: we'll deal first with pecuniary loss.

Loss of earnings

The claimant can claim for loss of earnings to date of trial and for loss of future earnings. Calculation of the former is straightforward. For the latter the court calculates the claimant's net annual loss, the multiplicand, and multiplies that by a figure based on the number of years the loss is likely to last, the multiplier. In this respect, see the case of *Herring v Ministry of Defence* [2004] 1 All ER 44 where the court discussed the approach to calculating future loss of earnings.

The multiplicand is found by taking gross earnings, allowing for increases in pay and promotion then deducting tax and social security contributions. The multiplier is not the duration of the disability, but a lower figure with a maximum of around 18, to take into account the 'general vicissitudes of life' and because the claimant has received money as a lump sum rather than over a period of years.

Note that damages cannot be awarded as periodical payments, except where both parties consent: *Burke v Tower Hamlets Health Authority* (1989) The Times 10 August, although s32A Supreme Court Act 1981 allows a provisional award to be made, even if there is a dispute between the parties as to the total award: *Hurditch v Sheffield Health Authority* [1989] 2 All ER 869. Note the restricted interpretation given to s32A in *Willson v Ministry of Defence* [1991] 1 All ER 638.

In *Kelly v Dawes* (1990) The Times 27 September a settlement was allowed in which the defendants invested part of the sum payable to the claimant in an annuity which provided the claimant with an index-linked annual sum for the rest of her life. A recent example where the courts have calculated damages in respect of personal injury is *Cooke v United Bristol Healthcare NHS Trust; Sheppard v Stibbe; Page v Lee* [2004] 1 All ER 797.

Lost years

That is, where the claimant has a reduced expectation of life. In *Pickett v British Rail Engineering* [1980] AC 136 the House of Lords allowed recovery for the lost years, although sums which the claimant would have spent exclusively on himself must be deducted: *Harris v Empress Motors* [1983] 3 All ER 561.

For very young claimants no award is likely because the process is too speculative: *Croke v Wiseman* [1981] 3 All ER 852.

Potential loss of earning capacity

The claimant may keep his pre-accident employment but run the risk that if he loses that job he will be at a disadvantage in the labour market: *Moeliker v Reyrolle* [1977] 1 All ER 9; *Smith v Manchester Corporation* (1974) 17 KIR 1.

Loss of pension rights

May accompany future loss of earnings.

Loss of housekeeping, DIY, etc, capacity

In *Daly* v *General Steam Navigation* [1980] 3 All ER 696, the claimant was not able to perform all her housekeeping duties, and it was held that she could recover the cost of domestic help. See also *Willson* (above).

Medical expenses

The claimant can recover private medical expenses despite the fact that treatment could be provided by the NHS: s2(4) Law Reform (Personal Injuries) Act 1948.

If the claimant is cared for by a member of his family, a realistic sum will be awarded in respect of that care: *Housecroft* v *Burnett* [1986] 1 All ER 332, although not where the services are rendered by the tortfeasor: *Hunt* v *Severs* [1994] 2 All ER 385.

Deductions

Loss of earnings may be made up from various sources. Section 82 Social Security Administration Act 1992 provides no payment shall be made for any personal injury unless the compensator obtains a certificate from the Secretary of State giving the benefits paid or likely to be paid in the five years from the accident. The compensator deducts this sum and gives the victim a certificate of deduction; the compensator then pays this deducted amount to the Secretary of State to reimburse the State. This applies to injuries suffered after 1 January 1989 and its precursor came into force on 3 September 1990. It does not apply to payments under the Fatal Accidents Act 1976 or to payments below £2,500. For accidents prior to 1 January 1989 s2 Law Reform (Personal Injuries) Act 1948 requires one-half social security benefits to be deducted from the damages and for this deduction to cease after five years; there is no reimbursement of deductions to the State.

For other benefits, the general rule is that a benefit is deducted where it truly reduces the loss suffered: *Parry* v *Cleaver* [1970] AC 1. Thus wages or sick pay are deducted, but not insurance sums: *Bradburn* v *Great Western Railway* (1874) LR10 Ex 1, nor charitable donations, nor ill-health awards nor higher pension benefits: *Smoker* v *London Fire and Civil Defence Authority* [1991] 2 All ER 449. Where the employer insures his employees, deduction of these insurance benefits depends on whether the benefits are a continuation of salary and thus in the nature of earnings: *Hussain* v *New Taplow Paper Mills* [1988] 2 WLR 266, or whether they are pure insurance benefits: *McCamley* v *Cammell Laird Shipbuilders* [1990] 1 All ER 854.

Similarly, a redundancy payment will be deducted where it is unlikely that the claimant would have been offered redundancy but for the accident: *Colledge* v *Bass Mitchells & Butlers* [1988] 1 All ER 536. See also *Wadey* v *Surrey County Council* [1999] 2 All ER 334 for an example.

The House of Lords in *Wisely* v *John Fulton (Plumbers) Ltd* [2000] 2 All ER 545 held that benefits received from the state must be disregarded in calculating interest.

Other pecuniary loss

For example, loss of ability to carry out a profitable hobby (see also *Meah* v *McCreamer* [1985] 1 All ER 367).

Where personal injuries result in divorce it is not clear whether the financial consequences of the divorce are recoverable: *Jones* v *Jones* [1985] QB 704 allowed recovery; *Pritchard* v *Cobden* [1988] Fam 22 did not. The Damages (Personal Injury) Order 2001, made under s1 of the Damages Act 1996, prescribes 2.5 per cent as the rate of return which courts are required to take into account when calculating damages for future pecuniary loss in an action for personal injury.

Hardwick v *Hudson* [1999] 3 All ER 426 provides an example of how the court calculated pecuniary loss.

Non-pecuniary loss

Pain and suffering

Recoverable, but not if the claimant is in a coma: *Wise* v *Kaye* [1962] 1 QB 638. This pain and suffering does not include sorrow or grief unless it amounts to nervous shock: *Kralj* v *McGrath* (above); *AB* v *South West Water Services* (above). In *Re The Herald of Free Enterprise* (1989) The Guardian 2 May it was held that post traumatic stress disorder and pathological grief which is in excess of normal grief are recognised psychiatric illnesses for which compensation can be awarded. This head of damages may also include a sum for loss of congenial employment ie loss of job satisfaction: *Champion* v *London Fire Authority* (1990) The Times 5 July.

Note s1(1)(b) Administration of Justice Act 1982 requires the court to take into account any suffering caused to the claimant by his awareness that his expectation of life has been reduced.

In *Heil* v *Rankin* [2000] 3 All ER 138, the Court of Appeal applied modest increases in calculating pain and suffering.

Loss of amenity

That is, loss of ability to engage in pre-accident activities. May be awarded even if the claimant is unaware of the loss: *West* v *Shepherd* [1964] AC 326; *Lim Poh Choo* v *Camden & Islington Area Health Authority* [1980] AC 174.

Loss of expectation of life

Abolished by s1(1) Administration of Justice Act 1982, and replaced by a statutory sum (£7,500 as from 1 April 1991) for bereavement for loss of spouse or child: see *Doleman* v *Deakin* (1990) The Times 30 January.

Injury itself

There is a tariff for loss of limbs or faculties; awards are tabulated in Kemp and Kemp *The Quantum of Damages* (Tolley's Practitioner Series, 2003) which helps to bring some consistency.

Interest

By s35A Supreme Court Act 1981 interest must be awarded for death or personal injury. It can only be claimed for losses to date of trial.

Pecuniary loss: one-half short term interest rate from date of accident to date of trial: *Jefford* v *Gee* [1970] 2 QB 130; *Cookson* v *Knowles* [1979] AC 556.

Non-pecuniary loss: 2 per cent from date of service of writ to date of trial: *Wright* v *British Railways Board* [1983] 2 AC 773.

In addition, every judgment debt carries interest from the date of judgment until payment: s17 Judgments Act 1838 and see *Thomas* v *Bunn* [1991] 2 WLR 27.

Death and tort

Two actions arise on death.

a) By s1(1) Law Reform (Miscellaneous Provisions) Act 1934 all causes vesting in the deceased survive for the benefit of his estate, ie the estate may sue the defendant.

   The case of *Cox* v *Hockenhull* [1999] 3 All ER 577 provides a useful example of this.

b) Under the Fatal Accidents Act 1976, dependants of the deceased may sue. The dependency must be calculated ie earnings less deceased's personal and living expenses and the multiplier is calculated as above. The chance of the widow remarrying or any benefits accruing as a result of the death are to be ignored but not the chance of divorce: *Martin* v *Owen* [1992] PIQR Q151: benefits include a pension and widow's allowance from an employer's pension fund payable on the death of the husband and are thus to be disregarded: *Pidduck* v *Eastern Scottish Omnibuses* [1990] 2 All ER 69.

   In *Jameson* v *Central Electricity Generating Board* [1999] 1 All ER 193 the House of Lords decided that the settlement of the deceased's claim before his death defeated a claim on behalf of his dependants under s1(1) of the FAA 1976.

   If a relative gives up employment to care for orphaned children, a claim may be made under the 1976 Act for the relative's loss of earnings: *Cresswell* v *Eaton* [1991] 1 All ER 484. See also *Watson* v *Willmot* [1991] 1 All ER 473 for the dependency of orphans.

Damage to property

Again the claimant must be put in the position as if the damage had not occurred: see *Swingcastle* v *Alastair Gibson* [1991] 2 All ER 353 for an example of this rule.

If goods are damaged, damages equal the loss in value: *The London Corporation* [1935] P 70. If goods are destroyed, damages equal market value at time of destruction: *The Liesbosch Dredger* v *SS Edison* [1933] AC 449; *BBMB Finance (Hong Kong)* v *Eda Holdings* [1991] 2 All ER 129.

If the goods were used to generate profits, damages equal loss of profit or cost of hire of substitute: *Martindale* v *Duncan* [1973] 1 WLR 574.

If business premises and machinery are destroyed, damages equal cost of new premises and replacement of machinery (not the acquisition cost of the machinery): see *Dominion Mosaics & Tile* v *Trafalgar Trading* [1990] 2 All ER 246.

Mitigation

The claimant is under a duty to act reasonably to mitigate his loss, and this mitigation will reduce his damages: *Darbishire* v *Warran* [1963] 1 WLR 1067; *Selvanayagam* v *University of the West Indies* [1983] 1 All ER 824.

Injunction

An equitable remedy only available at the discretion of the court. By s37 Supreme Court Act 1981 it must be 'just and reasonable' to grant the injunction. An injunction may be useful in (say) nuisance or trespass to land, but is not so useful in (say) negligence.

An injunction may be prohibitory; mandatory; quia timet; interlocutory.

The court may award damages in lieu of an injunction: see Chapter 12 for the principles involved.

Self-help

For example, in abating a nuisance, ejecting a trespasser, self-defence to battery, etc.

Limitation

By s2 Limitation Act 1980 an action in tort must be brought within six years from the date on which the action accrued (three years for personal injuries – s11 1980 Act).

If the tort is actionable per se, time runs from the date of the tort; if proof of damage is required, time runs from the date of damage. See *Nitrigin Eireann Teoranta* v *Inco Alloys* [1992] 1 All ER 854. For insidious personal injuries (eg asbestosis, noise-induced deafness) s11 1980 Act provides that time runs from the date of the claimant's knowledge of the damage, and s33 1980 Act allows the court discretion to proceed outside the three year period.

Note the effects of the Latent Damage Act 1986 on hidden damage – six years plus three years from date damage discovered, subject to an overall period of fifteen years from the date of negligence.

19.3 Key cases and statutes

- *AB* v *South West Water Services Ltd* [1993] 1 All ER 609
  Aggravated damages take into account the claimant's injured feelings

- *British Telecommunications plc and Another* v *One in a Million Ltd and Another* [1998] 4 All ER 476
  Court of Appeal considered the availability of injunctive relief

- *Cooke* v *United Bristol Healthcare NHS Trust; Sheppard* v *Stibbe; Page* v *Lee* [2004] 1 All ER 797
  Illustrates the method(s) employed by the court in calculating damages for personal injury

- *Cox* v *Hockenhull* [1999] 3 All ER 577
  The estate of the deceased may sue the defendant

- *Daly* v *General Steam Navigation Co Ltd* [1980] 3 All ER 696
  Damages were awarded for loss of housekeeping capacity

- *Hardwick* v *Hudson* [1999] 3 All ER 426
  Provides a recent example of how the court calculates pecuniary loss

- *Heil* v *Rankin* [2000] 3 All ER 138
  Court of Appeal applied modest increases in calculating pain and suffering (non-pecuniary loss)

- *Herring* v *Ministry of Defence* [2004] 1 All ER 44
  Approach to calculating future loss of earnings should be modelled on a likely career

- *Hunt* v *Severs* [1994] 2 All ER 885
  Claimant may recover all medical expenses

- *Hurditch* v *Sheffield Health Authority* [1989] 2 All ER 869
  Provisional awards may be possible, depending on the facts of the case and if both parties consent

- *Jameson* v *Central Electricity Generating Board* [1999] 1 All ER 193
  When a dependant of the deceased may exercise a right to sue

- *Khodaparast* v *Shad* [2000] 1 All ER 545
  Provides a useful illustration of the award of aggravated damages for malicious falsehood

- *Kuddus* v *Chief Constable of Leicestershire Constabulary* [2000] 3 All ER 193
  House of Lords awarded exemplary damages for misfeasance in public office

- *Moeliker* v *A Reyrolle Ltd* [1977] 1 All ER 9
  The courts may at times also grant damages to reflect the potential loss of earning capacity

- *Nykredit Mortgage Bank plc* v *Edward Erdman Group Ltd (No 2)* [1998] 1 All ER 305
  No interest can be awarded for losses before the date on which the cause of action arose

- *Patel* v *Hooper & Jackson* [1999] 1 All ER 992
  Court of Appeal considered the measure of damages to be paid

- *Pickett* v *British Rail Engineering Ltd* [1980] AC 136
  House of Lords allowed recovery for 'lost years'

- *Platform Home Loans Ltd* v *Oyster Shipways Ltd* [1999] 1 All ER 833
  Certain limitations operate on the recoverability of damages

- *Selvanayagam* v *University of the West Indies* [1983] 1 All ER 824
  Claimant is under a duty to reasonably mitigate his loss

- *Wadey* v *Surrey County Council* [1999] 2 All ER 334
  Court will deduct all payments and benefits received before calculating the final award

- *Wells* v *Wells; Thomas* v *Brighton Health Authority; Page* v *Sheerness Steel Co plc* [1998] 3 All ER 481
  House of Lords considered the correct method of calculating lump sum damages for the loss of future earnings and the cost of future care

- *Wisely* v *John Fulton (Plumbers) Ltd* [2000] 2 All ER 545
  Benefits received from the State must be disregarded in calculating interest

- Administration of Justice Act 1982 – court takes into account any suffering caused to the claimant owing to his/her expectation of life being reduced

- Damages Act 1996 – gave a statutory footing to certain types of damages

- Fatal Accidents Act 1976 – dependants of the deceased may sue

- Judgments Act 1838 – every judgment debt carries interest from date of judgment to date of payment

- Latent Damage Act 1986 – on hidden damage, an additional three years is added on top of the six years, from the date the damage is discovered

- Law Reform (Miscellaneous Provisions) Act 1934 – all causes of action vesting in the deceased survive for the benefit of his/her estate

- Law Reform (Personal Injuries) Act 1948 – allows the recovery of private medical expenses

- Limitation Act 1980 – actions in tort must be brought within six years from the date on which the cause of action accrued

- Social Security Administration Act 1992 – allows the State to recover all benefits paid to the victim prior to the court award

- Supreme Court Act 1981 – interest is awarded for death and personal injury actions; equitable remedy only available at the courts' discretion

19.4 Questions and suggested solutions

QUESTION ONE

Milly required major heart surgery. The operation was performed by Nora, a leading heart surgeon. She decided to use a new technique which avoided some of the risks of conventional surgery. It had never been performed in the United Kingdom, but Nora had observed it carried out in the United States. Nora told Milly how the operation would be performed, but not that it was a new technique. Although the operation was performed with reasonable care, Milly suffered brain damage. She is now severely disabled, unable to work and requires a great deal of care.

Milly was 22, had just obtained a degree in computer engineering and was about to undertake a graduate degree. Her mother Olivia, who is aged 45, and was a partner in a firm of city solicitors, has given up work to help care for her.

Advise (a) as to any claims in tort, (b) as to the assessment of damages and (c) as to the advantages and disadvantages of a structured settlement.

University of London LLB Examination
(for External Students) Law of Tort June 1999 Q2

General Comment

This question is relatively straightforward, provided candidates have revised remedies as well as substantive liability. Candidates should avoid any detailed examination of elements of negligence which are not in issue, such as whether a duty of care exists in this case. When discussing the advantages and disadvantages of structured settlements, do make sure that the points you raise are fully explained.

Skeleton Solution

a) Discuss Nora's liability in the tort of negligence, in particular the scope of the duty to disclose the risks involved in surgery under *Sidaway*, *Bolam* and *Bolitho* – discuss whether a breach of any duty by Nora caused Milly's loss.

b) Identify the aim of damages in tort and explain the heads of loss relevant to Milly's circumstances, under which damages will be assessed – make particular reference to future loss of earnings, and the provision of care by a relative.

c) Explain the nature of structured settlements, their advantages and disadvantages.

Suggested Solution

a) *Nora's liability in tort*

If Milly is to claim against Nora in tort, such a claim will be based in negligence upon Nora's duty to give her patient proper and skilled advice, rather than in trespass as a battery which lacks the patient's valid consent. Only if Nora had actively misled Milly concerning the fact that she was unpractised in the new technique for performing heart surgery would an action in battery be likely to arise: *Sidaway v Bethlem Royal Hospital Governors* [1985] AC 871.

It is well established that doctors owe duties of care to their patients, not only in the context of diagnosis and treatment, but also (in limited circumstances) to disclose the risks involved in a course of treatment. This was confirmed by the House of Lords in *Sidaway* and subsequently by the Court of Appeal in *Gold v Haringey Health Authority* [1988] QB 481.

In order to determine whether Nora is in breach of her duty to Milly, it is necessary to examine the scope of the duty she owes. The majority of their Lordships in *Sidaway* held that the proper test to apply in these circumstances is that established in *Bolam v Friern Hospital Management Committee* [1957] 1 WLR 582; in other words, the test is whether a reasonable doctor would have acted as the defendant had done. A doctor will be held to have acted reasonably if he acted in accordance with a practice accepted as proper by a responsible body of medical men skilled in that particular art. Not only would Nora's failure to inform Milly that she intended to use a new technique (with which she had no previous 'hands on' experience) have to accord with a practice accepted as proper by a responsible body of doctors, the court would also have to be satisfied that this practice of non-disclosure has a logical basis: *Bolitho v City and Hackney Health Authority* [1997] 4 All ER 771.

It would obviously be rare to find that a body of professional opinion lacked logical analysis. Lord Browne-Wilkinson in *Bolitho* said that a judge would not normally be able to draw such a conclusion without expert evidence, and if the body of opinion reflected an accepted practice in the profession, a judge would not be able to discard that practice unless it could not be logically supported at all.

It is difficult to speculate whether Nora's non-disclosure was in accordance with the commonly accepted practice of a body of responsible doctors. Nora did, after all, explain how the operation would be performed. One body of professional opinion might logically consider that such a disclosure would inhibit the introduction of new and unpractised procedures, as few patients might consent if they were aware that they were the first to be subjected to a new procedure. On the other hand, the court might conclude that it is illogical to assume that patients would not consent to a new procedure which offers a clear reduction in risks compared to conventional surgery.

It should be noted that the minority of their Lordships in *Sidaway* held that the disclosure of some risks are so obviously necessary to an informed choice on the part of a patient that no reasonable prudent medical man would fail to make them. The information not disclosed in this case might well be regarded as essential to allow a patient to make an informed choice; however, it is the view of the majority which has been followed in later cases. As such, there is no duty on the part of doctors to enable patients to make an informed choice in English law.

Assuming Nora were to have broken a duty of disclosure to Milly, it would also have to be proved that 'but for' the non-disclosure, Milly would not have consented to the new technique, and would not thereby have suffered brain damage: *Barnett v Chelsea and Kensington Hospital Management Committee* [1969] 1 QB 428.

b) *The assessment of damages*

Assuming Nora is in breach of a duty of care owed to Milly, Nora's employer will be vicariously liable to pay a lump sum of damages (unless the parties were to agree to a structured settlement: see (c) below). The aim of such an award will be to restore Milly, in so far as money will allow, to the position she was in before the negligence occurred. An award of damages is usually considered in two parts: 'special damages' covering precisely calculable losses, normally arising pre-trial, and 'general damages' which are not capable of precise mathematical calculation and normally arise post-trial. It is also customary to classify losses sustained as being either pecuniary or non-pecuniary.

Pecuniary losses: loss of earnings

These mostly arise post-trial in Milly's case, and will include prospective earnings during any 'lost years' due to a reduced life expectancy and loss of pension rights associated with a future loss of salary.

Milly's future loss of salary is clearly difficult to assess as she has not yet entered the job market. It is likely that, had Milly become fully qualified, she would have been extremely employable and would have attracted a high salary. The court will award Milly a lump sum which, when invested, will be sufficient to produce an income equal to the loss of her future salary. The calculation is approached in two stages. The court will first assess Milly's net annual loss. The difficulty here is knowing how much Milly would have earned upon her entry to the job market (possibly as a computer engineer). Nonetheless, the court will have to make some assumptions, most probably based upon evidence from someone with expert knowledge of Milly's future intended profession.

The court will then select a multiplier based upon the likely duration of the disability. However, this will not be the same as the number of years Milly will work before retirement following completion of her post-graduate course, because the courts apply a reduction to take account of the possibility that future events might have cut her working life short, eg early death or unemployment. The possibility that Milly might have taken a career break for several years in order to raise children will also be a limiting factor. A reduction is also applied to take account of the fact that a lump sum payment will produce an investment income of its own. Other factors, such as Milly's future promotion prospects, may well increase the multiplier. This factor, together with Milly's young age, means that she is likely to obtain a near-maximum multiplier, perhaps in the range of 16–18.

Medical expenses reasonably incurred

The cost of nursing care and travel expenses to and from hospital are recoverable. The cost of nursing care provided by Olivia can be recovered by Milly herself: *Hunt* v *Severs* [1994] 2 All ER 385. In *Housecroft* v *Burnett* [1986] 1 All ER 332 it was decided that where a relative gives up work to look after the claimant, the court will award reasonable recompense to the carer, but the ceiling on such an award is the commercial rate for providing such care. Thus Olivia will be unable to recover her full loss of earnings, given her former employment as a partner in a city firm of solicitors. The damages awarded in respect of the carer will be held on trust for Olivia by Milly: *Cunningham* v *Harrison* [1973] QB 942.

Non-pecuniary losses

Milly's non-pecuniary losses include the pain and suffering she has endured both pre and post-trial, her loss of amenity, ie the loss of capacity to engage in activities which she enjoyed before trial, and compensation for her actual injuries. The amounts awarded under these heads are usually assessed by reference to past cases.

c) *The structured settlement*

This type of settlement was developed following pressure from those involved in clinical negligence claims (eg lawyers and insurers) and from tax concessions made by the Inland Revenue. The Damages Act 1996 provided further statutory support. Structured settlements may be suitable in cases such as Milly's where substantial damages are payable, but they can only be made where both parties agree.

Once a lump sum figure has been agreed, the part of the award representing special damages to the date of settlement would be paid to Milly as a lump sum. The remainder is used by the defendant's insurers to purchase an annuity to provide a fixed income stream for the claimant. Variations in payments from the annuity can be built in to cater for various contingencies likely to arise during the life of the claimant.

Advantages of structured settlements

i)   Income from the annuity is tax free (benefiting higher rate taxpayers in particular) whereas income from the investment of a lump sum will be subject to income tax. Thus income payments from a structured settlement are likely to be larger.

ii) A structured settlement would provide certainty for Milly in respect of her future income, and would avoid the danger that a lump sum might be spent too quickly, leaving insufficient funds for later years.

iii) Milly is quite possibly unable to manage the investment of a lump sum herself given the extent of her disabilities, and would be reliant on the goodwill, good faith, and investment expertise of those who care for her to manage her affairs. The use of a structured settlement removes this responsibility from the claimant.

iv) Annuities can be set up to protect future income from the effects of inflation.

v)   The income from an annuity will be guaranteed to last for Milly's lifetime, even if she survived longer than her predicted life expectancy.

Disadvantages of structured settlements

i)   Even though there is flexibility within a structured settlement to vary payments to cater for various contingencies likely to arise during the life of the claimant, once agreed, a structured settlement cannot be modified. This means that there is extreme pressure to structure the settlement correctly at the outset. Predictions concerning Milly's future need for income and capital will have to be made straight away.

ii) The amounts payable under a structured settlement may still be inadequate if Milly's prognosis is incorrect.

QUESTION TWO

Fred is driving his sister Gail to the railway station on a dark evening so that she can catch an overnight train to Scotland for an important meeting. They have been held up in heavy traffic and Gail is convinced that she will be late. After they have waited at a red light for some time, Gail exclaims, 'You stupid fool. The lights have jammed. There's not a thing in sight. Get a move on.' Fred can see no traffic approaching and moves across the junction. He strikes a bicycle ridden at a fast speed by Harry, who is wearing black jeans and sweater. Gail is injured. Harry has unusually brittle bones and dies of his injuries.

Advise Gail and Harry's estate.

University of London LLB Examination
(for External Students) Law of Tort June 1997 Q8

General Comment

This type of question calls for an exposition of the various defences to negligence, as well as some discussion of joint liability and the extent of the remedies involved. With so many points to cover, some degree of economy on detail is needed, and planning of the answers is particularly important.

Skeleton Solution

Duty; breach; joint liability to Harry; contribution – Gail's claim against Fred; defences – volenti, contributory negligence, ex turpi causa – Harry's claim; defences – remoteness and the brittle bones – the claim by the estate.

Suggested Solution

The duty owed by one road user to another is so well established as to be beyond question. The real issues here are whether Gail will owe any duty towards Harry in addition to Fred, who obviously will, and whether there has been breach. Breach may be assumed because, even if the lights had broken down, it would have been prudent for Gail to get out of the car to have better visibility of other road users, but this would normally only show breach by Fred, as the driver. There is an argument here that Fred is acting in the furtherance of a common design in crossing the lights and this may be enough to bring down joint liability upon Gail for Fred's negligence as in *Brooke* v *Bool* [1928] 2 KB 578.

Alternatively, there may be an argument that Fred is acting as agent to Gail as principal and has committed a tort within his express authority, thus making her vicariously liable along the lines seen in *Ormrod* v *Crossville Motor Services Co Ltd* [1953] 1 WLR 1120. If this is the situation there would be nothing to prevent Fred's insurers (or the Motor Insurers Bureau if he were uninsured) seeking contribution against her under s1 Civil Liability (Contribution) Act 1978. A similar joint liability arose in *Scarsbrook* v *Mason* [1961] 3 All ER 767, although the House of Lords in *Morgans* v *Launchbury* [1973] AC 127 warned against too easy a recourse to agency principles in car cases where there was generally no fault on the part of the 'principal'. Here there seems to be primary fault on Gail's part.

Gail will be seeking recovery for her own injuries, probably against Fred and his insurers. Various defences may suggest themselves. Although the circumstances indicate that the absolute defence of volenti non fit injuria is in point, this defence is barred by s149(3) Road Traffic Act 1988 as against a passenger. This would not, of course, prevent a defence claim that Gail had contributed to her injuries by want of care for her own safety, and that the damages that she might be awarded should be reduced to reflect a just apportionment of her own blameworthiness under s1(1) Law Reform (Contributory Negligence) Act 1945. There might be a defence claim that, as the pair had agreed to do what is a criminal offence by the driver, her claim should be met by the defence of ex turpi causa non oritur actio. There is no doubt that injuries to, and torts against, the participants in illegal joint enterprises may sometimes be defended by ex turpi causa, but cases such as *Revill* v *Newberry* [1996] 2 WLR 239 and *Pitts* v *Hunt* [1991] 1 QB 24 show that a very restrictive view is taken of this defence, particularly where illegality is simply in the mode of driving a vehicle.

As to Harry's claim, there may be a possibility of defences of volenti and contributory negligence. We are not told whether Harry had lights on his bicycle but, assuming that he did not, this might support a claim that he was contributorily negligent. He seems to have been travelling quickly which might be adding to an impression of want of care. In *Tremayne* v *Hill* [1987] RTR 131 a pedestrian, who failed to watch out for cars going through traffic lights on red, was held not to be contributorily negligent, but it is by no means certain that the same result would follow where a cyclist is going quickly, without lights, in dark clothes at night. All that needs to be established for contributory negligence is a want of care for one's own safety: *Nance* v *British Columbia Electric Railway Co Ltd* [1951] AC 601. There seems little chance of establishing a volenti defence against Harry's claim because there must be some evidence that Harry was aware of the danger which was 'extreme and glaring' and, nevertheless, resolved to undertake the risk of it as in *Morris* v *Murray* [1991] 2 WLR 195. There is nothing equivalent to that here except as referred to below.

It may be that had Harry not had such brittle bones, he might have survived the incident, possibly with minor injuries. In the normal run of matters, a defendant cannot be heard to raise such a defence because the governing principle is that the tortfeasor must 'take his victim as he finds him', ie with his weaknesses (*Dulieu* v *White and Sons* [1901] 2 KB 669), and this principle extends liability to unexpected types of personal injury as in *Smith* v *Leech, Brain and Co* [1962] 2 QB 405, as well as to greater than expected degrees of damage. This must, of course, give way to the argument that if a person knows that he is extremely vulnerable to certain types of injury, this will, in a proper case, increase the possibility of a contributory negligence defence and, in a very extreme situation, the possible argument that he was volenti to an obvious, extreme and glaring risk.

The claim by Harry's estate will be brought under s1 Law Reform (Miscellaneous Provisions) Act 1934 on the same basis that he himself, had he survived, would have claimed for his personal injuries and damage to his bicycle, clothes, etc. The estate would not be able to claim for his 'lost years' earnings, but would be able to claim for funeral expenses: s1(2)(c). The claim for his personal injuries would be along conventional lines and much would depend upon what pain, suffering and loss of amenity he suffered prior to his death, as well as lost earnings up to that time. Had Harry any surviving dependants, those persons could bring an action under the Fatal Accidents Act 1976 for bereavement, funeral expenses and actual and future pecuniary losses based upon the valuation of the lost dependency when taken over the period that such a dependency was likely to last. The basis of the calculation for a wage earner is usually the earnings up to the accident less whatever part which was spent by the deceased on his own upkeep. A suitable multiplier is then worked out by reference to the projected length of the dependency, and a suitable discount applied for accelerated receipt of the award, but this claim is for the benefit of the dependants and does not go to the estate.

QUESTION THREE

David was driving at dusk at the maximum permitted speed. A large bird flew out suddenly and struck the windscreen of his car. David temporarily lost control and struck a pedal cycle which he was overtaking. The cyclist Paul suffered severe head injuries. He was aged 24, an articled clerk with a firm of City solicitors, unmarried and childless. He is now able to do only light unskilled work at a local supermarket. His expectation of life has probably not been reduced, but the medical experts are not agreed on this.

a) Has Paul a claim in tort against David? If so, how will the damages be assessed?

b) Do you think that English law provides a satisfactory method of compensation in such circumstances?

University of London LLB Examination
(for External Students) Law of Tort June 1993 Q3

General Comment

A question requiring analysis of the principles relating to the assessment of damages for personal injuries and a more general question on the adequacy of the English law in providing a satisfactory method of granting compensation.

Skeleton Solution

a) The claim: negligence – heads of damages – loss of earnings – pain and suffering – loss of amenity – other special and general damages – provisional damages.

b) Discussion of compensation, including structured settlements.

Suggested Solution

a) Paul's claim against David would be in negligence. As a road user, David owes a duty of care to other road users: *Nettleship* v *Weston* [1971] 2 QB 691. On the facts of this case it appears he is in breach of his duty. Firstly, he is driving at the maximum permitted speed. The speed at which a vehicle should be driven must be reasonable in the circumstances: *McLeod* v *Receiver of Metropolitan Police* [1971] Crim LR 364. Further, the Highway Code states that one's speed limit depends upon the conditions and we are told he is driving at dusk when visibility will be less.

Second, he is overtaking a cyclist. Again, he should have reduced speed and under the Highway Code a cyclist being overtaken should be given at least as much room as a car. Failure to observe the Highway Code can be relied upon to establish liability (the Road Traffic Act 1988 ss38–39). Therefore we can conclude that a reasonable driver would not have driven so fast at dusk and particularly when overtaking a cyclist.

It is not David's fault that a bird struck his windscreen, but we can argue that it is his fault that he was driving at such a speed and in such circumstances that a temporary loss of control caused an accident.

David's negligence has caused the accident and we are not told of anything that might allow a partial defence of contributory negligence.

Turning to the assessment of damages, the injuries are serious and the quantum is likely to be very high. The first head of damages is loss of earnings. His net annual loss (the multiplicand) is multiplied by a figure to denote the number of years' loss (the multiplier). This latter figure is not a 'real' number; Paul would probably have worked for another 30 or 40 years, but the multiplier will only be 15 or 16 in this case. Further, the multiplicand does not take into account promotion and so on, and also his likely earnings in the supermarket will be set off against the sum.

The second major head of damages will be for pain and suffering and/or loss of amenity and this figure is likely to be considerable. It is a matter for the court but there are numerous guideline cases which would allow Paul's advisers to predict quite closely what this amount should be. Both of these heads of damages are termed general damages and are largely speculative.

Paul will also claim for the special damages – quantifiable losses – incurred after the accident, such as damaged clothing, damage to his bicycle. Paul has no dependants and we are not told if his parents, for example, have incurred expenses in looking after him; if so, these would be recoverable. Similarly, any expenses likely to be incurred in the future can be claimed as general damages; for example, nursing care, special equipment.

Under the clawback rules, the accident having occurred after January 1989, any related benefits Paul has received would be deducted from the damages he receives. This is affirmed by the decision in *Hardwick* v *Hudson* [1999] 3 All ER 426 by the Court of Appeal, and again by the House of Lords in *Wisely* v *John Fulton (Plumbers) Ltd* [2000] 2 All ER 545.

Finally, there is lack of agreement as to his reduced life expectation. First, Paul can claim loss of future earnings not only for the period he is likely to survive but also for the 'lost years' and this is reflected in the multiplier: *Pickett* v *British Rail Engineering Ltd* [1980] AC 136. Second, s32A of the Supreme Court Act 1981 allows payment of provisional damages against the chance of further deterioration. An award is made now with power to make a further award if the deterioration occurs. It is submitted that this is unlikely in this case, since it is not his condition that will deteriorate and therefore justify a higher sum for pain and suffering or loss of amenity, but his expectation of life.

b) 'Damages for any tort are or ought to be fixed at a sum which will compensate the claimant, so far as money can do it, for all the injury which he has suffered': per Lord Reid, *Cassell* v *Broome* [1972] AC 1027.

There are various arguments to be made for and against the method of compensation provided for by English law in personal injury cases. It is based upon the idea that the claimant is given a lump sum, part of which relates exactly to expenses, both incurred and predicted. The remainder is the notional value given to the injury itself, being compensation for the pain, suffering and loss of amenity. One cannot quantify pain and suffering, so inevitably the figures are to that extent arbitrary. However, the claimant receives a 'once-and-for-all' payment to meet all his needs and requirements, whether it be for a broken finger or complete paralysis.

There are two obvious comments to be made. First, recovery of compensation depends upon proof of fault. Paul must prove, on the balance of probabilities, that David was negligent. That will also involve delay and expense, although legal costs will be largely recovered if the claimant is successful. A system of strict liability, while not necessarily altering the way quantum is apportioned, would remove that burden from the claimant.

Second, the current system involves, in the more serious cases, an estimate of the claimant's needs and life expectancy. What if the claimant proves long-lived and runs out of money or if his needs alter? While provisional damages meet this difficulty to a limited extent, structured settlements provide a fairer solution. Structured settlements were first approved in this country in *Kelly* v *Dawes* (1990) The Times 27 September but they are familiar within other jurisdictions, such as Canada. They involve periodic payments for life instead of a lump sum and are therefore more flexible as well as having other benefits (such as being tax-free in the claimant's hands).

That may go some way to solving the inequities of the more serious cases (to date, all structured settlements in this country have been in cases with a six-figure value) but the less serious cases, which form the great majority, remain as before. It is submitted that structured settlements could be appropriate for some less serious cases too, those involving some lack of amenity, for example, with periodic payments for a limited time.

However, the minor cases can only be dealt with by a lump sum and it is the procedure for awarding that sum which could be eased by removing the element of fault.

QUESTION FOUR

John was married to Primrose by whom he had two children: Timothy aged 19 years who is a first year university undergraduate and Fiona aged 14 who attends a boarding school. John was seriously injured in a road accident in which he was driving his car.

John's car was struck by one driven through a red traffic light by Stanley; John was not wearing a seat belt. John sustained severe brain damage. He never recovered consciousness but he lived for a further 18 months. At the date of the accident John was aged 48 years, he had been very fit and he had been employed as his company's chief production engineer at a gross annual salary of £25,000. His prospects for promotion had been good. What claims for damage may arise? By whom will they be brought?

Written by the Author

General Comment

This is a rather short question but it requires a thorough analysis of the law relating to the recovery of damages for personal injury. A sound knowledge of the relevant statutes is necessary. The defence of contributory neglilgence is also relevant.

Skeleton Solution

John – negligence of Stanley – loss of earnings – lost years – s4(2) AJA 1982 – *Wise* v *Kaye* – loss of amenity – contributory negligence – FAA – dependency – widow – children.

Suggested Solution

John was seriously injured in an accident involving Stanley and subsequently died as a result of his injuries. It seems clear that the accident was caused by the negligence of Stanley as we are told that he drove his car through a traffic light which was at red. We are not told that John brought an action against Stanley during his lifetime so the advice given here is based on the assumption that no such action was brought.

Where a tortious act results in the death of a person then there are two actions which may be brought. The first is under the Law Reform (Miscellaneous Provisions) Act 1934 (the 1934 Act) and the second is under the Fatal Accidents Act 1976 (the 1976 Act). We shall take each claim separately.

The 1934 Act provides for the survival for the benefit of the deceased's estate of any cause of action which was vested in the deceased at the time of his death. Such an action is brought by the personal representatives of the deceased's estate and any damages recovered are awarded to the estate to be distributed according to the will of the deceased or the rules of intestacy. The principles applicable to a claim under the 1934 Act are generally the same as in an ordinary personal injuries case.

Thus an action will be brought under the 1934 Act for both pecuniary loss and non-pecuniary loss. John appears to have suffered loss of earnings because we are not told that his employers continued to pay his wages. Had he brought an action before his death John could have recovered for his loss of earnings during the lost years, that is the period which he would have been alive and continued to earn had it not been for the tortious event: *Pickett v British Rail Engineering Ltd* [1980] AC 136. However s4(2) of the Administration of Justice Act 1982 provides that a claim for loss of earnings in the lost years can only be brought by a living claimant (reversing *Gammell* v *Wilson* [1982] AC 27). So the lost earnings will be confined to the 18 month period in which John was alive after the accident. In assessing John's net annual loss the court would start with John's gross annual earnings of £25,000 per annum. The court would, however, make an allowance for the possibility of an increase in pay or promotion. Here we are told that John's prospects for promotion had been good. In *Ratnasingam* v *Kow Ah Dek* [1983] 1 WLR 1235 the court made an allowance of one third for the chance that a teacher with a good academic record would pass an examination for promotion, even though he had failed the particular examination twice before and was on his last chance. Once this sum has been calculated then a deduction must be made for the tax which the claimant would have paid on his earnings and for social security contributions which he would have paid. A claim could also be made for any other pecuniary losses, such as medical expenses incurred and damage to property. The decision of the House of Lords in *Wisely* v *John Fulton (Plumbers) Ltd* [2000] 2 All ER 545 provides a useful illustration of this.

A claim can also be made for non-pecuniary loss. There is unlikely to be a claim for pain and suffering because in *Wise* v *Kaye* [1962] 1 QB 638 it was held that a claim could only be made for pain and suffering where the claimant was aware that he had suffered pain. Here we are told that John remained unconscious throughout so it is unlikely that he was aware of any pain and suffering. A claim could, however, be made for loss of amenity which is designed to compensate the claimant for the loss of his capacity to engage in activities which he enjoyed before his death. In *West* v *Shepherd* [1964] AC 326 it was held that the claimant was entitled to be compensated for his or her loss of amenities even though he or she was unaware of that loss. The case in many ways is a controversial one but it was later approved by the House of Lords in *Lim Poh Choo* v *Camden and Islington AHA* [1980] AC 174. However, the damages payable under this head will be reduced because of John's shortened life span because it was held in *West* that damages must be proportionate to the duration of the loss. More recently the Court of Appeal in *Heil* v *Rankin* [2000] 3 All ER 138 applied modest increases in calculating the question of damages for pain and suffering. Perhaps the trend is slowly changing.

John was, however, guilty of contributory negligence in failing to wear a seat belt. A failure to wear a seat belt was held to be contributory negligence in *Froom* v *Butcher* [1975] 3 WLR 379 and this common law rule has now been given statutory approval in s33A of the Road Traffic Act 1972 which makes the wearing of a seat belt mandatory. Thus damages would fall to be reduced by 20 per cent. Stanley may wish to argue that a failure to wear a seat belt was a novus actus interveniens as being an unreasonable act of the claimant, as in *McKew* v *Holland & Hannen & Cubitts (Scotland) Ltd* [1969] 3 All ER 1621, but such an argument is unlikely to succeed.

Second, a cause of action would accrue for the benefit of John's dependants under the 1976 Act. It should be noted that the defence of contributory negligence which would be available to Stanley in an action by John is also available as regards any action by the dependants. Dependants are defined in s1(2) and s1(4) of the 1976 Act as including the deceased's spouse and children and so would include Primrose, Timothy and Fiona. The dependants can bring an action for bereavement which is a statutory figure fixed at £7,500. The decision by the House of Lords in *Jameson* v *Central Electricity Generating Board* [1999] 1 All ER 193 exemplifies this point in more detail. If the dependants have in fact incurred funeral expenses in respect of John then these can be recovered from Stanley: s3(5) of the 1976 Act. In calculating the pecuniary loss which can be claimed by the dependants the court will calculate the deceased's earnings and then deduct a sum to represent the deceased's personal and living expenses. Only sums which would have been spent by the deceased exclusively upon himself fall to be deducted: *Harris* v *Empress Motors Ltd* [1983] 3 All ER 561. Once this has been done the court will assess the likely duration of the dependency. The duration of the dependency of the children is likely to be short as the dependency does not generally extend beyond the length of their full-time education and Timothy is already aged 19 and at university and Fiona is aged 14. The court will have to calculate how long the deceased would have continued to live had it not been for the accident with Stanley. In assessing the length of the dependency and damages the prospects of Primrose remarrying are to be ignored: s3(3) of the 1976 Act. Under s4 of the 1976 Act any benefits which have accrued or will accrue or may accrue to the dependants from the estate of the deceased or otherwise as a result of the death of the deceased are to be disregarded. Thus the damages payable to the estate in respect of loss of earnings during the 18 month period which John survived after the accident, any medical expenses and damages for loss of amenity will not be set off against the damages under the 1976 Act.

Revision Aids

Designed for the undergraduate, the 101 Questions & Answers series and the Suggested Solutions series are for all those who have a positive commitment to passing their law examinations. Each series covers a different examinable topic and comprises a selection of answers to examination questions and, in the case of the 101 Questions and Answers, interrograms. The majority of questions represent examination 'bankers' and are supported by full-length essay solutions. These titles will undoubtedly assist you with your research and further your understanding of the subject in question.

101 Questions & Answers Series

Only £7.95 Published December 2003

Constitutional Law
ISBN: 1 85836 522 8

Criminal Law
ISBN: 1 85836 432 9

Land Law
ISBN: 1 85836 515 5

Law of Contract
ISBN: 1 85836 517 1

Law of Tort
ISBN: 1 85836 516 3

Suggested Solutions to Past Examination Questions 2001–2002 Series

Only £6.95 Published December 2003

Company Law
ISBN: 1 85836 519 8

Employment Law
ISBN: 1 85836 520 1

European Union Law
ISBN: 1 85836 524 4

Evidence
ISBN: 1 85836 521 X

Family Law
ISBN: 1 85836 525 2

For further information or to place an order, please contact:

Mail Order
Old Bailey Press at Holborn College
Woolwich Road
Charlton
London
SE7 8LN

Telephone: 020 8317 6039
Fax: 020 8317 6004
Website: www.oldbaileypress.co.uk
E-Mail: mailorder@oldbaileypress.co.uk

Old Bailey Press

The Old Bailey Press Integrated Student Law Library is tailor-made to help you at every stage of your studies, from the preliminaries of each subject through to the final examination. The series of Textbooks, Revision WorkBooks, 150 Leading Cases and Cracknell's Statutes are interrelated to provide you with a comprehensive set of study materials.

You can buy Old Bailey Press books from your University Bookshop, your local Bookshop, directly using this form, or you can order a free catalogue of our titles from the address shown overleaf.

The following subjects each have a Textbook, 150 Leading Cases, Revision WorkBook and Cracknell's Statutes unless otherwise stated.

Administrative Law
Commercial Law
Company Law
Conflict of Laws
Constitutional Law
Conveyancing (Textbook and 150 Leading Cases)
Criminal Law
Criminology (Textbook and Sourcebook)
Employment Law (Textbook and Cracknell's Statutes)
English and European Legal Systems
Equity and Trusts
Evidence
Family Law
Jurisprudence: The Philosophy of Law (Textbook, Sourcebook and
   Revision WorkBook)
Land: The Law of Real Property
Law of International Trade
Law of the European Union
Legal Skills and System
   (Textbook)
Obligations: Contract Law
Obligations: The Law of Tort
Public International Law
Revenue Law (Textbook,
   Revision WorkBook and
   Cracknell's Statutes)
Succession (Textbook, Revision
   WorkBook and Cracknell's
   Statutes)

Mail order prices:	
Textbook	£15.95
150 Leading Cases	£12.95
Revision WorkBook	£10.95
Cracknell's Statutes	£11.95
Suggested Solutions 1999–2000	£6.95
Suggested Solutions 2000–2001	£6.95
Suggested Solutions 2001–2002	£6.95
101 Questions and Answers	£7.95
Law Update 2004	£10.95

Please note details and prices are subject to alteration.

To complete your order, please fill in the form below:

Module	Books required	Quantity	Price	Cost
		Postage		
		TOTAL		

For the UK and Europe, add £4.95 for the first book ordered, then add £1.00 for each subsequent book ordered for postage and packing.
For the rest of the world, add 50% for airmail.

ORDERING

By telephone to Mail Order at 020 8317 6039, with your credit card to hand.

By fax to 020 8317 6004 (giving your credit card details).

Website: www.oldbaileypress.co.uk
E-Mail: mailorder@oldbaileypress.co.uk

By post to: Mail Order, Old Bailey Press at Holborn College, Woolwich Road, Charlton, London, SE7 8LN.

When ordering by post, please enclose full payment by cheque or banker's draft, or complete the credit card details below. You may also order a free catalogue of our complete range of titles from this address.

We aim to despatch your books within 3 working days of receiving your order. All parts of the form must be completed.

Name

Address

E-Mail
Postcode   Telephone

Total value of order, including postage: £
I enclose a cheque/banker's draft for the above sum, or

charge my   ☐ Access/Mastercard   ☐ Visa   ☐ American Express

Cardholder: ....

Card number

☐☐☐☐ ☐☐☐☐ ☐☐☐☐ ☐☐☐☐

Expiry date   ☐☐☐☐

Signature: ....Date: ....